Stock Investing

FOR

DUMMIES®

3RD EDITION

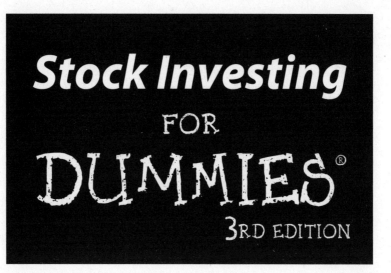

Stock Investing FOR DUMMIES® 3RD EDITION

by Paul Mladjenovic

WILEY

Wiley Publishing, Inc.

Stock Investing For Dummies®, 3rd Edition

Published by
Wiley Publishing, Inc.
111 River St.
Hoboken, NJ 07030-5774
www.wiley.com

For general information on our other products and services, please contact our Customer Care Department within the U.S. at 877-762-2974, outside the U.S. at 317-572-3993, or fax 317-572-4002.

For technical support, please visit www.wiley.com/techsupport.

Wiley also publishes its books in a variety of electronic formats. Some content that appears in print may not be available in electronic books.

Library of Congress Control Number: 2008942707

ISBN: 978-0-470-40114-9

Manufactured in the United States of America

10 9 8 7 6 5 4

WILEY

About the Author

Paul Mladjenovic is a certified financial planner practitioner, writer, and public speaker. His business, PM Financial Services, has helped people with financial and business concerns since 1981. In 1985 he achieved his CFP designation. Since 1983, Paul has taught thousands of budding investors through popular national seminars such as "The $50 Wealthbuilder" and "Stock Investing Like a Pro." Paul has been quoted or referenced by many media outlets, including Bloomberg, MarketWatch, Comcast, CNBC, and a variety of financial and business publications and Web sites. As an author, he has written the books *The Unofficial Guide to Picking Stocks* (Wiley, 2000) and *Zero-Cost Marketing* (Todd Publications, 1995). In 2002, the first edition of *Stock Investing For Dummies* was ranked in the top 10 out of 300 books reviewed by Barron's. In recent years, Paul accurately forecasted many economic events, such as the rise of gold, the decline of the U.S. dollar, and the housing crisis. At press time he had been warning his students and clients about the credit crisis on Wall Street. He edits the financial newsletter Prosperity Alert, available at no charge at www.supermoneylinks.com. Paul's personal Web site can be found at www.mladjenovic.com.

Dedication

For my fantastic wife Fran, my wonderful boys Adam and Joshua, and a loving, supportive family, I thank God for you.

I also dedicate this book to the millions of investors who deserve more knowledge and information to achieve lasting prosperity.

Author's Acknowledgments

First and foremost, I offer my appreciation and gratitude to the wonderful people at Wiley. It has been a pleasure to work with such a top-notch organization that works so hard to create products that offer readers tremendous value and information. I wish all of you continued success! Wiley has some notables whom I want to single out.

The first person is Georgette Beatty (my project editor). She has guided me from day one. Her patience, professionalism, and guidance have kept me sane and productive. Thanks for being great!

Todd Lothery (my copy editor) is a pro who took my bundle of words and turned them into worthy messages, and I thank him.

The technical editor, Juli Erhart-Graves, is a great financial pro whom I appreciate. She made sure that my logic is sound and my facts are straight. I wish her continued success.

My gratitude again goes out to my fantastic acquisitions editor, Stacy Kennedy, for making this 3rd edition happen. *For Dummies* books don't magically appear at the bookstore; they happen because of the foresight and efforts of people like Stacy. Wiley is fortunate to have her (and the others also mentioned)!

Fran, Lipa Zyenska, I appreciate your great support during the writing and updating of this book. It's not always easy dealing with the world, but with you by my side, I know that God has indeed blessed me. Te amo!

Lastly, I want to acknowledge you, the reader. Over the years, you've made the *For Dummies* books what they are today. Your devotion to these wonderful books helped build a foundation that played a big part in the creation of this book and many more yet to come. Thank you!

Publisher's Acknowledgments

We're proud of this book; please send us your comments through our Dummies online registration form located at `http://dummies.custhelp.com`. For other comments, please contact our Customer Care Department within the U.S. at 877-762-2974, outside the U.S. at 317-572-3993, or fax 317-572-4002.

Some of the people who helped bring this book to market include the following:

Acquisitions, Editorial, and Media Development

Senior Project Editor: Georgette Beatty

(Previous Edition: Jennifer Connolly)

Acquisitions Editor: Stacy Kennedy

Copy Editor: Todd Lothery

(Previous Edition: Sarah Faulkner)

Assistant Editor: Erin Calligan Mooney

Editorial Program Coordinator: Joe Niesen

Technical Editor: Juli Erhart-Graves

Editorial Manager: Michelle Hacker

Editorial Assistant: Jennette ElNaggar

Cover Photo: Image Farm

Cartoons: Rich Tennant
(`www.the5thwave.com`)

Composition Services

Senior Project Coordinator: Kristie Rees

Layout and Graphics: Stacie Brooks, Reuben W. Davis, Shawn Frazier, Melissa K. Jester, Christine Williams

Proofreader: C.M. Jones

Indexer: Sherry Massey

Publishing and Editorial for Consumer Dummies

Diane Graves Steele, Vice President and Publisher, Consumer Dummies

Kristin Ferguson-Wagstaffe, Product Development Director, Consumer Dummies

Ensley Eikenburg, Associate Publisher, Travel

Kelly Regan, Editorial Director, Travel

Publishing for Technology Dummies

Andy Cummings, Vice President and Publisher, Dummies Technology/General User

Composition Services

Gerry Fahey, Vice President of Production Services

Debbie Stailey, Director of Composition Services

Contents at a Glance

Introduction *1*

Part I: The Essentials of Stock Investing *9*

Chapter 1: Welcome to the World of Stock Investing 11

Chapter 2: Taking Stock of Your Current Financial Situation and Goals 19

Chapter 3: Defining Common Approaches to Stock Investing 37

Chapter 4: Recognizing the Risks 47

Chapter 5: Say Cheese: Getting a Snapshot of the Market with Indexes 63

Part II: Before You Start Buying *75*

Chapter 6: Gathering Information 77

Chapter 7: Going for Brokers 97

Chapter 8: Investing for Growth 109

Chapter 9: Investing for Income 123

Chapter 10: Getting a Grip on Economics 137

Part III: Picking Winners *149*

Chapter 11: Using Basic Accounting to Choose Winning Stocks 151

Chapter 12: Decoding Company Documents 167

Chapter 13: Analyzing Industries 179

Chapter 14: Emerging Sector Opportunities 189

Chapter 15: Money, Mayhem, and Votes 203

Part IV: Investment Strategies and Tactics *213*

Chapter 16: Choosing between Investing and Trading 215

Chapter 17: Selecting a Strategy That's Just Right for You 225

Chapter 18: Understanding Brokerage Orders and Trading Techniques 235

Chapter 19: Getting a Handle on DPPs, DRPs, and DCA . . . PDQ 251

Chapter 20: Corporate Skullduggery: Looking at Insider Activity 261

Chapter 21: Keeping More of Your Money from the Taxman 273

Part V: The Part of Tens 285

Chapter 22: Ten Ways to Profit before the Crowd Does 287
Chapter 23: Ten (Or So) Ways to Protect Your Stock Market Profits 293
Chapter 24: Ten Red Flags for Stock Investors 299
Chapter 25: Ten Challenges and Opportunities for Stock Investors.....................305

Part VI: Appendixes 311

Appendix A: Resources for Stock Investors 313
Appendix B: Financial Ratios..329

Index 339

Table of Contents

Introduction *1*

About This Book 1
Conventions Used in This Book..2
What You're Not to Read 3
Foolish Assumptions...3
How This Book Is Organized 4
    Part I: The Essentials of Stock Investing 4
    Part II: Before You Start Buying 4
    Part III: Picking Winners 5
    Part IV: Investment Strategies and Tactics................................6
    Part V: The Part of Tens 6
    Part VI: Appendixes 7
Icons Used in This Book 7
Where to Go from Here 8

Part 1: The Essentials of Stock Investing *9*

Chapter 1: Welcome to the World of Stock Investing 11

Understanding the Basics...12
Preparing to Buy Stocks 12
Knowing How to Pick Winners 13
    Recognizing stock value..13
    Understanding how market capitalization affects stock value......14
    Sharpening your investment skills 15
Boning Up on Strategies and Tactics 17

Chapter 2: Taking Stock of Your Current Financial Situation and Goals 19

Establishing a Starting Point by Preparing a Balance Sheet 20
    Step 1: Make sure you have an emergency fund............................21
    Step 2: List your assets in decreasing order of liquidity 22
    Step 3: List your liabilities 24
    Step 4: Calculate your net worth..26
    Step 5: Analyze your balance sheet......................................27
Funding Your Stock Program 29
    Step 1: Tally up your income..30
    Step 2: Add up your outgo 31

Step 3: Create a cash flow statement...................................32
Step 4: Analyze your cash flow.......................................33
Another option: Finding investment money in tax savings...........33
Setting Your Sights on Your Financial Goals..........................34

Chapter 3: Defining Common Approaches to Stock Investing......37

Matching Stocks and Strategies with Your Goals......................38
Investing for the Future 39
Focusing on the short term 39
Considering intermediate-term goals............................40
Preparing for the long term 41
Investing for a Purpose 42
Making loads of money quickly: Growth investing................42
Steadily making money: Income investing........................43
Investing for Your Personal Style 45
Conservative investing..45
Aggressive investing..46

Chapter 4: Recognizing the Risks 47

Exploring Different Kinds of Risk...................................48
Financial risk 48
Interest rate risk..49
Market risk...52
Inflation risk..54
Tax risk..54
Political and governmental risks 54
Personal risks 55
Emotional risk 56
Minimizing Your Risk...58
Gaining knowledge...58
Staying out until you get a little practice...................59
Putting your financial house in order 59
Diversifying your investments 60
Weighing Risk against Return 61

Chapter 5: Say Cheese: Getting a Snapshot
of the Market with Indexes 63

Knowing How Indexes Are Measured 63
Checking Out the Indexes...65
The Dow Jones Industrial Average 65
Standard & Poor's 500...68
Wilshire Total Market Index 69
Nasdaq indexes..69
Russell 3000 Index..70
International indexes..70

Using the Indexes Effectively 71
    Tracking the indexes 72
    Investing in indexes 72

Part II: Before You Start Buying 75

Chapter 6: Gathering Information 77

Looking to Stock Exchanges for Answers 78
Understanding Stocks and the Companies They Represent 79
    Accounting for taste and a whole lot more 79
    Understanding how economics affects stocks 80
Staying on Top of Financial News 84
    Figuring out what a company's up to 84
    Discovering what's new with an industry 85
    Knowing what's happening with the economy 85
    Seeing what politicians and government bureaucrats are doing 86
    Checking for trends in society, culture, and entertainment 86
Reading (And Understanding) Stock Tables 87
    52-week high 88
    52-week low 88
    Name and symbol 89
    Dividend 89
    Volume 89
    Yield 91
    P/E 91
    Day last 92
    Net change 92
Using News about Dividends 92
    Looking at important dates 93
    Understanding why these dates matter 94
Evaluating Investment Tips 95

Chapter 7: Going for Brokers 97

Defining the Broker's Role 97
Distinguishing between Full-Service and Discount Brokers 99
    Full-service brokers 99
    Discount brokers 101
Choosing a Broker 102
Discovering Various Types of Brokerage Accounts 103
    Cash accounts 103
    Margin accounts 104
    Option accounts 105
Judging Brokers' Recommendations 105
    Understanding basic recommendations 106
    Asking a few important questions 106

Chapter 8: Investing for Growth **109**

Becoming a Value-Oriented Growth Investor 110
Choosing Growth Stocks with a Few Handy Tips 111
Looking for leaders in megatrends 112
Comparing a company's growth to an industry's growth 113
Considering a company with a strong niche 113
Checking out a company's fundamentals 114
Evaluating a company's management 115
Noticing who's buying and/or recommending
a company's stock 117
Making sure a company continues to do well 118
Heeding investing lessons from history 119
Exploring Small Caps and Speculative Stocks 119
Know when to avoid IPOs 120
Make sure a small cap stock is making money 121
Analyze small cap stocks before you invest 122

Chapter 9: Investing for Income **123**

Understanding the Basics of Income Stocks 123
Getting a grip on dividends and dividend rates 124
Recognizing who's well-suited for income stocks 124
Checking out the advantages of income stocks 125
Watching out for the disadvantages of income stocks 125
Analyzing Income Stocks 127
Pinpointing your needs first 127
Checking out yield 128
Looking at a stock's payout ratio 130
Examining a company's bond rating 131
Diversifying your stocks 132
Exploring Some Typical Income Stocks 132
Utilities 133
Real estate investment trusts (REITs) 133
Royalty trusts 135

Chapter 10: Getting a Grip on Economics **137**

Breaking Down Microeconomics versus Macroeconomics 138
Microeconomics 138
Macroeconomics 139
Understanding Important Concepts in Economic Logic 139
Supply and demand 140
Wants and needs 140
Dynamic analysis versus static analysis 141
Cause and effect 142
Surveying a Few Schools of Economic Thought 142
The Marx school 142
The Keynes school 143
The Austrian school 145

Understanding Some Current Economic Issues
That Face Stock Investors...145
Inflation 146
Government intervention 146

Part III: Picking Winners 149

Chapter 11: Using Basic Accounting to Choose Winning Stocks...151

Recognizing Value When You See It...151
Understanding different types of value.......................................152
Putting the pieces together 154
Accounting for Value...155
Breaking down the balance sheet..156
Looking at the income statement 159
Tooling around with ratios..162

Chapter 12: Decoding Company Documents 167

Getting a Message from the Bigwigs: The Annual Report 167
Analyzing the annual report's anatomy......................................168
Going through the proxy materials 172
Getting a Second Opinion...172
Company documents filed with the SEC.....................................172
Value Line 174
Standard & Poor's...174
Moody's Investment Service 175
Brokerage reports: The good, the bad, and the ugly 175
Compiling Your Own Research Department.....................................177

Chapter 13: Analyzing Industries...............................179

Interrogating the Industries 180
Which category does the industry fall into? 180
Is the industry growing?..181
Are the industry's products or services in demand?...................183
What does the industry's growth rely on? 183
Is the industry dependent on another industry?.........................184
Who are the leading companies in the industry? 184
Is the industry a target of government action?............................185
Outlining Key Industries...185
Moving in: Real estate 186
Driving it home: Automotive 187
Talking tech: Computers and related electronics 187
Banking on it: Financials 188

Chapter 14: Emerging Sector Opportunities **189**

Bullish Opportunities...190
    Commodities 191
    Oil and gas 192
    Alternative energy 193
    Gold and other precious metals 194
    Healthcare...195
    Defending the nation 195
A Bearish Outlook...196
    Avoiding consumer discretionary sectors 196
    A warning on real estate 197
    The great credit monster 198
    Cyclical stocks...199
Important Considerations for Bulls and Bears 199
    Conservative and bullish 200
    Aggressive and bullish 200
    Conservative and bearish 201
    Aggressive and bearish 201

Chapter 15: Money, Mayhem, and Votes **203**

Tying Together Politics and Stocks.......................................204
    Seeing the general effects of politics on stock investing.............204
    Ascertaining the political climate....................................206
    Distinguishing between nonsystemic and systemic effects.........207
    Understanding price controls 209
Poking into Political Resources 209
    Government reports to watch out for...............................210
    Web sites to surf 212

Part IV: Investment Strategies and Tactics *213*

Chapter 16: Choosing between Investing and Trading **215**

The Differences between Investing and Trading....................215
    The time factor...216
    The psychology factor 217
    Checking out an example...217
Tools of the Trader 220
    Technical analysis 220
    Brokerage orders 221
    Advisory services 221
The Basic Rules of Trading...222

Chapter 17: Selecting a Strategy That's Just Right for You **225**

Laying Out Your Plans 225
    Living the bachelor life: Young single with no dependents 226
    Going together like a horse and carriage:
        Married with children..227

Getting ready for retirement: Over 40 and
either single or married..227
Kicking back in the hammock: Already retired............................228
Allocating Your Assets...228
Investors with less than $10,000......................................229
Investors with $10,000 to $50,000....................................230
Investors with $50,000 or more..230
Knowing When to Sell 231

**Chapter 18: Understanding Brokerage Orders
and Trading Techniques 235**
Checking Out Brokerage Orders...235
On the clock: Time-related orders...................................236
At your command: Condition-related orders 238
The joys of technology: Advanced orders.........................243
Buying on Margin...244
Examining marginal outcomes 245
Maintaining your balance 246
Striving for success on margin...246
Going Short and Coming Out Ahead 247
Setting up a short sale..248
Oops! Going short when prices grow taller.......................249
Feeling the squeeze 250

Chapter 19: Getting a Handle on DPPs, DRPs, and DCA . . . PDQ....251
Being Direct with DPPs 252
Investing in a DPP 252
Finding DPP alternatives...253
Recognizing the drawbacks 254
Dipping into DRPs..255
Getting a clue about compounding 255
Building wealth with optional cash payments...................256
Checking out the cost advantages....................................257
Weighing the pros with the cons 258
The One-Two Punch: Dollar Cost Averaging and DRPs 258

Chapter 20: Corporate Skullduggery: Looking at Insider Activity . . .261
Tracking Insider Trading..262
Looking at Insider Transactions 263
Breaking down insider buying...264
Picking up tips from insider selling..................................265
Considering Corporate Stock Buybacks.......................................266
Understanding why a company buys back shares......................267
Exploring the downside of buybacks 269
Stock Splits: Nothing to Go Bananas Over 269
Ordinary stock splits..270
Reverse stock splits...271

Chapter 21: Keeping More of Your Money from the Taxman **273**

Paying through the Nose: The Tax Treatment
of Different Investments 274
Understanding ordinary income and capital gains 274
Minimizing the tax on your capital gains.................................275
Coping with capital losses...276
Evaluating gains and losses scenarios 277
Sharing Your Gains with the IRS...277
Filling out forms 278
Playing by the rules 279
Discovering the Softer Side of the IRS: Tax Deductions for Investors.....279
Investment interest..280
Miscellaneous expenses..280
Donations of stock to charity 281
Knowing what you can't deduct 281
Taking Advantage of Tax-Advantaged Retirement Investing.................281
IRAs...282
401(k) plans 283

Part V: The Part of Tens **285**

Chapter 22: Ten Ways to Profit before the Crowd Does **287**

Use Your Instincts 287
Take Notice of Praise from Consumer Groups 288
Check Out Powerful Demographics 288
Look for a Rise in Earnings..289
Analyze Industries 289
Stay Aware of Positive Publicity for Industries 290
Watch Megatrends 290
Keep Track of Politics 290
Recognize Heavy Insider or Corporate Buying.....................................291
Follow Institutional Investors 292

**Chapter 23: Ten (Or So) Ways to Protect
Your Stock Market Profits** **293**

Accrue Cash 293
Spread Your Money across Several Stocks..293
Buy More of a Down (Yet Solid) Stock..294
Apply Long-Term Logic..294
Use the Almighty Stop-Loss Order 294
Use the Almighty Trailing Stop Order...295
Place a Limit Order...295
Set Up Broker Triggers...296
Consider the Put Option 296
Check Out the Covered Call Option 296
When All Else Fails, Sell 297

Chapter 24: Ten Red Flags for Stock Investors 299

Earnings Slow Down or Head South...299
Sales Slow Down 300
Debt Is Too High or Unsustainable 301
Analysts Are Exuberant Despite Logic..301
Insider Selling...302
A Bond Rating Cut 302
Increased Negative Coverage...302
Industry Problems 303
Political Problems 303
Funny Accounting: No Laughing Here!..303

Chapter 25: Ten Challenges and Opportunities
for Stock Investors 305

Debt, Debt, and More Debt..305
Derivatives..306
Real Estate 307
Inflation...307
Pensions and Unfunded Liabilities..308
The Growth of Government 308
Recession/Depression...309
Commodities 309
Energy 309
Dangers from Left Field..310

Part VI: Appendixes 311

Appendix A: Resources for Stock Investors 313

Financial Planning Sources..313
The Language of Investing..314
Textual Investment Resources 314
    Periodicals and magazines 314
    Books and pamphlets..315
    Special books of interest to stock investors 316
Investing Web Sites 317
    General investing Web sites 317
    Stock investing Web sites...318
Investor Associations and Organizations..319
Stock Exchanges 319
Finding Brokers...319
    Choosing brokers...320
    Brokers 320
Fee-Based Investment Sources 321
Dividend Reinvestment Plans 322

Sources for Analysis 323
  Earnings and earnings estimates 323
  Industry analysis 323
  Factors that affect market value 323
  Technical analysis 325
  Insider trading 325
Tax Benefits and Obligations 326
Fraud 326

Appendix B: Financial Ratios 329
Liquidity Ratios 330
  Current ratio 330
  Quick ratio 331
Operating Ratios 331
  Return on equity (ROE) 331
  Return on assets (ROA) 332
  Sales to receivables ratio (SR) 332
Solvency Ratios 333
  Debt to net equity ratio 333
  Working capital 334
Common Size Ratios 334
Valuation Ratios 335
  Price-to-earnings ratio (P/E) 335
  Price to sales ratio (PSR) 336
  Price to book ratio (PBR) 337

Index *339*

Introduction

Stock Investing For Dummies, 3rd Edition, has been an honor for me to write. I'm grateful that I can share my thoughts, information, and experience with such a large and devoted group of readers.

I think that this edition is my most important edition so far because so much change, volatility, and uncertainty have become a part of the stock market. It's not your parents' stock market anymore. The opportunities for great gains (and even greater losses) have reached an extreme. In some ways, today's market reminds me of Dickens' famous novel opener: "It was the best of times, it was the worst of times . . . ." In terms of what faces us in today's world — economic uncertainty, terrorism, war, political tensions, higher taxes, rising inflation, unemployment, and so on — these seem like the worst of times. Yet when I think of the tools, strategies, and investing vehicles available for you to build (and protect) wealth, these can be the best of times.

Successful stock investing takes diligent work and knowledge, like any other meaningful pursuit. This book can definitely help you avoid the mistakes others have made and can point you in the right direction. It will give you a heads up about trends and conditions that are found in few other stock investing guides. Explore the pages of this book and find the topics that most interest you within the world of stock investing. Let me assure you that I've squeezed over a quarter century of experience, education, and expertise between these covers. My track record is as good (or better) as the track records of the experts who trumpet their successes. More important, I share information to avoid common mistakes (some of which I made myself!). Understanding what not to do can be just as important as figuring out what to do.

In all the years that I've counseled and educated investors, the single difference between success and failure, between gain and loss, boils down to one word: knowledge. Take this book as your first step in a lifelong learning adventure.

About This Book

The stock market has been a cornerstone of the investor's passive wealth-building program for over a century and continues in this role. This decade has been one huge roller coaster ride for stock investors. Fortunes have been made and lost. With all the media attention, all the talking heads on radio and television, and the books with titles like *Dow at 36,000,* the investing public still didn't avoid losing trillions in a historic stock market debacle. Sadly, even the so-called experts who understand stocks didn't see the economic and geopolitical forces that acted like a tsunami on the market. With just a little more knowledge and a few wealth-preserving techniques, more investors could have held onto their hard-earned stock market fortunes. Cheer up, though: This book gives you an early warning on those megatrends and events that will affect your stock portfolio. While other books may tell you about stocks, this book tells you about stocks and what affects them.

This book is designed to give you a realistic approach to making money in stocks. It provides the essence of sound, practical stock investing strategies and insights that have been market-tested and proven from nearly 100 years of stock market history. I don't expect you to read it cover to cover, although I'd be delighted if you read every word! Instead, this book is designed as a reference tool. Feel free to read the chapters in whatever order you choose. You can flip to the sections and chapters that interest you or those that include topics that you need to know more about.

Stock Investing For Dummies, 3rd Edition, is also quite different from the "get rich with stocks" titles that have crammed the bookshelves in recent years. It doesn't take a standard approach to the topic; it doesn't assume that stocks are a sure thing and the be-all, end-all of wealth building. In fact, at times in this book, I tell you *not* to invest in stocks.

This book can help you succeed not only in up markets but also in down markets. Bull markets and bear markets come and go, but the informed investor can keep making money no matter what. To give you an extra edge, I've tried to include information about the investing environment for stocks. Whether it's politics or hurricanes (or both), you need to know how the big picture affects your stock investment decisions.

Conventions Used in This Book

To make navigating through this book easier, I've established the following conventions:

- ✔ **Boldface** text points out keywords or the main parts of bulleted items.
- ✔ *Italics* highlight new terms that are defined.
- ✔ `Monofont` is used for Web addresses.

When this book was printed, some Web addresses may have needed to break across two lines of text. If that happened, rest assured that I haven't put in any extra characters (such as hyphens) to indicate the break. So when using one of these Web addresses, just type in exactly what you see in this book, pretending as though the line break doesn't exist.

What You're Not to Read

Sidebars (gray boxes of text) in this book give you a more in-depth look at a certain topic. While they further illuminate a particular point, these sidebars aren't crucial to your understanding of the rest of the book. Feel free to read them or skip them. Of course, I'd love for you to read them all, but my feelings won't be hurt if you decide to skip them over.

The text that accompanies the Technical Stuff icon (see the forthcoming section "Icons Used in This Book") can be passed over as well. The text associated with this icon gives some technical details about stock investing that are certainly interesting and informative, but you can still come away with the information you need without reading this text.

Foolish Assumptions

I figure you've picked up this book for one or more of the following reasons:

- ✔ You're a beginner and want a crash course on stock investing that's an easy read.

- ✔ You're already a stock investor, and you need a book that allows you to read only those chapters that cover specific stock investing topics of interest to you.

- ✔ You need to review your own situation with the information in the book to see if you missed anything when you invested in that hot stock that your brother-in-law recommended.

- ✔ You need a great gift! When Uncle Mo is upset over his poor stock picks, you can give him this book so he can get back on his financial feet. Be sure to get a copy for his broker, too. (Odds are that the broker was the one who made those picks to begin with.)

How This Book Is Organized

The information is laid out in a straightforward format. The parts progress in a logical approach that any investor interested in stocks can follow very easily.

Part I: The Essentials of Stock Investing

This part is for everyone. Understanding the essentials of stock investing and investing in general will only help you, especially in uncertain economic times. Stocks may even touch your finances in ways not readily apparent. For example, stocks aren't only in individual accounts; they're also in mutual funds and pension plans.

An important point is that stocks are really financial tools that are a means to an end. Investors should be able to answer the question, "Why am I considering stocks at all?" Stocks are a great vehicle for wealth building, but only if investors realize what they can accomplish and how to use them. Chapter 2 explains how to take stock of your current financial situation and goals, and Chapter 3 defines common approaches to stock investing.

One of the essentials of stock investing is understanding risk. Most people are clueless about risk. Chapter 4, on risk, is one of the most important chapters that serious stock investors should read. You can't avoid every type of risk out there (life itself embodies risk). However, this chapter can help you recognize it and find ways to minimize it in your stock investing program.

Part II: Before You Start Buying

When you're ready to embark on your career as a stock investor, you need to use some resources to gather information about the stocks you're interested in. Fortunately, you live in the information age. I pity the investors from the 1920s who didn't have access to so many resources, but today's investors are in an enviable position. This part tells you where to find information and how to use it to be a more knowledgeable investor (a rarity in recent years!). For example, I explain that stocks can be used for both growth and income purposes, and I discuss the characteristics of each; see Chapters 8 and 9 for more information.

Chapter 6 is a great starting place for your information gathering; I show you how to stay on top of financial news and read stock tables, among other topics.

When you're ready to invest, you'll invariably have to turn to a broker. Several types of brokers are out there, so you should know which is which. The wrong broker can make you . . . uh . . . broker. Chapter 7 helps you choose.

New to this edition is Chapter 10, which gives you the lowdown on how a grasp of basic economics can make you more successful with your stock investing strategy.

Part III: Picking Winners

Part III is about picking good stocks by using microeconomics, meaning that you look at the stocks of individual companies. I explain how to evaluate a company's products, services, and other factors so that you can determine whether a company is strong and healthy.

One of the major differences with this edition versus earlier editions is the emphasis on emerging sector opportunities. If I can steer you toward those segments of the stock market that show solid promise for the coming years, that alone would make your stock portfolio thrive. Putting your money into solid companies in thriving industries has been the hallmark of superior stock investing throughout history. It's no different now. Check out Chapter 14 if you want to know more about emerging sector opportunities.

Where do you turn to find out about a company's financial health? In Chapters 11 and 12, I show you the documents you should review to make a more informed decision. When you find the information, you'll discover how to make sense of that data as well. While you're at it, check out Chapter 13 (on analyzing industries) and Chapter 15 (on how politics affects the art of stock picking).

I compare buying stock to picking goldfish. If you look at a bunch of goldfish to choose which ones to buy, you want to make sure that you pick the healthiest ones. With stocks, you also need to pick companies that are healthy. Part III can help you do that.

Part IV: Investment Strategies and Tactics

Even the stocks of great companies can fall in a bad investing environment. This is where you should be aware of the "macro." If stocks were goldfish, the macro would be the pond or goldfish bowl. In that case, even healthy goldfish can die if the water is toxic. Therefore, you should monitor the investing environment for stocks. Part IV reveals tips, strategies, and resources that you shouldn't ignore.

Investing is a long-term activity, but stocks can also be short-term opportunities, so I discuss stock trading in Chapter 16. In Chapter 17, I provide guidance on selecting an investing strategy that's right for your personal and financial situations.

After you understand stocks and the economic environment in which they operate, choose the strategy and the tactics to help steer you to your wealth-building objectives. Chapter 18 reveals some of my all-time favorite techniques for building wealth and holding onto your stock investment gains (definitely check it out).

You may be an investor, but that doesn't mean that you have deep pockets. Chapter 19 tells you how to buy stocks with low (or no) transaction costs. If you're going to buy the stock anyway, why not save on commissions and other costs?

As an investor, you must keep an eye on what company insiders are doing. In Chapter 20, I explain what it may mean if a company's management is buying or selling the same stock that you're considering.

After you spend all your time, money, and effort to grow your money in the world of stocks, you have yet another concern: holding onto your hard-earned gains. This challenge is summarized in one word: taxes. Sound tax planning is crucial for everyone who works hard. After all, taxes are the biggest expense in your lifetime (right after children!). See Chapter 21 for more information.

Part V: The Part of Tens

I wrap up the book with a hallmark of *For Dummies* books — the Part of Tens. These chapters give you a mini crash course in stock investing, including ten ways to protect yourself from fraud.

In this part, I offer some tips on how to profit with stocks before the crowd does (Chapter 22) and how to protect those profits (Chapter 23). I also provide a list of ten red flags for stock investors (Chapter 24), along with ten challenges and opportunities that face stock investors (Chapter 25).

Part VI: Appendixes

Don't overlook the appendixes. I pride myself on the resources I can provide my students and readers so that they can make informed investment decisions. Whether the topic is stock investing terminology, economics, or avoiding capital gains taxes, I include a treasure trove of resources to help you. Whether you go to a bookstore, the library, or the Internet, Appendix A gives you some great places to turn to for help. In Appendix B, I explain financial ratios. These important numbers help you better determine whether to invest in a particular company's stock.

Icons Used in This Book

 When you see this icon, I'm reminding you about some information that you should always keep stashed in your memory, whether you're new to investing or an old pro.

 The text attached to this icon may not be crucial to your success as an investor, but it may enable you to talk shop with investing gurus and better understand the financial pages of your favorite business publication or Web site.

 This icon flags a particular bit of advice that just may give you an edge over other investors.

 Pay special attention to this icon because the advice can prevent headaches, heartaches, and financial aches.

Where to Go from Here

You may not need to read every chapter to make you more confident as a stock investor, so feel free to jump around to suit your personal needs. Because every chapter is designed to be as self-contained as possible, it won't do you any harm to cherry-pick what you really want to read. But if you're like me, you may still want to check out every chapter because you never know when you may come across a new tip or resource that will make a profitable difference in your stock portfolio. I want you to be successful so that I can brag about you in the next edition!

Part I

The Essentials of Stock Investing

In this part . . .

The latest market turmoil and uncertainty tell investors to get back to square one. Your success is dependent on doing your homework before you invest your first dollar in stocks. Most investors don't realize that they should be scrutinizing their own situations and financial goals at least as much as they scrutinize stocks. How else can you know which stocks are right for you? Too many people risk too much simply because they don't take stock of their current needs, goals, and risk tolerance before they invest. The chapters in this part tell you what you need to know to choose the stocks that best suit you.

Chapter 1

Welcome to the World of Stock Investing

In This Chapter

▶ Knowing the essentials

▶ Doing your own research

▶ Recognizing winners

▶ Exploring investment strategies

Stock investing was the hot thing during the late 1990s — a trend just like the hula hoop and pet rocks. With the new millennium, however, a reversal of fortunes has occurred as the bear market of 2000–2002 rocked our world (a *bear market* is a prolonged period of falling prices — in this case, stock prices). This decade has been a wild roller coaster ride that saw the market hit new highs in 2007, although it's down in ugly fashion in 2008. During this time, the public figured out that stock investing isn't for wild-eyed amateurs or dart-throwers (or the worst . . . wild-eyed amateur dart-throwers!).

I wrote much of this 3rd Edition with current events and market conditions on my radar screen. The year 2008 witnessed some ominous events that will make stock investing very interesting (to say the least) for the time being. Don't let that scare you, though; informed investors have made money in all sorts of markets — good, bad, and even ugly. As I write this, the conditions are in place for an inflationary depression, but selecting stocks that can benefit from these challenging times could indeed make you much wealthier.

The purpose of this book is not only to tell you about the basics of stock investing but also to let you in on some solid strategies that can help you profit from the stock market. Before you invest your first dollar, you need to understand the basics of stock investing, which I introduce in this chapter.

Understanding the Basics

The basics are so basic that few people are doing them. Perhaps the most basic (and therefore most important) thing to grasp is the risk you face whenever you do anything (like putting your hard-earned money in an investment like a stock). When you lose track of the basics, you lose track of why you invested to begin with. Find out more about risk (and the different kinds of risk) in Chapter 4.

When the late comedian Henny Youngman was asked, "How is your wife?" he responded, "Compared to what?" This also applies to stocks. When you're asked, "How is your stock?" you can very well respond that it's doing well, especially when compared to an acceptable yardstick such as a stock index (like the S&P 500). Find out more about indexes in Chapter 5.

The bottom line in stock investing is that you shouldn't immediately send your money to a brokerage account or go to a Web site and click "buy stock." The first thing you should do is find out as much as you can about what stocks are and how to use them to achieve your wealth-building goals. Chapters 2 and 3 help you take stock of your current financial situation and help you understand common approaches to stock investing.

Before you continue, I want to get straight exactly what a stock is. *Stock* is a type of security that indicates ownership in a corporation and represents a claim on the part of that corporation's assets and earnings. The two primary types of stocks are common and preferred. *Common stock* (what I cover throughout this book) entitles the owner to vote at shareholders' meetings and receive any dividends that the company issues. *Preferred stock* doesn't usually confer voting rights, but it does include some rights that exceed those of common stock. Preferred stockholders, for example, have priority in certain conditions, such as receiving dividends before common stockholders in the event that the corporation is going bankrupt.

Preparing to Buy Stocks

Gathering information is critical in your stock-investing pursuits. You should gather information on your stock picks two times: before you invest and after. Obviously, you should become more informed before you invest your first dollar, but you also need to stay informed about what's happening to the company whose stock you buy, and also about the industry and the general economy. To find the best information sources, check out Chapter 6.

When you're ready to invest, you need a brokerage account. How do you know which broker to use? Chapter 7 provides some answers and resources to help you choose a broker.

Knowing How to Pick Winners

When you get past the basics, you can get to the meat of stock picking. Successful stock picking isn't mysterious, but it does take some time, effort, and analysis. And the effort is worthwhile because stocks are a convenient and important part of most investors' portfolios. Read the following sections and be sure to leapfrog to the relevant chapters to get the inside scoop on hot stocks.

Recognizing stock value

Imagine that you like eggs and you're buying them at the grocery store. In this example, the eggs are like companies, and the prices represent the prices that you would pay for the companies' stock. The grocery store is the stock market. What if two brands of eggs are similar, but one costs 50 cents a carton and the other costs 75 cents? Which would you choose? Odds are that you'd look at both brands, judge their quality, and if they're indeed similar, take the cheaper eggs. The eggs at 75 cents are overpriced. The same is true of stocks. What if you compare two companies that are similar in every respect but have different share prices? All things being equal, the cheaper price has greater value for the investor.

But the egg example has another side. What if the quality of the two brands of eggs is significantly different, but their prices are the same? If one brand of eggs is stale, of poor quality, and priced at 50 cents and the other brand is fresh, of superior quality, and also priced at 50 cents, which would you get? I'd take the good brand because they're better eggs. Perhaps the lesser eggs are an acceptable purchase at 10 cents, but they're definitely overpriced at 50 cents. The same example works with stocks. A poorly run company isn't a good choice if you can buy a better company in the marketplace at the same — or a better — price.

Comparing the value of eggs may seem overly simplistic, but doing so does cut to the heart of stock investing. Eggs and egg prices can be as varied as companies and stock prices. As an investor, you must make it your job to find the best value for your investment dollars. (Otherwise you get egg on your face. You saw that one coming, right?)

Understanding how market capitalization affects stock value

You can determine a company's value (and thus the value of its stock) in many ways. The most basic way is to look at the company's market value, also known as market capitalization (or market cap). *Market capitalization* is simply the value you get when you multiply all the outstanding shares of a stock by the price of a single share.

Calculating the market cap is easy. If a company has 1 million shares outstanding and its share price is $10, the market cap is $10 million.

Small cap, mid cap, and large cap aren't references to headgear; they're references to how large a company is as measured by its market value. Here are the five basic stock categories of market capitalization:

- **Micro cap (under $250 million):** These stocks are the smallest and hence the riskiest available.

- **Small cap ($250 million to $1 billion):** These stocks fare better than the microcaps and still have plenty of growth potential. The key word here is "potential."

- **Mid cap ($1 billion to $10 billion):** For many investors, this category offers a good compromise between small caps and large caps. These stocks have some of the safety of large caps while retaining some of the growth potential of small caps.

- **Large cap ($10 billion to $50 billion):** This category is usually best reserved for conservative stock investors who want steady appreciation with greater safety. Stocks in this category are frequently referred to as *blue chips.*

- **Ultra cap (over $50 billion):** These stocks are also called *mega caps* and obviously refer to companies that are the biggest of the big. Stocks such as General Electric and Exxon Mobil are examples.

From a safety point of view, a company's size and market value do matter. All things being equal, large cap stocks are considered safer than small cap stocks. However, small cap stocks have greater potential for growth. Compare these stocks to trees: Which tree is sturdier, a giant California redwood or a small oak tree that's just a year old? In a great storm, the redwood holds up well, while the smaller tree has a rough time. But you also have to ask yourself which tree has more opportunity for growth. The redwood may not have much growth left, but the small oak tree has plenty of growth to look forward to.

For beginning investors, comparing market cap to trees isn't so far-fetched. You want your money to branch out without becoming a sap.

Although market capitalization is important to consider, don't invest (or not invest) based solely on it. It's just one measure of value. As a serious investor, you need to look at numerous factors that can help you determine whether any given stock is a good investment. Keep reading — this book is full of information to help you decide.

Sharpening your investment skills

Investors who analyze a company can better judge the value of its stock and profit from buying and selling it. Your greatest asset in stock investing is knowledge (and a little common sense). To succeed in the world of stock investing, keep in mind these key success factors:

- ✔ Understand why you want to invest in stocks. Are you seeking appreciation (capital gains) or income (dividends)? Look at Chapters 8 and 9 for information on these topics.

- ✔ Get a good grounding in economics. It could save your financial life! In Chapter 10, I include some basic (but interesting) points on economics because I think that stock investors (as a group) are woefully undereducated in economics and are therefore at risk (translation: bad stock decisions!). Check it out — you'll be glad you did.

- ✔ Do some research. Look at the company whose stock you're considering to see whether it's a profitable business worthy of your investment dollars. Chapters 11 and 12 help you scrutinize companies.

- ✔ Choosing a winning stock also means that you choose a winning industry. You'll frequently see stock prices of mediocre companies in hot industries rise higher and faster than solid companies in floundering industries. Therefore, choosing the industry is very important. Find out more about analyzing industries in Chapter 13.

- ✔ Understand and identify megatrends. Doing so makes it easier for you to make money. This edition spends more time and provides more resources to help you see the opportunities in emerging sectors and avoid the problem areas (see Chapter 14 for details).

- ✔ Understand how the world affects your stock. Stocks succeed or fail in large part because of the environment in which they operate. Economics (see Chapter 10) and politics (see Chapter 15) make up that world, so you should know something about them.

Stock market insanity

Have you ever noticed a stock going up even though the company is reporting terrible results? How about seeing a stock nosedive despite the fact that the company is doing well? What gives? Well, judging the direction of a stock in a short-term period — over the next few days or weeks — is almost impossible.

Yes, in the short term, stock investing is irrational. The price of a stock and the value of its company seem disconnected and crazy. The key phrase to remember is "short term." A stock's price and the company's value become more logical over an extended period of time.

The longer a stock is in the public's view, the more rational the performance of the stock's price. In other words, a good company continues to draw attention to itself; hence, more people want its stock, and the share price rises to better match the company's value. Conversely, a bad company doesn't hold up to continued scrutiny over time. As more and more people see that the company isn't doing well, the share price declines. Over the long run, a stock's share price and the company's value eventually become equal for the most part.

✔ **Use investing strategies like the pros do.** In other words, how you go about investing can be just as important as what you invest in. Chapters 17, 18, and 19 highlight techniques for investing to help you make more money from your stocks.

✔ **Keep more of the money you earn.** After all your great work in getting the right stocks and making the big bucks, you should know about keeping more of the fruits of your investing. I cover taxes in stock investing in Chapter 21.

✔ Sometimes, what people tell you to do with stocks is not as revealing as what people are actually doing. This is why I like to look at company insiders before I buy or sell a particular stock. To find out more about insider buying and selling, read Chapter 20.

Actually, every chapter in this book offers you valuable guidance on some essential aspect of the fantastic world of stocks. The knowledge you pick up and apply from these pages has been tested over nearly a century of stock picking. The investment experience of the past — the good, the bad, and some of the ugly — is here for your benefit. Use this information to make a lot of money (and make me proud!). And don't forget to check out the appendixes, where I provide a wide variety of investing resources and financial ratios!

Boning Up on Strategies and Tactics

Successful investing isn't just what you invest in; it's also the way you invest. I'm very big on strategies such as trailing stops and limit orders. You can find out more in Chapter 18.

Buying stocks doesn't always mean that you must buy through a broker and that it must be 100 shares. You can buy stock for as little as $25 using programs such as dividend reinvestment plans. Chapter 19 tells you more.

 While you're at it, you may as well find out what the corporate insiders are doing. Why? Because corporate insiders are among the first to find out what's really going on inside a company, and that knowledge is reflected in their investing decisions, which you should pay attention to. You can find out more about insider trading and other management doings in Chapter 20.

Chapter 2

Taking Stock of Your Current Financial Situation and Goals

....

In This Chapter

▶ Preparing your personal balance sheet

▶ Looking at your cash flow statement

▶ Determining your financial goals

....

Yes, you want to make the big bucks. Or maybe you just want to get back the big bucks you lost in stocks during the bear market (a long period of falling prices) of 2000–2002, or perhaps in the tumultuous volatility of 2007 and early 2008. (Investors who followed the guidelines from the 1st and 2nd editions of this book did much better than the crowd!) Either way, you want your money to grow so that you can have a better life. But before you make reservations for that Caribbean cruise you're dreaming about, you have to map out your action plan for getting there. Stocks can be a great component of most wealth-building programs, but you must first do some homework on a topic that you should be very familiar with — yourself. That's right. Understanding your current financial situation and clearly defining your financial goals are the first steps in successful investing.

Let me give you an example. I met an investor at one of my seminars who had a million dollars worth of Procter & Gamble (PG) stock, and he was near-ing retirement. He asked me whether he should sell his stock and be more growth-oriented and invest in a batch of *small cap* stocks (stocks of a com-pany worth $250 million to $1 billion; see Chapter 1 for more information). Because he already had enough assets to retire on at that time, I said that he didn't need to get more aggressive. In fact, I told him that he had too much tied to a single stock, even though it was a solid, large company. What would happen to his assets if problems arose at PG? It seemed obvious to tell him to shrink his stock portfolio and put that money elsewhere, such as paying off debt or adding investment-grade bonds for diversification.

This chapter is undoubtedly one of the most important chapters in this book. At first, you may think it's a chapter more suitable for some general book on personal finance. Wrong! Unsuccessful investors' greatest weakness is not understanding their financial situation and how stocks fit in. Often, I counsel people to stay out of the stock market if they aren't prepared for the responsibilities of stock investing — they haven't been regularly reviewing the company's financial statements or tracking the company's progress.

Investing in stocks requires balance. Investors sometimes tie up too much money in stocks, putting themselves at risk of losing a significant portion of their wealth if the market plunges. Then again, other investors place little or no money in stocks and therefore miss out on excellent opportunities to grow their wealth. Investors should make stocks a part of their portfolios, but the operative word is *part.* You should let stocks take up only a *portion* of your money. A disciplined investor also has money in bank accounts, investment-grade bonds, precious metals, and other assets that offer growth or income opportunities. Diversification is the key to minimizing risk. (For more on risk, see Chapter 4.)

Establishing a Starting Point by Preparing a Balance Sheet

Whether you're already in stocks or you're looking to get into stocks, you need to find out about how much money you can afford to invest. No matter what you hope to accomplish with your stock investing plan, the first step you should take is to figure out how much you own and how much you owe. To do this, prepare and review your personal balance sheet. A *balance sheet* is simply a list of your assets, your liabilities, and what each item is currently worth so you can arrive at your net worth. Your net worth is total assets minus total liabilities. I know that these terms sound like accounting mumbo jumbo, but knowing your net worth is important to your future financial success, so just do it.

Composing your balance sheet is simple. Pull out a pencil and a piece of paper. For the computer savvy, a spreadsheet software program accomplishes the same task. Gather all your financial documents, such as bank and brokerage statements and other such paperwork — you need figures from these documents. Then follow the steps that I outline in the following sections. Update your balance sheet at least once a year to monitor your financial progress (is your net worth going up or down?).

Your personal balance sheet is really no different from balance sheets that giant companies prepare. (The main difference is a few zeros, but you can use my advice in this book to work on changing that.) In fact, the more you find out about your own balance sheet, the easier it is to understand the balance sheet of companies in which you're seeking to invest. See Chapter 11 for details on reviewing company balance sheets.

Step 1: Make sure you have an emergency fund

First, list cash on your balance sheet. Your goal is to have, in reserve, at least three to six months' worth of your gross living expenses in cash and cash equivalents. The cash is important because it gives you a cushion. Three to six months is usually enough to get you through the most common forms of financial disruption, such as losing your job.

If your monthly expenses (or *outgo*) are $2,000, you should have at least $6,000, and probably closer to $12,000, in a secure, FDIC-insured, interest-bearing bank account (or other, relatively safe interest-bearing vehicle such as a money market fund). Consider this account an emergency fund and not an investment. Don't use this money to buy stocks.

Too many Americans don't have an emergency fund, meaning that they put themselves at risk. Walking across a busy street while wearing a blindfold is a great example of putting yourself at risk, and in recent years, investors have done the financial equivalent. Investors piled on tremendous debt, put too much into investments (such as stocks) that they didn't understand, and had little or no savings. One of the biggest problems during this past decade was that savings were sinking to record lows while debt levels were reaching new heights. People then sold many stocks because they needed funds for — you guessed it — paying bills and debt.

Resist the urge to start thinking of your investment in stocks as a savings account generating over 20 percent per year. This is dangerous thinking! If your investments tank, or if you lose your job, you will have financial difficulty and that will affect your stock portfolio (you may have to sell some stocks in your account just to get money to pay the bills). An emergency fund helps you through a temporary cash crunch.

Step 2: List your assets in decreasing order of liquidity

Liquid assets aren't references to beer or cola (unless you're Anheuser-Busch). Instead, *liquidity* refers to how quickly you can convert a particular *asset* (something you own that has value) into cash. If you know the liquidity of your assets, including investments, you have some options when you need cash to buy some stock (or pay some bills). All too often, people are short on cash and have too much wealth tied up in *illiquid investments* such as real estate. *Illiquid* is just a fancy way of saying that you don't have the immediate cash to meet a pressing need. (Hey, we've all had those moments!) Review your assets and take measures to ensure that enough of them are liquid (along with your illiquid assets).

Listing your assets in order of liquidity on your balance sheet gives you an immediate picture of which assets you can quickly convert to cash and which ones you can't. If you need money *now,* you can see that cash in hand, your checking account, and your savings account are at the top of the list. The items last in order of liquidity become obvious; they're things like real estate and other assets that can take a long time to convert to cash.

Selling real estate, even in a seller's market, can take months. Investors who don't have adequate liquid assets run the danger of selling assets quickly and possibly at a loss because they scramble to accumulate the cash for their short-term financial obligations. For stock investors, this scramble may include prematurely selling stocks that they originally intended to use as long-term investments.

Table 2-1 shows a typical list of assets in order of liquidity. Use it as a guide for making your own asset list.

Table 2-1	John Q. Investor: Personal Assets as of December 31, 2008	
Asset Item	**Market Value**	**Annual Growth Rate %**
Current assets		
Cash on hand and in checking	$150	0
Bank savings accounts and certificates of deposit	$5,000	2%
Stocks	$2,000	11%

Asset Item	Market Value	Annual Growth Rate %
Mutual funds	$2,400	9%
Total current assets	**$9,790**	
Long-term assets		
Auto	$1,800	−10%
Residence	$150,000	5%
Real estate investment	$125,000	6%
Personal stuff (such as jewelry)	$4,000	
Total long-term assets	**$280,800**	
Total assets	**$290,590**	

Here's how to break down the information in Table 2-1:

- ✔ The first column describes the asset. You can quickly convert *current assets* to cash — they're more liquid; *long-term assets* have value, but you can't necessarily convert them to cash quickly — they aren't very liquid.

  Please take note — I have stocks listed as short-term in the table. The reason is that this balance sheet is meant to list items in order of liquidity. Liquidity is best embodied in the question, "How quickly can I turn this asset into cash?" Because a stock can be sold and converted to cash very quickly, it's a good example of a liquid asset. (However, that's not the main purpose for buying stocks.)

- ✔ The second column gives the current market value for that item. Keep in mind that this value isn't the purchase price or original value; it's the amount you would realistically get if you sold the asset in the current market at that moment.

- ✔ The third column tells you how well that investment is doing, compared to one year ago. If the percentage rate is 5 percent, that item increased in value by 5 percent from a year ago. You need to know how well all your assets are doing. Why? To adjust your assets for maximum growth or to get rid of assets that are losing money. Assets that are doing well are kept (consider increasing your holdings in these assets), and assets that are down in value should be scrutinized to see whether they're candidates for removal. Perhaps you can sell them and reinvest the money elsewhere. In addition, the realized loss has tax benefits (see Chapter 21).

Figuring the annual growth rate (in the third column) as a percentage isn't difficult. Say that you buy 100 shares of the stock Gro-A-Lot Corp. (GAL), and its market value on December 31, 2007, is $50 per share for a total market value of $5,000 (100 shares × $50 per share). When you check its value on December 31, 2008, you find out that the stock is at $60 per share for a total market value of $6,000 (100 shares × $60). The annual growth rate is 20 percent. You calculate this by taking the amount of the gain ($60 per share less $50 per share = $10 gain per share), which is $1,000 (100 shares times the $10 gain), and dividing it by the value at the beginning of the time period ($5,000). In this case, you get 20 percent ($1,000 ÷ $5,000).

What if GAL also generates a dividend of $2 per share during that period — now what? In that case, GAL generates a total return of 24 percent. To calculate the total return, add the appreciation ($10 per share × 100 shares = $1,000) and the dividend income ($2 per share × 100 shares = $200) and divide that sum ($1,000 + $200, or $1,200) by the value at the beginning of the year ($50 per share × 100 shares, or $5,000). The total is $1,200 ÷ $5,000, or 24 percent.

✔ The last line lists the total for all the assets and their current market value.

Step 3: List your liabilities

Liabilities are simply the bills that you're obligated to pay. Whether it's a credit card bill or a mortgage payment, a liability is an amount of money you have to pay back eventually (usually with interest). If you don't keep track of your liabilities, you may end up thinking that you have more money than you really do.

Table 2-2 lists some common liabilities. Use it as a model when you list your own. You should list the liabilities according to how soon you need to pay them. Credit card balances tend to be short-term obligations, while mortgages are long-term.

Table 2-2	Listing Personal Liabilities	
Liabilities	*Amount*	*Paying Rate %*
Credit cards	$4,000	15%
Personal loans	$13,000	10%
Mortgage	$100,000	8%
Total liabilities	**$117,000**	

Here's a summary of the information in Table 2-2:

- ✔ The first column names the type of debt. Don't forget to include student loans and auto loans if you have them.

    Never avoid listing a liability because you're embarrassed to see how much you really owe. Be honest with yourself — doing so helps you improve your financial health.

- ✔ The second column shows the current value (or current balance) of your liabilities. List the most current balance to see where you stand with your creditors.

- ✔ The third column reflects how much interest you're paying for carrying that debt. This information is an important reminder about how debt can be a wealth zapper. Credit card debt can have an interest rate of 18 percent or more, and to add insult to injury, it isn't even tax-deductible. Using a credit card to make even a small purchase costs you if you don't pay off the balance each month. Within a year, a $50 sweater at 18 percent costs $59 when you add in the potential interest you pay.

If you compare your liabilities in Table 2-2 and your personal assets in Table 2-1, you may find opportunities to reduce the amount you pay for interest. Say, for example, that you pay 15 percent on a credit card balance of $4,000 but also have a personal asset of $5,000 in a bank savings account that's earning 2 percent in interest. In that case, you may want to consider taking $4,000 out of the savings account to pay off the credit card balance. Doing so saves you $520; the $4,000 in the bank was earning only $80 (2 percent of $4,000), while you were paying $600 on the credit card balance (15 percent of $4,000).

If you can't pay off high-interest debt, at least look for ways to minimize the cost of carrying the debt. The most obvious ways include the following:

- ✔ **Replace high-interest cards with low-interest cards.** Many companies offer incentives to consumers, including signing up for cards with favorable rates (recently under 10 percent) that can be used to pay off high-interest cards (typically 12 to 18 percent or higher).

- ✔ **Replace unsecured debt with secured debt.** Credit cards and personal loans are *unsecured* (you haven't put up any collateral or other asset to secure the debt); therefore, they have higher interest rates because this type of debt is considered riskier for the creditor. Sources of *secured debt* (such as home equity line accounts and brokerage accounts) provide you with a means to replace your high-interest debt with lower-interest debt. You get lower interest rates with secured debt because it's less risky for the creditor — the debt is backed up by collateral (your home or your stocks).

✔ Replace variable-interest debt with fixed-interest debt. Think about how homeowners got blindsided when their monthly payments on adjustable-rate mortgages went up drastically in the wake of the housing bubble that popped during 2005–2008. If you can't lower your debt, at least make it fixed and predictable.

The year 2007 was the 11th consecutive year that personal bankruptcies surpassed the million mark in the United States. Corporate bankruptcies were also at record levels. Due to the fallout of the housing bubble, it's probably safe to say that by the time you read this, 2008 will also join the million-plus bankruptcies club, unfortunately. Make a diligent effort to control and reduce your debt; otherwise, the debt can become too burdensome. If you don't control it, you may have to sell your stocks just to stay liquid. Remember, Murphy's Law states that you *will* sell your stock at the worst possible moment! Don't go there.

Step 4: Calculate your net worth

Your *net worth* is an indication of your total wealth. You can calculate your net worth with this basic equation: total assets (Table 2-1) less total liabilities (Table 2-2) equal net worth (net assets or net equity).

Table 2-3 shows this equation in action with a net worth of $173,590 — a very respectable number. For many investors, just being in a position where assets exceed liabilities (a positive net worth) is great news. Use Table 2-3 as a model to analyze your own financial situation. Your mission (if you choose to accept it — and you should) is to ensure that your net worth increases from year to year as you progress toward your financial goals (I discuss financial goals later in this chapter).

Table 2-3	Figuring Your Personal Net Worth	
Totals	*Amounts ($)*	*Increase from Year Before*
Total assets (from Table 2-1)	$290,590	+5%
Total liabilities (from Table 2-2)	($117,000)	–2%
Net worth (total assets less total liabilities)	**$173,590**	**+3%**

I owe, I owe, so off to work I go

One reason you continue to work is probably so that you can pay off your bills. But many people today are losing their jobs because their company owes, too!

Debt is one of the biggest financial problems in America today. Companies and individuals holding excessive debt contributed to the stock market's massive decline in 2000 and the U.S. recession in 2001. If individuals managed their personal liabilities more responsibly, the general economy would be much better off.

One reason the U.S. appeared to be doing so well during the late 1990s was the fact that individuals and organizations went on an unprecedented spending binge, financed mostly by excessive debt. The economy looked unstoppable. However, sooner or later you have to pay the piper. Stock prices may go up and down, but debt stays up until it's either paid down or the debtor files for bankruptcy. As of the first quarter of 2008, U.S. debt has surpassed a mind-boggling $49 trillion, which means that consumers, businesses, and governments will continue dealing with challenging times through this decade and into the next. Yes, the stock market (and the stocks in your portfolio) will be affected!

Step 5: Analyze your balance sheet

Create a balance sheet based on the prior steps in this chapter to illustrate your current finances. Take a close look at it and try to identify any changes you can make to increase your wealth. Sometimes, reaching your financial goals can be as simple as refocusing the items on your balance sheet (use Table 2-3 as a general guideline). Here are some brief points to consider:

✔ **Is the money in your emergency (or rainy day) fund sitting in an ultra-safe account and earning the highest interest available?** Bank money market accounts or money market funds are recommended. The safest type of account is a U.S. Treasury money market fund. Banks are backed by the Federal Deposit Insurance Corporation (FDIC), while U.S. treasury securities are backed by the "full faith and credit" of the federal government. Shop around for the best rates.

✔ **Can you replace depreciating assets with appreciating assets?** Say that you have two stereo systems. Why not sell one and invest the proceeds? You may say, "But I bought that unit two years ago for $500, and if I sell it now, I'll get only $300." That's your choice. You need to decide what helps your financial situation more — a $500 item that keeps shrinking in value (a *depreciating asset*) or $300 that can grow in value when invested (an *appreciating asset*).

✔ **Can you replace low-yield investments with high-yield investments?** Maybe you have $5,000 in a bank certificate of deposit (CD) earning 3 percent. You can certainly shop around for a better rate at another bank, but you can also seek alternatives that can offer a higher yield, such as U.S. savings bonds or short-term bond funds. Just remember that if you already have a CD and you withdraw the funds before it matures, you may face a penalty (such as losing some interest).

✔ **Can you pay off any high-interest debt with funds from low-interest assets?** If, for example, you have $5,000 earning 2 percent in a taxable bank account, and you have $2,500 on a credit card charging 18 percent (nondeductible), you may as well pay off the credit card balance and save on the interest.

✔ **If you're carrying debt, are you using that money for an investment return that's greater than the interest you're paying?** Carrying a loan with an interest rate of 8 percent is acceptable if that borrowed money is yielding more than 8 percent elsewhere. Suppose that you have $6,000 in cash in a brokerage account. If you qualify, you can actually make a stock purchase greater than $6,000 by using margin (essentially a loan from the broker). You can buy $12,000 of stock using your $6,000 in cash, with the remainder financed by the broker. Of course, you pay interest on that margin loan. But what if the interest rate is 6 percent and the stock you're about to invest in has a dividend that yields 9 percent? In that case, the dividend can help you pay off the margin loan, and you keep the additional income. (For more on buying on margin, see Chapter 18.)

✔ **Can you sell any personal stuff for cash?** You can replace unproductive assets with cash from garage sales and auction Web sites.

✔ **Can you use your home equity to pay off consumer debt?** Borrowing against your home has more favorable interest rates, and this interest is still tax-deductible. (Be careful about your debt level. See Chapter 24 for warnings on debt and other concerns.)

Paying off consumer debt by using funds borrowed against your home is a great way to wipe the slate clean. What a relief to get rid of your credit card balances! Just don't turn around and run up the consumer debt again. You can get overburdened and experience financial ruin (not to mention homelessness). Not a pretty picture.

The important point to remember is that you can take control of your finances with discipline (and with the advice I offer in this book).

Funding Your Stock Program

If you're going to invest money in stocks, the first thing you need is . . . money! Where can you get that money? If you're waiting for an inheritance to come through, you may have to wait a long time, considering all the advances being made in healthcare lately. What's that? You were going to invest in healthcare stocks? How ironic. Yet, the challenge still comes down to how to fund your stock program.

Many investors can reallocate their investments and assets to do the trick. *Reallocating* simply means selling some investments or other assets and reinvesting that money into something else (such as stocks). It boils down to deciding what investment or asset you can sell or liquidate. Generally, you want to consider those investments and assets that give you a low return on your money (or no return at all). If you have a complicated mix of investments and assets, you may want to consider reviewing your options with a financial planner. Reallocation is just part of the answer; your cash flow is the other part.

Ever wonder why there's so much month left at the end of the money? Consider your cash flow. Your *cash flow* refers to what money is coming in (income) and what money is being spent (outgo). The net result is either a positive cash flow or a negative cash flow, depending on your cash management skills. Maintaining a positive cash flow (more money coming in than going out) helps you increase your net worth. A negative cash flow ultimately depletes your wealth and wipes out your net worth if you don't turn it around immediately. The following sections show you how to analyze your cash flow. The first step is to do a cash flow statement. With a cash flow statement, you ask yourself three questions:

- ✔ **What money is coming in?** In your cash flow statement, jot down all sources of income. Calculate income for the month and then for the year. Include everything: salary, wages, interest, dividends, and so on. Add them all up and get your grand total for income.

- ✔ **What is your outgo?** Write down all the things that you spend money on. List all your expenses. If possible, categorize them into essential and nonessential. You can get an idea of all the expenses that you can reduce without affecting your lifestyle. But before you do that, make as complete a list as possible of what you spend your money on.

- ✔ **What's left?** If your income is greater than your outgo, you have money ready and available for stock investing. No matter how small the amount seems, it definitely helps. I've seen fortunes built when people started to diligently invest as little as $25 to $50 per week or per month. If your outgo is greater than your income, you better sharpen your pencil. Cut down on nonessential spending and/or increase your income. If your budget is a little tight, hold off on your stock investing until your cash flow improves.

Dot-com-and-go

If you were publishing a book about negative cash flow, you could look for the employees of any one of 100 dot-com companies to write it. Their qualifications include working for a company that flew sky-high in 1999 and crashed in 2000 and 2001. Companies such as eToys.com, Pets.com, and DrKoop.com were given millions, yet they couldn't turn a profit and eventually closed for business. You may as well call them "dot-com-and-go." You can learn from their mistakes. (Actually, they could have learned from you.) In the same way that profit is the most essential single element in a business, a positive cash flow is important for your finances in general and for funding your stock investment program in particular.

 Don't confuse a cash flow statement with an income statement (also called a *profit and loss statement* or an *income and expense statement*). A cash flow statement is simple to calculate because you can easily track what goes in and what goes out. Income statements are a little different (especially for businesses) because they take into account things that aren't technically cash flow (such as depreciation or amortization). Find out more about income statements in Chapter 11.

Step 1: Tally up your income

Using Table 2-4 as a worksheet, list and calculate the money you have coming in. The first column describes the source of the money, the second column indicates the monthly amount from each respective source, and the last column indicates the amount projected for a full year. Include all income, such as wages, business income, dividends, interest income, and so on. Then project these amounts for a year (multiply by 12) and enter those amounts in the third column.

Table 2-4	Listing Your Income	
Item	*Monthly $ Amount*	*Yearly $ Amount*
Salary and wages		
Interest income and dividends		
Business net (after taxes) income		
Other income		
Total income		

This is the amount of money you have to work with. To ensure your financial health, don't spend more than this amount. Always be aware of and carefully manage your income.

Step 2: Add up your outgo

Using Table 2-5 as a worksheet, list and calculate the money that's going out. How much are you spending and on what? The first column describes the source of the expense, the second column indicates the monthly amount, and the third column shows the amount projected for a full year. Include all the money you spend: credit card and other debt payments; household expenses, such as food, utility bills, and medical expenses; and nonessential expenses such as video games and elephant-foot umbrella stands.

Table 2-5	Listing Your Expenses (Outgo)	
Item	*Monthly $ Amount*	*Yearly $ Amount*
Payroll taxes		
Rent or mortgage		
Utilities		
Food		
Clothing		
Insurance (medical, auto, homeowners, and so on)		
Telephone		
Real estate taxes		
Auto expenses		
Charity		
Recreation		
Credit card payments		
Loan payments		
Other		
Total		

Payroll taxes is just a category in which to lump all the various taxes that the government takes out of your paycheck. Feel free to put each individual tax on its own line if you prefer. The important thing is creating a comprehensive list that's meaningful to you.

You may notice that the outgo doesn't include items such as payments to a 401(k) plan and other savings vehicles. Yes, these items do impact your cash flow, but they're not expenses; the amounts that you invest (or your employer invests for you) are essentially assets that benefit your financial situation versus expenses that don't help you build wealth. To account for the 401(k), simply deduct it from the gross pay before you calculate the preceding worksheet. If, for example, your gross pay is $2,000 and your 401(k) contribution is $300, then use $1,700 as your income figure.

Step 3: Create a cash flow statement

Okay, you're almost to the end. The last step is creating a cash flow statement so that you can see (all in one place) how your money moves — how much comes in and how much goes out and where it goes.

Plug the amount of your total income (from Table 2-4) and the amount of your total expenses (from Table 2-5) into the Table 2-6 worksheet to see your *cash flow*. Do you have positive cash flow — more coming in than going out — so that you can start investing in stocks (or other investments), or are expenses overpowering your income? Doing a cash flow statement isn't just about finding money in your financial situation to fund your stock program. First and foremost, it's about your financial well-being. Are you managing your finances well or not?

Table 2-6	Looking at Your Cash Flow	
Item	Monthly $ Amount	Yearly $ Amount
Total income (from Table 2-4)		
Total outgo (from Table 2-5)		
Net inflow/outflow		

At the time of this writing, 2008 was shaping up to be yet another record year for personal and business bankruptcies. Personal debt and expenses far exceeded whatever income they generated. That announcement is another reminder to watch your cash flow; keep your income growing and your expenses and debt as low as possible.

Step 4: Analyze your cash flow

Use your cash flow statement in Table 2-6 to identify sources of funds for your investment program. The more you can increase your income and the more you can decrease your outgo, the better. Scrutinize your data. Where can you improve the results? Here are some questions to ask yourself:

- ✔ How can you increase your income? Do you have hobbies, interests, or skills that can generate extra cash for you?

- ✔ Can you get more paid overtime at work? How about a promotion or a job change?

- ✔ Where can you cut expenses?

- ✔ Have you categorized your expenses as either "necessary" or "nonessential"?

- ✔ Can you lower your debt payments by refinancing or consolidating loans and credit card balances?

- ✔ Have you shopped around for lower insurance or telephone rates?

- ✔ Have you analyzed your tax withholdings in your paycheck to make sure that you're not overpaying your taxes (just to get your overpayment back next year as a refund)?

Another option: Finding investment money in tax savings

According to the Tax Foundation, the average U.S. citizen pays more in taxes than in food, clothing, and shelter combined. Sit down with your tax advisor and try to find ways to reduce your taxes. A home-based business, for example, is a great way to gain new income and increase your tax deductions, resulting in a lower tax burden. Your tax advisor can make recommendations that work for you.

One tax strategy to consider is doing your stock investing in a tax-sheltered account such as a traditional Individual Retirement Account (IRA) or a Roth Individual Retirement Account (Roth IRA). Again, check with your tax advisor for deductions and strategies available to you. For more on the tax implications of stock investing, see Chapter 21.

Setting Your Sights on Your Financial Goals

Consider stocks as tools for living, just like any other investment — no more, no less. Stocks are the tools you use (one of many) to accomplish something — to achieve a goal. Yes, successfully investing in stocks is the goal that you're probably shooting for if you're reading this book. However, you must complete the following sentence: "I want to be successful in my stock investing program to accomplish _____." You must consider stock investing as a means to an end. When people buy a computer, they don't (or shouldn't) think of buying a computer just to have a computer. People buy a computer because doing so helps them achieve a particular result, such as being more efficient in business, playing fun games, or having a nifty paperweight (tsk, tsk).

Know the difference between long-term, intermediate-term, and short-term goals, and then set some of each (see Chapter 3 for more information).

- ✔ Long-term goals refer to projects or financial goals that need funding five or more years from now.

- ✔ Intermediate term refers to financial goals that need funding two to five years from now.

- ✔ Short-term goals need funding less than two years from now.

Stocks, in general, are best suited for long-term goals such as these:

- ✔ Achieving financial independence (think retirement funding)

- ✔ Paying for future college costs

- ✔ Paying for any long-term expenditure or project

Some categories of stock (such as conservative or large cap) may be suitable for intermediate-term financial goals. If, for example, you'll retire four years from now, conservative stocks can be appropriate. If you're optimistic (or *bullish*) about the stock market and confident that stock prices will rise, go ahead and invest. However, if you're negative about the market (you're *bearish*, or you believe that stock prices will decline), you may want to wait until the economy starts to forge a clear path. For more on investing in bull or bear markets, see Chapter 14.

Stocks generally aren't suitable for short-term investing goals because stock prices can behave irrationally in a short period of time. Stocks fluctuate from day to day, so you don't know what the stock will be worth in the near future. You may end up with less money than you expected. For investors seeking to reliably accrue money for short-term needs, short-term bank certificates of deposit or money market funds are more appropriate.

In recent years, investors have sought quick, short-term profits by trading and speculating in stocks. Lured by the fantastic returns generated by the stock market in the late 1990s, investors saw stocks as a get-rich-quick scheme. It's very important for you to understand the difference between *investing, saving, and speculating.* Which one do you want to do? Knowing the answer to this question is crucial to your goals and aspirations. Investors who don't know the difference tend to get burned. Here's some information to help you distinguish among these three actions:

- ✔ *Investing* **is the act of putting your current funds into securities or tangible assets for the purpose of gaining future appreciation, income, or both.** You need time, knowledge, and discipline to invest. The investment can fluctuate in price, but it has been chosen for long-term potential.

- ✔ *Saving* **is the safe accumulation of funds for a future use.** Savings don't fluctuate and are generally free of financial risk. The emphasis is on safety and liquidity.

- ✔ *Speculating* **is the financial world's equivalent of gambling.** An investor who speculates is seeking quick profits gained from short-term price movements in a particular asset or investment. (In recent years, many folks are trading stocks, which is in the realm of short-term speculating. Find out more about trading in Chapter 16.)

These distinctly different concepts are often confused, even among so-called financial experts. I know of one financial advisor who actually put a child's college fund money into an Internet stock fund, only to lose over $17,000 in less than ten months! This advisor thought that she was investing, but in reality, she was speculating. I know of another advisor who told a client to avoid savings accounts altogether because the client had a 401(k) plan. This particular advisor didn't catch the crucial difference between saving and investing. The client eventually found out the difference; his 401(k) fell by 40 percent when the bear market of 2000 arrived.

Fortunately, we can learn from these situations and get back on track. That child who lost the $17,000? He's my neighbor, and I helped the father reinvest the remaining funds. The portfolio doubled in value by the following year, and it's still growing. The second fellow who lost 40 percent in his 401(k) account? He became my student, he has recouped his losses, and his 401(k) plan is up (this occurred within two years). As of 2008, both investors have portfolios that are out-performing the general stock market.

Chapter 3

Defining Common Approaches to Stock Investing

In This Chapter

▶ Pairing stock strategies with investing goals

▶ Deciding what time frame fits your investment strategy

▶ Looking at your purpose for investing: growth versus income

▶ Determining your investing style: conservative versus aggressive

"**I**nvesting for the long term" isn't just some perfunctory investment slogan. It's a culmination of proven stock market experience that goes back many decades. Unfortunately, investor buying and selling habits have deteriorated in recent years due to impatience. Today's investors think that short term is measured in days, intermediate term is measured in weeks, and long term is measured in months. Yeesh! It's no wonder that so many folks are complaining about lousy investment returns. Investors have lost the profitable art of patience!

What should you do? Become an investor with a time horizon greater than one year. Give your investments time to grow. Everybody dreams about emulating the success of someone like Warren Buffett, but few emulate his patience (a huge part of his investment success).

Stocks are tools you can use to build your wealth. When used wisely, for the right purpose, and in the right environment, they do a great job. But when improperly applied, they can lead to disaster. In this chapter, I show you how to choose the right types of investments based on your short- and long-term financial goals. I also show you how to decide on your purpose for investing (growth or income investing) and your style of investing (conservative or aggressive).

Matching Stocks and Strategies with Your Goals

Various stocks are out there, as well as various investment approaches. The key to success in the stock market is matching the right kind of stock with the right kind of investment situation. You have to choose the stock and the approach that match your goals. (Refer to Chapter 2 for more on defining your financial goals.)

Before investing in a stock, ask yourself, "When do I want to reach my financial goal?" Stocks are a means to an end. Your job is to figure out what that end is — or, more important, when it is. Do you want to retire in ten years or next year? Must you pay for your kid's college education next year or 18 years from now? The length of time you have before you need the money you hope to earn from stock investing determines what stocks you should buy. Table 3-1 gives you some guidelines for choosing the kind of stock best suited for the type of investor you are and the goals you have.

Table 3-1	Stock Types, Financial Goals, and Investor Types	
Type of Investor	*Time Frame for Financial Goals*	*Type of Stock Most Suitable*
Conservative (worries about risk)	Long term (over 5 years)	Large cap stocks and mid cap stocks
Aggressive (high tolerance to risk)	Long term (over 5 years)	Small cap stocks and mid cap stocks
Conservative (worries about risk)	Intermediate term (2 to 5 years)	Large cap stocks, preferably with dividends
Aggressive (high tolerance to risk)	Intermediate term (2 to 5 years)	Small cap stocks and mid cap stocks
Short term	1 to 2 years	Stocks are not suitable for the short term. Instead, look at vehicles such as savings accounts and money market funds.
Very short term	Less than 1 year	Stocks? Don't even think about it! Well . . . you *can* invest in stocks for less than a year, but seriously, you're not really investing — you're either trading (see Chapter 16) or speculating (see Chapter 2). Instead, use savings accounts and money market funds.

Dividends are payments made to a stock owner (unlike *interest,* which is payment to a creditor). Dividends are a great form of income, and companies that issue dividends tend to have more stable stock prices as well. For more information on dividend-paying stocks, see the section "Steadily making money: Income investing," later in this chapter, and also see Chapter 9.

Table 3-1 gives you general guidelines, but not everyone fits into a particular profile. Every investor has a unique situation, set of goals, and level of risk tolerance. The terms *large cap, mid cap,* and *small cap* refer to the size (or *market capitalization,* also known as *market cap*) of the company. All factors being equal, large companies are safer (less risky) than small companies. For more on market caps, see the section "Investing for Your Personal Style," later in this chapter.

Investing for the Future

Are your goals long term or short term? Answering this question is important because individual stocks can be either great or horrible choices, depending on the time period you want to focus on. Generally, the length of time you plan to invest in stocks can be short term, intermediate term, or long term. The following sections outline what kinds of stocks are most appropriate for each term length.

Investing in quality stocks becomes less risky as the time frame lengthens. Stock prices tend to fluctuate on a daily basis, but they have a tendency to trend up or down over an extended period of time. Even if you invest in a stock that goes down in the short term, you're likely to see it rise and possibly exceed your investment if you have the patience to wait it out and let the stock price appreciate.

Focusing on the short term

Short term generally means one year or less, although some people extend the period to two years or less. Short-term investing isn't about making a quick buck on your stock choices — it refers to when you may need the money.

Every person has short-term goals. Some are modest, such as setting aside money for a vacation next month or paying for medical bills. Other short-term goals are more ambitious, such as accruing funds for a down payment to purchase a new home within six months. Whatever the expense or purchase, you need a predictable accumulation of cash soon. If this sounds like your situation, stay away from the stock market!

Because stocks can be so unpredictable in the short term, they're a bad choice for short-term considerations. I get a kick out of market analysts on TV saying things such as, "At $25 a share, XYZ is a solid investment, and we feel that its stock should hit our target price of $40 within six to nine months." You know that an eager investor hears that and says, "Gee, why bother with 3 percent at the bank when this stock will rise by more than 50 percent? I better call my broker." It may hit that target amount (or surpass it), or it may not. Most of the time, the stock doesn't reach the target price, and the investor is disappointed. The stock could even go down!

The reason that target prices are frequently missed is that it's difficult to figure out what millions of investors will do in the short term. The short term can be irrational because so many investors have so many reasons for buying and selling that it can be difficult to analyze. If you invest for an important short-term need, you could lose very important cash quicker than you think.

During the raging bull market (see more about bull markets in Chapter 14) of the late 1990s, investors watched as some high-profile stocks went up 20 to 50 percent in a matter of months. Hey, who needs a savings account earning a measly interest rate when stocks grow like that! Of course, when the bear market hit from 2000 to 2003 and those same stocks fell 50 to 85 percent, a savings account earning a measly interest rate suddenly didn't seem so bad.

Short-term stock investing is very unpredictable. Stocks — even the best ones — fluctuate in the short term. In a negative environment, they can be very volatile. No one can accurately predict the price movement (unless he or she has some inside information), so stocks are definitely inappropriate for any financial goal you need to reach within one year. You can better serve your short-term goals with stable, interest-bearing investments like certificates of deposit at your local bank. Check Table 3-1 for suggestions about your short-term strategies.

Considering intermediate-term goals

Intermediate term refers to the financial goals you plan to reach within five years. For example, if you want to accumulate funds to put money down for investment in real estate four years from now, some growth-oriented investments may be suitable. (I discuss growth investing in more detail later in this chapter.)

Although some stocks *may* be appropriate for a two- or three-year period, not all stocks are good intermediate-term investments. Some stocks are fairly stable and hold their value well, such as the stock of large or established dividend-paying companies. Other stocks have prices that jump all over the place, such as those of untested companies that haven't been in existence long enough to develop a consistent track record.

Short-term investing = speculating

My case files are littered with examples of long-term stock investors who morphed into short-term speculators. I know of one fellow who had $80,000 and was set to get married within 12 months and then put a down payment on a new home for him and his bride. He wanted to surprise her by growing his nest egg quickly so they could have a glitzier wedding and a larger down payment. What happened? The money instead shrunk to $11,000 as his stock choices pulled back sharply. Ouch! How

does that go again? For better or for worse . . . uh . . . for richer or for poorer? I'm sure they had to adjust their plans accordingly. I recall some of the stocks he chose, and now, years later, those stocks have recovered and gone on to new highs.

The bottom line is that investing in stocks for the short term is nothing more than speculating. Your only possible strategy is luck.

If you plan to invest in the stock market to meet intermediate-term goals, consider large, established companies or dividend-paying companies in industries that provide the necessities of life (like the food and beverage industry, or electric utilities). In today's economic environment, I strongly believe that stocks attached to companies that serve basic human needs should have a major presence in most stock portfolios. They're especially well-suited for intermediate investment goals.

Just because a particular stock is labeled as being appropriate for the intermediate term doesn't mean you should get rid of it by the stroke of midnight five years from now. After all, if the company is doing well and going strong, you can continue holding the stock indefinitely. The more time you give a well-positioned, profitable company's stock to grow, the better you'll do.

Preparing for the long term

Stock investing is best suited for making money over a long period of time. When you measure stocks against other investments in terms of five to (preferably) ten or more years, they excel. Even investors who bought stocks during the depths of the Great Depression saw profitable growth in their stock portfolios over a ten-year period. In fact, if you examine any ten-year period over the past fifty years, you see that stocks beat out other financial investments (such as bonds or bank investments) in almost every period when measured by total return (taking into account reinvesting and compounding of capital gains and dividends)!

Of course, your work doesn't stop at deciding on a long-term investment. You still have to do your homework and choose stocks wisely, because even in good times, you can lose money if you invest in companies that go out of business. Part III of this book shows you how to evaluate specific companies and industries and alerts you to factors in the general economy that can affect stock behavior. Appendix A provides plenty of resources you can turn to.

Because so many different types and categories of stocks are available, virtually any investor with a long-term perspective should add stocks to his investment portfolio. Whether you want to save for a young child's college fund or for future retirement goals, carefully selected stocks have proven to be a superior long-term investment.

Investing for a Purpose

When someone asked the lady why she bungee jumped off the bridge that spanned a massive ravine, she answered, "Because it's fun!" When someone asked the fellow why he dove into a pool chock-full of alligators and snakes, he responded, "Because someone pushed me." You shouldn't invest in stocks unless you have a purpose that you understand, like investing for growth or investing for income. Even if an advisor pushes you to invest, be sure that your advisor gives you an explanation of how each stock choice fits your purpose.

I know of a very nice, elderly lady who had a portfolio brimming with aggressive-growth stocks because she had an overbearing broker. Her purpose should've been conservative, and she should've chosen investments that would preserve her wealth rather than grow it. Obviously, the broker's agenda got in the way.

Stocks are just a means to an end. Figure out your desired end and then match the means. To find out more about dealing with brokers, go to Chapter 7.

Making loads of money quickly: Growth investing

When investors want their money to grow (versus just trying to preserve it), they look for investments that appreciate in value. *Appreciate* is just another way of saying *grow*. If you bought a stock for $8 per share and now its value is $30 per share, your investment has grown by $22 per share — that's appreciation. I know I would appreciate it.

Appreciation (also known as *capital gain*) is probably the number one reason people invest in stocks. Few investments have the potential to grow your wealth as conveniently as stocks. If you want the stock market to make you loads of money (and you can assume some risk), head to Chapter 8, which takes an in-depth look at investing for growth.

Stocks are a great way to grow your wealth, but they're not the only way. Many investors seek alternative ways to make money, but many of these alternative ways are more aggressive than stocks and carry significantly more risk. You may have heard about people who made quick fortunes in areas such as commodities (like wheat, pork bellies, or precious metals), options, and other more sophisticated investment vehicles. Keep in mind that you should limit these more risky investments to only a small portion of your portfolio, such as 10 percent of your investable funds. Experienced investors, however, can go as high as 20 percent.

Steadily making money: Income investing

Not all investors want to take on the risk that comes with making a killing. (Hey . . . no guts, no glory!) Some people just want to invest in the stock market as a means of providing a steady income. They don't need stock values to go through the ceiling. Instead, they need stocks that perform well consistently.

If your purpose for investing in stocks is to create income, you need to choose stocks that pay dividends. Dividends are typically paid quarterly to stockholders on record as of specific dates. How do you know if the dividend you're being paid is higher (or lower) than other vehicles (such as bonds)? The next sections will help you figure it out.

Distinguishing between dividends and interest

Don't confuse dividends with interest. Most people are familiar with interest because that's how you grow your money over the years in the bank. The important difference is that *interest* is paid to creditors, and *dividends* are paid to owners (meaning *shareholders* — and if you own stock you're a shareholder because shares of stock represent ownership in a publicly traded company).

When you buy stock, you buy a piece of that company. When you put money in a bank (or when you buy bonds), you basically loan your money. You become a creditor, and the bank or bond issuer is the debtor, and as such, it must eventually pay your money back to you with interest.

Recognizing the importance of an income stock's yield

When you invest for income, you have to consider your investment's yield and compare it with the alternatives. The *yield* is an investment's payout expressed as a percentage of the investment amount. Looking at the yield is a way to compare the income you expect to receive from one investment with the expected income from others. Table 3-2 shows some comparative yields.

Table 3-2	Comparing the Yields of Various Investments				
Investment	*Type*	*Amount*	*Pay Type*	*Payout*	*Yield*
Smith Co.	Stock	$50/share	Dividend	$2.50	5.0%
Jones Co.	Stock	$100/share	Dividend	$4.00	4.0%
Acme Bank	Bank CD	$500	Interest	$25.00	5.0%
Acme Bank	Bank CD	$2,500	Interest	$131.25	5.25%
Acme Bank	Bank CD	$5,000	Interest	$287.50	5.75%
Brown Co.	Bond	$5,000	Interest	$300.00	6.0%

To calculate yield, use the following formula:

Yield = Payout ÷ Investment amount

For the sake of simplicity, the following exercise is based on an annual percentage yield basis (compounding would increase the yield).

Jones Co. and Smith Co. are typical dividend-paying stocks. Looking at Table 3-2 and presuming that both companies are similar in most respects except for their differing dividends, how can you tell whether the $50 stock with a $2.50 annual dividend is better (or worse) than the $100 stock with a $4.00 dividend? The yield tells you.

Even though Jones Co. pays a higher dividend ($4.00), Smith Co. has a higher yield (5 percent). Therefore, if you had to choose between those two stocks as an income investor, you would choose Smith Co. Of course, if you truly want to maximize your income and don't really need your investment to appreciate a lot, you should probably choose Brown Co.'s bond because it offers a yield of 6 percent.

Dividend-paying stocks do have the ability to increase in value. They may not have the same growth potential as growth stocks, but at the very least, they have a greater potential for capital gain than CDs or bonds. Dividend-paying stocks (investing for income) are covered in Chapter 9.

Investing for Your Personal Style

Your investing style isn't a blue-jeans-versus-three-piece-suit debate. It refers to your approach to stock investing. Do you want to be conservative or aggressive? Would you rather be the tortoise or the hare? Your investment personality greatly depends on your purpose and the term over which you're planning to invest (see the previous two sections in this chapter). The following sections outline the two most general investment styles.

Conservative investing

Conservative investing means that you put your money in something proven, tried, and true. You invest your money in safe and secure places, such as banks and government-backed securities. But how does that apply to stocks? (Table 3-1 gives you suggestions.)

If you're a conservative stock investor, you want to place your money in companies that exhibit some of the following qualities:

- **Proven performance:** You want companies that have shown increasing sales and earnings year after year. You don't demand anything spectacular — just a strong and steady performance.

- **Large market size:** You want to invest in large cap companies (short for large capitalization). In other words, they should have a market value exceeding $5–$25 billion. Conservative investors surmise that bigger is safer.

- **Proven market leadership:** Look for companies that are leaders in their industries.

- **Perceived staying power:** You want companies with the financial clout and market position to weather uncertain market and economic conditions. It shouldn't matter what happens in the economy or who gets elected.

As a conservative investor, you don't mind if the companies' share prices jump (who would?), but you're more concerned with steady growth over the long term.

Aggressive investing

Aggressive investors can plan long term or look over only the intermediate term, but in any case, they want stocks that resemble jack rabbits — those that show the potential to break out of the pack.

If you're an aggressive stock investor, you want to invest your money in companies that exhibit some of the following qualities:

- ✔ **Great potential:** Choose companies that have superior goods, services, ideas, or ways of doing business compared to the competition.

- ✔ **Capital gains possibility:** Don't even consider dividends. If anything, you dislike dividends. You feel that the money dispensed in dividend form is better reinvested in the company. This, in turn, can spur greater growth.

- ✔ **Innovation:** Find companies that have innovative technologies, ideas, or methods that make them stand apart from other companies.

Aggressive investors usually seek out small capitalization stocks, known as *small caps,* because they can have plenty of potential for growth. Take the tree example, for instance: A giant redwood may be strong, but it may not grow much more, whereas a brand-new sapling has plenty of growth to look forward to. Why invest in big, stodgy companies when you can invest in smaller enterprises that may become the leaders of tomorrow? Aggressive investors have no problem buying stock in obscure businesses because they hope that such companies will become another IBM or McDonald's. Find out more about growth investing in Chapter 8.

Chapter 4

Recognizing the Risks

. . . .

In This Chapter

▶ Considering different types of risk

▶ Taking steps to reduce your risk

▶ Balancing risk against return

. . . .

Investors face many risks, most of which I cover in this chapter. The simplest definition of risk for investors is "the possibility that your investment will lose some (or all) of its value." Yet you don't have to fear risk if you understand it and plan for it. You must understand the oldest equation in the world of investing — risk versus return. This equation states the following:

> If you want a greater return on your money, you need to tolerate more risk. If you don't want to tolerate more risk, you must tolerate a lower rate of return.

This point about risk is best illustrated from a moment in one of my investment seminars. One of the attendees told me that he had his money in the bank but was dissatisfied with the rate of return. He lamented, "The yield on my money is pitiful! I want to put my money somewhere where it can grow." I asked him, "How about investing in common stocks? Or what about growth mutual funds? They have a solid, long-term growth track record." He responded, "Stocks? I don't want to put my money there. It's too risky!" Okay, then. If you don't want to tolerate more risk, then don't complain about earning less on your money. Risk (in all its forms) has a bearing on all your money concerns and goals. That's why it's so important that you understand risk before you invest.

This man — as well as the rest of us — needs to remember that risk is not a four-letter word. (Well, it is a four-letter word, but you know what I mean.) Risk is present no matter what you do with your money. Even if you simply stick your money in your mattress, risk is involved — several kinds of risk, in fact. You have the risk of fire. What if your house burns down? You have the risk of theft. What if burglars find your stash of cash? You also have relative risk. (In other words, what if your relatives find your money?)

Be aware of the different kinds of risk that I describe in this chapter, and you can easily plan around them to keep your money growing.

Exploring Different Kinds of Risk

Think about all the ways that an investment can lose money. You can list all sorts of possibilities. So many that you may think, "Holy cow! Why invest at all?"

Don't let risk frighten you. After all, life itself is risky. Just make sure that you understand the different kinds of risk that I discuss in the following sections before you start navigating the investment world. Be mindful of risk and find out about the effects of risk on your investments and personal financial goals.

Financial risk

The financial risk of stock investing is that you can lose your money if the company whose stock you purchase loses money or goes belly up. This type of risk is the most obvious because companies do go bankrupt.

You can greatly enhance the chances of your financial risk paying off by doing an adequate amount of research and choosing your stocks carefully (which this book helps you do — see Part III for details). Financial risk is a real concern even when the economy is doing well. Some diligent research, a little planning, and a dose of common sense help you reduce your financial risk.

In the stock investing mania of the late 1990s, millions of investors (along with many well-known investment gurus) ignored some obvious financial risks of many then-popular stocks. Investors blindly plunked their money into stocks that were bad choices. Consider investors who put their money in DrKoop. com, a health information Web site, in 1999 and held on during 2000. This company had no profit and was over-indebted. DrKoop.com went into cardiac arrest as it collapsed from $45 per share to $2 per share by mid-2000. By the time the stock was DOA, investors lost millions. RIP (risky investment play!).

Internet and tech stocks littered the graveyard of stock market catastrophes during 2000–2001 because investors didn't see (or didn't want to see?) the risks involved with companies that didn't offer a solid record of results (profits, sales, and so on). When you invest in companies that don't have a proven track record, you're not investing, you're speculating.

Fast forward to 2007–2008. New risks abound as the headlines rail on about the credit crisis on Wall Street and the subprime fiasco in the wake of the housing bubble popping. Think about how this crisis impacted investors as the market went through its stomach-churning roller-coaster ride. A good example of a casualty you didn't want to be a part of was Bear Stearns (BSC), which was caught in the subprime buzz saw. Bear Stearns was sky-high at $170 a share in early 2007, yet it crashed to $2 a share by March 2008. Yikes! Its problems arose from massive overexposure to bad debt, and investors could have done some research (the public data was revealing!) and avoided the stock entirely.

Investors who did their homework regarding the financial conditions of companies such as the Internet stocks (and Bear Stearns, among others) would have discovered that these companies had the hallmarks of financial risk — high debt, low (or no) earnings, and plenty of competition. They steered clear, avoiding tremendous financial loss. Investors who didn't do their homework were lured by the status of these companies and lost their shirts.

Of course, the individual investors who lost money by investing in these trendy, high-profile companies don't deserve all the responsibility for their tremendous financial losses; some high-profile analysts and media sources also should have known better. The late 1990s may someday be a case study of how euphoria and the herd mentality (rather than good, old-fashioned research and common sense) ruled the day (temporarily). The excitement of making potential fortunes gets the best of people sometimes, and they throw caution to the wind. Historians may look back at those days and say, "What *were* they thinking?" Achieving true wealth takes diligent work and careful analysis.

In terms of financial risk, the bottom line is . . . well . . . the bottom line! A healthy bottom line means that a company is making money. And if a company is making money, then you can make money by investing in its stock. However, if a company isn't making money, you won't make money if you invest in it. Profit is the lifeblood of any company. See Chapter 11 for the scoop on determining whether a company's bottom line is healthy.

Interest rate risk

You can lose money in an apparently sound investment because of something that sounds as harmless as "interest rates have changed." Interest rate risk may sound like an odd type of risk, but in fact, it's a common consideration for investors. Be aware that interest rates change on a regular basis, causing some challenging moments. Banks set interest rates, and the primary institution to watch closely is the Federal Reserve (the Fed), which is, in effect, the country's central bank. The Fed raises or lowers its interest rates, actions that, in turn, cause banks to raise or lower interest rates accordingly. Interest rate changes affect consumers, businesses, and, of course, investors.

Here's a generic introduction to the way fluctuating interest rate risk can affect investors in general: Suppose that you buy a long-term, high-quality corporate bond and get a yield of 6 percent. Your money is safe, and your return is locked in at 6 percent. Whew! That's 6 percent. Not bad, huh? But what happens if, after you commit your money, interest rates increase to 8 percent? You lose the opportunity to get that extra 2 percent interest. The only way to get out of your 6 percent bond is to sell it at current market values and use the money to reinvest at the higher rate.

The only problem with this scenario is that the 6 percent bond is likely to drop in value because interest rates rose. Why? Say that the investor is Bob and the bond yielding 6 percent is a corporate bond issued by Lucin-Muny (LM). According to the bond agreement, LM must pay 6 percent (called the *face rate* or *nominal rate*) during the life of the bond and then, upon maturity, pay the principal. If Bob buys $10,000 of LM bonds on the day they're issued, he gets $600 (of interest) every year for as long as he holds the bonds. If he holds on until maturity, he gets back his $10,000 (the principal). So far so good, right? The plot thickens, however.

Say that he decides to sell the bond long before maturity and that, at the time of the sale, interest rates in the market have risen to 8 percent. Now what? The reality is that no one is going to want his 6 percent bond if the market is offering bonds at 8 percent. What's Bob to do? He can't change the face rate of 6 percent, and he can't change the fact that only $600 is paid each year for the life of the bond. What has to change so that current investors get the *equivalent* yield of 8 percent? If you said, "The bond's value has to go down," . . . bingo! In this example, the bond's market value needs to drop to $7,500 so that investors buying the bond get an equivalent yield of 8 percent. (For simplicity's sake, I left out the time it takes for the bond to mature.) Here's how that figures:

New investors still get $600 annually. However, $600 is equal to 8 percent of $7,500. Therefore, even though investors get the face rate of 6 percent, they get a yield of 8 percent because the actual investment amount is $7,500. In this example, little, if any, financial risk is present, but you see how interest rate risk presents itself. Bob finds out that you can have a good company with a good bond, yet you still lose $2,500 because of the change in the interest rate. Of course, if Bob doesn't sell, he doesn't realize that loss. (For more on the how and why of selling your stock, review Chapters 17 and 18.)

Historically, rising interest rates have had an adverse effect on stock prices. I outline several reasons why in the following sections. Because our country is top-heavy in debt, rising interest rates are an obvious risk that threatens both stocks and fixed-income securities (such as bonds).

Hurting a company's financial condition

Rising interest rates have a negative impact on companies that carry a large current debt load or that need to take on more debt, because when interest rates rise, the cost of borrowing money rises, too. Ultimately, the company's profitability and ability to grow are reduced. When a company's profits (or earnings) drop, its stock becomes less desirable, and its stock price falls.

Affecting a company's customers

A company's success comes when it sells its products or services. But what happens if increased interest rates negatively impact its customers (specifically, other companies that buy from it)? The financial health of its customers directly affects the company's ability to grow sales and earnings.

For a good example, consider Home Depot (HD) during 2005–2008. The company had soaring sales and earnings during 2005 and into early 2006 as the housing boom hit its high point (record sales, construction, and so on). As the housing bubble popped and the housing and construction industries went into an agonizing decline, the fortunes of Home Depot followed suit because its success is directly tied to home building, repair, and improvement. By late 2006, HD's sales were slipping and earnings were dropping as the housing industry sunk deeper into its depression. This was bad news for stock investors. HD's stock went from over $44 in 2005 to $21 by October 2008 (a drop of about 52 percent). Ouch! No "home improvement" there.

Impacting investors' decision-making considerations

When interest rates rise, investors start to rethink their investment strategies, resulting in one of two outcomes:

✔ Investors may sell any shares in interest-sensitive stocks that they hold. Interest-sensitive industries include electric utilities, real estate, and the financial sector. Although increased interest rates can hurt these sectors, the reverse is also generally true: Falling interest rates boost the same industries. Keep in mind that interest rate changes affect some industries more than others.

✔ Investors who favor increased current income (versus waiting for the investment to grow in value to sell for a gain later on) are definitely attracted to investment vehicles that offer a higher yield. Higher interest rates can cause investors to switch from stocks to bonds or bank certificates of deposit.

Hurting stock prices indirectly

High or rising interest rates can have a negative impact on any investor's total financial picture. What happens when an investor struggles with burdensome debt, such as a second mortgage, credit card debt, or *margin debt* (debt from borrowing against stock in a brokerage account)? He may sell some stock to pay off some of his high-interest debt. Selling stock to service debt is a common practice that, when taken collectively, can hurt stock prices.

As this book goes to press, the stock market and the U.S. economy face perhaps the greatest challenge since the Great Depression — debt. In terms of Gross Domestic Product (GDP), the size of the economy is about $14 trillion (give or take $100 billion), but the debt level is about $49 trillion (this includes personal, corporate, mortgage, and government debt). This already enormous amount doesn't include $53 trillion of liabilities such as Social Security and Medicare. Additionally (Yikes! There's more?), some of our financial institutions hold over $100 trillion worth of derivatives. These can be very complicated and sophisticated investment vehicles that can backfire. Derivatives have, in fact, sunk some large organizations (such as Enron and Bear Stearns), and investors should be aware of them. Just check out the company's financial reports. (Find out more in Chapter 12.)

Because of the effects of interest rates on stock portfolios, both direct and indirect, successful investors regularly monitor interest rates in both the general economy and in their personal situations. Although stocks have proven to be a superior long-term investment (the longer the term, the better), every investor should maintain a balanced portfolio that includes other investment vehicles. A diversified investor has some money in vehicles that do well when interest rates rise. These vehicles include money market funds, U.S. savings bonds (series I), and other variable-rate investments whose interest rates rise when market rates rise. These types of investments add a measure of safety from interest rate risk to your stock portfolio. (I discuss diversification in more detail later in this chapter.)

Market risk

People talk about *the market* and how it goes up or down, making it sound like a monolithic entity instead of what it really is — a group of millions of individuals making daily decisions to buy or sell stock. No matter how modern our society and economic system, you can't escape the laws of supply and demand. When masses of people want to buy a particular stock, it becomes in demand, and its price rises. That price rises higher if the supply is limited. Conversely, if no one's interested in buying a stock, its price falls. Supply and demand is the nature of market risk. The price of the stock you purchase can rise and fall on the fickle whim of market demand.

Millions of investors buying and selling each minute of every trading day affect the share price of your stock. This fact makes it impossible to judge which way your stock will move tomorrow or next week. This unpredictability and seeming irrationality is why stocks aren't appropriate for short-term financial growth.

A good example of market risk with a stock is Apple (AAPL). Had you bought AAPL in early 2007, you could have gotten it for about $75 a share in January 2007 and watched it rise joyfully upward to hit $205 a share by December 2007. At that point some giddy investor may be thinking, "It's time to pop the champagne! I'll be able to buy Rhode Island!" Hold on a second! Within three months of that top, AAPL had a dizzying plunge to under $120 by March 2008. It's typical for stocks to take a relatively long time to climb, but they can fall in a relatively short time. In that example, a long-term patient investor would still be up, but some short-term folks that "jump in" and "jump out" would have been burned. I'm sure that some of them lived in Rhode Island (but probably renting).

Markets are volatile by nature; they go up and down, and investments need time to grow. Market volatility is an increasingly common condition that we have to live with. Investors should be aware of the fact that stocks in general (especially in today's marketplace) aren't suitable for short-term (one year or less) goals (see Chapters 2 and 3 for more on short-term goals). Despite the fact that companies you're invested in may be fundamentally sound, all stock prices are subject to the gyrations of the marketplace and need time to trend upward.

Investing requires diligent work and research before putting your money in quality investments with a long-term perspective. Speculating is attempting to make a relatively quick profit by monitoring the short-term price movements of a particular investment. Investors seek to minimize risk, whereas speculators don't mind risk because it can also magnify profits. Speculating and investing have clear differences, but investors frequently become speculators and ultimately put themselves and their wealth at risk. Don't go there!

Consider the married couple nearing retirement who decided to play with their money to see about making their pending retirement more comfortable. They borrowed a sizable sum by tapping into their home equity to invest in the stock market. (Their home, which they had paid off, had enough equity to qualify for this loan.) What did they do with these funds? You guessed it; they invested in the high-flying stocks of the day, which were high-tech and Internet stocks. Within eight months, they lost almost all their money.

Understanding market risk is especially important for people who are tempted to put their nest eggs or emergency funds into volatile investments such as growth stocks (or mutual funds that invest in growth stocks, or similar aggressive investment vehicles). Remember, you can lose everything.

Inflation risk

Inflation is the artificial expansion of the quantity of money so that too much money is used in exchange for goods and services. To consumers, inflation shows up in the form of higher prices for goods and services. Inflation risk is also referred to as *purchasing power risk*. This term just means that your money doesn't buy as much as it used to. For example, a dollar that bought you a sandwich in 1980 barely bought you a candy bar a few years later. For you, the investor, this risk means that the value of your investment (a stock that doesn't appreciate much, for example) may not keep up with inflation.

Say that you have money in a bank savings account currently earning 4 percent. This account has flexibility — if the market interest rate goes up, the rate you earn in your account goes up. Your account is safe from both financial risk and interest rate risk. But what if inflation is running at 5 percent? At that point you're losing money.

At the time of this writing, inflation is a very real and a very serious concern and it should not be ignored. I deal more with inflation in Chapter 10.

Tax risk

Taxes (such as income tax or capital gains tax) don't affect your stock investment directly. Taxes can obviously affect how much of your money you get to keep. Because the entire point of stock investing is to build wealth, you need to understand that taxes take away a portion of the wealth that you're trying to build. Taxes can be risky because if you make the wrong move with your stocks (selling them at the wrong time, for example), you can end up paying higher taxes than you need to. Because tax laws change so frequently, tax risk is part of the risk-versus-return equation, as well.

It pays to gain knowledge about how taxes can impact your wealth-building program before you make your investment decisions. Chapter 21 covers in greater detail the impact of taxes.

Political and governmental risks

If companies were fish, politics and government policies (such as taxes, laws, and regulations) would be the pond. In the same way that fish die in a toxic or polluted pond, politics and government policies can kill companies. Of course, if you own stock in a company exposed to political and governmental risks, you need to be aware of these risks. For some companies, a single new regulation or law is enough to send them into bankruptcy. For other companies, a new law could help them increase sales and profits.

What if you invest in companies or industries that become political targets? You may want to consider selling them (you can always buy them back later) or consider putting in stop-loss orders on the stock (see Chapter 18). For example, tobacco companies were the targets of political firestorms that battered their stock prices. Whether you agree or disagree with the political machinations of today is not the issue. As an investor, you have to ask yourself, "How do politics affect the market value and the current and future prospects of my chosen investment?" (See Chapter 15 for more on how politics can affect the stock market.)

Taking the preceding point a step further, I'd like to remind you that politics and government have a direct and often negative impact on the economic environment. And one major pitfall for investors is that many misunderstand even basic economics. Considering all the examples I could find in recent years, I could write a book! Or . . . uh . . . simply add it to this book. Chapter 10 goes into greater detail to help you make (and keep) stock market profits just by understanding rudimentary (and quite interesting) economics. (Don't worry; the dry stuff will be kept to a minimum!)

Personal risks

Frequently, the risk involved with investing in the stock market may not be directly involved with the investment or factors directly related to the investment; sometimes the risk is with the investor's circumstances.

Suppose that investor Ralph puts $15,000 into a portfolio of common stocks. Imagine that the market experiences a drop in prices that week and Ralph's stocks drop to a market value of $14,000. Because stocks are good for the long term, this type of decrease is usually not an alarming incident. Odds are that this dip is temporary, especially if Ralph carefully chose high-quality companies. Incidentally, if a portfolio of high-quality stocks *does* experience a temporary drop in price, it can be a great opportunity to get more shares at a good price. (Chapter 18 covers orders you can place with your broker to help you do that.)

Over the long term, Ralph would probably see the value of his investment grow substantially. But what if during a period when his stocks are declining, Ralph experiences financial difficulty and needs quick cash? He may have to sell his stock to get some money.

This problem occurs frequently for investors who don't have an emergency fund or a rainy day fund to handle large, sudden expenses. You never know when your company may lay you off or when your basement may flood, leaving you with a huge repair bill. Car accidents, medical emergencies, and other unforeseen events are part of life's bag of surprises — for anyone.

You probably won't get much comfort from knowing that stock losses are tax deductible — a loss is a loss (see Chapter 21 for more on taxes). However, you can avoid the kind of loss that results from prematurely having to sell your stocks if you maintain an emergency cash fund. A good place for your emergency cash fund is in either a bank savings account or a money market fund. Then you aren't forced to prematurely liquidate your stock investments to pay emergency bills. (Chapter 2 provides more guidance on having liquid assets for emergencies.)

Emotional risk

What does emotional risk have to do with stocks? Emotions are important risk considerations because the main decision makers are human beings. Logic and discipline are critical factors in investment success, but even the best investor can let emotions take over the reins of money management and cause loss. For stock investing, you're likely to be sidetracked by three main emotions: greed, fear, and love. You need to understand your emotions and what kinds of risk they can expose you to. If you get too attached to a sinking stock, then you don't need a stock investing book — you need Dr. Phil!

Paying the price for greed

In 1998–2000, millions of investors threw caution to the wind and chased highly dubious, risky dot-com stocks. The dollar signs popped up in their eyes (just like slot machines) when they saw that easy street was lined with dot-com stocks that were doubling and tripling in a very short time. Who cares about price/earnings (P/E) ratios and earnings when you can just buy stock, make a fortune, and get out with millions? (Of course, *you* care about making money with stocks, so you can flip to Chapter 11 and Appendix B to find out more about P/E ratios.)

Unfortunately, the lure of the easy buck can easily turn healthy attitudes about growing wealth into unhealthy greed that blinds investors and discards common sense (such as investing for quick short-term gains in dubious hot stocks rather than doing your homework and buying stocks of solid companies with strong fundamentals and a long-term focus, as I explain in Part III).

Recognizing the role of fear

Greed can be a problem, but fear is the other extreme. People who are fearful of loss frequently avoid suitable investments and end up settling for a low rate of return. If you have to succumb to one of these emotions, at least fear exposes you to less loss.

Investment lessons from September 11

September 11, 2001, was a horrific day that is burned in our minds and won't be forgotten in our lifetime. The acts of terrorism that day took over 3,000 lives and caused untold pain and grief. A much less important aftereffect was the hard lessons that investors learned that day. Terrorism reminds us that risk is more real than ever and that we should never let our guard down. What lessons can investors learn from the worst acts of terrorism to ever happen on U.S. soil? Here are a few pointers:

✔ **Diversify your portfolio.** Of course, the events of September 11 were certainly surreal and unexpected. But before the events occurred, investors should have made it a habit to assess their situations and see whether they had any vulnerabilities. Stock investors with no money outside the stock market are always more at risk. Keeping your portfolio diversified is a time-tested strategy that is more relevant than ever before. (I discuss diversification later in this chapter.)

✔ **Review and re-allocate.** September 11 triggered declines in the overall market, but specific industries, such as airlines and hotels, were hit particularly hard. In addition, some industries, such as defense and food, saw stock prices rise. Monitor your portfolio and ask yourself whether it's overly reliant on or exposed to events in specific sectors. If so, reallocate your investments to decrease your risk exposure.

✔ **Check for signs of trouble.** Techniques such as trailing stops (which I explain in Chapter 18) come in very handy when your stocks plummet because of unexpected events. Even if you don't use these techniques, you can make it a regular habit to analyze your stocks and check for signs of trouble, such as debts or P/E ratios that are too high. If you see signs of trouble (check out Chapter 24), consider selling anyway.

Also, keep in mind that fear is frequently a symptom of lack of knowledge about what's going on. If you see your stocks falling and don't understand why, fear will take over and you may act irrationally. When stock investors are affected by fear, the tendency is to sell their stocks and head for the exits and the life boats. When an investor sees his stock go down 20 percent, what goes through his head? Experienced, knowledgeable investors see that no bull market goes straight up. Even the strongest bull goes up in a zigzag fashion. Conversely, even bear markets don't go straight down, they zigzag down. Out of fear, inexperienced investors will sell good stocks if they see them go down temporarily (the "correction") while experienced investors see that temporary down move as a good buying opportunity to add to their positions. (Flip to Chapter 14 for details on dealing with bull and bear markets.)

Looking for love in all the wrong places

Stocks are dispassionate, inanimate vehicles, but people can look for love in the strangest places. Emotional risk occurs when investors fall in love with a stock and refuse to sell it, even when the stock is plummeting and shows all the symptoms of getting worse. Emotional risk also occurs when investors are drawn to bad investment choices just because they sound good, are popular, or are pushed by family or friends. Love and attachment are great in relationships with people but can be horrible with investments. To deal with this emotion, investors have to deploy techniques that take the emotion out. For example, you can use brokerage orders (such as trailing stops and limit orders), which can automatically trigger buy and sell transactions and leave some of the agonizing out. Hey, disciplined investing may just become your new passion!

Minimizing Your Risk

Now, before you go crazy thinking that stock investing carries so much risk that you may as well not get out of bed, take a breath. Minimizing your risk in stock investing is easier than you think. Although wealth building through the stock market doesn't take place without some amount of risk, you can practice the following tips to maximize your profits and still keep your money secure.

Gaining knowledge

Some people spend more time analyzing a restaurant menu to choose a $10 entrée than analyzing where to put their next $5,000. Lack of knowledge constitutes the greatest risk for new investors, but diminishing that risk starts with gaining knowledge. The more familiar you are with the stock market — how it works, factors that affect stock value, and so on — the better you can navigate around its pitfalls and maximize your profits. The same knowledge that enables you to grow your wealth also enables you to minimize your risk. Before you put your money anywhere, you want to know as much as you can. This book is a great place to start — check out Chapter 6 for a rundown of the kinds of information you want to know before you buy stocks, as well as the resources that can give you the information you need to invest successfully.

Staying out until you get a little practice

If you don't understand stocks, don't invest! Yeah, I know this book is about stock investing, and I think that some measure of stock investing is a good idea for most people. But that doesn't mean you should be 100 percent invested 100 percent of the time. If you don't understand a particular stock (or don't understand stocks, period), stay away until you do understand. Instead, give yourself an imaginary sum of money, such as $100,000, give yourself reasons to invest, and just make believe ("simulated stock investing or trading"). Pick a few stocks that you think will increase in value, track them for a while, and see how they perform. Begin to understand how the price of a stock goes up and down, and watch what happens to the stocks you choose when various events take place. As you find out more and more about stock investing, you get better and better at picking individual stocks, and you haven't risked — or lost — any money during your learning period.

A good place to do your imaginary investing is at Web sites such as Marketocracy (www.marketocracy.com) and Investopedia's simulator (http://simulator.investopedia.com). You can design a stock portfolio and track its performance with thousands of other investors to see how well you do.

Putting your financial house in order

Advice on what to do before you invest could be a whole book all by itself. The bottom line is that you want to make sure that you are, first and foremost, financially secure before you take the plunge into the stock market. If you're not sure about your financial security, look over your situation with a financial planner. (You can find more on financial planners in Appendix A.)

Before you buy your first stock, here are a few things you can do to get your finances in order:

- ✓ **Have a cushion of money.** Set aside three to six months' worth of your gross living expenses somewhere safe, such as in a bank account or treasury money market fund, in case you suddenly need cash for an emergency (see Chapter 2 for details).

- ✓ **Reduce your debt.** Overindulging in debt was the worst personal economic problem for many Americans in the late 1990s, and this has continued in recent years. The year 2001 was a record year for bankruptcy, with nearly 1.5 million people filing for bankruptcy. When the housing bubble popped, millions of foreclosures were the result as homeowners piled on too much debt.

✔ **Make sure that your job is as secure as you can make it.** Are you keeping your skills up to date? Is the company you work for strong and growing? Is the industry that you work in strong and growing?

✔ **Make sure that you have adequate insurance.** You need enough insurance to cover you and your family's needs in case of illness, death, disability, and so on.

Diversifying your investments

Diversification is a strategy for reducing risk by spreading your money across different investments. It's a fancy way of saying, "Don't put all your eggs in one basket." But how do you go about divvying up your money and distributing it among different investments? The easiest way to understand proper diversification may be to look at what you *shouldn't* do:

✔ **Don't put all your money in one stock.** Sure, if you choose wisely and select a hot stock, you may make a bundle, but the odds are tremendously against you. Unless you're a real expert on a particular company, it's a good idea to have small portions of your money in several different stocks. As a general rule, the money you tie up in a single stock should be money you can do without.

✔ **Don't put all your money in one industry.** I know people who own several stocks, but the stocks are all in the same industry. Again, if you're an expert in that particular industry, it could work out. But just understand that you're not properly diversified. If a problem hits an entire industry, you may get hurt.

✔ **Don't put all your money in one type of investment.** Stocks may be a great investment, but you need to have money elsewhere. Bonds, bank accounts, treasury securities, real estate, and precious metals are perennial alternatives to complement your stock portfolio. Some of these alternatives can be found in mutual funds or exchange-traded funds (ETFs). An *exchange-traded fund* is a fund with a fixed portfolio of stocks or other securities that tracks a particular index but is traded like a stock. By the way, I love ETFs and I think that every serious investor should consider them; see Chapter 14 for more information.

Better luck next time!

A little knowledge can be very risky. Consider the true story of one "lucky" fellow who played the California lottery in 1987. He discovered that he had a winning ticket, with the first prize of $412,000. He immediately ordered a Porsche, booked a lavish trip to Hawaii for his family, and treated his wife and friends to a champagne dinner at a posh Hollywood restaurant. When he finally went to collect his prize, he found out that he had to share first prize with over 9,000 other lottery players who also had the same winning numbers. His share of the prize was actually only $45! Hopefully, he invested that tidy sum based on his increased knowledge about risk.

Okay, now that you know what you *shouldn't* do, what *should* you do? Until you become more knowledgeable, follow this advice:

✔ **Keep only 10 percent (or less) of your investment money in a single stock.**

✔ **Invest in four or five (and no more than ten) different stocks that are in different industries.** Which industries? Choose industries that offer products and services that have shown strong, growing demand. To make this decision, use your common sense (which isn't as common as it used to be). Think about the industries that people need no matter what happens in the general economy, such as food, energy, and other consumer necessities. See Chapter 13 for more information about analyzing industries.

Weighing Risk against Return

How much risk is appropriate for you, and how do you handle it? Before you try to figure out what risks accompany your investment choices, analyze yourself. Here are some points to keep in mind when weighing risk versus return in your situation:

✔ **Your financial goal:** In five minutes with a financial calculator, you can easily see how much money you're going to need to become financially independent (presuming financial independence is your goal). Say that you need $500,000 in ten years for a worry-free retirement and that your financial assets (such as stocks, bonds, and so on) are currently worth $400,000. In this scenario, your assets need to grow by only 2.25 percent to hit your target. Getting investments that grow by 2.25 percent safely is easy to do because that's a relatively low rate of return.

The important point is that you don't have to knock yourself out trying to double your money with risky, high-flying investments; some run-of-the-mill bank investments will do just fine. All too often, investors take on more risk than is necessary. Figure out what your financial goal is so that you know what kind of return you realistically need. Flip to Chapters 2 and 3 for details on determining your financial goals.

✔ **Your investor profile:** Are you nearing retirement, or are you fresh out of college? Your life situation matters when it comes to looking at risk versus return.

- If you're just beginning your working years, you can certainly tolerate greater risk than someone facing retirement. Even if you lose big time, you still have a long time to recoup your money and get back on track.

- However, if you're within five years of retirement, risky or aggressive investments can do much more harm than good. If you lose money, you don't have as much time to recoup your investment, and the odds are that you'll need the investment money (and its income-generating capacity) to cover your living expenses after you're no longer employed.

✔ **Asset allocation:** I never tell retirees to put a large portion of their retirement money into a high-tech stock or other volatile investment. But if they still want to speculate, I don't see a problem as long as they limit such investments to 5 percent of their total assets. As long as the bulk of their money is safe and sound in secure investments (such as U.S. treasury bonds), I know I can sleep well (knowing that *they* can sleep well!).

Asset allocation beckons back to diversification, which I discuss earlier in this chapter. For people in their 20s and 30s, having 75 percent of their money in a diversified portfolio of growth stocks (such as mid cap and small cap stocks; see Chapter 1) is acceptable. For people in their 60s and 70s, it's not acceptable. They may, instead, consider investing no more than 20 percent of their money in stocks (mid caps and large caps are preferable). Check with your financial advisor to find the right mix for your particular situation.

Chapter 5

Say Cheese: Getting a Snapshot of the Market with Indexes

In This Chapter

▶ Defining index basics

▶ Looking at the Dow and other indexes

▶ Exploring indexes for practical use

"**H**ow's the market doing today?" is the most common question that interested parties ask about the stock market. "What did the Dow do?" "How about Nasdaq?" Invariably, people asking those questions expect an answer regarding how well the market performed that day. "Well, the Dow fell 157 points to 12,500, while Nasdaq was unchanged at 2,449." The Dow and Nasdaq are *indexes,* which are statistical measures that represent the value of a batch of stocks. You can use indexes as general gauges of stock market activity. From them, you get a basic idea of how well (or how poorly) the overall market (or a portion of it) is doing. In this chapter, I focus my attention on the major stock market indexes and how to use them.

Knowing How Indexes Are Measured

The oldest stock market index is the Dow Jones Industrial Average (DJIA or simply "The Dow"), which was created by Charles Dow (of Dow Jones fame) in 1896. The Dow covered only 12 stocks then, but the number increased to 30 stocks in 1928, and it remains the same to this day. Because Dow worked long before the age of computers, he kept the calculations of his stock market index simple and did them arithmetically by hand. Dow added up the stock prices of the 12 companies and then divided the sum by 12. Technically, this number is an *average* and not an index (hence the word "average" in the name). For simplicity's sake, I refer to it as an index. Besides, the number gets tweaked nowadays to account for things such as stock splits. (For more on stock splits, see Chapter 20.)

However, indexes and averages get calculated differently. The primary difference is the concept of weighting. *Weighting* refers to the relative importance of the items when they're computed within the index. Several kinds of indexes exist, including:

✔ **Price-weighted index:** This index tracks changes based on the change in the individual stock's price per share. For example, suppose you own two stocks: Stock A, worth $20 per share, and Stock B, worth $40 per share. A price-weighted index allocates a greater proportion of the index to the stock at $40 than to the one at $20. If the index contained only these two stocks, the index number would reflect the $40 stock as being 67 percent (two-thirds of the total), while the $20 stock would be 33 percent (one-third of the total). The Dow is a good example of a price-weighted index.

✔ **Market-value weighted index:** This index, also known as a *capitalization-weighted index,* tracks the proportion of a stock based on its market capitalization (or market value, also called market cap).

Say that in your portfolio, you have 10 million shares of a $20 stock (Stock A) and 1 million shares of a $40 stock (Stock B). Stock A's market cap is $200 million, while Stock B's market cap is $40 million. Therefore, in a market-value weighted index, Stock A represents 83 percent of the index's value because of its much larger market cap. An example of a market-value weighted index is the Nasdaq Composite Index.

✔ **Broad-based index:** The sample portfolios in the preceding bullets show only two stocks — obviously not a good representative index. Most investing professionals (especially money managers and mutual fund firms) use a broad-based index as a benchmark to compare their progress. A broad-based index provides a snapshot of the entire market. The S&P 500 and the Wilshire 5000 are good examples of broad-based indexes (they also happen to be market-value weighted indexes; see descriptions of both indexes later in this chapter.)

✔ **Composite index:** This index is a combination of several averages or indexes. An example is the New York Stock Exchange (NYSE) Composite, which tracks all the stocks on the NYSE. Another example is the Nasdaq Composite Index, which is a market-capitalization composite index of 3,000 companies on Nasdaq. (I discuss Nasdaq later in this chapter.)

✔ **Performance-based index:** This index includes not only the appreciation of the stocks represented in the index but also the dividends (and other cash payouts) issued to stockholders. The DAX (the most widely followed German index, composed of 30 major German companies) is a performance-based index.

Checking Out the Indexes

Although most people consider the Dow, Nasdaq, and Standard & Poor's 500 to be the stars of the financial press, you may find other indexes equally important to follow because they cover other significant facets of the market, such as small cap and mid cap stocks, or specific sectors and industries.

For example, if you invest in an Internet stock, you should check the Internet Stock Index to compare how your stock is doing when measured against the index. You can find indexes that cover industries such as transportation, brokerage firms, retailers, computer companies, and real estate firms. For a comprehensive list of indexes, go to www.djindexes.com (a Dow Jones & Co. Web site). The most reliable and most widely respected indexes are produced not only by Dow Jones but also Standard & Poor's and the major exchanges/ markets themselves, such as the New York Stock Exchange (NYSE), the American Stock Exchange (AMEX), and Nasdaq. Smaller exchanges also issue or provide indexes (such as the Philadelphia Exchange). Web sites for different exchanges can be found in Appendix A.

The Dow Jones Industrial Average

The most famous stock market barometer is my first example in the previous section — the Dow Jones Industrial Average (DJIA). When someone asks how the market is doing, most investors quote the DJIA (simply referred to as "the Dow"). The Dow is price weighted and tracks a basket of 30 of the largest and most influential public companies in the stock market. I list the stocks tracked on the Dow and discuss the Dow's drawbacks in the following sections.

The companies of the Dow

The following list shows the current roster of 30 stocks tracked on the DJIA (in alphabetical order by company, with their stock symbols in parentheses).

Alcoa (AA)

American Express Co. (AXP)

AT&T (T)

Bank of America (BAC)

Boeing (BA)

Caterpillar (CAT)

Chevron (CVX)

Citigroup (C)

Coca-Cola Co. (KO)

Disney & Co (DIS)

DuPont (DD)

Exxon Mobil (XOM)

General Electric (GE)

General Motors (GM)

Hewlett-Packard (HPQ)

Home Depot (HD)

Intel (INTC)

International Business Machines (IBM)

Johnson & Johnson (JNJ)

J.P. Morgan Chase (JPM)

Kraft Food Inc. (KFT)

McDonald's (MCD)

Merck (MRK)

Microsoft (MSFT)

Minnesota Mining and Manufacturing (also known as 3M) (MMM)

Pfizer (PFE)

Procter & Gamble (PG)

United Technologies (UTX)

Verizon (VZ)

Wal-Mart Stores (WMT)

The drawbacks of the Dow

The Dow has survived as a popular gauge of stock market activity for over a century because it was the first such statistical snapshot of the stock market, which helped it become quickly entrenched as a widely followed and quoted barometer. Although it's an important indicator of the market's progress, the Dow does have one major drawback: It tracks only 30 companies. Regardless of their status in the market, the companies in the Dow represent a limited sampling, so they don't communicate the true pulse of the market. For example, when the Dow surpassed the record 10,000 and 11,000 milestones during 1999 and 2000, the majority of (nonindex) companies showed lackluster or declining stock price movement. (See the "Dow Jones milestones" sidebar, later in this chapter, for more information.)

The roster of the Dow has changed many times during the 100-plus years of its existence. The only original company from 1896 is General Electric. Dow Jones made most of the changes because of company mergers and bankruptcy. However, Dow Jones also made some changes simply to reflect the changing times. In September 2008, as AIG Corp.'s stock was plummeting because of the credit crisis on Wall Street, it was quickly removed from the Dow and replaced with Kraft Foods. At that time, AIG fell from $25 per share to $3 per share within days. Had AIG stayed in the Dow, the Dow would have shown a larger drop, but it maintained a higher level because of the quick replacement. Investors unaware of such moves can be fooled regarding the market's health — another drawback of the Dow.

Dow Jones milestones

This table shows when the Dow Jones Industrial Average reached each of 14 1,000-point milestones and how long it took to reach that point:

Milestone	Date	How long it took
1,000	Nov. 14, 1972	76 years
2,000	Jan. 8, 1987	14 years
3,000	April 17, 1991	4 years
4,000	Feb. 23, 1995	4 years
5,000	Nov. 21, 1995	9 months
6,000	Oct. 14, 1996	11 months
7,000	Feb. 13, 1997	4 months
8,000	July 16, 1997	5 months
9,000	April 6, 1998	9 months
10,000	March 29, 1999	1 year
11,000	May 3, 1999	1 month
12,000	Oct. 19, 2006	7 years and 5 months
13,000	April 25, 2007	6 months
14,000	July 19, 2007	3 months

As you can see, the Dow took 76 years to hit its first milestone. But it took less and less time to hit each succeeding milestone because the higher the Dow is in a relative sense, the easier it is to jump 1,000 points. For example, it went from 6,000 to 7,000 in only four months.

As the table indicates, most of the milestones happened during the 1982–1999 bull market. But the Dow didn't reach a new milestone from 2000–2004. After the Dow hit a peak of 11,722 in January 2000, it entered a bear market that lasted three years. A new bull market started in 2003, and the Dow regained its traction and started an ascent to new highs. It finally hit the 12,000 mark in late 2006 (nearly 7½ years after hitting the 11,000 level). Despite hitting the 14,000 plateau in July 2007, it spent the subsequent 12-month period trading sideways in the 11,000–13,000 range. The Dow hit an all-time closing high of 14,164.53 on October 9, 2007 (Hey! That's my wedding anniversary!), although it is considerably lower a year later (under 9,300). Oh well . . . .

The Dow isn't a pure gauge of industrial activity because it also includes a hodgepodge of nonindustrial companies such as J.P. Morgan Chase and Citigroup (banks), Home Depot (retailing), and Microsoft (software). During this decade, true industrial sectors like manufacturing had difficult times, yet the Dow rose to record levels.

Given the Dow's shortcomings, serious investors also look at the following indexes:

✔ **Broad-based indexes:** The S&P 500 and the Wilshire 5000 are more realistic gauges of the stock market's performance than the Dow. (I discuss these indexes later in this chapter.)

✔ **Industry or sector indexes:** These indexes are better gauges of the growth (or lack of growth) of specific industries and sectors. If you buy a gold stock, for example, you should track the index for the precious metals industry.

Dow Jones has several averages, including the Dow Jones Transportation Average (DJTA) and the Dow Jones Utilities Average (DJUA). Dow Jones manages both of these indexes more strictly than the Dow, so they tend to be a more accurate barometer of the market they represent. Find out more about the Dow Jones indexes at `www.djindexes.com`.

Standard & Poor's 500

The Standard & Poor's 500 (S&P 500) tracks 500 leading publicly traded companies considered to be widely held. The publishing firm Standard & Poor's created this index (I bet you could've guessed that). Because it contains 500 companies, the S&P 500 more accurately represents overall market performance than the DJIA, with its 30 companies. Money managers and financial advisors actually watch the S&P 500 stock index more closely than the Dow. Most mutual funds especially like to measure their performance against the S&P 500 rather than any other index, although mutual funds that concentrate on small cap stocks usually prefer an index that has more small cap stocks in it, such as the Russell 2000 (which I discuss later in this chapter).

The S&P 500 doesn't attempt to cover the 500 biggest companies. Instead, it includes companies that are widely held and widely followed. The companies are also industry leaders in a variety of industries, including energy, technology, healthcare, and finance.

Although it's a reliable indicator of the market's overall status, the S&P 500 also has some limitations. Despite the fact that it tracks 500 companies, the top 50 companies make up 50 percent of the index's market value. This situation can be a drawback, because those 50 companies have a greater influence on the index's price movement than any other segment of companies. In other words, 10 percent of the companies have an equal impact to 90 percent of the companies on the same index. Therefore, although the index better represents the market than the DIJA, it doesn't give a perfectly accurate representation of the general market.

Standard & Poor's doesn't set the 500 companies it tracks in stone — S&P can add or remove companies when market conditions change, removing a company if it isn't doing well or goes bankrupt, for instance, and replacing it with a company that's doing better. You can find out more at `www.standard andpoors.com`.

Wilshire Total Market Index

The Wilshire 5000 Equity Index, often referred to as the Wilshire Total Market Index, is probably the largest stock index in the world. Wilshire Associates started out in 1980 tracking 5,000 stocks. Since then, the Wilshire 5000 has ballooned to cover more than 7,500 stocks. The advantage of the Wilshire 5000 is that it's very comprehensive, covering nearly the entire market (at the very least, the Wilshire 5000 tracks the largest publicly traded stocks). It includes all the stocks on the major stock exchanges (NYSE, AMEX, and the largest issues on Nasdaq), which by default also includes all the stocks covered by the S&P 500. Investors and analysts who seek the greatest representation/performance of the general market look to the Wilshire 5000.

The Wilshire 5000 is a market-value weighted index that also performs as a broad-based index. The Wilshire indexes are maintained by Wilshire Associates Incorporated, and you can find out more at `www.wilshire.com`.

Nasdaq indexes

Nasdaq became a formalized market in 1971. The name used to stand for "National Association of Securities Dealers Automated Quote" system, but now it's simply "Nasdaq" (as if it's a name like Ralph or Eddie). Nasdaq indexes are similar to other indexes in style and structure. The only difference is that, well, they cover companies traded on the Nasdaq (`www.nasdaq.com`). The Nasdaq has two indexes, both of which are reported in the financial pages:

- **Nasdaq Composite Index:** Most frequently quoted on the news, the Nasdaq Composite Index covers about 3,000 companies that trade on Nasdaq. The companies encompass a variety of industries, but the index's concentration is primarily technology, telecommunications, and related sectors. The Nasdaq Composite Index hit an all-time high of 5,048 in March 2000 before the worst bear market in its history occurred. The index dropped a whopping 77 percent by 2002 to bottom out at 1,114 in October 2002. As of early October 2008, the Nasdaq was at approximately 1,740 (still way below its all-time high, but higher than its bottom six years earlier).

✔ **Nasdaq 100 Index:** The Nasdaq 100 tracks the 100 largest companies in Nasdaq based on size in terms of market capitalization. This index is for investors who want to concentrate on the largest companies, which tend to be especially weighted in technology. It provides extra representation of technology-related companies such as Microsoft, Adobe, and Symantec.

Although these indexes track growth-oriented companies, the stocks of these companies are also very volatile and carry commensurate risk. The indexes themselves bear this risk out; in the bear market of 2000 and 2001 (and even extending into 2002), they fell more than 60 percent. You can find out more about Nasdaq's indexes at www.nasdaq.com.

Russell 3000 Index

The Russell 3000 Index is a great example of an index that seeks more comprehensive inclusion of U.S. companies. It's a performance-based index that includes the 3,000 largest publicly traded companies (nearly 98 percent of publicly traded stocks). The Russell 3000 is important because it includes many mid cap and small cap stocks. Most companies covered in the Russell 3000 have an average market value of a billion dollars or less.

Russell Investments Group created and maintains the Russell 3000 Index, as well as the Russell 1000 and the Russell 2000. The Russell 2000 contains the smallest 2,000 companies from the Russell 3000, while the Russell 1000 contains the largest 1,000 companies. The Russell indexes don't cover *micro cap stocks* (companies with a market capitalization under $250 million). You can find out more at www.russell.com.

International indexes

Investors need to remember that the whole world is a vast marketplace that interacts with and exerts tremendous influence on individual national economies and markets. Whether you have one stock or one mutual fund, keep tabs on how world markets affect your portfolio. The best way to get a snapshot of international markets is, of course, with indexes. Here are some of the more widely followed international indexes:

✔ **BSE SENSEX (India):** The most widely followed index of Indian stocks is also referred to as the "BSE 30 Index" and is a value-weighted index maintained by the Bombay Stock Exchange (www.bseindia.com).

✔ **CAC-40 (France):** This market-capitalization weighted index tracks 40 of the largest public stocks that trade on Paris's stock exchange, the Euronext Paris.

✔ **DAX (Germany):** This index is similar to our DJIA in that it tracks 30 blue chip stocks (the largest and most active that trade on the Frankfurt Exchange).

✔ **FTSE-100 (Great Britain):** Usually referred to as the "footsie," this market-value weighted index includes the top 100 public companies in the United Kingdom.

✔ **Halter USX China Index (China):** This index tracks a basket of 50 market-value weighted U.S. public companies that derive most of their revenues from China.

✔ **Hang Seng Index (Hong Kong):** This market-value weighted index tracks the top 45 companies on the Hong Kong Stock Exchange.

✔ **Nikkei (Japan):** This index is considered Japan's version of the Dow. If you're invested in Japanese stocks or in stocks that do business with Japan, you want to know what's up with the Nikkei.

✔ **SSE Composite Index (Shanghai):** This is an index of all the stocks that trade on the Shanghai Stock Exchange.

You can track these international indexes (among others) at major financial Web sites such as www.bloomberg.com and www.marketwatch.com. You may find international indexes useful in your analysis as you watch your stocks' progress. What if you have stock in a company that has most of its customers in Japan? Then the Nikkei can help you get a general snapshot of how well the major companies are doing in Japan, which in turn can be a general barometer of Japan's economic health. If your company's business partners or customers are in the Nikkei and it's plunging, you know it's probably "sayonara" for the company's stock price.

As for me, I'm still waiting for the "Galaxy 1 Million Index" — no point in being overweight with Earth stocks, you know.

Using the Indexes Effectively

You may be wondering which indexes you should be checking out and exactly what you should do with them. The sections that follow give you some idea of how to put all the pieces together.

Tracking the indexes

The bottom line is that indexes give investors an instant snapshot of how well the market is doing. Indexes offer a quick way to compare the performance of one investor's portfolio with the rest of the market. If the Dow goes up 10 percent in a year and your portfolio shows a cumulative gain of 12 percent, then you know you're doing well. Appendix A lists resources to help you keep up with various indexes.

The problem with indexes is that they can be misleading if you take them too literally as an accurate barometer of stock success. For example, the Dow has changed its roster of companies many times since 1896. Had it not, the Dow's general upward trajectory in the past few decades would have been much different. Laggard stocks have been dropped and replaced with stocks that have shown more promise. Many of the original companies that were in the DJIA in 1896 went out of business or were bought by other companies that aren't reflected in the index.

Investing in indexes

If the market is doing well but your specific stock isn't, can you find a way to invest in the index itself? Yes, and with investments based on indexes, you can invest in the general market or a particular industry.

Say you want to invest in the DJIA. After all, why try to beat the market if just matching it is sufficient to grow your wealth? Why not have a portfolio that directly mirrors the DJIA? Well, it's too impractical and expensive to invest in all 30 stocks in the DJIA. Fortunately, alternatives can accomplish the act of investing in indexes. Here are the best ways:

- ✔ **Index mutual funds:** An index mutual fund is much like a regular mutual fund except that it only invests in securities (in this case, stocks) that match as closely as possible the basket of stocks in that particular index. For example, you can find index mutual funds that track the DJIA and the S&P 500. Find out more about index mutual funds at places such as Morningstar (www.morningstar.com).

- ✔ **Exchange-traded funds (ETFs):** This is a particular favorite of mine. ETFs have similar characteristics to mutual funds except for a few key differences. An ETF can reflect a basket of stocks that mirror a particular index, but you can trade the ETF like a stock itself. You can transact ETFs like stocks in that you can buy, sell, or go short. You can put stop losses on them, and you can even purchase them on margin (see Chapter 18 for more on stop losses and buying on margin). ETFs can give you the diversification of mutual funds coupled with the versatility of stocks. Examples of ETFs that track indexes are the DJIA ETF (symbol DIA) and the ETF for Nasdaq (QQQ). You can find out more about ETFs at the American Stock Exchange (www.amex.com).

Part II
Before You
Start Buying

The 5th Wave   By Rich Tennant

EARLY INVESTORS TRACKING A STOCK

In this part . . .

When you're about to begin investing in stocks, you should know that different types of stocks exist for different objectives. If you can at least get a stock that fits your situation, you're that much ahead in the game. In this part, you can find out where to start gathering information and discover what stockbrokers can do for you. In addition, you'll find a fun chapter on the basics of economics (really!) that will keep you ahead of the curve because stock choices are made more intelligently when you know the economic environment.

Chapter 6

Gathering Information

In This Chapter

▶ Using stock exchanges to get investment information

▶ Applying accounting and economic know-how to your investments

▶ Exploring financial issues

▶ Deciphering stock tables

▶ Interpreting dividend news

▶ Recognizing good (and bad) investing advice

Knowledge and information are two critical success factors in stock investing. (Isn't that true about most things in life?) People who plunge headlong into stocks without sufficient knowledge of the stock market in general, and current information in particular, quickly learn the lesson of the eager diver who didn't find out ahead of time that the pool was only an inch deep (ouch!). In their haste to avoid missing so-called golden investment opportunities, investors too often end up losing money.

Opportunities to *make* money in the stock market will always be there, no matter how well or how poorly the economy and the market are performing in general. There's no such thing as a single (and fleeting) magical moment, so don't feel that if you let an opportunity pass you by, you'll always regret that you missed your one big chance.

For the best approach to stock investing, you want to build your knowledge and find quality information first. Then buy stocks and make your fortunes more assuredly. Basically, before you buy stock, you need to know that the company you're investing in is

✔ Financially sound and growing

✔ Offering products and services that are in demand by consumers

✔ In a strong and growing industry (and general economy)

Where do you start and what kind of information do you want to acquire? Keep reading.

Looking to Stock Exchanges for Answers

Before you invest in stocks, you need to be completely familiar with the basics of stock investing. At its most fundamental, stock investing is about using your money to buy a piece of a company that will give you value in the form of appreciation or income. Fortunately, many resources are available to help you find out about stock investing. Some of my favorite places are the stock exchanges themselves.

Stock exchanges are organized marketplaces for the buying and selling of stocks (and other securities). The New York Stock Exchange (NYSE), the premier stock exchange, provides a framework for stock buyers and sellers to make their transactions. The NYSE makes money not only from a piece of every transaction but also from fees (such as listing fees) charged to companies and brokers that are members of its exchanges. In 2007, the NYSE merged with Euronext, a major European exchange, but no material differences exist for stock investors.

The main exchanges for most stock investors are the NYSE and the American Stock Exchange (AMEX). Nasdaq is technically not an exchange, but it is a formal market that effectively acts as an exchange. These three encourage and inform people about stock investing. Because these exchanges/markets benefit from increased popularity of stock investing and continued demand for stocks, they offer a wealth of free (or low-cost) resources and information for stock investors. Go to their Web sites and you find useful resources such as:

✔ Tutorials on how to invest in stocks, common investment strategies, and so on

✔ Glossaries and free information to help you understand the language, practice, and purpose of stock investing

✔ A wealth of news, press releases, financial data, and other information about companies listed on the exchange or market, usually accessed through an on-site search engine

✔ Industry analysis and news

✔ Stock quotes and other market information related to the daily market movements of stocks, including data such as volume, new highs, new lows, and so on

✔ Free tracking of your stock selections (you can input a sample portfolio, or the stocks you're following, to see how well you're doing)

What each exchange/market offers keeps changing and is often updated, so go explore them at their Web sites:

✔ New York Stock Exchange: www.nyse.com

✔ American Stock Exchange: www.amex.com

✔ Nasdaq: www.nasdaq.com

Understanding Stocks and the Companies They Represent

Stocks represent ownership in companies. Before you buy individual stocks, you want to understand the companies whose stock you're considering and find out about their operations. It may sound like a daunting task, but you'll digest the point more easily when you realize that companies work very similarly to how you work. They make decisions on a day-to-day basis just as you do.

Think about how you grow and prosper as an individual or as a family, and you see the same issues with businesses and how they grow and prosper. Low earnings and high debt are examples of financial difficulties that can affect both people and companies. You'll understand companies' finances when you take the time to pick up some information in two basic disciplines: accounting and economics. These two disciplines play a significant role in understanding the performance of a firm's stock.

Accounting for taste and a whole lot more

Accounting. Ugh! But face it: Accounting is the language of business, and believe it or not, you're already familiar with the most important accounting concepts! Just look at the following three essential principles:

✔ **Assets minus liabilities equal net worth.** In other words, take what you own (your assets), subtract what you owe (your liabilities), and the rest is yours (net worth)! Your own personal finances work the same way as Microsoft's (except yours have fewer zeros at the end). See Chapter 2 to figure out how to calculate your own net worth.

A company's balance sheet shows you its net worth at a specific point in time (such as December 31). The net worth of a company is the bottom line of its asset and liability picture, and it tells you whether the company is *solvent* (has the ability to pay its debts without going out of business). The net worth of a successful company is regularly growing. To see whether your company is successful, compare its net worth with the net worth from the same point a year earlier. A firm that has a $4 million net worth on December 31, 2007, and a $5 million net worth on December 31, 2008, is doing well; its net worth has gone up 25 percent ($1 million) in one year.

✔ **Income less expenses equal net income.** In other words, take what you make (your income), subtract what you spend (your expenses), and the remainder is your *net income* (or net profit or net earnings — your gain).

A company's profitability is the whole point of investing in its stock. As it profits, the business becomes more valuable, and in turn, its stock price becomes more valuable. To discover a firm's net income, look at its income statement. Try to determine whether the company uses its gains wisely, either reinvesting them for continued growth or paying down debt.

✔ **Do a comparative financial analysis.** That's a mouthful, but it's just a fancy way of saying how a company is doing now compared with something else (like a prior period or a similar company).

If you know that the company you're looking at had a net income of $50,000 for the year, you may ask, "Is that good or bad?" Obviously, making a net profit is good, but you also need to know whether it's good compared to something else. If the company had a net profit of $40,000 the year before, you know that the company's profitability is improving. But if a similar company had a net profit of $100,000 the year before and in the current year is making $50,000, then you may want to either avoid that company or see what went wrong (if anything) with it.

Accounting can be this simple. If you understand these three basic points, you're ahead of the curve (in stock investing as well as in your personal finances). For more information on how to use a company's financial statements to pick good stocks, see Chapters 11 and 12.

Understanding how economics affects stocks

Economics. Double ugh! No, you aren't required to understand "the inelasticity of demand aggregates" (thank heavens!) or "marginal utility" (say what?). But a working knowledge of basic economics is crucial (and I mean crucial) to your success and proficiency as a stock investor. The stock market and the economy are joined at the hip. The good (or bad) things that happen to one have a direct effect on the other.

Getting the hang of the basic concepts

Alas, many investors get lost on basic economic concepts (as do some so-called experts that you see on TV). I owe my personal investing success to my status as a student of economics. Understanding basic economics helps me (and will help you) filter the financial news to separate relevant information from the irrelevant in order to make better investment decisions. Be aware of these important economic concepts:

- **Supply and demand:** How can anyone possibly think about economics without thinking of the ageless concept of supply and demand? *Supply and demand* can be simply stated as the relationship between what's available (the supply) and what people want and are willing to pay for (the demand). This equation is the main engine of economic activity and is extremely important for your stock investing analysis and decision-making process. I mean, do you really want to buy stock in a company that makes elephant-foot umbrella stands if you find out that the company has an oversupply and nobody wants to buy them anyway? (I discuss supply and demand in more detail in Chapter 10.)

- **Cause and effect:** If you pick up a prominent news report and read, "Companies in the table industry are expecting plummeting sales," do you rush out and invest in companies that sell chairs or manufacture tablecloths? Considering cause and effect is an exercise in logical thinking, and believe you me, logic is a major component of sound economic thought.

   When you read business news, play it out in your mind. What good (or bad) can logically be expected given a certain event or situation? If you're looking for an effect ("I want a stock price that keeps increasing"), you also want to understand the cause. Here are some typical events that can cause a stock's price to rise (see Chapter 10 for additional info on cause and effect):

   - **Positive news reports about a company:** The news may report that the company is enjoying success with increased sales or a new product.

   - **Positive news reports about a company's industry:** The media may be highlighting that the industry is poised to do well.

   - **Positive news reports about a company's customers:** Maybe your company is in industry A, but its customers are in industry B. If you see good news about industry B, that may be good news for your stock.

- **Negative news reports about a company's competitors:** If the competitors are in trouble, their customers may seek alternatives to buy from, including your company.

✔ **Economic effects from government actions:** Political and governmental actions have economic consequences. As a matter of fact, nothing (and I mean nothing!) has a greater effect on investing and economics than government. Government actions usually manifest themselves as taxes, laws, or regulations. They also can take on a more ominous appearance, such as war or the threat of war. Government can willfully (or even accidentally) cause a company to go bankrupt, disrupt an entire industry, or even cause a depression. It controls the money supply, credit, and all public securities markets. For more information on political effects, see Chapter 15.

Gaining insight from past mistakes

Because most investors ignored some basic observations about economics in the late 1990s, they subsequently lost trillions in their stock portfolios. During 2000–2008, the U.S. experienced the greatest expansion of total debt in history, coupled with a record expansion of the money supply. The Federal Reserve (or "the Fed"), the U.S. government's central bank, controls both. This growth of debt and money supply resulted in more consumer (and corporate) borrowing, spending, and investing. This activity hyperstimulated the stock market and caused stocks to rise 25 percent per year for five straight years during the late 1990s. When the stock market bubble popped during 2000–2002, it was soon replaced with the housing bubble, which popped during 2005–2006 and is still hurting the economy in 2008.

Of course, you should always be happy to earn 25 percent per year with your investments, but such a return can't be sustained and encourages speculation. This artificial stimulation by the Fed resulted in the following:

✔ More and more people depleted their savings. After all, why settle for 3 percent in the bank when you can get 25 percent in the stock market?

✔ More and more people bought on credit. If the economy is booming, why not buy now and pay later? Consumer credit hit record highs.

✔ More and more people borrowed against their homes. Why not borrow and get rich now? I can pay off my debt later.

✔ More and more companies sold more goods as consumers took more vacations and bought SUVs, electronics, and so on. Companies then borrowed to finance expansion, open new stores, and so on.

✔ More and more companies went public and offered stock to take advantage of more money that was flowing to the markets from banks and other financial institutions.

Know thyself before you invest in stocks

If you're reading this book, you're probably doing so because you want to become a successful investor. Granted, to be a successful investor, you have to select great stocks, but having a realistic understanding of your own financial situation and goals is equally important. I recall one investor who lost $10,000 in a speculative stock. The loss wasn't that bad because he had most of his money safely tucked away elsewhere. He also understood that his overall financial situation was secure and that the money he lost was "play" money — the loss wouldn't have a drastic effect on his life. But many investors often lose even more money, and the loss does have a major, negative effect on their lives. You may not be like the investor who can afford to lose $10,000. Take time to understand yourself, your own financial picture, and your personal investment goals before you decide to buy stocks.

In the end, spending started to slow down because consumers and businesses became too indebted. This slowdown in turn caused the sales of goods and services to taper off. However, companies had too much overhead, capacity, and debt because they expanded too eagerly. At this point, businesses were caught in a financial bind. Too much debt and too many expenses in a slowing economy mean one thing: Profits shrink or disappear. Companies, to stay in business, had to do the logical thing — cut expenses. What's usually the biggest expense for companies? People! To stay in business, many companies started laying off employees. As a result, consumer spending dropped further because more people were either laid off or had second thoughts about their own job security.

As people had little in the way of savings and too much in the way of debt, they had to sell their stock to pay their bills. This trend was a major reason that stocks started to fall in 2000. Earnings started to drop because of shrinking sales from a sputtering economy. As earnings fell, stock prices also fell.

The lessons from the 1990s are important ones for investors today:

- ✔ Stocks are not a replacement for savings accounts. Always have some money in the bank.

- ✔ Stocks should never occupy 100 percent of your investment funds.

- ✔ When anyone (including an expert) tells you that the economy will keep growing indefinitely, be skeptical and read diverse sources of information.

- ✔ If stocks do well in your portfolio, consider protecting your stocks (both your original investment and any gains) with stop-loss orders. (See Chapter 18 for more on these strategies.)

✔ Keep debt and expenses to a minimum.

✔ If the economy is booming, a decline is sure to follow as the ebb and flow of the economy's business cycle continues.

Staying on Top of Financial News

Reading the financial news can help you decide where or where not to invest. Many newspapers, magazines, and Web sites offer great coverage of the financial world. Obviously, the more informed you are, the better, but you don't have to read everything that's written. The information explosion in recent years has gone beyond overload, and you can easily spend so much time reading that you have little time left for investing. In the following sections, I describe the types of information you need to get from the financial news.

Appendix A of this book provides more information on the following resources, along with a treasure trove of some of the best publications, resources, and Web sites to assist you:

✔ The most obvious publications of interest to stock investors are *The Wall Street Journal* and *Investor's Business Daily.* These excellent publications report the news and stock data as of the prior trading day.

✔ Some of the more obvious Web sites are MarketWatch (`www.market watch.com`) and Bloomberg (`www.bloomberg.com`). These Web sites can actually give you news and stock data within 15 to 20 minutes after an event occurs.

✔ Don't forget the exchanges' Web sites that I list in the earlier section, "Looking to Stock Exchanges for Answers"!

Figuring out what a company's up to

Before you invest, you need to know what's going on with the company. When you read about the company, either from the firm's literature (its annual report, for example) or from media sources, be sure to get answers to some pertinent questions:

✔ **Is the company making more net income than it did last year?** You want to invest in a company that's growing.

✔ **Are the company's sales greater than they were the year before?** Remember, you won't make money if the company isn't making money.

✔ **Is the company issuing press releases on new products, services, inventions, or business deals?** All these achievements indicate a strong, vital company.

Knowing how the company is doing, no matter what's happening with the general economy, is obviously important. To better understand how companies tick, see Chapters 11 and 12.

Discovering what's new with an industry

As you consider investing in a stock, make it a point to know what's going on in that company's industry. If the industry is doing well, your stock is likely to do well, too. But then again, the reverse is also true.

Yes, I've seen investors pick successful stocks in a failing industry, but those cases are exceptional. By and large, it's easier to succeed with a stock when the entire industry is doing well. As you're watching the news, reading the financial pages, or viewing financial Web sites, check out the industry to see that it's strong and dynamic. See Chapter 13 for information on analyzing industries.

Knowing what's happening with the economy

No matter how well or how poorly the overall economy is performing, you want to stay informed about its general progress. It's easier for the value of stock to keep going up when the economy is stable or growing. The reverse is also true; if the economy is contracting or declining, the stock has a tougher time keeping its value. Some basic items to keep tabs on include the following:

✔ **Gross domestic product (GDP):** This is roughly the total value of output for a particular nation, measured in the dollar amount of goods and services. The GDP is reported quarterly, and a rising GDP bodes well for your stock. When the GDP is rising 3 percent or more on an annual basis, that's solid growth. If it rises at more than zero but less than 3 percent, that's generally considered less than stellar (or mediocre). A GDP under zero (or negative) means that the economy is shrinking (heading into recession).

✔ **The index of leading economic indicators (LEI):** The LEI is a snapshot of a set of economic statistics covering activity that precedes what's happening in the economy. Each statistic helps you understand the economy in much the same way that barometers (and windows!) help you understand what's happening with the weather. Economists don't just look at an individual statistic; they look at a set of statistics to get a more complete picture of what's happening with the economy.

Chapter 10 goes into greater detail on economics and its effect on stock prices.

Seeing what politicians and government bureaucrats are doing

Being informed about what public officials are doing is vital to your success as a stock investor. Because federal, state, and local governments pass literally thousands of laws every year, monitoring the political landscape is critical to your success. The news media report what the president and Congress are doing, so always ask yourself, "How does a new law, tax, or regulation affect my stock investment?"

Because government actions have a significant effect on your investments, it's a good idea to see what's going on. Laws being proposed or enacted by the federal government can be found through the Thomas legislative search engine, which is run by the Library of Congress (www.loc.gov). Also, some great organizations inform the public about tax laws and their impact, such as the National Taxpayers Union (www.ntu.org). Chapter 15 gives you more insights into politics and its effect on the stock market.

Checking for trends in society, culture, and entertainment

As odd as it sounds, trends in society, popular culture, and entertainment affect your investments, directly or indirectly. For example, a headline such as, "The Graying of America — More People Than Ever Before Will Be Senior Citizens" gives you some important information that can make or break your stock portfolio. With that particular headline, you know that as more and more people age, companies that are well positioned to cater to that growing market's wants and needs will do well — meaning a successful stock for you.

Keep your eyes open to emerging trends in society at large. What trends are evident now? Can you anticipate the wants and needs of tomorrow's society? Being alert, staying a step ahead of the public, and choosing stocks appropriately gives you a profitable edge over other investors. If you own stock in a solid company with growing sales and earnings, other investors eventually notice. As more investors buy up your company's stocks, you're rewarded as the stock price increases.

Reading (And Understanding) Stock Tables

The stock tables in major business publications such as *The Wall Street Journal* and *Investor's Business Daily* are loaded with information that can help you become a savvy investor — *if* you know how to interpret them. You need the information in the stock tables for more than selecting promising investment opportunities. You also need to consult the tables after you invest to monitor how your stocks are doing.

Looking at the stock tables without knowing what you're looking for or why you're looking is the equivalent of reading *War and Peace* backwards through a kaleidoscope — nothing makes sense. But I can help you make sense of it all (well, at least the stock tables!). Table 6-1 shows a sample stock table for you to refer to as you read the sections that follow.

Table 6-1		A Sample Stock Table						
52-Wk High	52-Wk Low	Name (Symbol)	Div	Vol	Yld	P/E	Day Last	Net Chg
21.50	8.00	SkyHighCorp (SHC)		3,143		76	21.25	+.25
47.00	31.75	LowDownInc (LDI)	2.35	2,735	5.9	18	41.00	−.50
25.00	21.00	ValueNowInc (VNI)	1.00	1,894	4.5	12	22.00	+.10
83.00	33.00	DoinBadly Corp (DBC)		7,601			33.50	−.75

Every newspaper's financial tables are a little different, but they give you basi-cally the same information. Updated daily, this section is not the place to start your search for a good stock; it's usually where your search ends. The stock tables are the place to look when you own a stock or know what you want to buy and you're just checking to see the most recent price.

Each item gives you some clues about the current state of affairs for that par-ticular company. The sections that follow describe each column to help you understand what you're looking at.

52-week high

The column in Table 6-1 labeled "52-Wk High" gives you the highest price that particular stock has reached in the most recent 52-week period. Knowing this price lets you gauge where the stock is now versus where it has been recently. SkyHighCorp's (SHC) stock has been as high as $21.50, while its last (most recent) price is $21.25, the number listed in the "Day Last" column. (Flip to the "Day last" section for more on understanding this information.) SkyHighCorp's stock is trading very high right now because it's hovering right near its overall 52-week high figure.

Now, take a look at DoinBadlyCorp's (DBC) stock price. It seems to have tumbled big time. Its stock price has had a high in the past 52 weeks of $83, but it's currently trading at $33.50. Something just doesn't seem right here. During the past 52 weeks, DBC's stock price fell dramatically. If you're think-ing about investing in DBC, find out why the stock price fell. If the company is strong, it may be a good opportunity to buy stock at a lower price. If the company is having tough times, avoid it. In any case, research the firm and find out why its stock has declined.

52-week low

The column labeled "52-Wk Low" gives you the lowest price that particular stock reached in the most recent 52-week period. Again, this information is crucial to your ability to analyze stock over a period of time. Look at DBC in Table 6-1, and you can see that its current trading price of $33.50 is close to its 52-week low of $33.

Keep in mind that the high and low prices just give you a range of how far that particular stock's price has moved within the past 52 weeks. They could alert you that a stock has problems, or they could tell you that a stock's price has fallen enough to make it a bargain. Simply reading the 52-Wk High and 52-Wk Low columns isn't enough to determine which of those two scenarios is hap-pening. They basically tell you to get more information before you commit your money.

Name and symbol

The "Name (Symbol)" column is the simplest in Table 6-1. It tells you the company name (usually abbreviated) and the stock symbol assigned to the company.

When you have your eye on a stock for potential purchase, get familiar with its symbol. Knowing the symbol makes it easier for you to find your stock in the financial tables, which list stocks in alphabetical order by the company's name. Stock symbols are the language of stock investing, and you need to use them in all stock communications, from getting a stock quote at your broker's office to buying stock over the Internet.

Dividend

Dividends (shown under the "Div" column in Table 6-1) are basically payments to owners (stockholders). If a company pays a dividend, it's shown in the dividend column. The amount you see is the annual dividend quoted for one share of that stock. If you look at LowDownInc (LDI) in Table 6-1, you can see that you get $2.35 as an annual dividend for each share of stock that you own. Companies usually pay the dividend in quarterly amounts. If I own 100 shares of LDI, the company pays me a quarterly dividend of $58.75 ($235 total per year). A healthy company strives to maintain or upgrade the dividend for stockholders from year to year. (I discuss additional dividend details later in this chapter.)

The dividend is very important to investors seeking income from their stock investment. For more about investing for income, see Chapter 9. Investors buy stock in companies that don't pay dividends primarily for growth. For more information on growth stocks, see Chapter 8.

Volume

Normally, when you hear the word "volume" on the news, it refers to how much stock is bought and sold for the entire market: "Well, stocks were very active today. Trading volume at the New York Stock Exchange hit 2 billion shares." Volume is certainly important to watch because the stocks that you're investing in are somewhere in that activity. For the "Vol" column in Table 6-1, though, the volume refers to the individual stock.

Volume tells you how many shares of that particular stock were traded that day. If only 100 shares are traded in a day, then the trading volume is 100. SHC had 3,143 shares change hands on the trading day represented in Table 6-1. Is that good or bad? Neither, really. Usually the business news media only mention volume for a particular stock when it's unusually large. If a stock normally has volume in the 5,000 to 10,000 range and all of a sudden has a trading volume of 87,000, then it's time to sit up and take notice.

Keep in mind that a low trading volume for one stock may be a high trading volume for another stock. You can't necessarily compare one stock's volume against that of any other company. The large cap stocks like IBM or Microsoft typically have trading volumes in the millions of shares almost every day, while less active, smaller stocks may have average trading volumes in far, far smaller numbers.

The main point to remember is that trading volume that is far in excess of that stock's normal range is a sign that something is going on with that stock. It may be negative or positive, but something newsworthy is happening with that company. If the news is positive, the increased volume is a result of more people buying the stock. If the news is negative, the increased volume is probably a result of more people selling the stock. What are typical events that cause increased trading volume? Some positive reasons include the following:

- **Good earnings reports:** The company announces good (or better-than-expected) earnings.

- **A new business deal:** The firm announces a favorable business deal, such as a joint venture, or lands a big client.

- **A new product or service:** The company's research and development department creates a potentially profitable new product.

- **Indirect benefits:** The business may benefit from a new development in the economy or from a new law passed by Congress.

Some negative reasons for an unusually large fluctuation in trading volume for a particular stock include the following:

- **Bad earnings reports:** Profit is the lifeblood of a company. When its profits fall or disappear, you see more volume.

- **Governmental problems:** The stock is being targeted by government action, such as a lawsuit or a Securities and Exchange Commission (SEC) probe.

✔ **Liability issues:** The media report that the company has a defective product or similar problem.

✔ **Financial problems:** Independent analysts report that the company's financial health is deteriorating.

Check out what's happening when you hear about heavier than usual volume (especially if you already own the stock).

Yield

In general, yield is a return on the money you invest. However, in the stock tables, *yield* ("Yld" in Table 6-1) is a reference to what percentage that particular dividend is to the stock price. Yield is most important to income investors. It's calculated by dividing the annual dividend by the current stock price. In Table 6-1, you can see that the yield du jour of ValueNowInc (VNI) is 4.5 percent (a dividend of $1 divided by the company's stock price of $22). Notice that many companies report no yield; because they have no dividends, their yield is zero.

Keep in mind that the yield reported in the financial pages changes daily as the stock price changes. Yield is always reported as if you're buying the stock that day. If you buy VNI on the day represented in Table 6-1, your yield is 4.5 percent. But what if VNI's stock price rises to $30 the following day? Investors who buy stock at $30 per share obtain a yield of just 3.3 percent. (The dividend of $1 divided by the new stock price, $30.) Of course, because you bought the stock at $22, you essentially locked in the prior yield of 4.5 percent. Lucky you. Pat yourself on the back.

P/E

The P/E ratio is the ratio between the price of the stock and the company's earnings. P/E ratios are widely followed and are important barometers of value in the world of stock investing. The P/E ratio (also called the "earnings multiple" or just "multiple") is frequently used to determine whether a stock is expensive (a good value). Value investors (such as yours truly) find P/E ratios to be essential to analyzing a stock as a potential investment. As a general rule, the P/E should be 10 to 20 for large cap or income stocks. For growth stocks, a P/E no greater than 30 to 40 is preferable. (See Chapter 11 for full details on P/E ratios.)

In the P/E ratios reported in stock tables, *price* refers to the cost of a single share of stock. *Earnings* refers to the company's reported earnings per share as of the most recent four quarters. The P/E ratio is the price divided by the earnings. In Table 6-1, VNI has a reported P/E of 12, which is considered a low P/E. Notice how SHC has a relatively high P/E (76). This stock is considered too pricey because you're paying a price equivalent to 76 times earnings. Also notice that DBC has no available P/E ratio. Usually this lack of a P/E ratio indicates that the company reported a loss in the most recent four quarters.

Day last

The "Day Last" column tells you how trading ended for a particular stock on the day represented by the table. In Table 6-1, LDI ended the most recent day of trading at $41. Some newspapers report the high and low for that day in addition to the stock's ending price for the day.

Net change

The information in the "Net Chg" column answers the question, "How did the stock price end today compared with its price at the end of the prior trading day?" Table 6-1 shows that SHC stock ended the trading day up 25 cents (at $21.25). This column tells you that SHC ended the prior day at $21. VNI ended the day at $22 (up 10 cents), so you can tell that the prior trading day it ended at $21.90.

Using News about Dividends

Reading and understanding the news about dividends is essential if you're an *income investor* (someone who invests in stocks as a means of generating regular income; see Chapter 9 for details). The following sections explain some basics about dividends you should know.

You can find news and information on dividends in newspapers such as *The Wall Street Journal, Investor's Business Daily,* and *Barron's* (you can find their Web sites online with your favorite search engine, or just check out Appendix A).

Looking at important dates

In order to understand how buying stocks that pay dividends can benefit you as an investor, you need to know how companies report and pay dividends. Some important dates in the life of a dividend are as follows:

- ✔ **Date of declaration:** This is the date when a company reports a quarterly dividend and the subsequent payment dates. On January 15, for example, a company may report that it "is pleased to announce a quarterly dividend of 50 cents per share to shareholders of record as of February 10." That was easy. The date of declaration is really just the announcement date. If you buy the stock before, on, or after the date of declaration, it won't matter in regard to receiving the stock's quarterly dividend. The date that matters is the date of record (see that bullet later in this list).

- ✔ **Date of execution:** This is the day you actually initiate the stock transaction (buying or selling). If you call up a broker (or contact her online) today to buy a particular stock, then today is the date of execution, or the date on which you execute the trade. You don't own the stock on the date of execution; it's just the day you put in the order. For an example, skip to the following section.

- ✔ **Closing date (settlement date):** This is the date on which the trade is finalized, which usually happens three business days after the date of execution. The closing date for stock is similar in concept to a real estate closing. On the closing date, you're officially the proud new owner (or happy seller) of the stock.

- ✔ **Date of record:** This is used to identify which stockholders qualify to receive the declared dividend. Because stock is bought and sold every day, how does the company know which investors to pay? The company establishes a cut-off date by declaring a date of record. All investors who are official stockholders as of the declared date of record receive the dividend on the payment date, even if they plan to sell the stock any time between the date of declaration and the date of record.

- ✔ **Ex-dividend date:** *Ex-dividend* means *without dividend.* Because it takes three days to process a stock purchase before you become an official owner of the stock, you have to qualify (that is, you have to own or buy the stock) *before* the three-day period. That three-day period is referred to as the "ex-dividend period." When you buy stock during this short time frame, you aren't on the books of record, because the closing (or settlement) date falls after the date of record. See the next section to see the effect that the ex-dividend date can have on an investor.

- ✔ **Payment date:** The date on which a company issues and mails its dividend checks to shareholders. Finally!

For typical dividends, the events in Table 6-2 happen four times per year.

Table 6-2	The Life of the Quarterly Dividend	
Event	*Sample Date*	*Comments*
Date of declaration	January 15	The date that the company declares the quarterly dividend
Ex-dividend date	February 7	Starts the three-day period during which, if you buy the stock, you don't qualify for the dividend
Record date	February 10	The date by which you must be on the books of record to qualify for the dividend
Payment date	February 27	The date that payment is made (a dividend check is issued and mailed to stockholders who were on the books of record as of February 10)

Understanding why these dates matter

Three business days pass between the date of execution and the closing date. Three business days also pass between the ex-dividend date and the date of record. This information is important to know if you want to qualify to receive an upcoming dividend. Timing is important, and if you understand these dates, you know when to purchase stock and whether you qualify for a dividend.

As an example, say that you want to buy ValueNowInc (VNI) in time to qualify for the quarterly dividend of 25 cents per share. Assume that the date of record (the date by which you have to be an official owner of the stock) is February 10. You have to execute the trade (buy the stock) no later than February 7 to be assured of the dividend. If you execute the trade right on February 7, the closing date occurs three days later, on February 10 — just in time for the date of record.

But what if you execute the trade on February 8, a day later? Well, the trade's closing date is February 11, which occurs *after* the date of record. Because you aren't on the books as an official stockholder on the date of record, you aren't getting that quarterly dividend. In this example, the February 7–10 period is called the *ex-dividend period*.

Fortunately, for those people who buy the stock during this brief ex-dividend period, the stock actually trades at a slightly lower price to reflect the amount of the dividend. If you can't get the dividend, you may as well save on the stock purchase. How's that for a silver lining?

Evaluating Investment Tips

Psssst. Have I got a stock tip for you! Come closer. You know what it is? Research! What I'm trying to tell you is to never automatically invest just because you get a hot tip from someone. Good investment selection means looking at several sources before you decide on a stock. No shortcut exists. That said, getting opinions from others never hurts — just be sure to carefully analyze the information you get. Here are some important points to bear in mind as you evaluate tips and advice from others:

✔ **Consider the source.** Frequently, people buy stock based on the views of some market strategist or market analyst. People may see an analyst being interviewed on a television financial show and take that person's opinions and advice as valid and good. The danger here is that the analyst may be biased because of some relationship that isn't disclosed on the show.

 It happens on TV all too often. The show's host interviews analyst U.R. Kiddingme from the investment firm Foollum & Sellum. The analyst says, "Implosion Corp. is a good buy with solid, long-term upside potential." You later find out that the analyst's employer gets investment banking fees from Implosion Corp. Do you really think that analyst would ever issue a negative report on a company that's helping to pay the bills? It's not likely.

✔ **Get multiple views.** Don't base your investment decisions on just one source unless you have the best reasons in the world for thinking that a particular, single source is outstanding and reliable. A better approach is to scour current issues of independent financial publications, such as *Barron's, Money* magazine, *SmartMoney,* and other publications (and Web sites) listed in Appendix A.

 ✔ **Gather data from the SEC.** When you want to get more objective information about a company, why not take a look at the reports that firms must file with the SEC? These reports are the same reports that the pundits and financial reporters read. Arguably, the most valuable report you can look at is the 10K. The 10K is a report that all publicly traded companies must file with the SEC. It provides valuable information on the company's operations and financial data for the most recent year, and it's likely to be less biased than the information a company includes in other corporate reports, such as an annual report. The next most important document from the SEC is the 10Q, which gives the investor similar detailed information but for a single quarter. (See Chapter 12 for more information about these documents.)

To access 10K and 10Q reports, go to the SEC Web site (www.sec. gov). From there, you can find the SEC's extensive database of public filings called EDGAR (Electronic Data Gathering, Analysis, and Retrieval system). By searching EDGAR, you can find companies' balance sheets, income statements, and other related information so that you can verify what others say and get a fuller picture of what a business is doing and what its financial condition is.

Chapter 7

Going for Brokers

In This Chapter

▶ Finding out what brokers do

▶ Comparing full-service and discount brokers

▶ Selecting a broker

▶ Exploring the types of brokerage accounts

▶ Evaluating the recommendations of brokers

When you're ready to dive in and start investing in stocks, you first have to choose a broker. It's kind of like buying a car: You can do all the research in the world and know exactly what kind of car you want, but you still need a venue to conduct the actual transaction. Similarly, when you want to buy stock, your task is to do all the research you can to select the company you want to invest in. Still, you need a broker to actually buy the stock, whether you buy over the phone or online. In this chapter, I introduce you to the intricacies of the investor/broker relationship.

For information on various types of orders you can place with a broker, such as market orders, stop-loss orders, and so on, flip to Chapter 18.

Defining the Broker's Role

The broker's primary role is to serve as the vehicle through which you either buy or sell stock. When I talk about brokers, I'm referring to companies such as Charles Schwab, Merrill Lynch, E*TRADE, and many other organizations that can buy stock on your behalf. Brokers can also be individuals who work for such firms. Although you can buy some stocks directly from the company that issues them (I discuss direct purchase plans in Chapter 19), to purchase most stocks, you still need a broker.

The distinction between institutional stockbrokers and personal stockbrokers is important:

- ✔ Institutional stockbrokers make money from institutions and companies through investment banking and securities placement fees (such as initial public offerings and secondary offerings), advisory services, and other broker services.

- ✔ Personal stockbrokers generally offer the same services to individuals and small businesses.

Although the primary task of brokers is the buying and selling of securities (the word *securities* refers to the world of financial or paper investments, and stocks are only a small part of that world), they can perform other tasks for you, including the following:

- ✔ **Providing advisory services:** Investors pay brokers a fee for investment advice. Customers also get access to the firm's research.

- ✔ **Offering limited banking services:** Brokers can offer features such as interest-bearing accounts, check writing, electronic deposits and withdrawals, and credit/debit cards.

- ✔ **Brokering other securities:** In addition to stocks, brokers can buy bonds, mutual funds, options, exchange-traded funds (ETFs), and other investments on your behalf.

Personal stockbrokers make their money from individual investors like you and me through various fees, including the following:

- ✔ **Brokerage commissions:** This fee is for buying and/or selling stocks and other securities.

- ✔ **Margin interest charges:** This interest is charged to investors for borrowing against their brokerage account for investment purposes. (I discuss margin accounts in more detail later in this chapter.)

- ✔ **Service charges:** These charges are for performing administrative tasks and other functions. Brokers charge fees to investors for Individual Retirement Accounts (IRAs) and for mailing stocks in certificate form.

Any broker you deal with should be registered with the Financial Industry Regulatory Authority (FINRA) and the Securities and Exchange Commission (SEC). In addition, to protect your money after you deposit it into a brokerage account, that broker should be a member of the Securities Investor Protection Corporation (SIPC). SIPC doesn't protect you from market losses; it protects your money in case the brokerage firm goes out of business. To find out whether the broker is registered with these organizations, contact FINRA (www.finra.org), SEC (www.sec.gov), or SIPC (www.sipc.org). See Appendix A for more information on these organizations.

Distinguishing between Full-Service and Discount Brokers

Stockbrokers fall into two basic categories: full-service and discount. The type you choose really depends on what type of investor you are. Here are the differences in a nutshell:

- ✔ *Full-service brokers* are suitable for investors who need some guidance and personal attention.

- ✔ *Discount brokers* are better for those investors who are sufficiently confident and knowledgeable about stock investing to manage with minimal help (usually through the broker's Web site).

Before you deal with any broker (either full-service or discount), get a free report on the broker from FINRA by calling 301-590-6500 or visiting its Web site at `www.finra.org`. FINRA can tell you whether any complaints or penalties have been filed against a brokerage firm or an individual rep.

Full-service brokers

Full-service brokers are just what the name indicates. They try to provide as many services as possible for investors who open accounts with them. When you open an account at a brokerage firm, a representative is assigned to your account. This representative is usually called an *account executive,* a *registered rep,* or a *financial consultant* by the brokerage firm. This person usually has a securities license (meaning that he or she is registered with the FINRA and the SEC) and is knowledgeable about stocks in particular and investing in general.

Examples of full-service brokers are Merrill Lynch and Morgan Stanley. Of course, all brokers now have full-featured Web sites to give you further information about their services. Get as informed as possible before you open your account. A full-service broker is there to help you build wealth, not make you . . . uh . . . broker.

What they can do for you

Your account executive is responsible for assisting you, answering questions about your account and the securities in your portfolio, and transacting your buy and sell orders. Here are some things that full-service brokers can do for you:

✔ **Offer guidance and advice.** The greatest distinction between full-service brokers and discount brokers is the personal attention you receive from your account rep. You get to be on a first-name basis with a full-service broker, and you disclose much information about your finances and financial goals. The rep is there to make recommendations about stocks and funds that are hopefully suitable for you.

✔ **Provide access to research.** Full-service brokers can give you access to their investment research department, which can give you in-depth information and analysis on a particular company. This information can be very valuable, but be aware of the pitfalls. (See the section "Judging Brokers' Recommendations," later in this chapter.)

✔ **Help you achieve your investment objectives.** A good rep gets to know you and your investment goals and *then* offers advice and answers your questions about how specific investments and strategies can help you accomplish your wealth-building goals.

✔ **Make investment decisions on your behalf.** Many investors don't want to be bothered when it comes to investment decisions. Full-service brokers can actually make decisions for your account with your authorization. This service is fine, but be sure to require them to explain their choices to you.

What to watch out for

Although full-service brokers, with their seemingly limitless assistance, can make life easy for an investor, you need to remember some important points to avoid problems:

✔ Brokers and account reps are salespeople. No matter how well they treat you, they're still compensated based on their ability to produce revenue for the brokerage firm. They generate commissions and fees from you on behalf of the company. (In other words, they're paid to sell you things.)

✔ Whenever your rep makes a suggestion or recommendation, be sure to ask why and request a complete answer that includes the reasoning behind the recommendation. A good advisor is able to clearly explain the reasoning behind every suggestion. If you don't fully understand and agree with the advice, don't take it.

✔ Working with a full-service broker costs more than working with a discount broker. Discount brokers are paid for simply buying or selling stocks for you. Full-service brokers do that and much more, like provide advice and guidance. Because of that, full-service brokers are more expensive (through higher brokerage commissions and advisory fees). Also, most full-service brokers expect you to invest at least $5,000 to $10,000 just to open an account.

✔ Handing over decision-making authority to your rep can be a possible negative because letting others make financial decisions for you is always dicey — especially when they're using *your* money. If they make poor investment choices that lose you money, you may not have any recourse because you authorized them to act on your behalf.

✔ Some brokers engage in an activity called churning. *Churning* is basically buying and selling stocks for the sole purpose of generating commissions. Churning is great for brokers but bad for customers. If your account shows a lot of activity, ask for justification. Commissions, especially by full-service brokers, can take a big bite out of your wealth, so don't tolerate churning or other suspicious activity.

Discount brokers

Perhaps you don't need any hand-holding from a broker (that'd be kinda weird anyway). You know what you want, and you can make your own investment decisions. All you need is a convenient way to transact your buy/sell orders. In that case, go with a discount broker. They don't offer advice or premium services — just the basics required to perform your stock transactions.

Discount brokers, as the name implies, are cheaper to engage than full-service brokers. Because you're advising yourself (or getting advice and information from third parties such as newsletters, hotlines, or independent advisors), you can save on costs that you'd incur if you used a full-service broker.

If you choose to work with a discount broker, you must know as much as possible about your personal goals and needs. You have a greater responsibility for conducting adequate research to make good stock selections, and you must be prepared to accept the outcome, whatever that may be. (See Part III for details on researching stock selections.)

For a while, the regular investor had two types of discount brokers to choose from: conventional discount brokers and Internet discount brokers. But the two are basically synonymous now, so the differences are hardly worth mentioning. Through industry consolidation, most of the conventional discount brokers today have fully featured Web sites, while Internet discount brokers have adapted by adding more telephone and face-to-face services.

Charles Schwab and TD Ameritrade are examples of conventional discount brokers that have adapted well to the Internet era. Internet brokers such as E*TRADE.com, TradeKing.com, Scottrade.com, and thinkorswim.com have added more conventional services.

What they can do for you

Discount brokers offer some significant advantages over full-service brokers, such as:

- ✔ **Lower cost:** This lower cost is usually the result of lower commissions, and it's the primary benefit of using discount brokers.

- ✔ **Unbiased service:** Because they don't offer advice, discount brokers have no vested interest in trying to sell you any particular stock.

- ✔ **Access to information:** Established discount brokers offer extensive educational materials at their offices or on their Web sites.

What to watch out for

Of course, doing business with discount brokers also has its downside, including the following:

- ✔ **No guidance:** Because you've chosen a discount broker, you *know* not to expect guidance, but the broker should make this fact clear to you anyway. If you're a knowledgeable investor, the lack of advice is considered a positive thing — no interference.

- ✔ **Hidden fees:** Discount brokers may shout about their lower commissions, but commissions aren't their only way of making money. Many discount brokers charge extra for services that you may think are included, such as issuing a stock certificate or mailing a statement. Ask whether they assess fees for maintaining IRAs or for transferring stocks and other securities (like bonds) in or out of your account, and find out what interest rates they charge for borrowing through brokerage accounts.

- ✔ **Minimal customer service:** If you deal with an Internet brokerage firm, find out about its customer service capability. If you can't transact business on its Web site, find out where you can call for assistance with your order.

Choosing a Broker

Before you choose a broker, you need to analyze your personal investing style (as I explain in Chapter 3), and then you can proceed to finding the kind of broker that fits your needs. It's almost like choosing shoes; if you don't know your size, you can't get a proper fit (and you can be in for a really uncomfortable future).

When it's time to choose a broker, keep the following points in mind:

✔ Match your investment style with a brokerage firm that charges the least amount of money for the services you're likely to use most frequently.

✔ Compare all the costs of buying, selling, and holding stocks and other securities through a broker. Don't compare only commissions; compare other costs, too, like margin interest and other service charges (see the earlier section, "Defining the Broker's Role," for more about these costs).

✔ Use broker comparison services available in financial publications such as *SmartMoney* and *Barron's* (and, of course, their Web sites).

Finding brokers is easy. They're listed in the Yellow Pages (or on directory sites like www.superpages.com), in many investment publications, and on many financial Web sites. Start your search by using the sources in Appendix A, which includes a list of the major brokerage firms.

Discovering Various Types of Brokerage Accounts

When you start investing in the stock market, you have to somehow actually *pay* for the stocks you buy. Most brokerage firms offer investors several types of accounts, each serving a different purpose. I present three of the most common types in the following sections. The basic difference boils down to how particular brokers view your creditworthiness when it comes to buying and selling securities. If your credit isn't great, your only choice is a cash account. If your credit is good, you can open either a cash account or a margin account. After you qualify for a margin account, you can (with additional approval) upgrade it to do options trades.

To open an account, you have to fill out an application and submit a check or money order for at least the minimum amount required to establish an account.

Cash accounts

A *cash account* (also referred to as a *Type 1 account*) means just what you think it means. You must deposit a sum of money along with the new account application to begin trading. The amount of your initial deposit varies from broker to broker. Some brokers have a minimum of $10,000; others let you open an account for as little as $500. Once in a while you may see a broker offering cash accounts with no minimum deposit, usually as part of a promotion. Use the resources in Appendix A to help you shop around. Qualifying for a cash account is usually easy, as long as you have cash and a pulse.

With a cash account, your money has to be deposited in the account before the closing (or settlement) date for any trade you make. The closing occurs three business days after the date you make the trade (the date of execution). You may be required to have the money in the account even before the date of execution. See Chapter 6 for details on these and other important dates.

In other words, if you call your broker on Monday, October 10, and order 50 shares of CashLess Corp. at $20 per share, then on Thursday, October 13, you better have $1,000 in cash sitting in your account (plus commission). Otherwise, the purchase doesn't go through.

In addition, ask the broker how long it takes deposited cash (such as a check) to be available for investing. Some brokers put a hold on checks for up to ten business days, regardless of how soon that check clears your account (that would drive me crazy!).

See whether your broker will pay you interest on the uninvested cash in your brokerage account. Some brokers offer a service in which uninvested money earns money market rates, and you can even choose between a regular money market account and a tax-free municipal money market account.

Margin accounts

A *margin account* (also called a *Type 2 account*) allows you to borrow money against the securities in the account to buy more stock. Because you can borrow in a margin account, you have to be qualified and approved by the broker. After you're approved, this newfound credit gives you more leverage so you can buy more stock or do short-selling. (You can read more about buying on margin and short-selling in Chapter 18.)

For stock trading, the margin limit is 50 percent. For example, if you plan to buy $10,000 worth of stock on margin, you need at least $5,000 in cash (or securities owned) sitting in your account. The interest rate you pay varies depending on the broker, but most brokers generally charge a rate that's several points higher than their own borrowing rate.

Why use margin? Margin is to stocks what mortgage is to buying real estate. You can buy real estate with all cash, but using borrowed funds often makes sense because you may not have enough money to make a 100 percent cash purchase, or you may just prefer not to pay all cash. With margin, you can, for example, buy $10,000 worth of stock with as little as $5,000. The balance of the stock purchase is acquired using a loan (margin) from the brokerage firm.

Personally, I'm not a big fan of margin, and I use it sparingly. Margin is a form of leverage that can work out fine if you're correct but can be very danger-ous if the market moves against you. It's best applied with stocks that are generally stable and dividend-paying. That way, the dividends help pay off the margin interest.

Option accounts

An *option account* (also referred to as a *Type 3 account*) gives you all the capa-bilities of a margin account (which in turn also gives you the capabilities of a cash account) plus the ability to trade options on stocks and stock indexes. To upgrade your margin account to an option account, the broker usually asks you to sign a statement that you're knowledgeable about options and familiar with the risks associated with them.

Options can be a very effective addition to a stock investor's array of wealth-building investment tools. A more comprehensive review of options is available in the book *Stock Options For Dummies* by Alan R. Simon (Wiley). I personally love to use options (as do my clients and students), and I think they can be a great tool in your wealth-building arsenal. I discuss options fur-ther in Chapter 16.

Judging Brokers' Recommendations

In recent years, Americans have become enamored with a new sport: the rating of stocks by brokers on the TV financial shows. Frequently, these shows feature a dapper market strategist talking up a particular stock. Some stocks have been known to jump significantly right after an influential analyst issues a buy recommendation. Analysts' speculation and opinions make for great fun, and many people take their views very seriously. However, most investors should be very wary when analysts, especially the glib ones on TV, make a recommendation. It's often just showbiz. In the following sections, I define basic broker recommendations and list a few important consider-ations for evaluating them.

Understanding basic recommendations

Brokers issue their recommendations (advice) as a general idea of how much regard they have for a particular stock. The following list presents the basic recommendations (or ratings) and what they mean to you:

- *Strong buy* and *buy:* Hot diggity dog! These ratings are the ones to get. The analyst loves this pick, and you would be very wise to get a bunch of shares. The thing to keep in mind, however, is that *buy* recommendations are probably the most common because (let's face it) brokers sell stocks.

- *Accumulate* and *market perform:* An analyst who issues these types of recommendations is positive, yet unexcited, about the pick. This rating is akin to asking a friend whether he likes your new suit and getting the response "It's nice" in a monotone voice. It's a polite reply, but you wish his opinion had been more definitive.

- *Hold* or *neutral:* Analysts use this language when their backs are to the wall, but they still don't want to say, "Sell that loser!" This recommendation reminds me of my mother telling me to be nice and either say something positive or keep my mouth shut. In this case, the rating is the analyst's way of keeping his mouth shut.

- *Sell:* Many analysts should have issued this recommendation during the bear market of 2000–2002 but didn't. What a shame. So many investors lost money because some analysts were too nice (or biased?) or just afraid to be honest, sound the alarm, and urge people to sell.

- *Avoid like the plague:* I'm just kidding about this one, but I wish that this recommendation was available. I've seen plenty of stocks that I thought were dreadful investments — stocks of companies that made no money, were in terrible financial condition, and should never have been considered at all. Yet investors gobble up billions of dollars' worth of stocks that eventually become worthless.

Asking a few important questions

Don't get me wrong. An analyst's recommendation is certainly a better tip than what you'd get from your barber or your sister-in-law's neighbor, but you want to view recommendations from analysts with a healthy dose of reality. Analysts have biases because their employment depends on the very companies that are being presented. What investors need to listen to when a broker talks up a stock is the reasoning behind the recommendation. In other words, why is the broker making this recommendation?

Keep in mind that analysts' recommendations can play a useful role in your personal stock investing research. If you find a great stock and *then* you hear analysts give glowing reports on the same stock, you're on the right track! Here are some questions and points to keep in mind:

✔ **How does the analyst arrive at a rating?** The analyst's approach to evaluating a stock can help you round out your research as you consult other sources such as newsletters and independent advisory services.

✔ **What analytical approach is the analyst using?** Some analysts use *fundamental analysis* — looking at the company's financial condition and factors related to its success, such as its standing within the industry and the overall market. Other analysts use *technical analysis* — looking at the company's stock price history and judging past stock price movements to derive some insight regarding the stock's future price movement. Many analysts use a combination of the two. Is this analyst's approach similar to your approach, or to those of sources that you respect or admire?

✔ **What is the analyst's track record?** Has the analyst had a consistently good record through both bull and bear markets? Major financial publications, such as *Barron's* and *Hulbert Financial Digest,* and Web sites, such as `MarketWatch.com`, regularly track recommendations from well-known analysts and stock pickers.

✔ **How does the analyst treat important aspects of the company's performance, such as sales and earnings?** How about the company's balance sheet? The essence of a healthy company is growing sales and earnings coupled with strong assets and low debt. (See Chapter 11 for more details on these topics.)

✔ **Is the industry that the company's in doing well?** Do the analysts give you insight on this important information? A strong company in a weak industry can't stay strong for long. The right industry is a critical part of the stock selection process (for more information, see Chapter 13).

✔ **What research sources does the analyst cite?** Does the analyst quote the federal government or industry trade groups to support her thesis? These sources are important because they help give a more complete picture regarding the company's prospects for success. Imagine that you decide on the stock of a strong company. What if the federal government (through agencies like the SEC) is penalizing the company for fraudulent activity? Or what if the company's industry is shrinking or has ceased to grow (making it tougher for the company to continue growing)? The astute investor looks at a variety of sources before buying stock.

✔ **Is the analyst rational when citing a target price for a stock?** When he says, "We think the stock will hit $100 per share within 12 months," is he presenting a rational model, such as basing the share price on a projected price/earnings ratio (see Chapter 11)? The analyst must be able to provide a logical scenario explaining why the stock has a good chance of achieving the cited target price within the time frame mentioned. You may not necessarily agree with the analyst's conclusion, but the explanation can help you decide whether the stock choice is well thought out.

✔ **Does the company that's being recommended have any ties to the analyst or the analyst's firm?** During 2000–2002, the financial industry got bad publicity because many analysts gave positive recommendations on stocks of companies that were doing business with the very firms that employed those analysts. This conflict of interest is probably the biggest reason that analysts were so wrong in their recommendations during that period. Ask your broker to disclose any conflict of interest.

✔ **What school of economic thought does the analyst adhere to?** This may sound like an odd question, and it may not be readily answered, but it's a good thing to know. If I had to choose between two analysts that were very similar except that Analyst A adhered to the Keynesian school of economic thought and Analyst B adhered to the Austrian school, guess what? I'd choose Analyst B because those who embrace the Austrian school have a much better grasp of real-world economics (which means better stock investment choices). For more discussion on this point, see Chapter 10.

The bottom line with brokerage recommendations is that you shouldn't use them to buy or sell a stock. Instead, use them to confirm your own research. I know that if I buy a stock based on my own research and later discover the same stock being talked up on the financial shows, that's just the icing on the cake. The experts may be great to listen to, and their recommendations can augment your own opinions, but they're no substitute for your own careful research. I devote Part III of this book to chapters on researching and picking winning stocks.

Chapter 8

Investing for Growth

In This Chapter

▶ Balancing growth and value

▶ Figuring out how to choose growth stocks

▶ Looking at small caps and other speculative investments

*W*hat's the number one reason people invest in stocks? To grow their wealth (also referred to as *capital appreciation*). Yes, some people invest for income (in the form of dividends), but that's a different matter (I discuss investing for income in Chapter 9). Investors seeking growth would rather see the money that could have been distributed as dividends be reinvested in the company so that (hopefully) a greater gain is achieved by seeing the stock's price rise or appreciate. People interested in growing their wealth see stocks as one of the convenient ways to do it. Growth stocks tend to be riskier than other categories of stocks, but they offer excellent long-term prospects for making the big bucks. If you don't believe me, just ask Warren Buffett, Peter Lynch, and other successful, long-term investors.

Although someone like Buffett is not considered a growth investor, his long-term, value-oriented approach has been a successful growth strategy. If you're the type of investor who has enough time to let somewhat risky stocks trend upward or who has enough money so that a loss won't devastate you financially, then growth stocks are definitely for you. As they say, no guts, no glory. The challenge is to figure out which stocks make you richer quicker; I give you tips on how to do so in this chapter.

Short of starting your own business, stock investing is the best way to profit from a business venture. I want to emphasize that to make money in stocks consistently over the long haul, you must remember that you're investing in a *company;* buying the stock is just a means for you to participate in the company's success (or failure). Why does it matter that you think of stock investing as buying a *company* versus buying a *stock?* Invest in a stock only if you're just as excited about it as you would be if you were the CEO and in charge of running the company. If you're the sole owner of the company, do you act differently than one of a legion of obscure stockholders? Of course you do. As the firm's owner, you have a greater interest in the company. You have a strong desire to know how the enterprise is doing. As you invest in stocks, make believe that you're the owner, and take an active interest in the company's products, services, sales, earnings, and so on. This attitude and discipline can enhance your goals as a stock investor. This approach is especially important if your investment goal is growth.

Becoming a Value-Oriented Growth Investor

A stock is considered a *growth stock* when it's growing faster and higher than the overall stock market. Basically, a growth stock performs better than its peers in categories such as sales and earnings. *Value stocks* are stocks that are priced lower than the value of the company and its assets — you can identify a value stock by analyzing the company's fundamentals and looking at key financial ratios, such as the price-to-earnings ratio. (For more on the topic of ratios, see Appendix B.) Growth stocks tend to have better prospects for growth for the immediate future (from one to four years), but value stocks tend to have less risk and more steady growth over a longer term.

Over the years, a debate has quietly raged in the financial community about growth versus value investing. Some people believe that growth and value are mutually exclusive. They maintain that large numbers of people buying stock with growth as the expectation tend to drive up the stock price relative to the company's current value. Growth investors, for example, aren't put off by price-to-earnings (P/E) ratios of 30, 40, or higher. Value investors, meanwhile, are too nervous buying a stock at those P/E ratio levels.

However, you *can* have both. A value-oriented approach to growth investing serves you best. Long-term growth stock investors spend time analyzing the company's fundamentals to make sure that the company's growth prospects lie on a solid foundation. But what if you have to choose between a growth stock and a value stock? Which do you choose? Seek value when you're buying the stock and analyze the company's prospects for growth. Growth includes but is not limited to the health and growth of the company's specific industry, the economy at large, and the general political climate (see Chapters 10, 13, 14, and 15).

The bottom line is that growth is much easier to achieve when you seek solid, value-oriented companies in growing industries. To better understand industries and how they affect stock value, see Chapter 13.

Value-oriented growth investing probably has the longest history of success compared to most stock investing philosophies. The track record for those people who use value-oriented growth investing is enviable. Warren Buffett, Benjamin Graham, John Templeton, and Peter Lynch are a few of the more well-known practitioners. Each may have his own spin on the concepts, but all have successfully applied the basic principles of value-oriented growth investing over many years.

Choosing Growth Stocks with a Few Handy Tips

Although the information in the previous section can help you shrink your stock choices from thousands of stocks to maybe a few dozen or a few hundred (depending on how well the general stock market is doing), the purpose of this section is to help you cull the so-so growth stocks to unearth the go-go ones. It's time to dig deeper for the biggest potential winners. Keep in mind that you probably won't find a stock to satisfy all the criteria presented here. Just make sure that your selection meets as many criteria as realistically possible. But hey, if you do find a stock that meets all the criteria cited, *buy as much as you can!*

For the record, my approach to choosing a winning growth stock is probably almost the reverse method of . . . uh . . . that screaming money guy on TV (I won't mention his name!). People watch his show for "tips" on "hot stocks." The frenetic host seems to do a rapid-fire treatment of stocks in general. You get the impression that he looks over thousands of stocks and says "I like this one" and "I don't like that one." The viewer has to decide. Sheesh.

Verifiably, 80 to 90 percent of my stock picks are profitable. People ask me how I pick a winning stock. I tell them that I don't just pick a stock and hope that it does well. In fact, my personal stock-picking research doesn't even begin with stocks; I first look at the investing environment (politics, economics, demographics, and so on) and choose which industry will benefit. After I know which industry will benefit and prosper accordingly, *then* I start to analyze and choose my stock(s).

After I choose a stock, I wait. Patience is more than just a virtue; it is to investing what time is to a seed that is planted in fertile soil. The legendary Jesse Livermore said that he didn't make his stock market fortunes by trading stocks; his fortunes were made "in the waiting." Why?

When I tell you to have patience and a long-term perspective, it isn't because I want you to wait years or decades for your stock portfolio to bear fruit. It's because you're waiting for a specific condition to occur: when the market discovers what you have! When you have a good stock in a good industry, it takes time for the market to discover it. The simple act that makes a stock rise is when it has more buyers than sellers. As time passes, more buyers find your stock. As the stock rises, this attracts more attention and therefore more buyers. The more time that passes, the better your stock looks to the investing public.

When you're choosing growth stocks, you should consider investing in a company only *if* it makes a profit and *if* you understand *how* it makes that profit and from *where* it generates sales. Part of your research means looking at the industry (see Chapter 13) and economic trends in general.

Looking for leaders in megatrends

A strong company in a growing industry is a common recipe for success. If you look at the history of stock investing, this point comes up constantly. Investors need to be on the alert for megatrends because they help ensure success.

A *megatrend* is a major development that has huge implications for much (if not all) of society for a long time to come. Good examples are the advent of the Internet and the aging of America. Both of these trends offer significant challenges and opportunities for our economy. Take the Internet, for example. Its potential for economic application is still being developed. Millions are flocking to it for many reasons. And census data tells us that senior citizens (over 65) will be the fastest-growing segment of our population during the next 20 years. How does the stock investor take advantage of a megatrend?

In 2008, the big news was the credit crisis that slammed the stock markets (in the U.S. and across the globe). A megatrend — indebtedness to the tune of trillions — hit as predicted in the previous edition of *Stock Investing For Dummies*. Investors who stayed alert were able to get their money out of harm's way by moving it out of sectors most affected by the credit crisis, such as bank and brokerage stocks. Stocks tied to human need (such as food and water) fared much better as a group.

In this 3rd edition, I plan to do what I did in the 2nd edition, which is to help you identify the megatrends that are in place to make it easier for you to pick winning stocks (you're welcome!). For emerging megatrends, check out Chapter 14.

Comparing a company's growth to an industry's growth

You have to measure the growth of a company against something to figure out whether it's a growth stock. Usually, you compare the growth of a company with growth from other companies in the same industry or with the stock market in general. In practical terms, when you measure the growth of a stock against the stock market, you're actually comparing it against a generally accepted benchmark, such as the Dow Jones Industrial Average (DJIA) or the Standard & Poor's 500 (S&P 500). For more on DJIA and S&P 500, see Chapter 5.

If a company has earnings growth of 15 percent per year over three years or more and the industry's average growth rate over the same time frame is 10 percent, then the stock qualifies as a growth stock. You can easily calculate the earnings growth rate by comparing a company's earnings in the current year and previous year and computing the difference as a percentage. For example, if the company's earnings (on a per share basis) were $1 last year and $1.10 this year, then earnings grew by 10 percent. Many analysts also look at a current quarter and compare the earnings to the same quarter from the previous year to see if earnings are growing.

A growth stock is called that not only because the company is growing but also because the company is performing well with some consistency. Having a single year where your earnings do well versus the S&P 500's average doesn't cut it. Growth must be consistently accomplished.

Considering a company with a strong niche

Companies that have established a strong niche are consistently profitable. Look for a company with one or more of the following characteristics:

- ✔ **A strong brand:** Companies such as Coca-Cola and Microsoft come to mind. Yes, other companies out there can make soda or software, but a business needs a lot more than a similar product to topple companies that have established an almost irrevocable identity with the public.

✔ **High barriers to entry:** United Parcel Service and Federal Express have set up tremendous distribution and delivery networks that competitors can't easily duplicate. High barriers to entry offer an important edge to companies that are already established. Examples of high barriers include high capital requirements (needing lots of cash to start) or special technology that's not easily produced or acquired.

✔ **Research and development (R&D):** Companies such as Pfizer and Merck spend a lot of money researching and developing new pharmaceutical products. This investment becomes a new product with millions of consumers who become loyal purchasers, so the company's going to grow. You can find out what companies spend on R&D by checking their financial statements and their annual reports (more on this in Chapter 12).

Checking out a company's fundamentals

When you hear the word *fundamentals* in the world of stock investing, it refers to the company's financial condition and related data. When investors (especially value investors) do *fundamental analysis,* they look at the company's fundamentals — its balance sheet, income statement, cash flow, and other operational data, along with external factors such as the company's market position, industry, and economic prospects. Essentially, the fundamentals indicate the company's financial condition. Chapter 11 goes into greater detail about analyzing a company's financial condition. However, the main numbers you want to look at include the following:

✔ **Sales:** Are the company's sales this year surpassing last year's? As a decent benchmark, you want to see sales at least 10 percent higher than last year. Although it may differ depending on the industry, 10 percent is a reasonable, general yardstick.

✔ **Earnings:** Are earnings at least 10 percent higher than last year? Earnings should grow at the same rate as sales (or, hopefully, better).

✔ **Debt:** Is the company's total debt equal to or lower than the prior year? The death knell of many a company has been excessive debt.

A company's financial condition has more factors than I mention here, but these numbers are the most important. I also realize that using the 10 percent figure may seem like an oversimplification, but you don't need to complicate matters unnecessarily. I know someone's computerized financial model may come out to 9.675 percent or maybe 11.07 percent, but keep it simple for now.

Evaluating a company's management

The management of a company is crucial to its success. Before you buy stock in a company, you want to know that the company's management is doing a great job. But how do you do that? If you call up a company and ask, it may not even return your phone call. How do you know whether management is running the company properly? The best way is to check the numbers. The following sections tell you the numbers you need to check. If the company's management is running the business well, the ultimate result is a rising stock price.

Return on equity

Although you can measure how well management is doing in several ways, you can take a quick snapshot of a management team's competence by checking the company's return on equity (ROE). You calculate the ROE simply by dividing earnings by equity. The resulting percentage gives you a good idea whether the company is using its equity (or net assets) efficiently and profitably. Basically, the higher the percentage, the better, but you can consider the ROE solid if the percentage is 10 percent or higher. Keep in mind that not all industries have identical ROEs.

To find out a company's earnings, check out the company's income statement. The *income statement* is a simple financial statement that expresses this equation: sales (or revenue) less expenses equal net earnings (or net income or net profit). You can see an example of an income statement in Table 8-1. (I give more details on income statements in Chapter 11.)

Table 8-1	Grobaby, Inc., Income Statement	
	2007 Income Statement	*2008 Income Statement*
Sales	$82,000	$90,000
Expenses	–$75,000	–$78,000
Net earnings	$7,000	$12,000

To find out a company's equity, check out that company's balance sheet. (See Chapter 11 for more details on balance sheets.) The *balance sheet* is actually a simple financial statement that illustrates this equation: total assets minus total liabilities equal net equity. For public stock companies, the net assets are called "shareholders' equity" or simply "equity." Table 8-2 shows a balance sheet for Grobaby, Inc.

Table 8-2	Grobaby, Inc., Balance Sheet	
	Balance Sheet for December 31, 2007	**Balance Sheet for December 31, 2008**
Total assets (TA)	$55,000	$65,000
Total liabilities (TL)	–$20,000	–$25,000
Equity (TA less TL)	$35,000	$40,000

Table 8-1 shows that Grobaby's earnings went from $7,000 to $12,000. In Table 8-2, you can see that Grobaby increased the equity from $35,000 to $40,000 in one year. The ROE for the year 2007 is 20 percent ($7,000 in earnings divided by $35,000 in equity), which is a solid number. The following year, the ROE is 30 percent ($12,000 in earnings divided by $40,000 equity), another solid number. A good minimum ROE is 10 percent, but 15 percent or more is preferred.

Equity and earnings growth

Two additional barometers of success are a company's growth in earnings and growth of equity.

- ✔ Look at the growth in earnings in Table 8-1. The earnings grew from $7,000 (in 2007) to $12,000 (in 2008), or a percentage increase of 71 percent ($12,000 less $7,000 equals $5,000, and $5,000 divided by $7,000 is 71 percent), which is excellent. At a minimum, earnings growth should be equal or better to the rate of inflation, but because that's not always a reliable number, I like at least 10 percent.

- ✔ In Table 8-2, Grobaby's equity grew by $5,000 (from $35,000 to $40,000), or 14 percent, which is very good — management is doing good things here. I like to see equity increasing by 10 percent or better.

Insider buying

Watching management as it manages the business is important, but another indicator of how well the company is doing is to see whether management is buying stock in the company as well. If a company is poised for growth, who knows better than management? And if management is buying up the company's stock en masse, then that's a great indicator of the stock's potential. See Chapter 20 for more details on insider buying.

Noticing who's buying and/or recommending a company's stock

You can invest in a great company and still see its stock go nowhere. Why? Because what makes the stock go up is demand — having more buyers than sellers of the stock. If you pick a stock for all the right reasons and the market notices the stock as well, that attention causes the stock price to climb. The things to watch for include the following:

- ✔ **Institutional buying:** Are mutual funds and pension plans buying up the stock you're looking at? If so, this type of buying power can exert tremendous upward pressure on the stock's price. Some resources and publications track institutional buying and how that affects any particular stock. (You can find these resources in Appendix A.) Frequently, when a mutual fund buys a stock, others soon follow. In spite of all the talk about independent research, a herd mentality still exists.

- ✔ **Analysts' attention:** Are analysts talking about the stock on the financial shows? As much as you should be skeptical about an analyst's recommendation (given the stock market debacle of 2000–2002 and the market problems in 2008), it offers some positive reinforcement for your stock. Don't ever buy a stock solely on the basis of an analyst's recommendation. Just know that if you buy a stock based on your own research, and analysts subsequently rave about it, your stock price is likely to go up. A single recommendation by an influential analyst can be enough to send a stock skyward.

- ✔ **Newsletter recommendations:** Independent researchers usually publish newsletters. If influential newsletters are touting your choice, that praise is also good for your stock. Although some great newsletters are out there (find them in Appendix A) and they offer information that's as good or better than the research departments of some brokerage firms, don't use a single tip to base your investment decision on. But it should make you feel good if the newsletters tout a stock that you've already chosen.

- ✔ **Consumer publications:** No, you won't find investment advice here. This one seems to come out of left field, but it's a source that you should notice. Publications such as *Consumer Reports* regularly look at products and services and rate them for consumer satisfaction. If a company's offerings are well received by consumers, that's a strong positive for the company. This kind of attention ultimately has a positive effect on that company's stock.

Protecting your downside

I become a Johnny-one-note on one topic: trailing stops. (See Chapter 18 for a full explanation of trailing stops.) *Trailing stops* are stop losses that you regularly manage with the stock you invest in. I usually advocate using them, especially if you're new to the game of buying growth stocks. Trailing stops can help you, no matter how good or bad the economy is (or how good or bad the stock you're investing in is).

Suppose that you had invested in Enron, a classic example of a phenomenal growth stock that went bad. In 1999 and 2000, when its stock soared, investors were as happy as chocoholics at Hershey. Along with many investors who forgot that sound investing takes discipline and research, Enron investors thought, "Downside risk? What downside risk?"

Here's an example of how a stop-loss order would have worked if you had invested in Enron. Suppose that you bought Enron in 2000 at $50 per share and put in a stop-loss order with your broker at $45. (Remember to make it a good-till-canceled, or GTC, order. If you do, the stop-loss order stays on indefinitely.) As a general rule, I like to place the stop-loss order at 10 percent below the market value. As the stock went up, you kept the stop loss trailing upward like a tail. (Now you know why it's called a "trailing" stop;

it trails the stock's price.) When Enron hit $70, your stop loss was changed to, say, $63, and so on. At $84, your new stop loss was at $76. Then what?

When Enron started its perilous descent, you got out at $76. The new price of $76 triggered the stop loss, and the stock was automatically sold — you stopped the loss! Actually, in this case, you could call it a "stop and cash in the gain" order. Because you bought the stock at $50 and sold at $76, you pocketed a nice capital gain of $26 (52 percent appreciation — a-do-en-ron, a-do-en-ron!). Then you safely stepped aside and watched the stock continue its plunge.

But what if the market is doing well? Are trailing stops a good idea? Because these stops are placed below the stock price, you're not stopping the stock from rising upward indefinitely. All you're doing is protecting your investment from loss. That's discipline! The stock market of 2004–2008 was fairly good to stock investors as the bear market that started in 2000 took a break. If a bear market continues, trailing stop strategies will again become very useful because a potential decline in the stock price will become a greater risk.

Making sure a company continues to do well

A company's financial situation does change, and you, as a diligent investor, need to continue to look at the numbers for as long as the stock is in your portfolio. You may have chosen a great stock from a great company with great numbers in 2006, but chances are pretty good that the numbers have changed since then.

Great stocks don't always stay that way. A great selection that you're drawn to today may become tomorrow's pariah. Information, both good and bad, moves like lightning. Keep an eye on your stock company's numbers! To help minimize the downside risk, see the nearby sidebar for an example. For more information on a company's financial data, check out Chapter 11.

Heeding investing lessons from history

A growth stock isn't a creature like the Loch Ness monster — always talked about but rarely seen. Growth stocks have been part of the financial scene for nearly a century. Examples abound that offer rich information that you can apply to today's stock market environment. Look at past market winners, especially those of the 1970s and 1980s, and ask yourself, "What made them profitable stocks?" I mention these two decades because they offer a stark contrast to each other. The '70s were a tough, bearish decade for stocks, while the '80s were booming bull times. (See Chapter 14 for details on bear and bull markets.)

Being aware and acting logically is as vital to successful stock investing as it is to any other pursuit. Over and over again, history gives you the formula for successful stock investing:

- ✔ Pick a company that has strong fundamentals, including signs such as rising sales and earnings and low debt. (See Chapter 11.)

- ✔ Make sure that the company is in a growing industry. (See Chapter 13.)

- ✔ Be fully invested in stocks during a bull market, when prices are rising in the stock market and in the general economy. (See Chapter 14.)

- ✔ During a bear market, switch more of your money out of growth stocks (such as technology) and into defensive stocks (such as utilities).

- ✔ Monitor your stocks. Hold onto stocks that continue to have growth potential, and sell those stocks with declining prospects. (See Chapter 24 for some red flags for stock investors.)

Exploring Small Caps and Speculative Stocks

Everyone wants to get in early on a hot new stock. Why not? You buy Shlobotky, Inc., at $1 per share and hope it zooms to $98 before lunchtime. Who doesn't want to buy a stock that could become the next IBM or Microsoft? This possibility is why investors are attracted to small cap stocks.

Small cap (or small capitalization) is a reference to the company's market size, as I explain in Chapter 1. *Small cap stocks* are stocks that have a market value under $1 billion. Investors may face more risk with small caps, but they also have the chance for greater gains.

Out of all the types of stocks, small cap stocks continue to exhibit the greatest amount of growth. In the same way that a tree planted last year has more opportunity for growth than a mature 100-year-old redwood, small caps have greater growth potential than established large cap stocks. Of course, a small cap doesn't exhibit spectacular growth just because it's small. It grows when it does the right things, such as increasing sales and earnings by producing goods and services that customers want.

For every small company that becomes a Fortune 500 firm, hundreds of companies don't grow at all or go out of business. When you try to guess the next great stock before any evidence of growth, you're not investing — you're speculating. Have you heard that one before? (If not, flip to Chapter 2 for details.) Of course you have, and you'll hear it again. Don't get me wrong — there's nothing wrong with speculating. But it's important to *know* that you're speculating when you're doing it. If you're going to speculate in small stocks hoping for the next Google, then use the guidelines I present in the following sections to increase your chances of success.

Know when to avoid IPOs

Initial public offerings (IPOs) are the birthplace of public stocks, or the proverbial ground floor. The *IPO* is the first offering to the public of a company's stock. The IPO is also referred to as "going public." Because a company's going public is frequently an unproven enterprise, investing in an IPO can be risky. Here are the two types of IPOs:

- ✔ **Start-up IPO:** This is a company that didn't exist before the IPO. In other words, the entrepreneurs get together and create a business plan. To get the financing they need for the company, they decide to go public immediately by approaching an investment banker. If the investment banker thinks that it's a good concept, the banker will seek funding (selling the stock to investors) via the IPO.

- ✔ **A private company that decides to go public:** In many cases, the IPO is done for a company that already exists and is seeking expansion capital. The company may have been around for a long time as a smaller private concern, but it decides to seek funding through an IPO to grow even larger (or to fund a new product, promotional expenses, and so on).

Which of the two IPOs do you think is less risky? That's right — the private company going public. Why? Because it's already a proven business, which is a safer bet than a brand-new start-up. Some great examples of successful IPOs in recent years are United Parcel Service and Google (they were both established companies *before* they went public).

Great stocks started as small companies going public. You may be able to recount the stories of Federal Express, Dell, AOL, Home Depot, and hundreds of other great successes. But do you remember an IPO by the company Lipschitz & Farquar? No? I didn't think so. It's among the majority of IPOs that don't succeed.

IPOs have a poor track record of success in their first year. Studies periodically done by the brokerage industry have revealed that IPOs (more times than not) actually decline in price 60 percent of the time during the first 12 months. In other words, an IPO has a better than even chance of dropping in price. For investors, the lesson is clear: Wait until a track record appears before you invest in a company. If you don't, you're simply rolling the dice (in other words, you're speculating, not investing!). Don't worry about missing that great opportunity; if it's a bona fide opportunity, you'll still do well after the IPO.

Make sure a small cap stock is making money

I emphasize two points when investing in stocks:

- ✔ Make sure that a company is established. (Being in business for at least three years is a good minimum.)
- ✔ Make sure that a company is profitable.

These points are especially important for investors in small stocks. Plenty of start-up ventures lose money but hope to make a fortune down the road. A good example is a company in the biotechnology industry. Biotech is an exciting area, but it's esoteric, and at this early stage, companies are finding it difficult to use the technology in profitable ways. You may say, "But shouldn't I jump in now in anticipation of future profits?" You may get lucky, but understand that when you invest in unproven, small cap stocks, you're speculating.

Analyze small cap stocks before you invest

The only difference between a small cap stock and a large cap stock is a few zeros in their numbers and the fact that you need to do more research with small caps. By sheer dint of size, small caps are riskier than large caps, so you offset the risk by accruing more information on yourself and the stock in question. Plenty of information is available on large cap stocks because they're widely followed. Small cap stocks don't get as much press, and fewer analysts issue reports on them. Here are a few points to keep in mind:

- ✔ **Understand your investment style.** Small cap stocks may have more potential rewards, but they also carry more risk. No investor should devote a large portion of his capital to small cap stocks. If you're considering retirement money, you're better off investing in large cap stocks, exchange-traded funds (ETFs), investment-grade bonds, bank accounts, and mutual funds. For example, retirement money should be in investments that are either very safe or have proven track records of steady growth over an extended period of time (five years or longer).

- ✔ **Check with the Securities and Exchange Commission (SEC).** Get the financial reports that the company must file with the SEC (such as its 10Ks and 10Qs — see Chapter 6 for more details). These reports offer more complete information on the company's activities and finances. Go to the SEC Web site at www.sec.gov and check its massive database of company filings at EDGAR (Electronic Data Gathering, Analysis, and Retrieval system). You can also check to see whether any complaints have been filed against the company.

- ✔ **Check other sources.** See whether brokers and independent research services, such as Value Line, follow the stock. If two or more different sources like the stock, it's worth further investigation. Check the resources in Appendix A for further sources of information before you invest.

Chapter 9

Investing for Income

In This Chapter
▶ Getting familiar with income stock fundamentals
▶ Selecting income stocks with a few criteria in mind
▶ Checking out utilities, REITs, and royalty trusts

*I*nvesting for income means investing in stocks that provide you with regular cash payments (dividends). Income stocks may not seem to offer stellar growth potential, but they're good for a steady infusion of cash. If you have a low tolerance for risk, or if your investment goal is anything less than long term, income stocks are your best bet. In this chapter, I explain the basics of income stocks, show you how to analyze income stocks with a few handy formulas, and describe several typical income stocks.

Getting your stock portfolio to yield more income is easier than you think. Many investors increase income using proven techniques such as covered call writing. Covered call writing is beyond the scope of this book, but I encourage you to find out more about this technique and whether it applies to your situation. Talk to your financial advisor or read up on it — it's covered more fully in *Stock Options For Dummies* by Alan R. Simon (Wiley). You can also find great educational material on this option strategy (and many others) at the Chicago Board Options Exchange (www.cboe.com).

Understanding the Basics of Income Stocks

I certainly think that dividend-paying stocks are a great consideration for those investors seeking greater income in their portfolios. I especially like stocks with higher-than-average dividends (typically 4 percent or greater) that are known as *income stocks*. Income stocks take on a dual role in that they can appreciate but also provide regular income. The following sections take a closer look at dividends and income stocks.

Getting a grip on dividends and dividend rates

When people talk about gaining income from stocks, they're usually talking about dividends. A *dividend* is nothing more than money paid out to the owner of stock. You purchase dividend stocks primarily for income — not for spectacular growth potential.

A dividend is quoted as an annual number but is usually paid on a quarterly basis. For example, if a stock pays a dividend of $4, you're probably paid $1 every quarter. If, in this example, you have 200 shares, you're paid $800 every year (if the dividend doesn't change during that period), or $200 per quarter. Getting that regular dividend check every three months (for as long as you hold the stock) can be a nice perk.

A good income stock has a higher-than-average dividend (typically 4 percent or higher).

Dividend rates aren't guaranteed — they can go up or down, or in some extreme cases, the dividend can be discontinued. Fortunately, most companies that issue dividends continue them indefinitely and actually increase dividend payments from time to time. Historically, dividend increases have equaled (or exceeded) the rate of inflation.

Recognizing who's well-suited for income stocks

What type of person is best suited to income stocks? Income stocks can be appropriate for many investors, but they're especially well-suited for the following individuals:

- **Conservative and novice investors:** Conservative investors like to see a slow-but-steady approach to growing their money while getting regular dividend checks. Novice investors who want to start slowly also benefit from income stocks.

- **Retirees:** Growth investing (which I describe in Chapter 8) is best suited for long-term needs, while income investing is best suited to current needs. Retirees may want some growth in their portfolios, but they're more concerned with regular income that can keep pace with inflation.

- **Dividend reinvestment plan (DRP) investors:** For those investors who like to compound their money with DRPs, income stocks are perfect. For more information on DRPs, see Chapter 19.

Checking out the advantages of income stocks

Income stocks tend to be among the least volatile of all stocks, and many investors view them as defensive stocks. *Defensive stocks* are stocks of companies that sell goods and services that are generally needed no matter what shape the economy is in. (Don't confuse defensive stocks with *defense stocks,* which specialize in goods and equipment for the military.) Food, beverage, and utility companies are great examples of defensive stocks. Even when the economy is experiencing tough times, people still need to eat, drink, and turn on the lights. Companies that offer relatively high dividends also tend to be large firms in established, stable industries.

Some industries in particular are known for high-dividend stocks. Utilities (such as electric, gas, and water), real estate investment trusts (REITs), and the energy sector (oil and gas royalty trusts) are places where you definitely find income stocks. Yes, you can find high-dividend stocks in other industries, but you find a high concentration of them in these industries. For more details, see the sections highlighting these industries later in this chapter.

Watching out for the disadvantages of income stocks

Before you say, "Income stocks are great! I'll get my checkbook and buy a batch right now," take a look at some potential disadvantages (ugh!). Income stocks do come with some fine print.

What goes up . . .

Income stocks can go down as well as up, just as any stock can. The factors that affect stocks in general — politics (Chapter 15), economic trends (Chapter 10), industry changes (Chapter 13), and so on — affect income stocks, too. Fortunately, income stocks don't get hit as hard as other stocks when the market is declining, because high dividends tend to act as a support to the stock price. Therefore, income stocks' prices usually fall less dramatically than other stocks' prices in a declining market.

Interest-rate sensitivity

Income stocks can be sensitive to rising interest rates. When interest rates go up, other investments (such as corporate bonds, U.S. treasury securities, and bank certificates of deposit) are more attractive. When your income stock yields 4 percent and interest rates go up to 5 percent, 6 percent, or higher, you may think, "Hmm. Why settle for a 4 percent yield when I can get 5 percent or better elsewhere?" As more and more investors sell their low-yield stock, the prices for those stocks fall.

Another point to remember is that rising interest rates may hurt the company's financial strength. If the company has to pay more interest, that may affect the company's earnings, which in turn may affect the dividend.

Dividend-paying companies that are experiencing consistent falling revenues tend to cut dividends. In this case, "consistent" means two years or more.

The effect of inflation

Although many companies raise their dividends on a regular basis, some don't. Or if they do raise their dividends, the increases may be small. If income is your primary consideration, you want to be aware of this fact. If you're getting the same dividend year after year and this income is important to you, rising inflation becomes a problem.

Say that you have XYZ stock at $10 per share with an annual dividend of 30 cents (the yield is 30 cents divided by $10, or 3 percent). If you have a yield of 3 percent two years in a row, how do you feel when inflation rises 6 percent one year and 7 percent the next year? Because inflation means your costs are rising, inflation shrinks the value of the dividend income you receive. Fortunately, studies show that in general, dividends do better in inflationary environments than bonds and other fixed-rate investments. Usually, the dividends of companies that provide consumer staples (food, energy, and so on) meet or exceed the rate of inflation.

Playing it safe with alternatives for generating income

If you're an investor seeking income and you're nervous about potential risks with income stocks, here are some non-stock alternatives:

- **U.S. Treasury securities:** Issued by the federal government, these securities are considered the safest investments in the world. Examples of treasury securities are U.S. savings bonds and treasury bonds. They pay interest and are an ideal addition to any income investor's portfolio.

- **Bank certificates of deposit (CDs):** These investments are backed by the Federal Deposit Insurance Corporation (FDIC) and are considered very safe.

- **Income mutual funds:** Many mutual funds, such as treasury bond mutual funds and corporate bond funds, are designed for income investors. They offer investors diversification and professional management, and you can usually invest with as little as $1,000. For more details, refer to *Mutual Funds For Dummies* by Eric Tyson (published by Wiley).

Uncle Sam's cut

The government usually taxes dividends as ordinary income. Fortunately, recent tax legislation has favored dividend-paying stock. See Chapter 21 for more information on taxes for stock investors.

Analyzing Income Stocks

As I explain in the previous section, even conservative income investors can be confronted with different types of risk. (Chapter 4 covers the topic of risk in greater detail.) Fortunately, this section helps you carefully choose income stocks so that you can minimize potential disadvantages.

Look at income stocks in the same way you do growth stocks when assessing the financial strength of a company. Getting nice dividends comes to a screeching halt if the company can't afford to pay them. If your budget depends on dividend income, then monitoring the company's financial strength is that much more important. You can apply the same techniques I list in Chapter 8 for assessing the financial strength of growth stocks to your assessment of income stocks.

Pinpointing your needs first

You choose income stocks primarily because you want or need income now. As a secondary point, income stocks have the potential for steady, long-term appreciation. So if you're investing for retirement needs that won't occur for another 20 years, maybe income stocks aren't suitable for you — better to invest in growth stocks because they're more likely to grow your money faster over your stated lengthy investment term. (I explain who's best suited to income stocks earlier in this chapter.)

If you're certain you want income stocks, do a rough calculation to figure out how big a portion of your portfolio you want income stocks to occupy. Suppose that you need $25,000 in investment income to satisfy your current financial needs. If you have bonds that give you $20,000 in interest income and you want the rest to come from dividends from income stocks, you need to choose stocks that pay you $5,000 in annual dividends. If you have $80,000 left to invest, you need a portfolio of income stocks that yields 6.25 percent ($5,000 divided by $80,000 equals a yield of 6.25 percent; I explain yield in more detail in the following section).

Minding your dividends and interest

Dividends are sometimes confused with interest. However, *dividends* are payouts to owners, while *interest* is a payment to a creditor. A stock investor is considered a part owner of the company he invests in and is entitled to dividends when they're issued. A bank, on the other hand, considers you a creditor when you open an account. The bank borrows your money and pays you interest on it.

You may ask, "Why not just buy $80,000 of bonds [for instance] that yield at least 6.25 percent?" Well, if you're satisfied with that $5,000 and inflation for the foreseeable future is zero, then you have a point. Unfortunately, inflation will probably be with us for a long time. Fortunately, steady growth that income stocks provide is a benefit to you.

If you have income stocks and don't have any immediate need for the dividends, consider reinvesting the dividends in the company's stock. For more details on this kind of reinvesting, see Chapter 19.

Every investor is different. If you're not sure about your current or future needs, your best choice is to consult with a financial planner. Flip to Appendix A for helpful financial planning resources.

Checking out yield

Because income stocks pay out dividends — income — you need to assess which stocks can give you the highest income. How do you do that? The main thing to look for is *yield,* which is the percentage rate of return paid on a stock in the form of dividends. Looking at a stock's dividend yield is the quickest way to find out how much money you'll earn versus other dividend-paying stocks (or even other investments, such as a bank account). Table 9-1 illustrates this point. Dividend yield is calculated in the following way:

Dividend yield = Dividend income ÷ Stock investment

The next two sections use the information in Table 9-1 to compare the yields from different investments and to show how evaluating yield helps you choose the stock that earns you the most money.

Table 9-1	Comparing Yields			
Investment	**Type**	**Investment Amount**	**Annual Investment Income (Dividend)**	**Yield (Annual Investment Income ÷ Investment Amount)**
Smith Co.	Common stock	$20 per share	$1.00 per share	5%
Jones Co.	Common stock	$30 per share	$1.50 per share	5%
Wilson Bank	Savings account	$1,000 deposit	$40 (interest)	4%

Don't stop scrutinizing stocks after you acquire them. You may make a great choice that gives you a great dividend, but that doesn't mean the stock stays that way indefinitely. Monitor the company's progress for as long as it's in your portfolio by using resources such as www.bloomberg.com and www.marketwatch.com (see Appendix A for more resources).

Examining changes in yield

Most people have no problem understanding yield when it comes to bank accounts. If I tell you that my bank certificate of deposit (CD) has an annual yield of 3.5 percent, you can easily figure out that if I deposit $1,000 in that account, a year later I'll have $1,035 (slightly more if you include compounding). The CD's market value in this example is the same as the deposit amount — $1,000. That makes it easy to calculate.

How about stocks? When you see a stock listed in the financial pages, the dividend yield is provided, along with the stock's price and annual dividend. The dividend yield in the financial pages is always calculated as if you bought the stock on that given day. Just keep in mind that based on supply and demand, stock prices change every day (virtually every minute!) that the market's open, so the yield changes daily as well. So keep the following two things in mind when examining yield:

> ✔ **The yield listed in the financial pages may not represent the yield you're receiving.** What if you bought stock in Smith Co. (see Table 9-1) a month ago at $20 per share? With an annual dividend of $1, you know your yield is 5 percent. But what if today Smith Co. is selling for $40 per share? If you look in the financial pages, the yield quoted would be 2.5 percent. Gasp! Did the dividend get cut in half?! No, not really. You're

still getting 5 percent because you bought the stock at $20 rather than the current $40 price; the quoted yield is for investors who purchase Smith Co. today. They pay $40 and get the $1 dividend, and they're locked into the current yield of 2.5 percent. Although Smith Co. may have been a good income investment for you a month ago, it's not such a hot pick today because the price of the stock doubled, cutting the yield in half. Even though the dividend hasn't changed, the yield changed dramatically because of the stock price change.

✔ **Stock price affects how good of an investment the stock may be.** Another way to look at yield is by looking at the investment amount. Using Smith Co. in Table 9-1 as the example, the investor who bought, say, 100 shares of Smith Co. when they were $20 per share only paid $2,000 (100 shares times $20 — leave out commissions to make the example simple). If the same stock is purchased later at $40 per share, the total investment amount is $4,000 (100 shares times $40). In either case, the investor gets a total dividend income of $100 (100 shares times $1 dividend per share). Which investment is yielding more — the $2,000 investment or the $4,000 investment? Of course, it's better to get the income ($100 in this case) with the smaller investment (a 5 percent yield is better than a 2.5 percent yield).

Comparing yield between different stocks

All things being equal, choosing Smith Co. or Jones Co. is a coin toss. It's looking at your situation and each company's fundamentals and prospects that will sway you. What if Smith Co. is an auto stock (similar to General Motors in 2008) and Jones Co. is a utility serving the Las Vegas metro area? Now what? In 2008, the automotive industry struggled tremendously, but utilities were generally in much better shape. In that scenario, Smith Co.'s dividend is in jeopardy while Jones Co.'s dividend is more secure. Another issue is the payout ratio (see the next section). Therefore, companies whose dividends have the same yield may still have different risks.

Looking at a stock's payout ratio

You can use the payout ratio to figure out what percentage of a company's earnings is being paid out in the form of dividends (earnings equal sales minus expenses). Keep in mind that companies pay dividends from their net earnings. Therefore, the company's earnings should always be higher than the dividends the company pays out. Here's how to figure a payout ratio:

Dividend (per share) ÷ Earnings (per share) = Payout ratio

Say that the company CashFlow Now, Inc. (CFN), has annual earnings of $1 million. Total dividends are to be paid out of $500,000, and the company has 1 million outstanding shares. Using those numbers, you know that CFN's earnings per share (EPS) is $1 ($1 million in earnings divided by 1 million shares) and that it pays an annual dividend of 50 cents per share ($500,000 divided by 1 million shares). The dividend payout ratio is 50 percent (the 50-cent dividend is 50 percent of the $1 EPS). This number is a healthy dividend payout ratio because even if CFN's earnings fall by 10 percent or 20 percent, it still has plenty of room to pay dividends.

People concerned about their dividend income's safety should regularly watch the payout ratio. The maximum acceptable payout ratio should be 80 percent, and a good range is 50–70 percent. A payout ratio of 60 percent and lower is considered very safe (the lower the percentage, the safer the dividend).

When a company suffers significant financial difficulties, its ability to pay dividends is compromised. (Good examples of stocks that have had their dividends cut in recent years due to financial difficulties are mortgage companies in the wake of the housing bubble bursting and the fallout from the subprime debt fiasco. Mortgage companies received less and less income due to mortgage defaults, which forced the lowering of dividends as cash inflow shrunk.) So if you need dividend income to help you pay your bills, you better be aware of the dividend payout ratio.

Examining a company's bond rating

Bond rating? Huh? What's that got to do with dividend-paying stocks? Actually, a company's bond rating is very important to income stock investors. The bond rating offers insight into the company's financial strength. Bonds get rated for quality for the same reasons that consumer agencies rate products like cars or toasters. Standard & Poor's (S&P) is the major independent rating agency that looks into bond issuers. S&P looks at the bond issuer and asks, "Does this bond issuer have the financial strength to pay back the bond and the interest as stipulated in the bond indenture?"

To understand why this rating is important, consider the following:

✔ A good bond rating means that the company is strong enough to pay its obligations. These obligations include expenses, payments on debts, and declared dividends. If a bond rating agency gives the company a high rating (or if it raises the rating), that's a great sign for anyone holding the company's debt or receiving dividends.

- ✔ If a bond rating agency lowers the rating, that means the company's financial strength is deteriorating — a red flag for anyone who owns the company's bonds or stock. A lower bond rating today may mean trouble for the dividend later on.

- ✔ A poor bond rating means that the company is having difficulty paying its obligations. If the company can't pay all its obligations, it has to choose which ones to pay. More times than not, a financially troubled company chooses to cut dividends or (in a worst case scenario) not pay dividends at all.

The highest rating issued by S&P is AAA. The grades AAA, AA, and A are considered *investment grade,* or of high quality. Bs and Cs indicate a poor grade, and anything lower than that is considered very risky (the bonds are referred to as *junk bonds*). So if you see a XXX rating, then . . . gee . . . you better stay away! (You may even get an infection.)

Diversifying your stocks

If most of your dividend income is from stock in a single company or single industry, consider reallocating your investment to avoid having all your eggs in one basket. Concerns about diversification apply to income stocks as well as growth stocks. If all your income stocks are in the electric utility industry, then any problems in that industry are potential problems for your portfolio as well. See Chapter 4 for more on diversification.

Exploring Some Typical Income Stocks

Although virtually every industry has stocks that pay dividends, some industries have more dividend-paying stocks than others. You won't find too many dividend-paying income stocks in the computer or biotech industries, for instance. The reason is that these types of companies need a lot of money to finance expensive research and development (R&D) projects to create new products. Without R&D, the company can't create new products to fuel sales, growth, and future earnings. Computer, biotech, and other innovative industries are better for growth investors. Keep reading for the scoop on stocks that work well for income investors.

Utilities

Utilities generate a large cash flow. (If you don't believe me, look at your gas and electric bills!) Cash flow includes money from income (sales of products and/or services) and other items (such as the selling of assets, for example). This cash flow is needed to cover expenses, loan payments, and dividends. Utilities are considered the most common type of income stocks, and many investors have at least one utility company in their portfolio. Investing in your own local utility isn't a bad idea — at least it makes paying the utility bill less painful.

Before you invest in a public utility, consider the following:

- **The utility company's financial condition:** Is the company making money, and are its sales and earnings growing from year to year? Make sure the utility's bonds are rated A or higher (I cover bond ratings in the "Examining a company's bond rating" section, earlier in this chapter).

- **The company's dividend payout ratio:** Because utilities tend to have a good cash flow, don't be too concerned if the ratio reaches 70 percent. From a safety point of view, however, the lower the rate, the better. See the "Looking at a stock's payout ratio" section, earlier in this chapter, for more on payout ratios.

- **The company's geographic location:** If the utility covers an area that's doing well and offers an increasing population base and business expansion, that bodes well for your stock. A good resource for researching population and business data is the U.S. Census Bureau (www.census.gov).

Real estate investment trusts (REITs)

Real estate investment trusts (REITs) are a special breed of stock. A *REIT* is an investment that has elements of both a stock and a *mutual fund* (a pool of money received from investors that's managed by an investment company).

- A REIT resembles a stock in that it's a company whose stock is publicly traded on the major stock exchanges, and it has the usual features that you expect from a stock — it can be bought and sold easily through a broker, income is given to investors as dividends, and so on.

✔ A REIT resembles a mutual fund in that it doesn't make its money selling goods and services; it makes its money by buying, selling, and managing an investment portfolio of real estate investments. It generates revenue from rents and property leases, as any landlord does. In addition, some REITs own mortgages, and they gain income from the interest.

REITs are called trusts only because they meet the requirements of the Real Estate Investment Trust Act of 1960. This act exempts REITs from corporate income tax and capital gains taxes as long as they meet certain criteria, such as dispensing 95 percent of their net income to shareholders. This provision is the reason why REITs generally issue generous dividends. Beyond this status, REITs are, in a practical sense, like any other publicly traded company.

The main advantages to investing in REITs include the following:

✔ Unlike other types of real estate investing, REITs are easy to buy and sell. You can buy a REIT by making a phone call to a broker or visiting a broker's Web site, just as you can to purchase any stock.

✔ REITs have higher-than-average yields. Because they must distribute at least 95 percent of their income to shareholders, their dividends usually yield a return of 5 to 12 percent.

✔ REITs involve a lower risk than the direct purchase of real estate because they use a portfolio approach diversified among many properties. Because you're investing in a company that buys the real estate, you don't have to worry about managing the properties — the company's management does that on a full-time basis. Usually, the REIT doesn't just manage one property; it's diversified in a portfolio of different properties.

✔ Investing in a REIT is affordable for small investors. REIT shares usually trade in the $10 to $40 range, meaning that you can invest with very little money.

REITs do have disadvantages. Although they tend to be diversified with various properties, they're still susceptible to risks tied to the general real estate sector. Real estate investing reached manic, record-high levels during 2000–2007, which meant that a downturn was likely. Whenever you invest in an asset (like real estate or REITs in recent years) that has already skyrocketed due to artificial stimulants (in the case of real estate, very low interest rates and too much credit and debt), the potential losses can offset any potential (unrealized) income.

When you're looking for a REIT to invest in, analyze it the way you'd analyze a property. Look at the location and type of property. If shopping malls are booming in California and your REIT buys and sells shopping malls in California, then hopefully you'll do well. However, if your REIT invests in office buildings across the country and the office building market is overbuilt and having tough times, you'll have a tough time, too. In 2009 and for the next few years, it will pay for investors to be extra selective regarding REIT investments because the difficulties in the real estate industry aren't over yet.

Royalty trusts

In recent years, the oil and gas sector has generated much interest as people and businesses experience much higher energy prices. Due to a variety of bullish factors, such as increased international demand from China and other emerging industrialized nations, oil and gas prices have zoomed to record highs. Some income investors have capitalized on this price increase by investing in energy stocks called royalty trusts.

Royalty trusts are companies that hold assets such as oil-rich and/or gas-rich land and generate high fees from companies that seek access to these properties for exploration. The fees paid to the royalty trusts are then disbursed as high dividends to their shareholders. By the first half of 2008, dividend-rich royalty trusts sported yields in the 9 to 15 percent range, which is very enticing given how low the yields have been in this decade for other investments like bank accounts and bonds. You can research royalty trusts in generally the same venues as regular stocks (see Appendix A).

Although energy has been a hot field in recent years and royalty trusts have done well, keep in mind that their payout ratios are very high (often in the 90 to 100 percent range), so dividends will suffer should their cash flow shrink.

Chapter 10

Getting a Grip on Economics

. . . .

In This Chapter

▶ Distinguishing between microeconomics and macroeconomics

▶ Boning up on key economic concepts

▶ Exploring the major schools of economic thought

▶ Keeping an eye on a couple of current economic issues

. . . .

"Stock prices have reached what looks like a permanently high plateau," said the celebrated economist Irving Fisher on October 17, 1929, shortly before history's most famous single-day stock market plunge. Nobody should have listened to Irving Fisher — not even Irving Fisher. He lost a ton of money in the stock market and filed for bankruptcy at the start of the Great Depression. Sooooo . . . if you don't think understanding economics is important to your stock investing strategy, then by gum you'd be as wrong as Irving.

This chapter isn't full of economic gobbledygook; I won't beat you over the head with phrases like "inelastic demand aggregates" and "marginal statistical utility" (whatever that means). (You're breathing a sigh of relief, aren't you?) Presented properly, economics really is quite interesting. Understanding economics helps you make better decisions involving your investment choices. All of my successful stock picks were first grounded in common sense economics. Economics also helped me avoid bad choices; Internet stocks in the late 1990s and mortgage and financial stocks during 2006–2008 didn't make economic sense, and ultimately shareholders lost most (or all) of their money as stock prices sank into oblivion. Always ask yourself: "Does this stock pick make economic sense?" I find economics fascinating, and I hope you find this chapter beneficial and, uh, tolerable.

Don't repeat the mistakes of the past! Be an informed stock investor. Here are some sources to help you understand economics more fully:

✔ American Institute for Economic Research: www.aier.org

✔ Dismal Scientist: www.dismal.com

- ✔ Financial Sense: `www.financialsense.com`
- ✔ Foundation for Economic Education: `www.fee.org`
- ✔ The Mises Institute: `www.mises.org`
- ✔ Shadow Government Statistics: `www.shadowstats.com`

Breaking Down Microeconomics versus Macroeconomics

You can divide the field of economics into two categories: microeconomics and macroeconomics. For stock investors,

- ✔ *Microeconomics* is looking at the economic small picture, such as the fundamentals of a company.
- ✔ *Macroeconomics* is looking at the economic big picture, such as the health of the general economy.

Microeconomics

It may not always dawn on you that economics isn't about alien, arcane data and statistics. Economics is the rudimentary stuff of financial life such as sales, expenses, profit, debt, and so on. Your own household is the first and best example of microeconomics in action. If the money coming in is greater than the money going out, that's certainly good. If you have lots of debt (liabilities) and very little in the way of things you own (assets), then your net worth is negative (dead meat!) and the microeconomics of your household aren't good at all.

Much of this book covers microeconomics in terms of choosing your stock. After all, if you're going to put your hard-earned money in a stock, you have to familiarize yourself with the company represented by that stock. Is the company in good economic shape? You find out by checking the company's microeconomic indicators, such as its income statement (or the P&L), balance sheet, and cash flow. You find more information about these indicators in Chapter 11.

Macroeconomics

If you're only familiar with the microeconomic and don't notice the big picture, you could see your portfolio crumble. Macroeconomics is an important part of your investment decision-making process because stocks aren't chosen in a vacuum. Even the best stocks in the world will go down if the economy is experiencing major problems. This is especially true for stocks of companies that offer products and services.

One of the most helpful macroeconomic indicators is the index of Leading Economic Indicators (LEI), which is an economic gauge that covers a broad array of statistics intended to estimate future economic activity. It's calculated by the Conference Board (`www.conference-board.org`), and it's a useful gauge for investors because it gives you an idea of how the economy is progressing.

A flaw with the analysis of the investing pundits on financial TV shows is that although they're usually very good at microeconomics, because of certain factors (a lack of education, bias, and so on), they aren't proficient at macroeconomics. They may tell you about a great stock in sector X, but they're missing what will hit that sector (and that stock) because of factors elsewhere in the economy. A good example is homebuilding stocks. In 2006, I watched as a financial advisor extolled the virtues of a particular homebuilding company ("Great financials, great profit margin — this stock is a definite buy!"). However, the housing sector was about to be slammed by a huge wave of defaults and foreclosures because of mortgage problems and a slowing general economy. In the following months, that stock plummeted by 60 percent even though its microeconomic picture looked nice.

Understanding Important Concepts in Economic Logic

To keep yourself grounded with the right data and logic for your stock investing decisions, I discuss a few points that you ought to be familiar with in the following sections.

Supply and demand

Doing a chapter on economics without mentioning supply and demand is like doing a chapter on graceful aging without mentioning Pat Boone and Dick Clark. Supply and demand are the quintessential duo in the economic universe, and the more you understand how they work, the more successful your investment decisions will be.

Here are definitions for these two concepts (from my perspective, of course):

- ✔ **Supply.** What's being offered or produced? How much is there? How desirable or necessary is it? Are there substitutes? How limited or plentiful is the supply in question? What factors affect supply, and do those factors affect it directly or indirectly?

- ✔ **Demand.** This refers to the market that will ultimately buy what's offered. Who are they? How many are they? Are they willing and able to buy? Are they individuals, small organizations, or large organizations? Do they merely want what's offered, or do they need it? What factors affect demand, and do those factors affect it directly or indirectly?

We count on supply and demand to tell us how well a product or service will sell. This in turn tells us if the company providing the supply (again, product or service) has enough customers (demand) to be profitable and successful.

How do supply and demand relate to your investing decisions? Here's a simple example: A company sells medical equipment that's necessary for an aging population, and the aging population is a growing segment of society. Therefore, demand is strong and probably growing, so the stock of the company providing supply (the medical equipment) is probably a good bet.

Sometimes the laws of supply and demand can be overcome or temporarily suspended in the short term by something powerful such as government action (a good example is price controls, which I cover in Chapter 15). However, in the long term, supply and demand trump all.

Wants and needs

One of my favorite definitions of economics is a very pithy one: "Economics is humanity dealing with scarcity." After all, to "economize" is to use resources wisely and to make choices about what to do with time, effort, and money. As humans, we know that we must use our resources (such as time, effort, and money) to voluntarily exchange with others to acquire goods and services that meet our wants and needs (or both).

When times are good and we're doing well financially, we're not that concerned about our needs, and we have a greater ability to address our wants, such as a new car or a better vacation. When times are good, we have an easier time with stock investing; many stocks tend to do well when times are good because more money flows toward both wants and needs.

But what if times are bad (or simply not as good)? When economic times are tough or uncertain, common sense kicks in for stock investors. Demand for products and services that people merely want but don't need is weak or negative. However, demand for those things that are needed in our lives (such as food or energy) are a safer choice for stock investors.

As I write this, times are difficult, and the data tells me that 2009 and beyond will be economically hazardous and difficult for our economy. Therefore, investors would be prudent to stick to investment choices tied to human needs.

Dynamic analysis versus static analysis

Economics isn't about dry statistics; it's about human behavior with incentives and disincentives. In other words, when it comes to economics, people behave in a way that usually suits their self-interest. For example, say you're driving down the highway and you notice two gas stations. Gas station A has gasoline at $3.00 per gallon while gas station B has the same gas at $2.80. Which one is more profitable? All things being equal, gas station B (the one with the lower price) will make more money.

Dynamic analysis takes human behavior into account, such as in that example. However, someone using *static analysis* would conclude that gas station A would be more profitable by assuming that it would make an extra 20 cents per gallon. If the world were a static place and if people were automatons, then the latter situation could possibly prove correct. But look . . . we're human! Everyone loves a bargain. Gas A is more expensive, so more people will buy gas B, resulting in higher profits for the lower-priced station.

Dynamic analysis takes into account how people or organizations act differently given incentives (such as discounts) or disincentives (such as sales taxes), while static analysis doesn't.

We're all faced with choices about what to do with our money. I'm certain that you'd find the same product cheaper at a big box store than at a haughty boutique in Beverly Hills. Yet which one would make greater overall profits? Ask yourself how people would behave with the choices they face in the marketplace. Those companies that deliver with greater efficiency and value are a good bet for stock investing.

Cause and effect

Cause and effect is an exercise in logic that stock investors should embrace. If something is a growing problem (or a growing opportunity), what is its possible cause? And, in turn, what effect will it have? The credit crisis of 2008 is a great example of this. When banks were overburdened with debt and much of that debt was discovered to be low-quality (risky) debt, this situation caused several effects, among them major losses and potential bankruptcies. Wary investors see that too much debt in an uncertain economy can certainly cause some undesired effects. Individual companies suffer and their stock price goes down, which, of course, has a negative effect on your portfolio.

Surveying a Few Schools of Economic Thought

Adhering to a particular economic philosophy can make you or break you as a stock investor. Be sure to discover which ones have withstood the test of time and which ones are the kiss of economic death. In the following sections, I introduce a few major schools found in the world today.

Even if you aren't proficient in understanding different schools of thought, be sure to find out the school of thought of the financial planners you work with and the resources you use. By knowing a planner's school of thought, you can understand his general outlook and see whether it's a fit with your outlook. If a financial planner isn't aware of the schools of thought or answers "Keynesian," that indicates to me that he doesn't fully understand how government policy and economics affect the stock-picking process.

The Marx school

Frankly, the Marx school of economic thought (named after Karl Marx) makes me shudder. I was born in a communist country (Yugoslavia then, Croatia now, who knows what it will be tomorrow). I joke in my seminars that being born in a communist country is what made me a raving capitalist. In a communist country, the government runs everything. When the government runs everything, economic activity is controlled by a centralized, pervasive bureaucracy. And history has shown that such economies eventually collapse. Yugoslavia and the Soviet Union are examples of this.

Part of the reason that centralized planning doesn't work is that no single bureaucrat or committee of bureaucrats has the ability to see and meet the complex and constantly changing wants and needs of millions of diverse individuals. Centralized planning of an economy eventually leads to misallocation of resources, and that has always led to intractable economic problems. I can write volumes on the subject because my family has experienced it, and I've studied the topic for over 30 years. But a full treatment is beyond the scope and purpose of this book.

How does this relate to stocks? Marxist/socialist/communist economic thought is, at its core, antithetical to a healthy free market economy, which is necessary for stock investing. Stock investing requires a free market, one in which the functions of business (such as profit) can operate with minimal interference. Businesses must be allowed to be formed, and they must bear the burden of risk and reward. Poorly run businesses fail, while well-run companies are rewarded with profit (good for stockholders).

Although profit sometimes gets bad press, it is in fact the most necessary element of a successful economy. In other chapters of this book, you find out that profit is necessary for companies, but notice that I've extended that thought to the overall economy. Think about it for a moment. Profit is vital for economic growth. Profit is what makes an economy expand. Profit is an economic incentive missing from communist economies (and sorely missing from socialist ones). Profit is (and should be) a reward for innovation, risk, and the proper allocation of resources.

History has shown us conclusively that every country that has adopted a totalitarian, command-and-control economic model (communism, fascism, and so on) has ended in economic decline and abject failure. The bottom line is that Groucho Marx knows more about economics than Karl. Nuff said.

The Keynes school

The economic philosophy of John Maynard Keynes (a British economist in the early 20th century) has been the dominant school of thought in American politics and governmental economic policy matters for over a half-century. What a shame! What many don't realize is that, after decades of this policy being implemented, the long-term effect of Keynesian economics is now becoming evident.

Keynesian economics is an economic theory with the central idea that active government intervention in the marketplace and in monetary policy (managing the country's currency) is the best method of ensuring economic growth and stability. Believers in Keynesian economics think that it's the government's job to smooth out the ebbs and flows in the business cycle. In bad times, intervention takes the form of increased spending by the government and tax cuts to stimulate the economy. In good times, the government intervenes by a reduction in spending and increases in taxes to curb potential inflation.

The problem is that the government intervention at the heart of Keynesian economics is now finally seen as the great flaw. The intervention actually causes the recessions, depressions, and artificial booms that it was originally supposed to remedy. As government continues to spend and allows total government debt to keep rising, the situation must eventually be addressed. When flaws in his theory were pointed out and shown to be a huge problem in the long run, Keynes was famously quoted as saying, "In the long run, we will all be dead." Well, he certainly is dead, but his ideas live on and continue to wreak havoc on our economy today. Government intervention, massive bailouts, economic dislocation, and rising inflation are being dealt with right now. (Another quote attributed to Keynes was, "It is better to be roughly right than precisely wrong." Looks like he has been precisely wrong and it sure has been rough!)

What does Keynesian economics have to do with the stock market? This is the ideology that ends up causing artificial booms ("asset bubbles") and the resulting decline. Keynesian thinking is what drove the government (through the Federal Reserve) to increase liquidity (that is, increase the money supply and expand credit), which resulted in the bubbles that our society has witnessed in recent years. In the early stages of a bubble, everyone's happy as the value of their assets (such as stocks or real estate) rises and provides the illusion that has come to be known as "the wealth effect." People felt wealthy in the late 1990s when the stock market (especially Internet and tech stocks) went up dramatically. However, because bubbles are created by artificial means (the injection of credit), prices are bid up to unnatural levels and must ultimately come down. The stock market bubble popped in 2000, and millions of people lost trillions of dollars. Then the housing bubble inflated (again, by artificial stimulus via credit expansion by the Fed), and this has in recent years caused massive pain as record levels of defaults and foreclosures took place.

As I write this, the latest bubble in credit and derivatives has started to deflate and wreak havoc on the stock market (especially financial stocks like banks and brokerage firms). Bubbles have become the visible legacy of the rampant credit and money expansion which resulted from applying Keynesian economics. (By the way, most politicians are Keynesians. Ha! Need I say more?)

The Austrian school

In my humble opinion, the most useful school of economic thought for investors (anyone, actually) is the Austrian school. After 100 years of experience, the Austrian school has been proven consistently right.

The leading voice of this school was Ludwig von Mises, an Austrian economist in the early 20th century (now you know where the name of the school comes from!). He accurately forecast the Great Depression, the collapse of the Soviet Union, and other economic events.

The Austrian school emphasizes free markets, limited government, private property rights, and a sound currency tied to the gold standard. This last point is important given what can happen when a government issues currency without limit — how this leads to currency debasement and, ultimately, collapse. In addition, the Austrian school provides research on how asset bubbles (such as the recent stock and housing market bubbles) form and the problems that can ensue when these bubbles cause booms and the inevitable bust.

How does this help you with stocks? In 1999, I recall reading an article about asset bubbles on `www.mises.org`, the site that showcases the work of Mises and other Austrian economists (such as Murray Rothbard and Henry Hazlitt). That article explained how the stock market was a bubble and why. Armed with this knowledge, I informed students and clients about ways to protect against the stock market bubble. That forewarning saved many of my clients and students from the bear market of 2000–2002, and it was a concrete lesson in understanding (and applying) sound economic principles. Are you taking notes?

Understanding Some Current Economic Issues That Face Stock Investors

As I told you earlier in this chapter, I won't provide an all-encompassing, extensive, voluminous coverage of economics, but I am committed to your investment success. The following are a few economic issues that you *must* be aware of in the coming months and years if you're intent on successful stock investing.

Inflation

Inflation is an issue that could easily be lumped into the chapter on politics (Chapter 15, so you know) because it's as much a governmental phenomenon as it is an economic one. In modern economies, you and I use currencies (such as the dollar) to transact in our day-to-day lives. It's our medium of exchange; we use currencies to trade with so that we can obtain goods and services. The issuance of currency is a government matter; the central bank (in the U.S. it's the Federal Reserve) issues the currency and manages its quantity (the money supply). When you hear the term "monetary policy," that's just the official way of saying that the Federal Reserve manages our official supply of money — the dollar as our national currency.

Since 2001, the Federal Reserve has been increasing the money supply at a double-digit rate. In recent years, much of this came in the form of credit that went into assets (such as stocks and real estate), but much of it has been (and is) going into the price of goods and services. This means that the result has been (and will be) high and higher prices.

Inflation is effectively a hidden tax which hurts most consumers, especially those on fixed incomes. Stock investors should be aware of inflation and invest in ways that will benefit them. This is part of the reason why I repeatedly tell folks to invest in human need. As these prices go up, you need to be in the stocks of companies that will either benefit from inflation or (at the very least) not be hurt by it. Examples of human need include food, water, energy, and so on. Consider stocks in these necessary areas.

Government intervention

Stock investing was actually an easy pursuit in the 1980s and the early 1990s. The market was generally unfettered, and economic logic was easy to apply. However, a major sea change has occurred during the past 10–15 years that has made stock investing more precarious, unpredictable, and hazardous. That sea change was driven by government intervention, which is akin to betting on a basketball game but finding out that the referees are interfering in the game. Government intervention comes in a variety of flavors, and it's usually an outgrowth of political considerations, so spend some in Chapter 15, where I discuss the relationship between politics and stock investing in more detail.

9,000,000 percent inflation!

In a seminar in 2008, I asked my students to name the top-performing stock market in the world last year (from a nominal point of view). They blurted out "China," "Brazil," and other guesses, but they weren't even close. "Zimbabwe," I said to the puzzled class. That's right, a fairly obscure country in central Africa. Its stock market was up an astonishing 12,000 percent. Whew! Yet, the country is mired in poverty under an oppressive regime. How can that be? When socialist dictator Robert Mugabe took control of the country, he put in strict controls on the economy. Among those controls: Citizens couldn't have foreign accounts, couldn't buy gold or other alternative forms of money, and could only use the official currency, the Zimbabwean dollar. He then began to hyper-inflate the currency to initially benefit himself and his allies. After years of abuse, the inflation rate hit horrific levels. On paper, Zimbabwe had more multimillionaires per capita than any other nation even though most of the populace was destitute. By the summer of 2008, the inflation rate surpassed 9 million percent, as 40 billion Zimbabwean dollars equaled one U.S. dollar. Recently, the country's economic minister told the United Nations that the inflation rate was beyond calculation. Zimbabwe's fate regarding this extreme condition is yet to be clear. Stay tuned!

Part III
Picking Winners

The 5th Wave   By Rich Tennant

"I read about investing in a company called Unihandle Ohio, but I'm uneasy about a stock that's listed on the NASDAQ as UhOh."

In this part . . .

Now that you have the basics down, it's time to become a pro at picking individual stocks. When you consider investing in a company, you need to gain insight into what makes a particular stock's price rise. And because the stock market doesn't operate in a vacuum, I introduce political and governmental factors that can have a huge effect on the stock market. The chapters in this part steer you to key financial information and important company documents and show you how to interpret the information you find.

Chapter 11

Using Basic Accounting to Choose Winning Stocks

In This Chapter

▶ Determining a company's value

▶ Using accounting principles to understand a company's financial condition

Successful stock picking sometimes seems like plucking a rabbit out of a hat or watching the Amazing Kreskin do some Houdini trick. In other words, it seems like you need sleight of hand to choose a stock. Perhaps stock picking is more art than science. The other guy seems to always pick winners while you're stuck with losers. What does it take — a crystal ball or some system from a get-rich-quick-with-stocks book?

Well, with the book in your hands now and a little work on your part, I think you'll succeed. This chapter takes the mystery out of the numbers behind the stock. The most tried-and-true method for picking a good stock starts with picking a good company. Picking the company means looking at its products, services, industry, and financial strength (the numbers). Considering the problems that the market has witnessed in recent years — such as subprime debt problems and derivative meltdowns wreaking havoc on public companies and financial firms — this chapter is more important than ever. Understanding the basics behind the numbers can save your portfolio.

Recognizing Value When You See It

If you pick a stock based on the value of the company that issues it, you're a *value investor* — an investor who looks at a company's value and judges whether he can purchase the stock at a good price. Companies have value the same way many things have value, such as eggs or elephant-foot umbrella stands. And there's such a thing as a fair price to buy them at, too. Take eggs, for example. You can eat them and have a tasty treat while getting nutrition as well. But would you buy an egg for $1,000 (and no, you're not a starving millionaire on a deserted island)? Of course not. But what if you could buy an egg for 5 cents? At that point, it has value *and* a good price. This kind of deal is a value investor's dream.

Value investors analyze a company's *fundamentals* (earnings, assets, and so on) and see whether the information justifies purchasing the stock. They see whether the stock price is low relative to these verifiable, quantifiable factors. Therefore, value investors use *fundamental analysis,* while other investors may use *technical analysis.* Technical analysis looks at stock charts and statistical data, such as trading volume and historical stock prices (I take a closer look at technical analysis in Chapter 16). Some investors use a combination of both strategies.

History has shown that the most successful long-term investors have typically been value investors using fundamental analysis as their primary investing approach. The most consistently successful long-term investors were and are predominately value investors (yes, I count myself in this crowd as well).

In the following sections, I describe different kinds of value and explain how to spot a company's value in several places.

Understanding different types of value

"Value" may seem like a murky or subjective term, but it's the essence of good stock picking. You can measure value in different ways, so you need to know the differences and understand the impact that value has on your investment decisions.

Market value

When you hear someone quoting a stock at $47 per share, that price reflects the stock's market value. The total market valuation of a company's stock is also referred to as its *market cap* or *market capitalization.* How do you determine a company's market cap? With the following simple formula:

Market capitalization = Share price × Number of shares outstanding

If Bolshevik Corp.'s stock is $35 per share and it has 10 million shares outstanding (or shares available for purchase), its market cap is $350 million. Granted, $350 million may sound like a lot of money, but Bolshevik Corp. is considered a small cap stock. (For more information about small cap stocks, dip into Chapter 8.)

Who sets the market value of stock? The market, of course! Millions of investors buying and selling directly and through intermediaries such as mutual funds determine the market value of any particular stock. If the market perceives that the company is desirable, investor demand for the company's stock pushes up the share price.

The problem with market valuation is that it's not always a good indicator of a good investment. In recent years, plenty of companies have had astronomical market values, yet they proved to be very risky investments. For example, think about Bear Stearns. During 2007, it hit a stock price of $170; its market cap was measured in billions. Yet its stock price plunged to only $2 per share in the spring of 2008. Yikes! Because market value is a direct result of the buying and selling of stock investors, it can be a fleeting thing. This is why investors must understand the company behind the stock price.

Book value

Book value (also referred to as *accounting value*) looks at a company from a balance sheet perspective (assets minus liabilities equal net worth, or *stockholders' equity*). It's a way of judging a firm by its net worth to see whether the stock's market value is reasonable compared to the company's intrinsic value. *Intrinsic value* is value tied to what the market price would be of a company's assets, both tangible (such as equipment) and intangible (such as patents), if they were sold.

Generally, market value tends to be higher than book value. If market value is substantially higher than book value, the value investor becomes more reluctant to buy that particular stock because it's overvalued. The closer the stock's market capitalization is to the book value, the safer the investment.

I like to be cautious with a stock whose market value is more than twice its book value. If the market value is $1 billion or more and the book value is $500 million or less, that's a good indicator that the business may be overvalued, or valued at a higher price than its book value and ability to generate a profit. Just understand that the farther the market value is from the company's book value, the more you'll pay for the company's real potential value. And the more you pay for the company's real value, the greater the risk that the company's market value can decrease (the stock price, that is).

Sales and earnings value

A company's intrinsic value is directly tied to its ability to make money. In that case, many analysts like to value stocks from the perspective of the company's income statement. Two common barometers of value are expressed in ratios: the price to sales ratio (PSR) and the price-to-earnings ratio (P/E). In both instances, the price is a reference to the company's market value (as reflected in its share price). Sales and earnings are references to the firm's ability to make money. These two ratios are covered more fully in the section "Tooling around with ratios," later in this chapter.

For investors, the general approach is clear. The closer the market value is to the company's intrinsic value, the better. And, of course, if the market value is lower than the company's intrinsic value, you have a potential bargain worthy of a closer look. Part of looking closer means examining the company's income statement, also called the *profit and loss statement,* or simply, the *P&L.* A low price to sales ratio is 1, a medium PSR is between 1 and 2, and a high PSR is 3 or higher.

Putting the pieces together

When you look at a company from a value-oriented perspective, here are some of the most important items to consider (see the later section "Accounting for Value" for more information):

- ✔ **The balance sheet, to figure out the company's net worth:** A value investor doesn't buy a company's stock because it's cheap; she buys it because it's *undervalued* (the company is worth more than the price its stock reflects — its market value is as close as possible to its book value).

- ✔ **The income statement, to figure out the company's profitability:** A company may be undervalued from a simple comparison of the book value and the market value, but that doesn't mean it's a screaming buy. For example, what if you find out that a company is in trouble and losing money this year? Do you buy its stock then? No, you don't. Why invest in the stock of a losing company? (If you do, you aren't investing — you're gambling or speculating.) The heart of a firm's value, besides its net worth, is its ability to generate profit.

- ✔ **Ratios that let you analyze just how well (or not so well) the company is doing:** Value investors basically look for a bargain. That being the case, they generally don't look at companies that everyone is talking about, because by that point, the stock of those companies ceases to be a bargain. The value investor searches for a stock that will eventually be discovered by the market and then watches as the stock price goes up. But before you bother digging into the fundamentals to find that bargain stock, first make sure that the company is making money.

Value investors can find thousands of companies that have value, but they can probably buy only a handful at a truly good price. The number of stocks that can be bought at a good price is relative to the market. In mature bull markets (markets in a prolonged period of rising prices), a good price is hard to find because most stocks have probably seen significant price increases, but in bear markets (markets in a prolonged period of falling prices), good companies at bargain prices are easier to come by.

The more ways that you can look at a company and see value, the better. The first thing I look at is the P/E ratio. Does the company have one? (It sounds dumb, but if it's losing money, it may not have one.) Does the P/E ratio look reasonable, or is it in triple-digit, nose-bleed territory? Is it reasonable or too high?

Next, look at the company's debt load (the total amount of liabilities). Is it less than the company's equity? Are sales healthy and increasing from the prior year? Does the firm compare favorably in these categories versus other companies in the same industry?

Simplicity to me is best. You'll notice that the number 10 comes up frequently as I measure a company's performance, juxtaposing all the numbers that you need to be aware of. If net income is rising by 10 percent or more, that's fine. If the company is in the top 10 percent of its industry, that's great. If the industry is growing by 10 percent or better (sales and so on), that's terrific. If sales are up 10 percent or more from the prior year, that's wonderful. A great company doesn't have to have all these things going for it, but it should have as many of these things happening as possible to ensure greater potential success.

Does every company/industry have to neatly fit these criteria? No, of course not. But it doesn't hurt you to be as picky as possible. You need to find only a handful of stocks from thousands of choices. (Hey, this approach has worked for me, my clients, and my students for nearly 2$^1/_2$ decades — 'nuff said.)

Accounting for Value

Profit is to a company what oxygen is to you and me. That's neither good nor bad; it just is. Without profit, a company can't survive, much less thrive. Without profit, it can't provide jobs, pay taxes, and invest in new products, equipment, or innovation. Without profit, the company eventually goes bankrupt, and the value of its stock evaporates.

In the heady days leading up to the bear market of 2000–2002, many investors lost a lot of money simply because they invested in stocks of companies that weren't making a profit. Lots of public companies ended up like bugs that just didn't see the windshield coming their way. Companies such as Enron, WorldCom, and Global Crossing entered the graveyard of rather-be-forgotten stocks. Stock investors as a group lost trillions of dollars investing in glitzy companies that sounded good but weren't making money. When their brokers were saying, "buy, buy, buy," their hard-earned money was saying, "bye, bye, bye!" What were they thinking?

Crash-test dummy candidate?

From 2001–2003, consumers were buying up SUVs ... uh ... ASAP. Demand was very high for those popular gas-guzzling vehicles, and auto giant General Motors (GM) was racking up record sales. Investors noticed GM's success, and its stock surpassed $76 in 2001. However, the numbers (and the times) were catching up with GM. Their zero-interest financing program started to sputter. Debts and human resource liabilities (such as employee health and retirement commitments) started accelerating. Energy costs rose, making SUVs less attractive. The red flags came out. GM's 2004 year-end balance sheet showed debt of over $451 billion, while total shareholder equity was only $27.7 billion. GM's net income fell to just 1 percent of net sales, and its price-to-earnings (P/E) ratio ballooned to a lofty 39. The stock price hit $25 by April 2005. Although the price rebounded to the mid-$30s by July 2005, investors had skid marks on their portfolio as the stock lost nearly two-thirds of its value during that time frame. By

September 2005, GM reported a net loss (good-bye P/E ratio). In my reckoning, GM is no longer an investment; it's now a speculation. At this rate, it may go from SUV to DOA ASAP.

As a contrasting point, look at Exxon Mobil (XOM) during that same time frame. Its stock price went from about $35 in early 2001 to $60 in July 2005 (it had a 2-for-1 stock split in mid-2001). XOM's net income was a healthy 8 percent of sales, and the P/E ratio was only 14. In its 2004 year-end balance sheet, total shareholder equity of $101.7 billion comfortably exceeded its total liabilities of $89.5 billion. A sound company with sound numbers. (Ya hear me?)

The point here is that the stock price ultimately reflects the financial health and vitality of the company, and you can easily find and evaluate that information. You don't need luck or a crystal ball. Again, just a little work in the form of fundamental analysis is sufficient.

Stock investors need to pick up some rudimentary knowledge of accounting to round out their stock-picking prowess and to be sure that they're getting a good value for their investment dollars. Accounting is the language of business. If you don't understand basic accounting, then you'll have difficulty being a successful investor. Investing without accounting knowledge is like traveling without a map. However, if you can run a household budget, using accounting analysis to evaluate stocks is easier than you think.

Finding the relevant financial data on a company isn't difficult in the age of information. Web sites such as www.nasdaq.com can give you the most recent balance sheets and income statements of most public companies. You can find out more about public information and research on companies in Chapter 6.

Breaking down the balance sheet

A company's balance sheet gives you a financial snapshot of what the company looks like in terms of the following equation:

Assets – liabilities = Net worth (or net equity)

In the following sections, I list the questions that a balance sheet can answer and explain how to judge a company's strength over time from a balance sheet.

Answering a few balance sheet questions

Analyze the following items that you find on the balance sheet:

- **Total Assets:** Have they increased from the prior year? If not, was it because of the sale of an asset or a write-off (uncollectable accounts receivable, for example)?

- **Financial Assets:** In recent years, many companies (especially banks and brokerage firms) had questionable financial assets (such as sub-prime mortgages and specialized bonds) that went bad, and they had to write them off as unrecoverable losses. Does the company you're analyzing have a large exposure to financial assets that are low-quality (hence risky) debt?

- **Inventory:** Is inventory higher or lower than last year? If sales are flat but inventory is growing, that may be a potential problem.

- **Debt:** Debt is the biggest weakness on the corporate balance sheet. Make sure that debt isn't a growing item and that it's under control. In recent years, debt has become a huge problem.

- **Derivatives:** A *derivative* is a speculative and complex financial instrument that doesn't constitute ownership of an asset (such as a stock, bond, or commodity) but a promise to convey ownership. Some derivatives are quite acceptable because they're used as protective or hedging vehicles (this isn't my primary concern). However, they're frequently used to generate income and can then carry risks that can increase liabilities. Standard options and futures are examples of derivatives on a regulated exchange, but the derivatives I talk about here are a different animal and in an unregulated part of the financial world. They have a book value exceeding $600 trillion and can easily devastate a company, sector, or market (as the credit crisis of 2008 has shown).

  Find out whether the company dabbles in these complicated, dicey, leveraged financial instruments. Find out (from the company's 10K report; see Chapter 12) whether it has derivatives and, if so, the total amount. If a company has derivatives that are valued higher than the company's net equity, it may cause tremendous problems. Derivatives problems sank many organizations ranging from stodgy banks (Barings Bank of England) to affluent counties (Orange County, California) to once-respected hedge funds (LTCM) to infamous corporations (Enron).

- **Equity:** Equity is the company's net worth (what's left in the event that all the assets are used to pay off all the company debts). The stock-holders' equity should be increasing steadily by at least 10 percent per year. If not, find out why.

By looking at a company's balance sheet, you can address the following questions:

- ✔ **What does the company own (assets)?** The company can own assets, which can be financial, tangible, and/or intangible. An _asset_ is anything that has value or that can be converted to or sold for cash. Financial assets can be cash, investments (such as stocks or bonds of other companies), or accounts receivable. Assets can be tangible things such as inventory, equipment, and/or buildings. They can also be intangible things such as licenses, trademarks, or copyrights.

- ✔ **What does the company owe (liabilities)?** A _liability_ is anything of value that the company must ultimately pay to someone else. Liabilities can be invoices (accounts payable) or short-term or long-term debt.

- ✔ **What is the company's net equity (net worth)?** After you subtract the liabilities from the assets, the remainder is called _net worth, net equity,_ or _net stockholders' equity._ This number is critical when calculating a company's book value.

Assessing a company's financial strength over time

The assets/liabilities relationship for a company has the same logic as the assets and liabilities in your own household. When you look at a snapshot of your own finances (your personal balance sheet), how can you tell whether you're doing well? Odds are that you would start by comparing some numbers. If your net worth is $5,000, you may say, "That's great!" But a more appropriate remark is something like, "That's great compared to, say, a year ago."

Compare a company's balance sheet at a recent point in time to a past time. You should do this comparative analysis with all the key items on the balance sheet. You do this analysis to see the company's progress. Is it growing its assets and/or shrinking its debt? Most important, is the company's net worth growing? Is it growing by at least 10 percent from a year ago? All too often, investors stop doing their homework after they make an initial investment. You should continue to look at the firm's numbers on a regular basis so that you can be ahead of the curve. If the business starts having problems, you can get out before the rest of the market starts getting out (which causes the stock price to fall).

To judge the financial strength of a company, ask yourself the following questions:

- ✔ Are the company's assets greater in value than they were three months ago, a year ago, or two years ago? Compare current asset size to the most recent two years to make sure that the company is growing in size and financial strength.

✔ How do the individual items compare with prior periods? Some particular assets that you want to take note of are cash, inventory, and accounts receivable.

✔ Are liabilities such as accounts payable and debt about the same, lower, or higher compared to prior periods? Are they growing at a similar, faster, or slower rate than the company's assets? Debt that rises faster and higher than items on the other side of the balance sheet is a warning sign of pending financial problems.

✔ Is the company's net worth or equity greater than the previous year? And is that year's equity greater than the year before? In a healthy company, the net worth is constantly rising. As a general rule, in good economic times, net worth should be at least 10 percent higher than the previous year. In tough economic times (such as a recession), 5 percent is acceptable. Seeing the net worth growing at 15 percent or higher is great.

Looking at the income statement

Where do you look if you want to find out what a company's profit is? Check out the firm's income statement. It reports, in detail, a simple accounting equation that you probably already know:

> Sales – expenses = Net profit (or net earnings, or net income)

Look at the following figures found on the income statement:

✔ **Sales:** Are they increasing? If not, why not? By what percentage are sales increasing? Preferably, they should be 10 percent higher than the year before. Sales are, after all, where the money is coming from to pay for all the company's activities (such as expenses) and subsequent profit.

✔ **Expenses:** Do you see any unusual items? Are total expenses reported higher than the prior year, and by how much? If the total is significantly higher, why? A company with large, rising expenses will see profits suffer, which isn't good for the stock price.

✔ **Research and development (R&D):** How much is the company spending on R&D? Companies that rely on new product development (such as pharmaceuticals or biotech firms) should spend at least as much as they did the year before (preferably more) because new products mean future earnings and growth.

✔ **Earnings:** This figure reflects the bottom line. Are total earnings higher? How about earnings from operations (leaving out expenses such as taxes and interest)? The earnings section is the heart and soul of the income statement and of the company itself. Out of all the numbers in the financial statements, earnings have the greatest single impact on the company's stock price.

Looking at the income statement, an investor can try to answer the following questions:

- **What sales did the company make?** Businesses sell products and services that generate revenue (known as *sales* or *gross sales*). Sales also are referred to as the *top line*.

- **What expenses did the company incur?** In generating sales, companies pay expenses such as payroll, utilities, advertising, administration, and so on.

- **What is the net income?** Also called earnings or net profit, net income is the *bottom line*. After paying for all expenses, what profit did the company make?

The information you glean should give you a strong idea about a firm's current financial strength and whether it's successfully increasing sales, holding down expenses, and ultimately maintaining profitability. You can find out more about sales, expenses, and profits in the sections that follow.

Sales

Sales refers to the money that a company receives as customers buy its goods and/or services. It's a simple item on the income statement and a useful number to look at. Analyzing a business by looking at its sales is called *top line analysis*.

As an investor, you should take into consideration the following points about sales:

- **Sales should be increasing.** A healthy, growing company has growing sales. They should grow at least 10 percent from the prior year, and you should look at the most recent three years.

- **Core sales (sales of those products or services that the company specializes in) should be increasing.** Frequently, the sales figure has a lot of stuff lumped into it. Maybe the company sells widgets (what the heck is a widget, anyway?), but the core sales shouldn't include other things, such as the sale of a building or other unusual items. Take a close look. Isolate the firm's primary offerings and ask whether these sales are growing at a reasonable rate (such as 10 percent).

- **Does the company have odd items or odd ways of calculating sales?** In the late 1990s, many companies boosted their sales by aggressively offering affordable financing with easy repayment terms. Say you find out that Suspicious Sales Inc. (SSI) had annual sales of $50 million, reflecting a 25 percent increase from the year before. Looks great! But what if you find out that $20 million of that sales number comes from sales made on credit that the company extended to buyers? Some companies that use this approach later have to write off losses as uncollectable debt because the customers ultimately can't pay for the goods.

If you want to get a good clue whether a company is artificially boosting sales, check its *accounts receivable* (listed in the asset section of its balance sheet). Accounts receivable refers to money that is owed to the company for goods that customers have purchased on credit. If you find out that sales went up by $10 million (great!) but accounts receivable went up by $20 million (uh-oh), then something just isn't right. That may be a sign that the financing terms were too easy, and the company may have a problem collecting payment (especially in a recession).

Expenses

What a company spends has a direct relationship on its profitability. If spending isn't controlled or held at a sustainable level, it may spell trouble for the business.

When you look at a company's expense items, consider the following:

- ✔ **Compare expense items to the prior period.** Are expenses higher, lower, or about the same from the prior period? If the difference is significant, you should see commensurate benefits elsewhere. In other words, if overall expenses are 10 percent higher compared to the prior period, are sales at least 10 percent more during the same period?

- ✔ **Are some expenses too high?** Look at the individual expense items. Are they significantly higher than the year before? If so, why?

- ✔ **Have any unusual items been expensed?** Sometimes an unusual expense isn't necessarily a negative. Expenses may be higher than usual if a company writes off uncollectable accounts receivable as a bad debt expense. Doing so inflates the total expenses and subsequently results in lower earnings. Pay attention to nonrecurring charges that show up on the income statement and determine whether they make sense.

Profit

Earnings or profit is the single most important item on the income statement. It's also the one that receives the most attention in the financial media. When a company makes a profit, it's usually reported as earnings per share (EPS). So if you hear that XYZ Corporation beat last quarter's earnings by a penny, here's how to translate that news. Suppose that the company made $1 per share this quarter and 99 cents per share last quarter. If that company had 100 million shares of stock outstanding, its profit this quarter is $100 million (the EPS times the number of shares outstanding), which is $1 million more than it made in the prior quarter ($1 million is 1 cent per share times 100 million shares).

Don't simply look at current earnings as an isolated figure. Always compare current earnings to earnings in past periods (usually a year). For example, if you're looking at a retailer's fourth quarter results, you can't compare that with the retailer's third quarter. Doing so is like comparing apples to oranges. What if the company usually does well during the December holidays but poorly in the fall? In that case, you don't get a fair comparison.

A strong company should show consistent earnings growth from the period before (such as the year or the same quarter from the prior year), and you should check the period before that, too, so that you can determine whether earnings are consistently rising over time. Earnings growth is an important barometer of the company's potential growth and bodes well for the stock price.

When you look at earnings, here are some things to consider:

- **Total earnings:** This item is the most watched. Total earnings should grow year to year by at least 10 percent.

- **Operational earnings:** Break down the total earnings and look at a key subset — that portion of earnings derived from the company's core activity. Is the company continuing to make money from its primary goods and services?

- **Nonrecurring items:** Are earnings higher (or lower) than usual or than expected, and why? Frequently, the difference results from items such as the sale of an asset or a large depreciation write-off.

I like to keep percentages as simple as possible. Ten percent is a good number because it's easy to calculate and it's a good benchmark. However, 5 percent isn't unacceptable if you're talking about tough times, such as a recession. Obviously, if sales, earnings, and/or net worth are hitting or passing 15 percent, that's great.

Tooling around with ratios

A ratio is a helpful numerical tool that you can use to find out the relationship between two or more figures found in a company's financial data. A ratio can add meaning to a number or put it in perspective. Ratios sound complicated, but they're easier to understand than you think.

Say that you're considering a stock investment and the company you're looking at has earnings of $1 million this year. You may think that's a nice profit, but in order for this amount to be meaningful, you have to compare it to something. What if you find out that the other companies in the industry (of similar size and scope) had earnings of $500 million? Does that change your thinking? Or what if you find out that the same company had earnings of $75 million in the prior period? Does that change your mind?

Two key ratios to be aware of are

- ✔ Price-to-earnings ratio (P/E)
- ✔ Price to sales ratio (PSR)

Every investor wants to find stocks that have a 20 percent average growth rate over the past five years and have a low P/E ratio (sounds like a dream). Use stock screening tools available for free on the Internet to do your research. Many brokers have them at their Web sites (such as Charles Schwab at www. schwab.com and E*TRADE at www.etrade.com). Some excellent stock screening tools can also be found at Yahoo! (finance.yahoo.com), Business Week (www.businessweek.com), Nasdaq (www.nasdaq.com), and MarketWatch (www.marketwatch.com). A *stock screening tool* lets you plug in numbers such as sales or earnings and ratios such as the P/E ratio or the debt to equity ratio and then click! — up come stocks that fit your criteria. This is a good starting point for serious investors. Check out Appendix B for even more on ratios.

The P/E ratio

The price-to-earnings (P/E) ratio is very important in analyzing a potential stock investment because it's one of the most widely regarded barometers of a company's value, and it's usually reported along with the company's stock price in the financial page listing. The major significance of the P/E ratio is that it establishes a direct relationship between the bottom line of a company's operations — the earnings — and the stock price.

The *P* in P/E stands for the stock's current price. The *E* is for earnings per share (typically the most recent 12 months of earnings). The P/E ratio is also referred to as the "earnings multiple" or just "multiple."

You calculate the P/E ratio by dividing the price of the stock by the earnings per share. If the price of a single share of stock is $10 and the earnings (on a per-share basis) are $1, then the P/E is 10. If the stock price goes to $35 per share and the earnings are unchanged, then the P/E is 35. Basically, the higher the P/E, the more you pay for the company's earnings.

Why would you buy stock in one company with a relatively high P/E ratio instead of investing in another company with a lower P/E ratio? Keep in mind that investors buy stocks based on expectations. They may bid up the price of the stock (subsequently raising the stock's P/E ratio) because they feel that the company will have increased earnings in the near future. Perhaps they feel that the company has great potential (a pending new invention or lucrative business deal) that will eventually make it more profitable. More profitability in turn has a beneficial impact on the firm's stock price. The danger with a high P/E is that if the company doesn't achieve the hopeful results, the stock price could fall.

You should look at two types of P/E ratios to get a balanced picture of the company's value:

- ✔ **Trailing P/E:** This P/E is the most frequently quoted because it deals with existing data. The trailing P/E uses the most recent 12 months of earnings in its calculation.

- ✔ **Forward P/E:** This P/E is based on projections or expectations of earnings in the coming 12-month period. Although this P/E may seem preferable because it looks into the near future, it's still considered an estimate that may or may not prove to be accurate.

The following example illustrates the importance of the P/E ratio. Say that you want to buy a business and that I'm selling a business. If you come to me and say, "What do you have to offer?" I may say, "Have I got a deal for you! I operate a retail business downtown that sells spatulas. The business nets a cool $2,000 profit per year." You reluctantly say, "Uh, okay, what's the asking price for the business?" I reply, "You can have it for only $1 million! What do you say?"

If you're sane, odds are that you politely turn down that offer. Even though the business is profitable (a cool $2,000 a year), you'd be crazy to pay a million bucks for it. In other words, the business is way overvalued (too expensive for what you're getting in return for your investment dollars). The million dollars would generate a better rate of return elsewhere and probably with less risk. As for the business, the P/E ratio of 500 ($1 million divided by $2,000) is outrageous. This is definitely a case of an overvalued company — and a lousy investment.

What if I offered the business for $12,000? Does that price make more sense? Yes. The P/E ratio is a more reasonable 6 ($12,000 divided by $2,000). In other words, the business pays for itself in about 6 years (versus 500 years in the prior example).

Looking at the P/E ratio offers a shortcut for investors asking the question, "Is this stock overvalued?" As a general rule, the lower the P/E, the safer (or more conservative) the stock is. The reverse is more noteworthy: The higher the P/E, the greater the risk.

When someone refers to a P/E as high or low, you have to ask the question, "Compared to what?" A P/E of 30 is considered very high for a large cap electric utility but quite reasonable for a small cap, high-technology firm. Keep in mind that phrases such as "large cap" and "small cap" are just a reference to the company's market value or size (see Chapter 1 for details on these terms). "Cap" is short for "capitalization" (the total number of shares of stock outstanding times the share price).

The following basic points can help you evaluate P/E ratios:

- Compare a company's P/E ratio with its industry. Electric utility industry stocks, for example, generally have a P/E that hovers in the 9–14 range. Therefore, an electric utility with a P/E of 45 indicates that something is wrong with that utility. (I explain how to analyze industries in Chapter 13.)

- Compare a company's P/E with the general market. If you're looking at a small cap stock on the Nasdaq that has a P/E of 100 but the average P/E for established companies on the Nasdaq is 40, find out why. You should also compare the stock's P/E ratio with the P/E ratio for major indexes such as the Dow Jones Industrial Average (DJIA), the Standard & Poor's 500 (S&P 500), and the Nasdaq Composite (for more on market indexes, see Chapter 5).

- Compare a company's current P/E with recent periods (such as this year versus last year). If it currently has a P/E ratio of 20 and it previously had a P/E ratio of 30, you know that either the stock price has declined or that earnings have risen. In this case, the stock is less likely to fall. That bodes well for the stock.

- Low P/E ratios aren't necessarily a sign of a bargain, but if you're looking at a stock for many other reasons that seem positive (solid sales, strong industry, and so on) and it also has a low P/E, that's a good sign.

- High P/E ratios aren't necessarily bad, but they do mean that you should investigate further. If a company is weak and the industry is shaky, heed the high P/E as a warning sign. Frequently, a high P/E ratio means that investors have bid up a stock price, anticipating future income. The problem is that if the anticipated income doesn't materialize, the stock price could fall.

- Watch out for a stock that doesn't have a P/E ratio. In other words, it may have a price (the *P*), but it doesn't have earnings (the *E*). No earnings means no P/E, meaning that you're better off avoiding it. Can you still make money buying a stock with no earnings? You can, but you aren't investing; you're speculating.

The PSR

The price to sales ratio (PSR) is a company's stock price divided by its sales. Because the sales number is rarely expressed as a per-share figure, it's easier to divide a company's total market value (I explain what this term means earlier in this chapter) by its total sales for the last 12 months.

As a general rule, stock trading at a PSR of 1 or less is a reasonably priced stock worthy of your attention. For example, say that a company has sales of $1 billion and the stock has a total market value of $950 million. In that case, the PSR is 0.95. In other words, you can buy $1 of the company's sales for only 95 cents. All things being equal, that stock may be a bargain.

Analysts frequently use the PSR as an evaluation tool in the following circumstances:

- ✔ In tandem with other ratios to get a more well-rounded picture of the company and the stock.

- ✔ When they want an alternate way to value a business that doesn't have earnings.

- ✔ When they want a true picture of the company's financial health, because sales are tougher for companies to manipulate than earnings.

- ✔ When they're considering a company offering products (versus services). PSR is more suitable for companies that sell items that are easily counted (such as products). Firms that make their money through loans, such as banks, aren't usually valued with a PSR because deriving a usable PSR for them is more difficult.

Compare the company's PSR with other companies in the same industry, along with the industry average, so that you get a better idea of the company's relative value.

Chapter 12

Decoding Company Documents

In This Chapter
▶ Paging through an annual report
▶ Reviewing other information sources for a second opinion
▶ Organizing your own research library

inancial documents — good grief! Some people would rather suck a hospital mop than read some dry corporate or government report. Yet if you're serious about choosing stocks, you should be serious about your research. Fortunately, it's not as bad as you think (put away that disgusting mop). When you see that some basic research helps you build wealth, it gets easier.

In this chapter, I discuss the basic documents that you come across (or should come across) most often in your investing life. These documents include essential information that all investors need to know, not only at the time of the initial investment decision, but also for as long as that stock remains in their portfolio.

If you plan to hold a stock for the long haul, reading the annual report and other reports covered in this chapter will be very helpful. If you intend to get rid of the stock soon or plan to hold it only for the short term, reading these reports diligently isn't that important.

Getting a Message from the Bigwigs: The Annual Report

When you're a regular stockholder, the company sends you its annual report. If you're not already a stockholder, contact the company's shareholder service department for a hard copy.

You can often view a company's annual report at its Web site. Any major search engine can help you find it. Downloading or printing the annual report should be easy.

You need to carefully analyze an annual report to find out the following:

- ✔ **How well the company is doing.** Are earnings higher, lower, or the same as the year before? How are sales doing? These numbers should be clearly presented in the annual report's financial section.

- ✔ **Whether the company is making more money than it's spending.** How does the balance sheet look? Are assets higher or lower than the year before? Is debt growing, shrinking, or about the same as the year before? For more details on balance sheets, see Chapter 11.

- ✔ **What management's strategic plan is for the coming year.** How will management build on the company's success? This plan is usually covered in the beginning of the annual report — frequently in the letter from the chairman of the board.

Your task boils down to figuring out where the company has been, where it is now, and where it's going. As an investor, you don't need to read the annual report like a novel — from cover to cover. Instead, approach it like a newspaper and jump around to the relevant sections to get the answers you need to decide whether you should buy or hold onto the stock. I describe the makeup of the annual report and proxy materials in the following sections.

Analyzing the annual report's anatomy

Not every company puts its annual report together in exactly the same way — the style of presentation varies. Some annual reports have gorgeous graphics or coupons for the company's products, while others are in a standard black-and-white typeface with no cosmetic frills at all. But every annual report does include common basic content, such as the income statement and the balance sheet. The following sections present typical components of an average annual report. (Keep in mind that not every annual report will have the sections in the same order.)

The letter from the chairman of the board

The first thing you see is usually the letter from the chairman of the board. It's the "Dear Stockholder" letter that communicates views from the head muckety-muck. The chairman's letter is designed to put the best possible perspective on the company's operations during the past year. Be aware of this bias; no one in upper management wants to panic stockholders. If the company is doing well, the letter will certainly point it out. If the company is having hard times, the letter will probably put a positive spin on the company's difficulties. If the *Titanic* had an annual report, odds are that the last letter would have reported, "Great news! A record number of our customers participated in our spontaneous moonlight swimming program. In addition, we confidently project no operating expenses whatsoever for the subsequent fiscal quarter." You get the point.

To get a good idea of what issues the company's management team feels are important and what goals they want to accomplish, keep the following questions in mind:

- ✔ What does the letter say about changing conditions in the company's business? How about in the industry?

- ✔ If any difficulties exist, does the letter communicate a clear and logical action plan (cutting costs, closing money-losing plants, and so on) to get the company back on a positive track?

- ✔ What's being highlighted and why? For example, is the firm focusing on research and development for new products or on a new deal with China?

- ✔ Does the letter offer apologies for anything the company did? If, for example, it fell short of sales expectations, does the letter offer a reason for the shortcoming?

- ✔ Did the company make (or will it make) new acquisitions or major developments (selling products to China, or a new marketing agreement with a Fortune 500 company)?

You should read an annual report (or any messages from upper management) in the same way you read or hear anything from a politician — be more concerned with means than ends. In other words, don't tell me what the goal is (greater profitability, or peace on earth), tell me how you're going to get there. Executives may say that "we will increase sales and profits," but saying "we will increase sales and profits by doing X, Y, and Z" is a better message, because you can then decide for yourself if the road map makes sense.

The company's offerings

This section of an annual report can have various titles (such as "Sales and Marketing"), but it generally covers what the company sells. You should understand the products or services (or both) that the business sells and why customers purchase them. If you don't understand what the company offers, then understanding how it earns money, which is the driving force behind its stock, is more difficult.

Are the company's core or primary offerings selling well? If the earnings of McDonald's are holding steady but earnings strictly from burgers and fries are fizzling, that's a cause for concern. If a business ceases making money from its specialty, you should become cautious. Here are some other questions to ask:

- ✔ How does the company distribute its offerings — through a Web site, malls, representatives, or some other means? Does it sell only to the U.S. market, or is its distribution international? Generally, the greater the distribution, the greater the potential sales and, ultimately, the higher the stock price.

- ✔ Are most of the company's sales to a definable marketplace? For example, if most of the sales are to a war-torn or politically unstable country, you should worry. If the company's customers aren't doing well, that has a direct impact on the company and, eventually, its stock.

- ✔ How are sales doing versus market standards? In other words, is the company doing better than the industry average? Is it a market leader in what it offers? The firm should be doing better than (or as well as) its peers in the industry. If the company is falling behind its competitors, that doesn't bode well for the stock in the long run.

- ✔ Does the report include information on the company's competitors and related matters? You should know who the company's competitors are because they have a direct effect on the company's success. If customers are choosing the competitor over your firm, the slumping sales and earnings will ultimately hurt the stock's price.

Financial statements

Look over the various financial statements and find the relevant numbers. Every annual report should have (at the very least) a balance sheet and an income statement. Catching the important numbers on a financial statement isn't that difficult to do. However, it certainly helps when you pick up some basic accounting knowledge. Chapter 11 can give you more details on evaluating financial statements.

First, review the income statement (also known as the profit and loss statement, or simply P&L). It gives you the company's sales, expenses, and the result (net income or net loss). Next, look at the balance sheet. It provides a snapshot of a point in time (annual reports usually provide a year-end balance sheet) that tells you what the company owns (assets), what it owes (liabilities), and the end result (net worth). For a healthy company, assets should always be greater than liabilities.

Carefully read the footnotes to the financial statements. Sometimes big changes are communicated in small print. In current times, especially be wary of small print pointing out other debt or derivatives. *Derivatives* are complicated and (lately) very risky vehicles. Problems with derivatives were one of the major causes of the market turmoil that destroyed financial firms on

Wall Street during late 2008. AIG, for example, is a major insurer that had to be bailed out by the Federal Reserve before it went bankrupt (shareholders suffered huge losses).

Summary of past financial figures

The summary of past financial figures gives you a snapshot of the company's overall long-term progress. How many years does the annual report summarize? Some reports summarize three years, while most go back two years.

Management issues

The annual report's management issues section includes a reporting of current trends and issues, such as new developments happening in the industry that affect the company. See whether you agree with management's assessment of economic and market conditions that affect the firm's prospects. What significant developments in society does management perceive as affecting the company's operations? Does the report include information on current or pending lawsuits?

CPA opinion letter

Annual reports typically include comments from the company's independent accounting firm. It may be an opinion letter or a simple paragraph with the accounting firm's views regarding the financial statements.

The CPA opinion letter should offer an opinion about the accuracy of the financial data presented and information on how the statements were prepared. Check to see whether the letter includes any footnotes regarding changes in certain numbers or how they were reported. For example, a company that wants to report higher earnings may use a conservative method of measuring depreciation instead of a more aggressive approach. In any case, you should verify the numbers by looking at the company's 10K document filed with the Securities and Exchange Commission (SEC; I describe this document in more detail later in this chapter).

Company identity data

The company identity data section informs you about the company's subsidiaries (or lesser businesses that it owns), brands, and addresses. It also contains standard data such as the headquarters location and names of directors and officers. Many reports also include data on the directors' and officers' positions in stock ownership at year's end.

Stock data

The stock data section may include a history of the stock price, along with information such as what exchange the stock is listed on, the stock symbol, the company's dividend reinvestment plan (if any), and so on. It also includes information on stockholder services and who to contact for further information.

Going through the proxy materials

As a shareholder (or stockholder — same thing), you're entitled to vote at the annual shareholders meeting. If you ever get the opportunity to attend one, do so. You get to meet other shareholders and ask questions of management and other company representatives. Usually, the shareholder services department provides you with complete details. At the meetings, shareholders vote on company matters, such as approving the new accounting firm or deciding whether a proposed merger with another company will go forward.

If you can't attend (which is usually true for the majority of shareholders), you can vote by proxy. *Voting by proxy* essentially means that you vote by mail. You indicate your votes on the proxy statement (or card) and authorize a representative to vote at the meeting on your behalf. The proxy statement is usually sent to all shareholders, along with the annual report, just before the meeting.

Getting a Second Opinion

A wealth of valuable information is available for your investing pursuits. The resources in this section are just a representative few — a good representation, though. To get a more balanced view of the company and its prospects, take a look at several different sources of information for the stocks you're researching.

The information and research they provide can be expensive if you buy or subscribe on your own, but fortunately, most of the resources mentioned are usually available in the business reference section of a well-stocked public library.

Company documents filed with the SEC

The serious investor doesn't overlook the wealth of information that he can cull from documents filed with the SEC. Take the time and effort to review these documents, because they offer great insight regarding the company's activities.

Here's how to obtain the main documents that investors should be aware of:

✔ **Drop by the company itself.** Stockholder service departments keep these publicly available documents on hand and usually give them out at no cost to interested parties.

✔ **Visit the SEC, either in person or online.** These documents are available for public viewing at the SEC offices. You can find out more by contacting the Securities and Exchange Commission, Publications Unit, 450 Fifth St. NW, Washington, DC 20549.

At the SEC's Web site (`www.sec.gov`), you can check out EDGAR (Electronic Data Gathering, Analysis, and Retrieval system) to search public documents filed. It's a tremendous source of documents that date back to 1994. You can search, print, or download documents very easily. Documents can be located either by document number or keyword search.

✔ **Check out the Public Register's Annual Report Service (`www.prars.com`).** This organization maintains an extensive collection of annual reports.

✔ **Review the Annual Report Service (`www.annualreportservice.com`).** This site maintains an extensive database of annual reports.

✔ **Use *The Wall Street Journal* free annual report service.** If you read this newspaper's financial pages and see a company with the club symbol (like the one you see on a playing card), then you can order that company's annual report by calling 800-654-2582 or visiting the Web site (`www.wsj.com`).

Form 10K

Gee, how intimidating. Just the report name alone makes you scratch your head. To some people, 10K refers to running a race of 10 kilometers. But if you're reading (not running) a 10K, you may wish you were running one instead.

Form 10K is a report that companies must file with the SEC annually. It works like the annual report that you get from the company, except that it provides more detailed financial information. It can be a little intimidating because the text can be dry and cumbersome. It's not exactly Shakespeare (although 10K reports would've also driven Lady Macbeth insane); then again, the data isn't laden with as much spin as the annual report the company sends to shareholders. Without going crazy, go through each section of the 10K. Take some extra time to scrutinize the section on financial data. Ask the same questions that you do when you're looking at the annual report.

The following Web sites can help you make sense of 10K reports:

✔ FreeEDGAR (`www.freeedgar.com`)

✔ 10K Wizard (`www.10Kwizard.com`)

✔ Edgar Online, Inc. (`www.edgar-online.com`)

Form 10Q

This form is a quarterly report that gives you the same basic information as the 10K, but it details only three months' worth of activity. Because a long time can pass between 10Ks (after all, it is a year), don't wait 12 months to see how your company is progressing. Make a habit of seeing how the company is doing by comparing its recent 10Q with one that covers the same quarter last year. Is the profit higher or lower? How about sales? Debt?

Keep in mind that not every company has the same fiscal year. A company with a calendar year fiscal year (ending December 31) files a 10Q for each of the first three quarters and files a 10K for the final quarter. The company reports its fourth quarter data in the 10K, along with the statistics for the full year.

Insider reports

Two types of insiders exist: those who work within a company and those outside the company who have a significant (10 percent or more) ownership of company stock. Tracking insider activity is very profitable for investors who want to follow in the footsteps of the people in the know. See Chapter 20 for information about monitoring and benefiting from insider activity.

Every time an insider (such as the CEO or controller) buys or sells stock, the transaction has to be reported to the SEC. The insider actually reports the trade prior to transacting it. These reports are publicly available documents that allow you to see what the insiders are actually doing. Hearing what they say in public is one thing, but seeing what they're actually doing with their stock transactions is more important.

Value Line

The Value Line Investment Survey, one of many information products provided by Value Line Publishing, Inc., is considered a longtime favorite by many stock investing professionals. You can look it over at any library that has a good business reference department. In the survey, Value Line covers the largest public companies and ranks them according to financial strength and several other key business factors. To get more information about Value Line, either head to the library or visit www.valueline.com.

Standard & Poor's

Another ubiquitous and venerable publisher is Standard & Poor's (S&P). Although it has a number of quality information products and services for both individual and institutional investors, the three you should take a look at are the following:

✔ *S&P Stock Reports:* Available at many libraries, this guide comes out periodically and reports on stocks on the New York Stock Exchange, American Stock Exchange, and the largest firms listed on Nasdaq. It gives a succinct, two-page summary of each stock, offering a snapshot of the company's current finances, along with a brief history and commentary on the company's activities. This guide also rates companies based on their financial strength.

✔ *The S&P Industry Survey:* S&P gives detailed reports on the top industries, cramming a lot of information about a given industry in four to seven pages. This annual publication provides a nice summary of what's happened in each industry in the past 12 months, what the industry looks like today, and what the prospects are for the coming year. It also provides the important numbers (earnings, sales, and industry ranking) for the top 50 to 100 firms in each industry.

✔ *S&P Bond Reports:* Yes, I know this book is about stocks. But a company's bond rating is invaluable for stock investors. S&P analyzes the strength of the bond issuer and ranks the bond for creditworthiness. If S&P gives a company a high rating, you have added assurance that the company is financially strong. You want the company to have a bond rating of AAA, AA, or A, because these ratings tell you that the company is "investment-grade."

Check out S&P's Web site at www.standardandpoors.com for more information about its publications.

Moody's Investment Service

Another stalwart publisher, Moody's offers vital research on stocks and bonds. *Moody's Handbook of Common Stocks* is usually available in the reference section of a well-stocked library. It offers stock and bond guides similar to S&P and also provides an independent bond-rating service. A stock rated highly by both Moody's and S&P is a great choice for investors hunting for value investments.

Brokerage reports: The good, the bad, and the ugly

Clint Eastwood, where are you? Traditionally, brokerage reports have been a good source of information for investors seeking informed opinions about stocks. And they still are, but in recent years some brokers have been penalized for biased reports. Brokers should never be the sole source of information. Otherwise, Clint may ask them whether they're lucky punks.

The good

Research departments at brokerage firms provide stock reports and make them available for their clients and investment publications. The firms' analysts and market strategists generally prepare these reports. Good research is critical, and brokerage reports can be very valuable. What better source of guidance than full-time experts backed up by million-dollar research departments? Brokerage reports have some strong points:

- ✔ The analysts are professionals who should understand the value of a company and its stock. They analyze and compare company data every day.

- ✔ They have at their disposal tremendous information and historical data that they can sift through to make informed decisions.

- ✔ If you have an account with the firm, you can usually access the information at no cost.

The bad

Well, brokerage reports may not be bad in every case, but at their worst, they're quite bad. Brokers make their money from commissions and investment banking fees (nothing bad here). However, they can find themselves in the awkward position of issuing brokerage reports on companies that are (or could be) customers of the brokerage firm that employs them (hmmm — could be bad). Frequently, this relationship results in a brokerage report that paints an overly positive picture of a company that can be a bad investment (yup, that's bad).

The ugly

During 1998–2000, an overwhelming number of brokerage reports issued glowing praise of companies that were either mediocre or dubious. Investors bought up stocks such as tech stocks and Internet stocks. The sheer demand pushed up stock prices, which gave the appearance of genius to analysts' forecasts, yet the stock prices rose essentially as a self-fulfilling prophecy. The stocks were way overvalued and were cruisin' for a bruisin.' Analysts and investors were feeling lucky.

Investors, however, lost a ton of money (ooh, ugly). Money that people painstakingly accumulated over many years of work vanished in a matter of months as the bear market of 2000 hit (ooh, ugly). Retirees who had trusted the analysts saw nest eggs lose 40 to 70 percent in value (yikes, very ugly). In total, investors lost over $5 trillion during 2000–2002, much of it needlessly.

During that bear market, a record number of lawsuits and complaints were filed against brokerage firms. Wall Street and Main Street learned some tough lessons. Regarding research reports from brokerage firms, the following points can help you avoid getting a bad case of the uglies:

✔ Always ask yourself, "Is the provider of the report a biased source?" In other words, is the broker getting business in any way from the company he's recommending?

✔ Never, never, NEVER rely on just one source of information, especially if it's the same source that's selling you the stock or other investment.

✔ Do your research first before you rely on a brokerage report.

✔ Do your due diligence before you buy stocks anyway. Look at the chapters in Parts I and II to understand your need for diversification, risk tolerance, and so on.

✔ Verify the information provided to you with a trip to the library or Web sites (see Appendix A).

Although I generally don't rely on Wall Street brokerage analysts, I do track some independent investment analysts. You'll find some of my favorites mentioned in Appendix A.

Compiling Your Own Research Department

You don't need to spend an excessive amount of time or money, but you should maintain your own library of resources. You may only need one shelf (or a small amount of memory on your computer's hard drive), but why not have a few investment facts and resources at your fingertips? I maintain my own library loaded with books, magazines, newsletters, and tons of great stuff downloaded on my computer for easy search and reference. When you start your own collection, follow these tips:

✔ Keep some select newspapers. *Barron's, The Wall Street Journal,* and *Investor's Business Daily* regularly have some editions that are worth keeping. For example, *The Wall Street Journal* and *Investor's Business Daily* usually publish a year-in-review issue the first business week in January. *Barron's* has special issues reviewing brokers and financial Web sites.

✔ Subscribe to financial magazines. Publications such as *Forbes* and *SmartMoney* offer great research and regularly review stocks, brokers, and resources for investors.

✔ Keep annual reports. Regarding the stocks that are the core holdings in your portfolio, keep all the annual reports (at the very least, the most recent three).

✔ Go to the library's business reference section periodically to stay updated. Hey, you pay the taxes that maintain the public library — you may as well use it to stay informed.

✔ Use the Internet for research. The Web offers plenty of great sites to peruse; I list some of the best in Appendix A.

Financial reports are very important and easier to read than most people think. An investor can easily avoid a bad investment by simply noticing the data in what seems like a jumble of numbers. Figure out how to read them. For a great book to help you with reading financial reports (without needless technicality), check out *How to Read a Financial Report: Wringing Vital Signs Out of the Numbers,* 6th Edition, by John A. Tracy (published by Wiley).

Chapter 13

Analyzing Industries

· ·

In This Chapter

▶ Selecting industries by asking a few important questions

▶ Keeping an eye on four major industries

· ·

Suppose that you have to bet your entire nest egg on a one-mile race. All you need to do is select a winning group. Your choices are the following:

Group A: Thoroughbred race horses

Group B: Overweight Elvis impersonators

Group C: Lethargic snails

This isn't a trick question, and you have one minute to answer. Notice that I didn't ask you to pick a single winner out of a giant mush of horses, Elvii, and snails; I only asked you to pick the winning group in the race. The obvious answer is the thoroughbred race horses (and no, they weren't ridden by the overweight Elvis impersonators because that would take away from the eloquent point being made). In this example, even the slowest member of group A easily outdistances the fastest member of either group B or C.

Industries, like groups A, B, and C in my example, aren't equal, and life isn't fair. After all, if life were fair, Elvis would be alive and the impersonators wouldn't exist. Fortunately, picking stocks doesn't have to be as difficult as picking a winning racehorse. The basic point is that it's easier to pick a successful stock from a group of winners (a growing, vibrant industry). Understanding industries only enhances your stock-picking strategy.

A successful, long-term investor looks at the industry just as carefully as he looks at the individual stock. Luckily, choosing a winning industry to invest in is easier than choosing individual stocks, as you find out in this chapter. I know some investors who can pick a winning stock in a losing industry, and I also know investors who've chosen a losing stock in a winning industry (the former is far outnumbered by the latter). Just think how well you do when you choose a great stock in a great industry! Of course, if you repeatedly choose bad stocks in bad industries, you may as well get out of the stock market altogether (maybe your calling is instead to be a celebrity impersonator!).

Interrogating the Industries

Your common sense is an important tool in choosing industries with winning stocks. The following sections explore some of the most important questions to ask yourself when you're choosing an industry.

Keep in mind that an industry isn't the same as a sector. Even some market pros use the two words almost interchangeably. A *sector* is basically a "mega-industry," or a group of interrelated industries. For example, pharmaceuticals and HMOs are each an industry, but both are part of the healthcare sector. An *industry* is typically a category of business that performs a precise activity (such as manufacturing computer chips, or trucking). Not all industries in a sector perform equally in the same market conditions. See Chapter 14 for full details on sectors.

Which category does the industry fall into?

Most industries can neatly be placed in one of two categories: cyclical and defensive. In a rough way, these categories generally translate into what society wants and what it needs. Society buys what it *wants* when times are good and holds off when times are bad. It buys what it *needs* in both good and bad times. A want is a "like to have," while a need is a "must have." Kapish?

Cyclical industries

Cyclical industries are industries whose fortunes rise and fall with the economy's rise and fall. In other words, if the economy is doing well and the stock market is doing well, consumers and investors are confident and tend to spend and invest more money than usual, so cyclical industries tend to do well. Real estate and automobiles are great examples of cyclical industries.

Your own situation offers you some common-sense insight into the concept of cyclical industries. Think about your behavior as a consumer and you get a revealing clue into the thinking of millions of consumers. When you (and millions of others) feel good about your career, your finances, and your future, you have a greater tendency to buy more (and/or more expensive) stuff. When people feel financially strong, they're more apt to buy a new house or car or make some other large financial commitment. Also, people take on more debt because they feel confident that they can pay it back. In light of this behavior, what industries do you think would do well?

The same point holds for business spending. When businesses think that economic times are good and foresee continuing good times, they tend to spend more money on large purchases such as new equipment or technology. They think that when they're doing well and are flush with financial success, it's a good idea to reinvest that money in the business to increase future success.

Defensive industries

Defensive industries are industries that produce goods and services that are needed no matter what's happening in the economy. Your common sense kicks in here, too. What do you buy even when times are tough? Think about what millions of people buy no matter how bad the economy gets. A good example is food — people still need to eat regardless of good or bad times. Other examples of defensive industries are utilities and healthcare.

In bad economic times, defensive stocks tend to do better than cyclical stocks. However, when times are good, cyclical stocks tend to do better than defensive stocks. Defensive stocks don't do as well in good times because people don't eat twice as much or use up more electricity.

So how do defensive stocks grow? Their growth generally relies on two factors:

- **Population growth:** As more and more consumers are born, more people become available to buy.

- **New markets:** A company can grow by seeking out new groups of consumers to buy their products and services. Coca-Cola, for example, found new markets in Asia during the 1990s. As communist regimes fell from power and more societies embraced a free market and consumer goods, the company sold more beverages, and its stock soared.

One way to invest in a particular industry is to take advantage of exchange-traded funds (ETFs), which have become very popular in recent years. ETFs are structured much like mutual funds but are fixed portfolios that trade like a stock. If you find a winning industry but you can't find a winning stock (or don't want to bother with the necessary research), then ETFs are a great consideration. You can find out more about ETFs at the American Stock Exchange Web site (www.amex.com).

Is the industry growing?

The question may seem obvious, but you still need to ask it before you purchase stock. The saying "the trend is your friend" applies when choosing an industry in which to invest, as long as the trend is an upward one. If you look at three different stocks that are equal in every significant way but you find that stock A is in an industry growing 15 percent per year while the other two stocks are in industries that have either little growth or are shrinking, which stock would you choose?

Sometimes the stock of a financially unsound or poorly run company goes up dramatically because the industry it's in is very exciting to the public. The most obvious example is Internet stocks from 1998–2000. Stocks such as Pets. com shot up to incredible heights because investors thought the Internet was the place to be. Sooner or later, however, the measure of a successful company is its ability to be profitable (Pets.com went bankrupt in 2000). Serious investors look at the company's fundamentals (see Chapter 11 to find out how to do this) and the prospects for the industry's growth before settling on a particular stock.

To judge how well an industry is doing, various information sources monitor all the major industries and measure their progress. The more reliable sources include the following:

- MarketWatch (www.marketwatch.com)
- Standard & Poor's (www.standardpoor.com)
- Hoover's (www.hoovers.com)
- Yahoo! Finance (http://finance.yahoo.com)
- *The Wall Street Journal* (www.wsj.com)

The preceding sources generally give you in-depth information about the major industries. Visit their Web sites to read their current research and articles along with links to relevant sites for more details. For example, *The Wall Street Journal* (published by Dow Jones & Co.), whose Web site is updated daily, publishes indexes for all the major sectors and industries so that you can get a useful snapshot of how well an industry is doing, including information about whether a stock is up or down and how it's performing year-to-date.

Standard and Poor's (S&P) Industry Survey is an especially excellent source of information on U.S. industries. Besides ranking and comparing industries and informing you about their current prospects, the survey also lists the top companies by size, sales, earnings, and other key information. What I like is that each industry is covered in a few pages, so you get the critical information you need without reading a novel. The survey and other S&P publications are available on the S&P Web site or in the business reference section of most libraries (your best bet is to head for the library because the survey is rather expensive).

Are the industry's products or services in demand?

Look at the products and services that an industry provides. Do they look like things that society will continue to want? Are there products and services on the horizon that could replace them? Does the industry face a danger of potential obsolescence?

When evaluating future demand, look for a *sunrise industry* — one that's new or emerging or has promising appeal for the future. Good examples of sunrise industries in recent years are biotech and Internet companies. In contrast, a *sunset industry* is one that's either declining or has little potential for growth. For example, you probably shouldn't invest in the videocassette manufacturing industry as demand for DVDs increases. Owning stock in a strong, profitable company in a sunrise industry is obviously the most desirable choice.

Current research unveils the following megatrends:

- **The aging of the U.S.:** More senior citizens than ever before will be living in the U.S. Because of this fact, financial and healthcare services will prosper.

- **Advances in high technology:** Internet, telecom, medical, and biotechnology innovations will continue.

- **Increasing need for basic materials:** As society advances here and in the rest of the world, building blocks such as metals and other precious commodities will be in demand.

- **Security concerns:** Terrorism and other international tensions mean more attention for national defense, homeland security, and related matters.

- **Energy challenges:** Traditional and nontraditional sources of energy (such as solar, fuel cells, and so on) will demand society's attention as it faces Peak Oil (shrinking supplies of the world's available cheap crude oil; see Chapter 14 for details).

What does the industry's growth rely on?

An industry doesn't exist in a vacuum. External factors weigh heavily on its ability to survive and thrive. Does the industry rely on an established megatrend? Then it will probably be strong for a while. Does it rely on factors that are losing relevance? Then it may begin to decline soon. Technological and demographic changes are other factors that may contribute to an industry's growth or fall.

Perhaps the industry offers great new medical products for senior citizens. What are the prospects for growth? The graying of the U.S. is an established megatrend. As millions of Americans climb past age 50, profitable opportunities await companies that are prepared to cater to them.

Is the industry dependent on another industry?

This twist on the prior question is a reminder that industries frequently are intertwined and can become codependent. When one industry suffers, you may find it helpful to understand which industries will subsequently suffer. The reverse can also be true — when one industry is doing well, other industries may reap the benefits.

In either case, if the stock you choose is in an industry that's highly dependent on other industries, you should know about it. If you're considering stocks of resort companies and you see the headlines blaring, "Airlines losing money as public stops flying," what do you do? This type of question forces you to think logically and consider cause and effect. Logic and common sense are powerful tools that frequently trump all the number-crunching activity performed by analysts.

Who are the leading companies in the industry?

After you've chosen the industry, what types of companies do you want to invest in? You can choose from two basic types:

- ✔ **Established leaders:** These companies are considered industry leaders or have a large share of the market. Investing in these companies is the safer way to go; what better choice for novice investors than companies that have already proven themselves?

- ✔ **Innovators:** If the industry is hot and you want to be more aggressive in your approach, investigate companies that offer new products, patents, or technologies. These companies are probably smaller but have a greater potential for growth in a proven industry.

Is the industry a target of government action?

You need to know if the government is targeting an industry, because intervention by politicians and bureaucrats (rightly or wrongly) can have an impact on an industry's economic situation. For example, would you invest in a tobacco company now that the government has issued all its regulations and warnings?

Investors need to take heed when political "noise" starts coming out about a particular industry. An industry can be hurt either by direct government intervention or by the threat of it. Intervention can take the form of lawsuits, investigations, taxes, regulations, or sometimes an outright ban. In any case, being on the wrong end of government intervention is the greatest external threat to a company's survival.

Sometimes, government action helps an industry. Generally, beneficial action takes two forms:

- **Deregulation and/or tax decreases:** Government sometimes reduces burdens on an industry. In 1979, the federal government deregulated the airlines, an action that caused a boom in travel. The airline industry subsequently experienced tremendous growth because more people flew than ever before. This increase in the number of airline passengers spurred growth for the lodging and resort industries. Likewise, telecom deregulation in the mid-1990s helped that industry to boom.

- **Direct funding:** Government has the power to steer taxpayer money toward business as well. In recent years, federal and state governments have provided tax credits and other incentives for alternative energy such as solar power.

Outlining Key Industries

Not all industries go up and down in tandem. Indeed, at any given time, some industry is successful no matter what's happening with the general economy. In fact, investors have made a lot of money simply by choosing an industry that benefits from economic trends.

For example, the economy was in bad shape during the 1970s. It was a period of *stagflation* — low growth, high unemployment, and high inflation. This decade was the worst time for the economy since the Great Depression;

most industries (and therefore most stocks) were having tough times. But some industries did well — in fact, some flourished. Real estate and precious metals, for example, performed well in this environment. Because the inflation rate soared into double digits, inflationary hedges such as gold and silver did very well. During the '70s, gold skyrocketed from $35 an ounce to $850 an ounce over the course of the decade. Silver went from under $2 to over $50 in the same period. What do you think happened to stocks of gold and silver mining companies? That's right — they skyrocketed as well. Gold stocks gave investors spectacular returns.

In the 1980s, the economy was rejuvenated when taxes were cut, regulations were decreased, and inflation fell. Most industries did well, but even in a growing economy, some industries struggle. Examples of industries that struggled during that time include precious metals and energy stocks.

Now fast forward to 2008. Think about the industries that have recently struggled and those that have performed well during the past few years. Stocks involved in energy, agriculture, and general commodities have done very well. In the same time frame, industries like airlines, housing, and financials (such as banks and brokerage firms) have had a rough time. Choosing the right industries (or avoiding the wrong ones) has always been a major factor in successful stock picking.

In the following sections, I list some of the largest industries you can invest in and provide tips on how to tell when they're doing well . . . and not so well. (To research these industries, use the resources mentioned earlier in this chapter, as well as those listed in Appendix A.)

Moving in: Real estate

I include real estate as a key industry because it's a cyclical *bellwether industry* — one that has a great effect on many other industries that may be dependent on it. Real estate is looked at as a key component of economic health because so many other industries — including building materials, mortgages, household appliances, and contract labor services — are tied to it. A booming real estate industry bodes well for much of the economy.

Housing starts are one way to measure real estate activity. This data is an important leading indicator of health in the industry. Housing starts indicate new construction, which means more business for related industries.

Keep an eye on the real estate industry for negative news that could be bearish for the economy and the stock market. Because real estate is purchased with mortgage money, investors and analysts watch the mortgage market for trouble signs such as rising delinquencies and foreclosures. These statistics serve as a warning for general economic weakness.

In recent years, the real estate mania hit its zenith during 2005–2006. A *mania* is typically the final (and craziest) part of a mature bull market. In a mania, the prices of the assets experiencing the bull market (such as stock or real estate) skyrocket to extreme levels, which excites more and more investors to jump in, causing prices to rise even further. It gets to the point where seemingly everyone thinks that it's easy to get rich by buying this particular asset, and almost no one notices that the market has become unsustainable. After prices are exhausted and start to level off, investor excitement dies down, and then investors try to exit by selling their holdings to realize some profit. As more and more sell off their holdings, demand decreases while supply increases. The mania dissipates and the bear market appears. This is definitely what happened to real estate in 2007–2008, when the industry fell on hard times as the housing bubble popped.

Driving it home: Automotive

Cars are big-ticket items and are another barometer of people's economic well-being — people buy new cars when they're doing well financially. When sales of cars are up, it's usually a positive indicator for the economy.

Conversely, trouble in the auto industry is a red flag for trouble in the general economy. For instance, an increase in auto repossessions and car loan delinquencies translates to a warning about general economic weakness. During 2007–2008, some major difficulty definitely showed up in the auto industry as GM and Ford experienced financial troubles. When the auto industry struggles, other industries tied to it also struggle. These include consumer credit and numerous manufacturing subcategories that cater to the auto industry (such as base metals and electrical components).

Talking tech: Computers and related electronics

In recent years, technology stocks have become very popular with investors. Indeed, technology is a great sector, and its impact on the economy's present and future success can't be underestimated. The share price of technology companies can rise substantially because investors buy shares based on expectations — today's untested, unproven companies may become the Googles and Apples of tomorrow.

In spite of the sector's potential, companies can still fail if customers don't embrace their products. Even in technology stocks, you still must apply the rules and guidelines about financially successful companies that I discuss throughout this book. Pick the best in a growing industry and you'll succeed over the long haul. But because technology still hasn't recovered from its recent bear market, weakness in the industry means that investors need to be very picky and cautious.

Banking on it: Financials

Banking and financial services are an intrinsic part of any economy. Debt is the most telling sign of this industry for investors. If a company's debt is growing faster than the economy, you need to watch how that debt impacts stocks and mutual funds. If debt gets out of control, it can be disastrous for the economy. As credit specialist Doug Noland points out (you can find his column at www.prudentbear.com), the amount of debt and debt-related securities recently reached historic and troublesome levels. This trend means that many financial stocks are at risk if a recession hits anytime soon. As this book goes to press, financial stocks have experienced a tough market as debt and defaults on debt (like subprime debt) have become head-line news. Because this is a multitrillion-dollar issue and it weighs heavily across the economic landscape, problems will persist well into the future, and investors should avoid this sector or be very wary and selective.

Chapter 14

Emerging Sector Opportunities

. . . .

In This Chapter

▶ Checking out bullish opportunities

▶ Understanding your bearish opportunities

▶ Getting investment pointers for your unique situation

. . . .

I'm thrilled to include this chapter again in this 3rd edition of *Stock Investing For Dummies*. Had you read this chapter in the previous edition and acted accordingly, you could have made a fortune (I kid you not). So I think that it earns an encore. A lot of this book is about making your own decisions and doing your own research, but what the heck — if I can save you some time and effort, why not? You can thank me later. Anyway, it's time to make you privy to what my research tells me are unfolding megatrends that offer the greatest potential rewards (or risks) for stock investors.

Only a handful of changes in your portfolio over the past four decades would have made you tremendously rich. Had you put your money into natural resources (such as gold, silver, and oil) at the beginning of the 1970s and stayed put until the end of the decade, you would have made a fortune. Then, had you cashed in and switched to Japanese stocks in 1980 and held them for the rest of the decade, you would have made another fortune. Then, had you switched in 1990 to U.S. stocks for the entire decade, you would have made yet another fortune. What if you had cashed in your stocks in 2000? Well, for starters, you would have avoided huge losses in the down bear market. How about being bullish? What looks like a strong bull market for this decade?

By and large, this decade seems to be a repeat of the '70s. The general realm of natural resources looks to be the primary bull market for this decade. Why? First, look at what this decade has in common with the '70s:

 ✔ Problems with energy (rising costs, supply disruptions, and so on)

 ✔ Rising inflation (as the dollar and other currencies are increased in supply)

- International conflict (Iraq, Afghanistan, Iran, and so on)
- Sluggish or recessionary domestic economy
- Rising prices for natural resources (grains, metals, energy, lumber, and so on)

However, this decade has more to consider, including the following:

- Debt, debt, and more debt ($49 trillion as of September 2008, and three and a half times the U.S. gross domestic product (GDP) total of $14 trillion). The U.S. is now the world's largest debtor nation.
- The U.S. as a major importer (versus being an exporter in the '70s)
- China, Russia, Brazil, and India as major economic competitors (and consumers of resources)
- The threat of terrorism affecting the U.S. within its borders
- $600 + trillion worth of derivatives (20 times larger than the world's total GDP)! Many of these derivatives, which are complicated investment vehicles, are arcane and ultra-risky.
- Social Security and Medicare liabilities that are now projected to exceed $90 trillion (rising costs started in 2008 as the oldest baby boomers started to retire at age 62, and they'll escalate in 2011 and beyond as many turn 65).

This list isn't comprehensive (due to space limitations). The preceding points are enough to make you understand that this investing environment has changed dramatically, and you need to refocus your overall game plan to keep your money growing. It also makes you want to race off to Gilligan's island!

You'll see two types of opportunities in this chapter: bullish and bearish. I think that you would also benefit from reading Chapter 13 on industries as well. If I can't help you find the winning stocks, then by golly I can at least show you what potential problem areas to stay away from.

Bullish Opportunities

Being bullish (or going "long") is the natural inclination for most investors. It's an easy concept — buy low, sell high. No rocket science there. The following sections don't identify every bullish opportunity, but they do cover the most obvious ones (at least to me).

In the examples in the following sections, I reference time frames of several years. Why? You would have seen these stocks dip by 10 or 20 percent or more over a given short time frame such as a few weeks or a few months. But investing wisely means that time ultimately will get the stock price to higher ground, especially if you ride the megatrends.

As you research this area for places to help your investments grow, let me just mention two words that should guide you along the way: human need. As long as most (or even all) of your portfolio is geared toward those goods and services that the public will need no matter how good or bad the economy is, you should do well in the long run. Remember, not *want,* but *need* — it's a safer bet in the coming years.

Commodities

Two countries that figure to have a mega-impact on the world in the near future are China and India. In the past ten years, these countries have put their economies on the fast track. Consider the following:

- ✔ They've generally turned away from socialism and a command economy and have turned to a free market or more capitalistic system.
- ✔ Industrialization, privatization, and profit incentives have ignited tremendous booms in these countries.
- ✔ Both nations' populations have continued to grow, with nearly 3 billion people combined.

What do these facts mean for stock investors? Somebody has to sell them what they need. China, for example, has a voracious appetite for natural resources like building materials, energy, copper, grain, and so on. Companies that have provided these needed goods and services do very well. Take, for example, Bunge Limited (BG). You could have bought BG in late 2005 for about $39 per share. As of September 2008, BG hit $70 for a nice gain of 79 percent (not including dividends). In that same time frame, the S&P 500 was only up by about 3 percent (basically flat for three years).

Another great example is Reliance Steel & Aluminum Co. (RS). It provides the building blocks of infrastructure that society needs for bridges and other structures. This steel stock was a real steal at about $18 per share in late 2005. In September 2008, it was at $47 for a total gain of over 160 percent, while the S&P 500 floundered in the same time frame. Though many (most?) investors saw their portfolios go up a little, down a little, or flatline, resource investors saw their stocks do very well.

Of course, China and India are only a part of the world's emerging markets, but they're certainly the most important to Americans (in terms of economic impact). They are indeed megatrends that will either help (or hurt) your portfolio. In the coming years, demand will likely continue to be strong, and investors will see the obvious positive implications for solid companies that meet this demand.

To find out more, check out the resources in Appendix A, such as Jim Rogers's book entitled *Hot Commodities*. You can also conduct research at sites such as www.futuresource.com, the commodities section of www.marketwatch.com, and www.bloomberg.com.

Oil and gas

As I write this, triple-digit prices for oil and $4-per-gallon gas have become startling realities. Recent headlines tell me that the costs of energy are a major challenge for the economy. For decades, U.S. society has benefited from cheap oil, but global supply and demand (among other things) have caught up with us. A barrel of oil has gone from $67 in August 2005 to $116 only three years later (an increase of 74 percent). Gasoline has experienced a similar rise, and Peak Oil is much in the news (for more on this condition, check out the nearby sidebar, "Taking a peek at Peak Oil"). Energy investors must become familiar with Peak Oil because it has weighed, and will continue to weigh, *very* heavily on the economy because people are so dependent on oil for their modern lifestyle. Higher energy prices are here to stay. If you're going to pay more for energy, you may as well benefit.

As energy prices have risen strongly over the past few years, how have stocks fared? The general stock market (as represented by the Dow Jones Industrial Average and the S&P 500 index) didn't do much from 2005 to mid-2008. How about energy stocks? For an example, look at Schlumberger Limited (SLB), a major oil drilling and services firm whose fortunes are certainly tied to the energy market. Here's a company that you could have bought in late 2005 for about $30 per share. How has SLB fared during this time frame? Despite pulling back from a high of $115 in 2007, its stock is at $88 as of September 2008 for a solid gain of 167 percent.

The bottom line is that stock investors will either have to consider energy in their investment strategies or risk having energy prices steamroll over their potential gains. Investment opportunities are plentiful in companies that provide, sell, distribute, or explore energy. But you may want to consider energy alternatives as well. The U.S. and the rest of the world will be forced to turn to alternative energy sources in the coming years. As conventional oil and gas become scarce, the U.S. will look into gaining energy from sources such as wind, solar, fuel cell technologies, and Canada's oil sands, among others. (See the next section for more about alternative energy.)

Taking a peek at Peak Oil

In the late 1950s and early 1960s, geologist Marion King Hubbert conducted landmark studies related to the global supply of oil. His research indicated that the life of a particular underground reserve of oil goes through two phases. During the first phase, the oil can be easily and inexpensively extracted. However, after you get past the 50 percent mark, the remaining oil is very difficult (and hence very expensive) to extract. That 50 percent mark has come to be known as "Hubbert's Peak," and experts have come to call this condition Peak Oil. Hubbert correctly made forecasts of when the major oil-producing countries of the world would hit this peak. So far the forecasts have been accurate. The U.S. hit Hubbert's Peak in the early 1970s (American dependence on foreign oil grew significantly after that). Current industry research suggests that world production hit its peak in 2005. In August 2008, the top 100 largest oil fields in the world entered a period of declining production. To find out more about Peak Oil, check out Web sites such as the Association for the Study of Peak Oil & Gas (www.aspo-usa.com) and www.peakoil.net.

As you read this chapter, you may not be sure about what particular company you should invest in. If that's the case, why not consider a convenient way to invest in an entire industry or sector? A good consideration is an exchange-traded fund (ETF). Buying an ETF is like buying a whole portfolio of stocks as if it were a single stock. An example is an ETF with the symbol XLE. XLE has a cross section of the largest public oil and gas companies such as Exxon Mobil, Chevron, and others. In 2003, I bought XLE for $18 per share. By September 2008, it hit $70. To find out more about ETFs, go to the American Stock Exchange (www.amex.com) for all the details.

Alternative energy

Because a traditional energy source like oil has its supply issues (oil's days are numbered), it makes sense to anticipate what's next on the horizon that can logically fulfill America's energy needs. These changes must happen, and stock investors should benefit from what will be a historic shift into alternative energy. Alternative energy includes (but isn't limited to) nuclear energy, solar, wind, fuel cell, geothermal, and ocean currents. You can find many stocks and ETFs now that are among the myriad choices for investors to gain exposure in a sector that will become more and more prominent in the coming months and years. Check out Appendix A for general resources to help you research this great sector.

Gold and other precious metals

Over the ages, gold has come to be synonymous with wealth. In modern times, gold has become known as an inflation hedge and investment insurance, especially during times of inflation and geopolitical uncertainty. After being in a 20-year bear market (from its high of $850 in 1980 to its low of $252 in 2000), gold is in a powerful bull market. Aggressive investors should be investigating gold stocks and ETFs. Why now?

According to many (if not most) gold market analysts such as Bill Murphy of the Gold Anti-Trust Action Committee (www.gata.org), as well as sites that specialize in the gold market like www.lemetropolecafe.com, www.gold-eagle.com, and www.kitco.com, the fundamentals for gold are more bullish than ever. In recent years, demand has begun to significantly exceed supply. The shortfall has been filled from gold sales by central banks. Because of continued and growing demand both in the U.S. and abroad (most notably Russia, India, and China), total worldwide annual demand is outstripping supply by anywhere from 1000–2000 tons (depending on whose estimates you believe). Juxtapose this demand with current economic conditions (such as the declining value of the dollar and other paper currencies) and geopolitical instability, and you can see that gold and gold-related investments (such as quality gold stocks and ETFs) show bullish potential.

Because gold does well in an inflationary environment, understanding inflation itself is important. Inflation isn't the price of things going up; it's the value of the currency going down. The reason it goes down in value is primarily because the government can print money at will (the money supply). When you significantly increase the money supply, you create a bullish environment for hard assets such as gold. (For more about inflation, see Chapter 10.)

Gold analysts such as Bill Murphy, Doug Casey, Jay Taylor, James Sinclair, and many others accurately forecast that the price of gold would hit four figures (it did in March 2008) and that the current environment sees gold zigzagging to new highs in the coming years. If that's the case, gold mining stocks and ETFs will perform fantastically well (not unlike their heyday in the late 1970s). For conservative investors, consider the large, established mining firms such as Newmont Mining (NEM), Gold Corp. (GG), and Agnico-Eagle (AEM). For the more daring, consider junior mining stocks. Do your research using the Web sites mentioned in this section.

As an additional note, the general precious metals market is strong and is a good consideration for solid gains because of the current inflationary environment. I think that silver and even uranium (for energy) offer investors good opportunities. To find out more, check out my book *Precious Metals Investing For Dummies* (published by Wiley).

Healthcare

I'm sure you've heard much about the "graying of America." This phrase obviously represents a firm megatrend in place. For stock investors, this megatrend is a purely demographic play, and the numbers are with them. The number of people over the age of 50, and especially those considered senior citizens, represents the fastest growing segment of American society. The same megatrend is in place in all corners of the world (especially Europe). As more and more people move into this category, the idea that companies that serve this segment will also prosper becomes a no-brainer. Well-managed companies that run nursing homes and eldercare services will see their stocks rise.

 Be careful about which healthcare firms you select because this sector includes stocks that are defensive and also some that are cyclical. Companies that sell expensive equipment (such as CAT scans or MRI technology) may not do that well in an economic downturn because hospitals and other healthcare facilities may not want to upgrade or replace their equipment. Therefore, healthcare companies that sell big-ticket items can be considered cyclical. On the other hand, businesses that sell necessary items like medicine and bandages (such as pharmaceuticals and drug retailers) can be considered defensive. People who need medicine (such as aspirin or antacids) will buy it no matter how bad the economy is. In fact, people will probably buy even more aspirin and antacids in bad economic times.

 Also be wary of political trends as they affect healthcare. The U.S. may be slowly lurching toward socialized medicine. If this possibility develops, turn your bullish expectations into bearish ones. History (and my experience) tells me that a government takeover of an industry like healthcare spells danger for investors (and patients, too).

 To find out more about healthcare opportunities, check out the industry and main stocks by using the resources in Appendix A.

Defending the nation

The horrific events of September 11, 2001, remind the world how vulnerable America is as a free and open society. It has been a brave new world ever since. Americans watch their TV screens and listen to their radios to discover that terrorism's wretched tentacles reach across the globe. The most obvious way the country can respond is to increase security at home while deploying forces across the world to combat terrorists and tangle with the countries that support them. Foes of the U.S. aren't singular nations that are easily defined, fought, and defeated within a few months or a few years. Instead, they're implacable and virulent, and they're spread out over many countries.

In addition to terrorism, geopolitical developments pose potential problems for the U.S. Russia, China, and Iran are among the hot spots that will continue to challenge Americans economically as well as militarily.

As the U.S. continues to retool its military and seek ways to monitor, track, and attack terrorists, defense companies that sell certain products and services will benefit. For publications that do a great job informing investors and speculators regarding the war economy, check out the U.S. & World Early Warning Report (www.chaostan.com).

A Bearish Outlook

Stocks are versatile in that you can even make money when they go down in value. Techniques range from using put options to going short, or doing a short sale of stock. (See Chapter 18 regarding going short, and find out more about put options at www.cboe.com.) For traditional investors, the more appropriate strategy is first and foremost to avoid or minimize losses. Making money betting that a stock will fall is closer to speculating than actual investing. So all I want is that investors see the pitfalls and act accordingly. The following sections offer cautionary alerts to keep you away from troubled areas in the economy (or find speculative opportunities to short stocks).

The Dow Jones Industrial Average (DJIA) hit a high of 11,722 in January 2000 and, after seven roller-coaster years, hit an all-time high of 14,164.53 on October 9, 2007. (As I write this, the DJIA is about 8,400.) As you can see, the general market since January 2000 has been mediocre. Although some stock groups have grown quite well, stocks in general have struggled, and some sectors have done rather poorly. Choosing the right sector is critical for your stock investing success.

Avoiding consumer discretionary sectors

When the economy is struggling or contracting and people are concerned about their financial situation, some sectors will undoubtedly suffer. If you have money tied up in stocks attached to companies in these sectors, you may suffer as well. In today's economic environment, I would generally avoid sectors such as "consumer discretionary," which refers to companies that sell products or services that people may want but usually don't need. In other words, when consumers (both individuals and organizations) have to make hard choices on tighter budgets, the first areas of spending that will logically shrink are those goods and services that simply aren't that necessary in people's daily lives.

Here's an example: In trying times, those who typically eat at fancy, expensive restaurants will cut back. Maybe they'll eat at fast food places or simply opt for good ol' home cooking. Multiply this choice by millions of consumers and you see that high-end restaurants (and their stocks, if they're public companies) will see their fortunes sink. Your logic and common sense are very useful here.

A warning on real estate

In the second edition of this book, I warned you to stay away from housing because it became an enormous (and dangerous) bubble during 2002–2006. It has since sunk into its own depression. Although buying opportunities are plenty and sellers are having a difficult time, my warning on housing and the general real estate market (of course, all stocks associated with this sector) is still on. Be very cautious here and wait for a rebound. "But Paul," you may ask, "isn't the worst over? Isn't 2009 the bottom?" Possibly, but just understand that more credit problems still hang over the market.

Some recent industry data indicates that during 2007, one out of every seven homes purchased was underwater as of mid-2008. In other words, one out of every seven homeowners has a mortgage more valuable than the property purchased! Yikes! That means that some homebuyer out there has, say, a $250,000 mortgage on a property that has seen its market price decline to less than $250,000. How many homeowners will keep paying a mortgage that's worth more than the property itself, especially if times are tough and people are struggling or have lost a job?

In addition, think about *mortgage resets.* What does that mean? During the middle of this decade (2004–2007), many people purchased property with adjustable-rate mortgages (ARMs). These ARMs typically had an introductory period with a fixed monthly payment during the first few years (usually two to five years) and then were adjusted afterward. Many folks got into ARMs with the expectation that real estate would continue rising and that they'd be able to handle the new (higher) monthly payments later, or perhaps move out before the fixed introductory period ended. These ARMs became ticking time bombs. Many of them hit homeowners and forced sales, which made real estate prices drop as sales outnumbered purchases and the national inventory of available homes for sale ballooned to record levels. The ARMs aren't finished being adjusted, as many more are due to be adjusted during 2009–2011.

You can see that the real estate industry, with the ARMs issues and record levels of defaults and foreclosures, will need more time to heal and get back on a growth path. For stock investors, the point is obvious. Stocks related to real estate such as homebuilders, property developers, construction firms, and mortgage companies are too speculative at this point. Wait until the coast is clear.

To find out more about what's going on with this sector, check out www. realtor.com and www.realestatetopsites.com.

The great credit monster

Too much debt means that someone will get hurt. The unprecedented explosion in debt may have given the economy a huge boost in the late 1990s, but debt now poses great dangers for the rest of this decade. This massive debt problem is obviously tied to real estate. However, it goes much further. Individuals, companies, and government agencies are carrying too much debt for comfort. It's not just mortgage debt; it's also consumer, business, government, and margin debt. With total debt now in the vicinity of more than $45 trillion, saying that a lot of this debt won't be repaid is probably a safe bet. Individual and institutional defaults will rock the economy and the financial markets. Bankruptcy is (and will continue to be) a huge issue (in spite of bankruptcy reforms that became law on October 17, 2005).

Debt will (and does) weigh heavily on stocks, either directly or indirectly. Because every type of debt is now at record levels, no one is truly immune. Say you have a retail stock of a company that has no debt whatsoever. Are you immune? Not really, because consumer debt (credit cards, personal loans, and so on) is at an all-time high. If consumer spending declines, the retailer's sales go down, its profits shrink, and ultimately, its stock goes down.

Exposure to debt is quite pervasive. Check your 401(k) plan, your bond funds, and your insurance company's annuity. Why? Remember those mortgages I talk about earlier in this chapter? Banks and mortgage companies issued trillions of dollars' worth of those mortgages in recent years, but after the mortgages were issued, they were sold to other financial institutions. A huge number of mortgages were sold to the most obvious buyers, the Federal National Mortgage Association (FNM) and the Federal Mortgage Assurance Corporation (FRE). These giant, government-sponsored entities are usually referred to as "Fannie Mae" and "Freddie Mac." They were taken over in 2008 by the federal government because of gross mismanagement and overindebtedness (in the trillions!). Hmm . . . there goes that alarmist robot with the flailing arms again.

What's a stock investor to do?

✔ Well, remember that first commandment to avoid or minimize losses? Make sure that you review your portfolio and sell stocks that may get pulverized by the credit monster. That includes many banks and brokerage firms.

✔ Make sure that the companies themselves have no debt, low debt, or at least manageable debt. (Check their financial reports; see Chapter 12 for more details.)

✔ For the venturesome, seek shorting opportunities in those companies most exposed to the dangers of debt. (For more information on shorting, go to Chapter 18.)

Cyclical stocks

Another type of stock that I think you should be cautious about is cyclical stocks. Heavy equipment, automobiles, and technology tend to be cyclical and are very susceptible to downturns in the general economy. Conversely, cyclical stocks do very well when the economy is growing or on an upswing (hence the label).

As individuals and corporations get squeezed with more debt and less disposable income, hard choices need to be made. Ultimately, the result is that people buy fewer big-ticket items. That means that a company selling those items ends up selling less and earning less profit. This loss of profit, in turn, makes that company's stock go down.

Firms that experience lagging sales often turn to aggressive discounting. Recently, General Motors Corporation (GM) and Ford Motor Company (F) offered employee discount sales to the public. Both companies have been experiencing plunging sales and profits and ballooning debt in recent years. Subsequently, both companies have seen their stocks plummet to single digit levels in 2008.

In a struggling, recessionary economy, investing in cyclical stocks is like sunbathing on an anthill and using jam instead of sunblock — not a pretty picture.

Important Considerations for Bulls and Bears

I don't presume that stocks go straight up or that they zigzag upward indefinitely. Your due diligence is necessary for your success. Make sure that you're investing appropriately for your situation. If you're 35, heading into your peak earnings years, want to ride a home-run stock, and you understand the risks, then go ahead and speculate with that small cap gold mining stock or the solar power technology junior stock.

But if you're more risk averse or your situation is screaming out loud for you to be conservative, then don't speculate. Go instead with a more diversified portfolio of large cap stocks or get the ETF for that particular sector. And don't forget the trailing stop loss strategy (see Chapter 18). 'Nuff said.

For those people who want to make money by going short in those sectors that look bearish, again take a deep breath and remember what's appropriate. Conservative investors simply avoid the risky areas. Aggressive investors or speculators may want to deploy profitable bearish strategies (with a portion of their investable funds). Here are some highlights for all of you.

Conservative and bullish

Being conservative and bullish is proper when you're in (or near) retirement, have a family to support, or live in a very large shoe with so many kids that you don't know what to do. After you choose a promising sector, just select large cap companies that are financially strong, are earning a profit, have low debt, and are market leaders. This entire book shows you how to do just that.

However, you may not like the idea of buying stocks directly. In that case, consider either sector mutual funds or ETFs. That way you can choose the industry and effectively buy a basket of the top stocks in that area. ETFs have been a hot item lately, and I think that they're a great choice for most investors because they offer some advantages over mutual funds. For example, you can put stop-loss orders on them or borrow against them in your stock portfolio. Check with your financial advisor to see whether ETFs are appropriate for you.

Aggressive and bullish

If you're aggressive and bullish, you want to buy stocks directly. For real growth potential, look at mid caps or small caps. Remember that you're speculating, so you understand the downside risk but are willing to tolerate it because the upside potential can reward you so handsomely. Few things in the investment world give you a better gain than a supercharged stock in a hot sector.

Conservative and bearish

For many (if not most) investors, making money on a falling market isn't generally a good idea. Doing so takes a lot of expertise and risk tolerance. Really, for conservative investors, the key word is safety. Analyze your portfolio with an advisor you trust and sell the potentially troubled stocks. If you're not sure what to do on a particular stock, then (at the very least) put in stop-loss orders and make them GTC (good-till-canceled). (See Chapter 18 for details.) As odd as it sounds, sometimes losing less than others makes you come out ahead if you play it right.

For example, look at the bear market that hit the U.S. in the mid-1970s. In 1974–1975, the stock market fell 45 percent. Stocks didn't recover until 1982. If you had a stock that was at $100, it would have fallen to $55 and not returned to $100 until seven or eight years later. Whew! Sometimes just burying your money in the backyard sounds like genius. What if you had a stop loss at $90? You would have gotten out with a minimal loss and could have reinvested the money elsewhere (such as in bonds or CDs) and looked much brighter than your neighbor feverishly digging for money in his backyard.

Aggressive and bearish

Being aggressive in a bearish market isn't for the faint of heart. However, this is where the quickest fortunes have been made by some of history's greatest investors. Going short can make you great money when the market is bearish, but it can sink you if you're wrong. I usually don't tell my clients and students to short a stock because it can backfire. Yes, ways to go short with less risk are out there, but I prefer to buy put options.

Put options are a way to make money with limited risk when you essentially make a bet that an investment (such as stocks) will go down. Obviously, options go beyond the scope of this book, but at least let me give you some direction, because there's an appropriate options strategy for most stock portfolios. You can find great (free) tutorials on using options at Web sites such as the Chicago Board Options Exchange (www.cboe.com) and the Options Industry Council (www.888options.com).

Chapter 15

Money, Mayhem, and Votes

In This Chapter

▶ Looking at the effects of politics and government on stocks

▶ Checking out a few handy political resources

*P*olitics can be infuriating, disruptive, meddlesome, corrupting, and harmful. Don't let that fool you — it does have its bad side, too! Even if politics doesn't amuse or interest you, you can't ignore it. If you aren't careful, it can wreak great havoc on your portfolio. Politics wields great influence on the economic and social environment, which in turn affects how companies succeed or fail. This success or failure in turn either helps or hurts your stock's price. Politics (manifested in taxes, regulations, price controls, capital controls, and other government actions) can make or break a company or industry quicker than any other external force.

What people must understand (especially government policy makers) is that a new tax, law, regulation, or government action has a *macro* effect on a stock, an industry, or even an entire economic system, whereas a company has a *micro* effect on an economy. The following gives you a simple snapshot of these effects:

> Politics → policy → economy → industry → the company → the stock → stock investor

Now, this chapter doesn't moralize about politics or advocate a political point of view; after all, this book is about stock investing. In general, policies can be good or bad regardless of their effect on the economy — some policies are enacted to achieve greater purposes even if they kick you in the wallet. However, in the context of this chapter, politics is covered from a cause-and-effect perspective: How does politics affect prosperity in general and stock investing in particular?

A proficient stock investor can't — must not — look at stocks as though they exist in a vacuum. My favorite example of this rule is the idea of fish in a lake. You can have a great fish (your stock) among a whole school of fish (the stock market) in a wonderful lake (the economy). But what if the lake gets polluted (bad policy)? What happens to the fish? Politics controls the lake and can make it hospitable — or dangerous — for the participants. You get the point. The example may sound too simple, yet it isn't. So many people — political committees, corporate managers, bureaucrats, and politicians — still get this picture so wrong time and time again, to the detriment of the economy and stock investors. Heck, I don't mind if they get it wrong with *their* money, but their actions make it tough for *your* money.

Although the two inexorably get intertwined, I do what I can to treat politics and economics as separate issues. Economics gets its own spotlight in Chapter 10.

Tying Together Politics and Stocks

The campaigns heat up. Democrats, Republicans, and smaller parties vie for your attention and subsequent votes. Conservatives, liberals, socialists, moderates, and libertarians joust in the battlefield of ideas. But after all is said and done, voters make their decisions. Election Day brings a new slate of politicians into office, and they in turn joust and debate on new rules and programs in the legislative halls of power. Before and after election time, investors must keep a watchful eye on the proceedings. In the following sections, I explain some basic political concepts that relate to stock investing.

Seeing the general effects of politics on stock investing

For stock investors, politics manifests itself as a major factor in investment-making decisions in ways shown in Table 15-1.

Table 15-1	Politics and Investing
Possible Legislation	***Effect on Investing***
Taxes	Will a new tax affect a particular stock (industry or economy)? Generally, more or higher taxes ultimately have a negative impact on stock investing. Income taxes and capital gains taxes are good examples.
Laws	Will Congress (or, in some instances, state legislatures) pass a law that will have a negative impact on a stock, the industry, or the economy? Price controls — laws that set the price of a product, service, or commodity — are examples of negative laws. I discuss price controls in more detail later in this chapter.
Regulations	Will a new (or existing) regulation have a negative (or positive) effect on the stock of your choice? Generally, more or tougher regulations have a negative impact on stocks.
Government spending and debt	If government agencies spend too much or misallocate resources, they may create greater burdens on society, which in turn will be bearish for the economy and the stock market.
Money supply	The U.S. money supply — the dollars you use — is controlled by the Federal Reserve. It's basically a governmental agency that serves as America's central bank. How can it affect stocks? Increasing or decreasing the money supply results in either an inflationary or a deflationary environment, which can help or hurt the economy, specific industries, and stock picks.
Interest rates	The Federal Reserve has crucial influence here. It can raise or lower key interest rates that in turn can have an effect on the entire economy and the stock market. When interest rates go up, it makes credit more expensive for companies. When interest rates go down, companies can get cheaper credit, which can be better for profits.
Government bailouts	This is when the government intervenes directly in the marketplace and uses either tax money or borrowed money to bail out a troubled enterprise. This is generally a negative because funds are diverted by force from the healthier private economy to an ailing enterprise.

The seeds of financial disaster in the last decade

As I write this book, the financial headlines are blaring away about the trillion-dollar financial and credit catastrophes unfolding on Wall Street. Government-sponsored enterprises (GSEs) such as Fannie Mae (FNM) and Freddie Mac (FRE) have collapsed, and shareholders have been wiped out. Large financial entities such as AIG and Merrill Lynch have been rocked by multibillion-dollar losses. Politicians and pundits give indignant speeches about the failures of capitalism. But what really happened?

Gang, I predicted this mess years ago in the 2nd edition of *Stock Investing For Dummies*. Politically popular policies and regulations enacted by the federal government during the late 1990s and the early part of this decade laid the groundwork for today's massive financial mess. The Federal Reserve in 2001 lowered interest rates to artificially low levels, removed lending standards (to boost home ownership), greatly increased the money supply, and expanded credit on a massive scale. This fueled a historic mortgage boom that created the housing bubble. Trillions of mortgage money was loaned out, much of it to home buyers of *very* questionable credit quality. These subprime mortgages were repackaged as bonds and sold to financial entities on Wall Street and across the globe. When the mortgages went bad, financial entities lost billions.

Now, politicians rail about what government should do, but what they don't understand is that the root of the problem is what government had done years before. The lesson is that political/government intervention can unleash unintended consequences that can destroy a company whose stock you own.

When many of the factors in Table 15-1 work in tandem, they can have a magnified effect that can have tremendous consequences for your stock portfolio. Alert investors keep a constant vigil when the legislature is open for business, and they adjust their portfolios accordingly.

Ascertaining the political climate

The bottom line is that you ignore political realities at your own (economic) risk. To be and stay aware, ask yourself the following questions about the stock of each company in which you invest:

- ✔ What laws will directly affect my stock investment adversely?
- ✔ Will any laws affect the company's industry?
- ✔ Will any current or prospective laws affect the company's sources of revenue?
- ✔ Will any current or prospective laws affect the company's expenses or supplies?

✔ Am I staying informed about political and economic issues that may possibly have a negative impact on my investment?

✔ Will such things as excessive regulations, price controls, or new taxes have a negative impact on my stock's industry?

Here's an example: Oil and gas service and exploration companies benefited from the U.S. need for more energy supplies. But investment opportunities didn't stop there. As oil and gas supplies became costly and problematic, alternative energy sources gained national attention. The debate was rekindled on solar power and exciting new technologies, such as fuel cells. As traditional sources of energy (sweet crude) became more expensive, alternative sources became more economical. Investors who anticipated the new interest in alternative energy sought companies that would logically benefit. In the world of politics, Congress for years had a ban on offshore drilling, but the alternative energy industry received tax credits. With that wind at its back, along with public acceptance of clean energy technologies, alternative energy is something that investors should take notice of.

Distinguishing between nonsystemic and systemic effects

Politics can affect your investments in two basic ways: nonsystemic and systemic.

✔ *Nonsystemic* means that the system isn't affected but a particular participant is affected.

✔ *Systemic* means that all the players in the system are affected.

In this case, the system is the economy at large. Politics imposes itself (through taxes, laws, regulations, and so on) and has an undue influence on all the members of that system.

Nonsystemic

Say that you decide to buy stock in a company called Golf Carts Unlimited, Inc. (GCU). You believe that the market for golf carts has great potential and that GCU stands to grow substantially. How can politics affect GCU?

What if politicians believe that GCU is too big and that it controls too much of the golf cart industry? Maybe they view GCU as a monopoly and want the federal government to step in to shrink GCU's reach and influence for the benefit of competition and consumers. Maybe the government believes that GCU engages in unfair or predatory business practices and that it's in violation of antitrust (or antimonopoly) laws. If the government acts against GCU, the action is a nonsystemic issue: The action is directed toward the participant (in this case, GCU) and not the golf cart industry in general. (See the nearby sidebar for more about monopolies.)

What happens if you're an investor in GCU? Does your stock investment suffer as a result of government action directed against the company? Let's just say that the stock price will hook left and end up in the lake.

Systemic

Say that politicians want to target the golf industry for intervention because they maintain that golf should be free or close to free for all to participate in and that a law must be passed to make it accessible to all, especially those people who can't afford to play. So to remedy the situation, the following law is enacted: "Law #67590305598002 declares that from this day forward, all golf courses must charge only one dollar for any golfer who chooses to participate."

That law sounds great to any golfer. But what are the unintended effects when such a law becomes reality? Many people agree with the sentiment of the law, but what about the cause-and-effect aspects of it? Obviously, all things being equal, golf courses will be forced to close. Staying in business is uneconomical if their costs are higher than their income. If they can't charge any more than a dollar, how can they possibly stay open? Ultimately (and ironically), no one can play golf.

Playing monopoly

Government action against large companies for real (or alleged) abuses has happened many times. Longtime investors remember how companies such as IBM (in the 1970s) and Microsoft (during 1999 and 2000) faced monopolistic allegations. And in 2004, the New York attorney general targeted insurer American International Group, Inc. (AIG) for fraud, bid-rigging, and accounting irregularities. In a few months, AIG's stock fell from $74 to a low of $50 in April 2005. How irony moves in strange ways! In 2008, the federal government bailed out AIG with an $80 billion loan as the company was pulled away from the brink of collapse. As for AIG's stock? It went DOA . . . uh . . . ASAP. OK?

The federal government is a massive entity, and it has trillions of taxpayer dollars at its disposal. When it targets a company, regardless of the merits of the case, avoid investing in that company (until the trouble has passed). Investors should be wary when the government starts making noise about any company and potential legal actions against it.

What happens to investors of Golf Carts Unlimited, Inc.? If the world of golf shrinks, demand for golf carts shrinks as well. The value of GCU's stock will certainly be stuck in a sand trap.

Examples of politics creating systemic problems are endless, but you get the point.

Understanding price controls

Stock investors should be very wary of price controls, which are a great example of regulation. A *price control* is a fixed price on a particular product, commodity, or service mandated by the government.

Price controls have been tried continuously throughout history, and they've continuously been removed because they ultimately do more harm than good. It's easy to see why. Imagine that you run a business that sells chairs, and a law is passed that states, "From this point onward, chairs can be sold only for $10." If all your costs stay constant at $9 or less, the regulation isn't that bad. However, price controls put two dynamics in motion:

- First, the artificially lower price encourages consumption — more people buy chairs.
- Second, production is discouraged. What company wants to make chairs if it can't sell them for a decent profit?

What happens to the company with a fixed sales price (in this example, $10) and rising costs? Profits shrink, and depending on how long the price controls are in effect, the company eventually experiences losses. The chair producer is eventually driven out of business. The chair-building industry shrinks, and the result is a chair shortage. Profits (and jobs) soon vanish. So what happens if you own stock in a company that builds chairs? I'll just say that if I tell you which way the stock price is going, you better be sitting down (if, of course, you have a chair).

Poking into Political Resources

Ignoring what's going on in the world of politics is like sleepwalking near the Grand Canyon — a bad idea! You have to be aware of what's going on. Governmental data, reports, and political rumblings are important clues to the kind of environment that's unfolding for the economy and financial markets. Do your research with the following resources so you can stay a step ahead in your stock-picking strategies.

Government reports to watch out for

The best analysts look at economic reports from both private and government sources. The following sections list some reports/statistics issued by the government to watch out for. For private reports on the economy, investors can turn to sources such as the American Institute for Economic Research (www.aier.org) and Moody's (www.economy.com).

Alas, government reports aren't totally reliable because errors and/or purposeful fudging happen and usually have a political component to them. Take the gross domestic product (GDP), for instance. In the second quarter of 2008, the GDP was reported at a surprisingly robust 3.3 percent — a very healthy number given the fact that the economy was struggling at the time. A closer examination reveals that the GDP was calculated using a very low inflation rate of just 1.2 percent, a ten-year low. Yet in a separate report for the same quarter, the same agency (the Bureau of Labor Statistics) reported that inflation was at 5.6 percent, a 17-year high! Had the BLS used this more believable inflation rate, the GDP would have actually been at –1.1 percent. I doubt that the fact that 2008 is an election year is a coincidence because games like this have been played by administrations of all stripes dating back to Franklin Roosevelt's day. A good way to round out your economic analysis is to compare government data from other sources that scrutinize the same data. One that I like is Shadow Government Statistics (www.shadowstats.com).

GDP

Gross domestic product (GDP), which measures a nation's total output of goods and services for the quarter, is considered the broadest measure of economic activity. Although the U.S. GDP is measured in dollars (it hit $14 trillion by January 2008), it's usually quoted as a percentage. You typically hear a news report that says something like, "The economy grew by 2.5 percent last quarter." Because the GDP is an important overall barometer of the economy, it should be a positive number. The report on the GDP is released quarterly by the U.S. Department of Commerce (www.commerce.doc).

You should regularly monitor the GDP along with economic data that relates directly to your stock portfolio. The following list gives some general guidelines for evaluating the GDP:

✔ **Over 3 percent:** This number indicates strong growth and bodes well for stocks. At 5 percent or higher, the economy is sizzling!

✔ **1 to 3 percent:** This figure indicates moderate growth and can occur either as the economy is rebounding from a recession or as it's slowing down from a previously strong period.

✔ **0 percent or negative (as low as –3 percent):** This number isn't good and indicates that the economy is either not growing or is actually shrinking a bit. A negative GDP is considered *recessionary* (meaning that the economy's growth is receding).

✔ **Under –3 percent:** A GDP this low indicates a very difficult period for the economy. A GDP under –3 percent, especially for two or more quarters, indicates a serious recession or possibly a depression.

Looking at a single quarter isn't that useful. Track the GDP over many quarters to see which way the general economy is trending. When you look at the GDP for a particular quarter of a year, ask yourself whether it's better (or worse) than the quarter before. If it's better (or worse), then ask yourself to what extent it has changed. Is it dramatically better (or worse) than the quarter before? Is the economy showing steady growth, or is it slowing? If several quarters show solid growth, the overall economy is generally bullish.

Traditionally, if two or more consecutive quarters show negative growth (economic output is shrinking), the economy is considered to be in a recession. A recession can be a painful necessity; it usually occurs when the economy can't absorb the total amount of goods being produced because of too much excess production. A bear market in stocks usually accompanies a recession.

The GDP is just a rough estimate at best. It can't possibly calculate all the factors that go into economic growth. For example, crime has a negative effect on economic growth, but it's not reflected in the GDP. Still, most economists agree that the GDP provides a ballpark snapshot of the overall economy's progress.

Unemployment

The National Unemployment Report is provided by the Bureau of Labor Statistics (www.bls.gov). It gives investors a snapshot of the health and productivity of the economy.

The Consumer Price Index

The Consumer Price Index (CPI) is a statistic that tracks the prices of a representative basket of goods and services on a monthly basis. This statistic, which is also computed by the Bureau of Labor Statistics, is meant to track price inflation. Investors should pay attention to the CPI because a low-inflation environment is good for stocks (and bonds, too), while high inflation is generally more favorable for sectors such as commodities and precious metals.

Web sites to surf

To find out about new laws being passed or proposed, check out Congress and what's going on at its primary Web sites: the U.S. House of Representatives (www.house.gov) and the U.S. Senate (www.senate.gov). For presidential information and proposals, check the White House's Web site at www.whitehouse.gov.

You also may want to check out THOMAS, the service provided by the Library of Congress, at http://thomas.loc.gov. THOMAS is a search engine that helps you find any piece of legislation, either by bill number or keyword. This search engine is an excellent way to find out whether an industry is being targeted for increased regulation or deregulation. In the late 1980s, real estate was hit hard when the government passed new regulations and tax rules (related stocks went down). When the telecom industry was deregulated in the mid-1990s, the industry grew dramatically (related stocks went up).

Turn to the following sources for economic data:

- Conference Board, www.conferenceboard.org
- U.S. Department of Commerce, www.doc.gov
- The Federal Reserve, www.federalreserve.gov
- Free Lunch, www.freelunch.com

You can find more resources in Appendix A. The more knowledge you pick up about how politics and government actions can help (or harm) an investment, the better you'll be at growing (and protecting) your wealth.

Part IV
Investment Strategies and Tactics

The 5th Wave   By Rich Tennant

"I take it your stocks are still trading high on the 'yawn index.'"

In this part . . .

Successful stock investing is more than choosing a particular stock — it's also how you go about doing it. Successful investors go beyond merely picking good stocks and watching the financial news. They implement techniques and strategies that help them either minimize losses or maximize gains (hopefully both). The chapters in this part introduce some of the most effective investing techniques and describe some smart ways to hold onto more of your profits when tax time rolls around.

Chapter 16

Choosing between Investing and Trading

. . . .

In This Chapter

▶ Understanding the differences between investing and trading

▶ Checking out the tools of stock trading

▶ Sticking to important rules for safe trading

. . . .

*Y*ou may have heard of stock trading and wondered how it compares to stock investing. Rest assured that trading and investing are two different animals. Trading is advantageous when you're looking to profit from short-term swings in the market due to volatility. However, trading can be dangerous because the market's short-term movements can be quite unpredictable. The only reason I'm including trading in this book is because you, dear reader, should get some do's and don'ts in this short-term venture. If you're going to trade stocks, you should have some guidelines to keep the downside to a minimum. I explain what you need to know in this chapter.

The Differences between Investing and Trading

Stock investing and stock trading may sound similar, but they're actually pretty different:

✔ Investing looks primarily at fundamentals (earnings, sales, industry outlook, and so on), which tend to be long-term drivers of stock prices. The long-term investor waits out the zigzags as long as the bullish outlook and the general uptrend are intact. The good part is that investing involves fewer transaction costs (you aren't constantly buying and selling stock) and usually lower taxes (long-term capital gains typically are taxed at a lower rate than short-term gains). The bad part is that sometimes the stock can correct (go down temporarily) or have periods of flat performance, which the long-term investor has to patiently tolerate.

✔ In trading, much more activity takes place during a range of a few days, weeks, or months. Traders may dump losers immediately and cash out winners to lock in some profit before the next dip in price. Trading can mean more costs due to frequent commissions and short-term taxable gains. For trading, the fundamentals are either not a factor or at best a secondary or minor factor because short-term movements in a stock price are more geared to momentum and sentiment, which is reflected in the data found in charts along with price and volume statistics.

The following sections give you the full scoop on the differences between investing and trading.

The time factor

When I first started investing in stocks, it was easy to delineate what was *short term, intermediate term,* and *long term:*

✔ Short term was less than one year.

✔ Intermediate term was usually one to three years or one to five years, depending on your personal outlook.

✔ Long term was beyond that time frame.

In recent years, however, investors have become very impatient. For some investors, short term is now measured in days, intermediate term in weeks, and long term in months. In the old days, investors were akin to cooks using the crock pot; today, they use the microwave. But these people are actually traders, not investors. If an investment does well, they sell it immediately and move on to (hopefully) another profitable investment. If the investment is down, they sell it immediately and move on to (hopefully) greener pastures elsewhere.

There's no such thing as a three-month investment when it comes to stocks. Stocks require time for the marketplace to discover them. Sometimes great stocks see their prices move very little because the market (again, millions of individual and institutional investors) hasn't noticed them yet. In trading, on the other hand, you jump in and out relatively quickly. Typical trades occur over the span of a few days or a few weeks. Of course, if a position you take on grows more profitable and your expectations are positive, you can stay in longer. But many experienced traders won't tempt fate and stay in too long because a reversal of fortune can always occur, so don't be shy about cashing out and taking a profit.

The psychology factor

In investing, you can be very analytical. You can look at a stock and its fundamentals and then at the prospects for the stock's industry and the general economy, and you can make a good choice knowing that you're not worried about the price going up or down a few percentage points in the next few days or weeks. If you've done your homework, your stock will eventually go up and do well over the long haul.

Trading is different. Trading involves looking at stocks that have the ability to move quickly, regardless of the direction. The reason is that seasoned traders want to make money quickly and capitalize on crowd psychology. It matters little whether investors are bidding up or down; the trader is primarily looking for a stock with momentum.

Checking out an example

The stock investor takes the long view and stays patient and focused. As I try to stress throughout this book, investing should be measured in years, and the stock's *fundamentals* (a company's profits, sales, industry, and so on) are the foundation. A patient and successful investor holds on as the stock zigzags upward. When the inevitable correction occurs, a successful investor either just waits it out or takes that moment as a buying opportunity and adds shares to her holdings. In a bullish (up) outlook, the investor expects the stock to generally trend upward. If the investor expects a stock to have a downward path, then obviously she simply avoids it.

The stock trader sees things differently. The trader may indeed be just as bullish on a particular stock but may also bet on the occasional pullback or correction that's typical of most stocks. The trader may buy 100 shares of a stock and keep it as a core holding, but he may also make different bets on its price movement.

For an example, take a look at the chart in Figure 16-1. This is a chart of Zig Zag Corporation (ZZC), and it's helpful in showing you how investing and trading behave differently during the same time frame.

An investor would have bought ZZC stock in 2006 and held on. As long as the fundamentals don't change, the investor just "buys right and sits tight." Although some traders may smirk at such a simple strategy, it's a time-tested approach. Look at billionaire Warren Buffet for a great example of this. He has been known to hold stocks for decades. Many investors (and traders, too) envy his extraordinary success, but relatively few try to emulate it.

Patience and discipline aren't always popular or fashionable in investing, but a patient, disciplined approach has proven to be superior to many trading systems that tell you to jump in and jump out.

Looking at Figure 16-1, how would successful traders have performed with ZZC? The trader may start off as an investor and make that initial investment in the stock. As time passes, the trader would be watching technical indicators to time an entry or exit point. A *technical indicator* is a result of a mathematical calculation based on prices and the volume of trading, typically displayed as a chart. (See the "Technical analysis" section later in this chapter.)

Stock traders typically use options (such as calls and puts) because they're cheap and can provide a magnified move with the underlying stock. In other words, options are a form of leverage, meaning that the price swing can be greater (up or down) than the move in the underlying stock. If a stock moves up 10 percent, then an option (in this case a call option) could go up 20 percent or more. Of course, if the stock goes down 10 percent, then that same option could easily go down 20 percent or more.

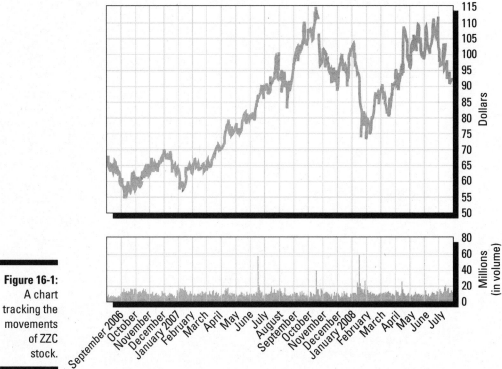

Figure 16-1:
A chart
tracking the
movements
of ZZC
stock.

What are call and put options?

- A *call option* is a bet that a particular stock (or exchange-traded fund) will go up during the life of the option.

- A *put option* is a bet that a particular stock (or exchange-traded fund) will go down during the life of the option.

Think of the following (very rough) rule of thumb:

- If the stock goes up 10 percent, a call option on that stock could go up 20 percent. Of course, a put option on that same stock would lose 20 percent (or more).

- If the stock goes down 10 percent, a call option could go down 20 percent. Of course, a put option on that same stock would gain 20 percent (or more).

- If the stock stays flat or neutral, both the call and put options would start to lose value because options have a finite life and can potentially be worthless by the time they expire.

Referring back to Figure 16-1, the trader may have seen his stock rise during October and November 2006 from about $55 per share to $70. Technical indicators may have flashed that the stock is overbought. Some traders would have cashed in and sat with the cash, waiting for the next opportunity. Other traders would have kept the stock but cashed in any call options that were purchased before that time frame for a nice profit. The money from cashing out the sale of the call options would sit waiting for the next entry point. Perhaps the trader would then use the money to purchase put options, betting that a correction was soon due. Then you see the huge move up by ZZC starting at about $55 in December 2006 and hitting $115 in October 2007 before correcting in a zigzag fashion down to about $73 in January 2008.

Had the trader employed both calls and puts, he would have had plenty of opportunities for profit. During the summer of 2007, the call options would have been profitable and could have been cashed out. In that scenario, a call option could easily reward the astute trader with triple-percentage gains. Of course, the puts in the same time frame would have greatly lost value. Heading into the September 2007–January 2008 period, the bearish strategies would have paid off because put options would rise in value as the underlying asset (in this case the stock of ZZC) declined.

As you can see, the successful trader must diligently monitor his positions and frequently enter more than one position on the same stock to try to capitalize on the stock's movements. Whenever you take opposing positions on the same security, you're doing a form of hedging. Hedging takes into consideration the idea that the market can easily go against you, which is an especially likely scenario if the market is volatile. In that case, why not profit from the move?

Keep in mind that any profits are offset by any losses from options that lose value (or expire worthless) and by transaction costs.

Scores of books have been written about options, so I won't go into great detail here, but you should get familiar with options, especially if short-term speculating or trading greatly interests you. You can start with *Stock Options For Dummies* by Alan R. Simon and *Trading Options For Dummies* by George A. Fontanills, both published by Wiley.

Tools of the Trader

As you can judge from the example I provide earlier in this chapter, successful trading requires lots of diligent attention. Because stocks can go all over the place, the trader uses various tools to determine entry and exit points. I cover some of those tools and strategies in the following sections.

Technical analysis

The most common tool of short-term speculators and traders is technical analysis. *Technical analysis* looks at the recent price movements and volume of trading for particular securities and commodities. The price movements are depicted on charts, so "charting a security" is a common practice among those who use technical analysis.

The technical analyst uses some useful short-term indicators, including

- ✔ *Moving averages* to gauge the general trend for a particular stock. Typical moving averages are the 10-day, 20-day, 50-day, and 200-day averages. Stocks that stay above these averages tend to be bullish, while stocks that keep falling below these averages tend to be bearish.

- ✔ *Relative Strength Indicators (RSI)* to see if a stock is considered oversold or overbought. A technical analyst sees an oversold stock as a buying opportunity and an overbought stock as a selling opportunity.

Technical analysis is a complex topic, and I just can't do it justice in this solitary chapter. I don't mean to shortchange it, as it's worthy of study for serious traders. I mention it here because traders should be aware of it, regardless of how extensively they use it. I strongly recommend that serious traders do some extensive research on the topic. Consider starting your research with *Technical Analysis For Dummies* by Barbara Rockefeller (Wiley).

As most longtime readers probably know by now, I'm not an ardent fan of technical analysis. Don't get me wrong; I respect it as a short-term trading tool. It can be remarkably useful over a period of a few weeks or months. However, it's not that useful for long-term investing. Yes, you can use it to maximize an entry or exit point, but over the long haul, a company's fundamentals are the primary drivers of the stock's price. When you look at the pantheon of consistently successful investors in history, it's no accident that most of them use fundamental analysis and are into some form of value investing.

Brokerage orders

Because trading in the market's short-term gyrations can be a fast-moving activity, it pays to get proficient with brokerage orders and trading triggers to help you manage your trading portfolio and take advantage of the market's swift moves.

The moment after a diligent trader buys a stock or an option, she'll enter her next order very quickly — often even before the stock has made a major move. For example, if she buys a stock for $50 at 10 a.m. on a weekday morning, she may enter a stop-loss order at, say, $45 at 11 a.m. and simultaneously put in a sell order at $60. That way she can limit the loss to $5 per share and maybe catch a $10 profit on the upside. These moves are possible now due to the sophisticated technology that most brokers have on their Web sites.

That's just an example of what you can do with brokerage orders. Find out more about brokerage orders and trade triggers in Chapter 18.

Advisory services

You don't have to go it alone with your trading strategies because the world is filled with advisory services, newsletters, and Web sites that cater to the art and science of short-term trading. Some notable ones that I respect include Elliott Wave International (www.elliottwave.com) and Roger Wiegand's Trader Tracks (www.tradertracks.com). A monthly publication that covers the realm of trading is *Stock, Futures and Options* magazine (www.sfomag.com). Of course, you can do your own diligent research at the library and on the Internet (check Appendix A for resources).

The Basic Rules of Trading

If you're going to trade, adhere to some golden rules to help you maximize your success (or at least minimize potential losses):

- ✔ **Don't commit all your cash at once:** In a fast-moving market, opportunities come up all the time. Try to keep some cash on hand to take advantage of those opportunities.

- ✔ **Have a plan:** Try to have predetermined points at which you cut losses or take profits.

- ✔ **Taking profits is not a sin:** Sometimes, a bird in the hand is worth two in the bush. Markets can reverse fairly quickly. If you have a stock position sitting there with a fat profit, it can't hurt to take the profit. This gives you cash for the next opportunity.

- ✔ **Discover hedging techniques:** Just because you're bullish doesn't mean that you can't also put on a bearish position. Hedging techniques protect you when the market moves against you.

- ✔ **Find out which events move markets:** Research the market and discover what types of events tend to move it (either up or down). Serious short-term traders keep one eye on their positions and the other on what's going on in the world. Keep informed by regularly reading financial publications and Web sites (see Appendix A for resources).

- ✔ **Check the stock's trading history:** Charts and related data tell you how a particular stock has moved in recent weeks, months, and years. Do you see any seasonality or reliable patterns that may help you judge future movements?

- ✔ **Use stop-loss and limit orders:** Using trade orders are an integral part of the trader's overall strategy. Find out more in Chapter 18.

- ✔ **Use discipline and patience versus emotion and panic:** Part of the human equation in the world of financial markets is that fear and greed can become an irrational, short-term driver of prices. Instead of joining the crowd, watch them to give you an advantage in assessing a stock's price movements. Stick with your plan and use discipline and patience.

- ✔ **Minimize transaction costs:** Keep in mind that because trading is typically active and short term, transaction costs are significant. Active trading can mean lots of brokerage commissions, even in this age of Internet-based brokerage firms. Therefore, traders should shop around for brokerage firms that charge low commissions for those that trade frequently (check out brokerage firms in Appendix A). In addition, short-term trading leads to short-term capital gains, which are taxed at a higher rate than long-term transactions.

✔ **Understand the beta of a stock:** The volatility of a stock is an important consideration for traders. The more volatile a stock is, the greater its ups and downs are. Therefore, traders should regularly check the stock's beta. *Beta* is a statistical measure of how volatile a particular stock is relative to a market standard (such as the S&P 500 index).

How is it measured? The S&P 500 (for example) is given a beta of 1. A stock with a beta of 2 is considered twice as volatile as the index. In other words, if the index falls by 10 percent, the stock in question has the potential of falling by 20 percent. A stock with a beta of 0.5 is considered to be half as volatile as the index. In other words, if the index falls by 10 percent, that low-beta stock would only be expected to fall 5 percent.

Traders looking for fast (and hopefully profitable) movement look for high-beta opportunities. A stock's beta can be found on various financial Web sites (see resources in Appendix A).

✔ **Read and learn from top traders:** Last (but not least), learn from the great ones out there, such as the legendary Jesse Livermore. You can read all about his trading exploits in the book *Reminiscences of a Stock Operator* by Edwin Lefevre (Wiley).

Because trading can be very risky, you need to know as much as you can. Don't use your rent money or retirement money, and for crying out loud, don't break open your kid's piggy bank. Trading should only be done with *risk capital* (money that, if lost, doesn't hurt your lifestyle). And don't forget the advice from the immortal Will Rogers: "Don't gamble; take all your savings and buy some good stock and hold it till it goes up, then sell it. If it don't go up, don't buy it."

Chapter 17

Selecting a Strategy That's Just Right for You

In This Chapter

▶ Basing your investing strategy on your needs and time frame

▶ Deciding where and how to allocate your assets

▶ Recognizing when to unload your stocks

S tocks are a means to an end. What end are you seeking? You should look at stocks as tools for wealth building. Sometimes they're great tools, and sometimes they're awful. The results you get depend on your approach. Some stocks are appropriate for a conservative approach, while others are more suitable for an aggressive approach. Sometimes stocks aren't a good idea at all. Golly! A stock investing book that suggests that stocks aren't always the answer! That's like a teenager saying, "Dad, I respectfully decline your generous offer of money for my weekend trip, and I'd be glad to mow the lawn."

In this chapter, I help you select a stock-investing strategy based on your personal circumstances and the amount of money you have to invest. I also provide tips on when to sell your stocks.

Laying Out Your Plans

A senior citizen in one of my investment seminars in 2000 wanted to be more aggressive with his portfolio, and his broker was more than happy to cater to his desire for growth stocks. Of course, stocks got clobbered in the volatile bear market of 2000–2002, and yes, he did lose lots of money. However, I soon discovered that even after the losses, he still had a substantial stock portfolio valued at over $1 million. He had more than enough to ensure a comfortable retirement. He sought aggressive growth even though it was really unnecessary for his situation. If anything, the aggressive strategy could have put his portfolio (and hence his retirement) in jeopardy.

Growth is desirable even in your twilight years because inflation can eat away at a fixed-income portfolio. But different rates of growth exist, and the type you choose should be commensurate with your unique situation and financial needs. Notice that I say "needs," not "wants." These perspectives are entirely different. You may *want* to invest in aggressive stocks regardless of their suitability (after all, it's your money), but your financial situation may dictate that you *need* to take another approach. Just understand the difference.

Stocks can play a role in all sorts of investment strategies, but in this chapter, I discuss only a few well-known approaches. Keep in mind that your stock-investing strategy can change based on the major changes in your life and the lifestyle that you lead, such as the ones I present in the following sections.

Living the bachelor life: Young single with no dependents

If you're young (age 20–40) and single, with no children or other dependents, being more aggressive with your stock selection is fine (as long as you don't use your rent money for investments). The reasoning is that if you do make riskier choices and they backfire, individuals dependent on you won't get hurt. In addition, if you're in this category, you can usually bounce back a lot easier over the long term even if you have financial challenges or if a bear (down) market hits your stocks.

Safety first: Examining savings bonds

For the next few years, fixed-interest bonds and other debt instruments (like corporate bonds) generally aren't the right place to be because excessive debt, low interest rates, and rising inflation are problematic for investors. A nice oasis in the valley of death known as America's debt load (currently $44+ trillion, which dwarfs our national GDP of about $14 trillion!) is U.S. Treasury-issued savings bonds, which can be purchased for as little as $25. Two types are out there — EE and I bonds. The interest rate for the EE bond is fixed, while the I bond's interest rate changes every six months, as it's tied to the official inflation rate referred to as the Consumer Price Index (CPI). If rates go up, the U.S. Treasury automatically updates the interest rate on your I savings bonds every six months so you aren't locked in to low rates when market rates are rising. Savings bonds are ultra safe, convenient, and inexpensive to buy, and they're free from state and local taxes. Find out more at the U.S. Treasury Web site (www.savingsbonds.gov).

Consider a mix of small cap, mid cap, and large cap growth stocks in growth industries (see Chapter 1 for an explanation of small cap, mid cap, and large cap stocks; I provide information on industries in Chapter 13). Invest some of your money in five to seven stocks and the remainder in growth-stock mutual funds. You can revise your investment allocations along the way as the general economy and/or your personal situation changes (like when you finally say "I do" to the love of your life).

Going together like a horse and carriage: Married with children

Married couples with children must follow a more conservative investing strategy, regardless of whether one spouse works or both spouses work. Children change the picture drastically (believe me; I have them — and the baggy eyes to prove it). You need more stable growth in your portfolio (and unbreakable furniture in your home).

 Consider a mix of large cap growth stocks and dividend-paying defensive stocks. (See Chapter 9 for more on defensive stocks.) Invest some of your money in five to seven stocks and the remainder in growth and income mutual funds. Of course, you can tweak your allocations along the way according to changes in the general economic conditions or your personal situation. Consider setting aside money for college in a growth-oriented mutual fund and in other vehicles such as savings bonds (as early as possible). For more information on financing college, check out *529 & Other College Savings Plans For Dummies* by Margaret A. Munro (published by Wiley).

Getting ready for retirement: Over 40 and either single or married

Whether you're over 40 and single or over 40 and married — and if married, whether one or both of you work — you should start to slowly convert your portfolio from aggressive growth to conservative growth. Shift more of your money out of individual stocks and into less-volatile investments such as balanced funds, investment-grade bonds, and bank certificates of deposit.

Devote some time and effort (with a financial planner if necessary) to calculating what your potential financial needs will be at retirement time. This step is critical in helping you decide what age to target for financial independence. (What's that? I can stop working?! Yee-ha!)

Consider five to seven large cap stocks that are predominantly dividend-paying defensive stocks in stable and needed industries (such as utilities, food and beverage, and so on). Put the remainder of your investment money in balanced mutual funds and short-term investment-grade bond funds. Don't invest all your money — keep about 10 to 15 percent of it in something very secure, such as savings bonds and bank vehicles (savings accounts and certificates of deposit). Keep savings in at least two separate institutions if possible to be diversified in today's uncertain economy. Remember that you can revise your allocations in the future as necessary.

Kicking back in the hammock: Already retired

If you're retired, you're probably in your 60s or older. Safe, reliable income and wealth preservation form the crux of your investment strategy. Some growth-oriented investments are okay as long as they're conservative and don't jeopardize your need for income. At one time, financial planners told their retired clients to replace growth-oriented investments with safe income-oriented investments. However, times have changed as senior citizens live longer than ever before.

Issues such as longevity and inflation (steadily increasing costs of living) mean that today's (and tomorrow's) retirees need growth in their portfolios. To be safe, make sure that 5–20 percent of your retirement portfolio has some growth-oriented securities such as stocks to make sure that you continue meeting your financial needs as the years pass. You should perform an annual review to see whether the stock allocation needs to be adjusted.

Consider a mix of large cap stocks dominated by dividend-paying defensive stocks in stable industries. Spread your money over three to six stocks, balanced mutual funds, and short-term investment-grade bond funds. Have a portion of your money in savings bonds and bank investments. You need to monitor and tweak your investment portfolio along the way to account for changes in either the general economic environment or your lifestyle needs.

Allocating Your Assets

Asset allocation is really an attempt to properly implement the concept of diversification — the key to safety and stability. *Diversification* is the inclusion in your portfolio of different (and frequently offsetting) investments to shield your wealth from most types of current risk while planning for future growth. To achieve proper diversification, you need to analyze your entire portfolio to look for glaring weaknesses or vulnerable areas. I don't discuss your total investment plan here — only the stock portion.

Investors frequently believe that having different stocks in different industries constitutes proper diversification. Well . . . not quite. Stocks in closely related industries tend to be affected (in differing degrees) by the same economic events, government policies, and so on. It's best to invest in stocks across different sectors. A *sector* is essentially a group of related industries; water, gas, and electric services are industries, but together they (plus a few other industries) make up the utilities sector. For more on analyzing industries to pick winning stocks, see Chapter 13.

Earlier in this chapter, I talk about some basics for investing, depending on your lifestyle, but how do you know how much you need to invest to meet your financial goals? In the following sections, I present some typical amounts most typical investors can (and should) devote to stock investing.

Investors with less than $10,000

If you have $10,000 or less to allocate to stocks, you may want to consider a mutual fund rather than individual stocks because that sum of money may not be enough to properly diversify. But if you're going to invest a sum that small, consider allocating it equally into two to four stocks in two different sectors that look strong for the foreseeable future. For small investors, consider sectors that are defensive in nature (such as food and utilities).

Because $10,000 or less is a small sum in the world of stock investing, you may have to purchase in odd lots. (*Odd lots* usually mean 99 shares or fewer. A block of 100 shares is considered a *round lot,* and 200 shares would be considered two round lots.) Say that you're buying four stocks, and all of them are priced at $50 per share. Obviously, your $10,000 won't buy you 100 shares of each. You may have to consider investing $2,500 in each stock, which means that you end up buying only 50 shares of each stock (not including commissions). Whether you buy an odd lot or a round lot, find out whether the company has a dividend reinvestment plan (DRP), and use the dividend money you earn to buy more shares of stock. (I discuss DRPs more fully in Chapter 19.)

Try to avoid the temptation of getting into initial public offerings (IPOs; see Chapter 8), penny stocks, and other speculative issues. Participation in them may cost little (stock prices are often under $10 per share and can be under $1), but the risk exposure is too high for inexperienced investors. If you can't buy 100 shares of a large-cap stock, consider buying fewer shares, because commissions are still relatively low. In general, it's safer to buy 50 shares of a large, established company than the same amount in a smaller, riskier company.

Investors with $10,000 to $50,000

If you have between $10,000 and $50,000 to invest, you have more breathing space for diversification. Consider buying four to six stocks in two or three different sectors. If you're the cautious type, defensive stocks will do. For growth investors, seek the industries in those sectors that have proven growth. This approach gets you off to a good start, and the section "Knowing When to Sell," later in this chapter, can help you maintain your portfolio by changing your strategy when necessary.

Does diversification mean that you shouldn't, under any circumstances, have all your stocks in one sector? It depends on you. For example, if you've worked all your life in a particular field and you're knowledgeable and comfortable with the sector, having a greater exposure is okay because your greater personal expertise offsets the risk. If you worked in retail for 20 years and know the industry inside and out, you probably know more about the good, the bad, and the ugly of the retail sector than most Wall Street analysts. Use your insight for more profitability. You still shouldn't invest all your money in that single sector, however, because diversification is still vital.

Investors with $50,000 or more

If you have $50,000 or more to invest, have no more than five to ten stocks in two or three different sectors. It's difficult to thoroughly track more than two or three sectors and do it successfully — best to keep it simple. For example, Warren Buffett, considered the greatest stock market investor of all time, has never invested in Web site businesses because he doesn't understand them. He invests only in businesses that he understands. If that strategy works for billionaire investors, then, by golly, it can't be that bad for smaller investors.

I suggest investing in no more than seven to ten stocks, because there is such a thing as overdiversification. The more stocks you have, the tougher it is to keep track of them. Owning more stocks means you need to do more research, read more annual reports and news articles, and follow the business news of more companies. Even in the best of times, you need to regularly monitor your stocks because successful investing requires diligent effort.

Consider whether to hire a personal money manager (a person that manages investment portfolios for a fee). If you have $50,000 to $100,000 or more, doing so may make sense. Get a referral from a financial planner and carefully weigh the benefits against the costs. Here are some points to consider:

- **Make sure that the money manager has a philosophy and an approach that you agree with.** Ask her to give you a copy of her written investment philosophy. How does she feel about small cap stocks versus large caps, or income investing versus growth investing?

- **Find out whether you're comfortable with how the money manager selects stocks.** Is he a value investor or a growth investor? Is he aggressive or conservative? Does he analyze a stock based on its fundamentals (sales, earnings, book value, and so on), or does he use stock price charts?

- **Ask the money manager to explain her strategy.** A good way to evaluate the success (or failure) of the money manager's strategy is to ask her for her past recommendations. Did she pick more winners than losers?

- **Ask the money manager to describe his economic philosophy.** Is it Keynesian, Austrian, or some other school of thought? Yes, it does matter, and Chapter 10 gives you some details about this (I happen to be in the Austrian school of thought).

Knowing When to Sell

The act of buying stock is relatively easy. However, the act of selling stock can be an agonizing decision for investors. But it's agonizing only in two instances: when you've made money with your stock and when you've lost it. That about covers it. It sounds like a bad joke, but it's not that far from the truth.

The idea of selling stock when it has appreciated (the stock price has increased in value) comes with the following concerns:

- **Tax implications:** This concern is a good reason to consider selling. See Chapter 21 for information about how selling stocks under given circumstances can affect your taxes.

- **Emotional baggage:** "That stock was in our family for years." Believe it or not, investors cite this personal reason (or one of a dozen other personal reasons) for agonizing over the sale of an appreciated stock.

The following is a list of issues that investors should be aware of when they're selling a stock that has lost money:

- ✓ **Tax benefits:** This issue is a good reason to consider selling a stock. See Chapter 21 for more on timing your stock sales to minimize your tax burden.

- ✓ **Pride:** "If I sell, I'll have to admit I was wrong" (followed by silent sobbing). So what? The best investors in history have made bad investments (some that have been quite embarrassing, in fact). Losing a little pride is cheaper than losing your money.

- ✓ **Doubt:** "If I sell my stock now, it may rebound later." Frequently, when an investor buys a stock at $50 and it goes to $40, the investor believes that if he sells, the stock will make an immediate rebound and go to $60, and then he'll be kicking himself. That may happen, but usually the stock price goes lower.

- ✓ **Separation anxiety:** "But I've had this stock so long that it's become a part of me." People hang onto a losing stock for all sorts of illogical reasons. Being married to a person is great; being married to a stock is ludicrous. If a stock isn't helping your goals, then it's hurting your goals.

People have plenty more reasons to agonize over the sale of a bad stock, but you can learn to handle the stock sale in a disciplined manner.

You have only two reasons to consider selling a stock, regardless of whether the stock price has gone up or down:

- ✓ **You need the money.** Obviously, if you need the money for a bona fide reason — such as paying off debt, wiping out a tax bill, or buying a home — then you need the money. This reason is easy to see. After all, regardless of investment or tax considerations, stocks are there to serve you. I hope you do some financial planning so that you don't need to sell your stocks for these types of expenses, but you can't avoid unexpected expenditures.

- ✓ **The stock ceases to perform as you desire.** If the stock isn't serving your wealth-building goals or fulfilling your investment objectives, it's time to get rid of it and move on to the next stock. Just as soon as you get a stiff upper lip and resolve to unload this losing stock, a little voice saying, "If I sell my stock now, it may rebound later," starts to haunt you. So you hang onto the stock, but then — bam! — before you know it, you lose more money.

Selling a stock shouldn't require a psychologist, but it does require discipline, which is why I'm a big proponent of trailing stops (see Chapter 18 for more on stop orders). Trailing stops take the agony out of selling the stock. All else being equal, you shouldn't sell a winning stock. If it's doing well, why sell it? Keep it as long as possible. But if it stops being a winning stock, sell it. If you don't know how or when to sell it, then apply a stop-loss order at 5 or 10 percent below the market value and let the market action take its course.

Chapter 18

Understanding Brokerage Orders and Trading Techniques

In This Chapter

▶ Looking at different types of brokerage orders

▶ Trading on margin to maximize profits

▶ Making sense of going short

*I*nvestment success isn't just about *which* stocks to choose; it's also about *how* you choose those stocks. Frequently, investors think that good stock picking means doing your homework and then making that buy (or sell). However, you can take it a step further to maximize profits (or minimize losses). As a stock investor, you can take advantage of techniques and services available through your standard brokerage account (see Chapter 7 for details). This chapter presents some of the best ways you can use these powerful techniques, which are useful whether you're buying or selling stock.

Just before the stock market bubble of 2000 popped, I warned my students and readers that a bear market was on the way. All the data warned me about it, and undoubtedly, it seemed like a time for caution. Investors didn't have to necessarily believe me, but they could have (at the very least) used trailing stops and other techniques to ensure greater investing success. Investors who used stop-loss orders avoided the carnage of trillions of dollars in stock losses. In this chapter, I show you how to use these techniques to maximize your investing profit.

Checking Out Brokerage Orders

Orders you place with your stockbroker fit neatly into three categories:

✓ Time-related orders

✓ Condition-related orders

✓ Advanced orders

At the very least, get familiar with the first two types of orders because they're easy to implement, and they're invaluable tools for wealth building and (more importantly) wealth saving! Advanced orders usually are combinations of the first two types.

Using a combination of orders helps you fine-tune your strategy so that you can maintain greater control over your investments. Speak with your broker about the different types of orders you can use to maximize the gains (or minimize the losses) from your stock investing activities. You also can read the broker's policies on stock orders at the brokerage Web site.

On the clock: Time-related orders

Time-related orders are just that — the order has a time limit. Typically, investors use these orders in conjunction with condition-related orders, which I describe later in this chapter. The two most common time-related orders are day orders and good-till-canceled (or GTC) orders.

Day order

A *day order* is an order to buy or sell a stock that expires at the end of that particular trading day. If you tell your broker, "Buy BYOB, Inc., at $37.50 and make it a day order," you mean that you want to purchase the stock at $37.50. But if the stock doesn't hit that price, your order expires, unfilled, at the end of the trading day. Why would you place such an order? Maybe BYOB is trading at $39, but you don't want to buy it at that price because you don't believe the stock is worth it. Consequently, you have no problem not getting the stock that day.

When would you use day orders? It depends on your preferences and personal circumstances. I rarely use day orders because few events cause me to say, "Gee, I'll just try to buy or sell between now and the end of today's trading action." However, you may feel that you don't want a specified order to linger beyond today's market action. Perhaps you want to test a price. ("I want to get rid of stock A at $39 to make a quick profit, but it's currently trading at $37.50. However, I may change my mind tomorrow.") A day order is the perfect strategy to use in this case.

If you make a trade and don't specify time with the order, most (if not all) brokers automatically treat it as a day order.

Good-till-canceled (GTC) order

A good-till-canceled (GTC) order is the most commonly requested order by investors. The GTC order means just what it says: The order stays in effect until it's transacted or until the investor cancels it. Although GTC orders are time-related, they're always tied to a condition, such as when the stock achieves a certain price.

Although the order implies that it can run indefinitely, most brokers have a limit of 30 or 60 days (or more). By that time, either the broker cancels the order or contacts you to see whether you want to extend it. Ask your broker about his particular policy.

A GTC order is usually coupled with condition-related orders. For example, say that you want to buy ASAP Corp. stock but you don't want to buy it at the current price of $48 per share. You've done your homework on the stock, including looking at the stock's price-to-earnings ratio, price to book ratio, and so on (see Appendix B for more on ratios), and you say, "Hey, this stock isn't worth $48 a share. I'd only buy it at $36 per share." You think the stock would make a good addition to your portfolio but not at the current market price. (It's overpriced or overvalued according to your analysis.) How should you proceed? Your best bet is to ask your broker to do a GTC order at $36. This request means that your broker will buy the shares if and when they hit the $36 mark (unless you cancel the order). Just make sure that your account has the funds available to complete the transaction.

GTC orders are very useful, so you should become familiar with your broker's policy on them. While you're at it, ask whether any fees apply. Many brokers don't charge for GTC orders because if they happen to result in a buy (or sell) order, they generate a normal commission just as any stock transaction does. Other brokers may charge a small fee.

To be successful with GTC orders, you need to know

- ✔ **When you want to buy:** In recent years, people have had a tendency to rush into buying a stock without giving some thought to what they could do to get more for their money. Some investors don't realize that the stock market can be a place for bargain-hunting consumers. If you're ready to buy a quality pair of socks for $16 in a department store but the sales clerk says that those same socks are going on sale tomorrow for only $8, what would you do — assuming that you're a cost-conscious consumer? Unless you're barefoot, you're probably better off waiting. The same point holds true with stocks.

Say that you want to buy SOX, Inc., at $26, but it's currently trading at $30. You think that $30 is too expensive, but you're happy to buy the stock at $26 or lower. However, you have no idea whether the stock will move to your desired price today, tomorrow, next week, or even next month (maybe never). In this case, a GTC order is appropriate.

✔ **When you want to sell:** What if you buy some socks at a department store and you discover that they have holes (darn it!)? Wouldn't you want to get rid of them? Of course you would. If a stock's price starts to unravel, you want to be able to get rid of it as well.

Perhaps you already own SOX at $25 but are concerned that market conditions may drive the price lower. You're not certain which way the stock will move in the coming days and weeks. In this case, a GTC order to sell the stock at a specified price is a suitable strategy. Because the stock price is $25, you may want to place a GTC order to sell it if it falls to $22.50, to prevent further losses. Again, in this example, GTC is the time frame, and it accompanies a condition (sell when the stock hits $22.50).

At your command: Condition-related orders

A condition-related order (also known as a conditional order) is an order that's executed only when a certain condition is met. Conditional orders enhance your ability to buy stocks at a lower price, to sell at a better price, or to minimize potential losses. When stock markets become bearish or uncertain, conditional orders are highly recommended.

A good example of a conditional order is a *limit order*. A limit order may say, "Buy Mojeski Corp. at $45." But if Mojeski Corp. isn't at $45 (this price is the condition), then the order isn't executed. I discuss limit orders, as well as market orders and stop orders, in the following sections.

Market orders

When you buy stock, the simplest type of order is a *market order* — an order to buy or sell a stock at the market's current best available price. Orders don't get any more basic than that. Here's an example: Kowalski, Inc., is available at the market price of $10. When you call up your broker and instruct her to buy 100 shares "at the market," the broker will implement the order for your account, and you pay $1,000 plus commission.

I say "current best available price" because the stock's price is constantly moving, and catching the best price can be a function of the broker's ability to process the stock purchase. For very active stocks, the price change can happen within seconds. It's not unheard of to have three brokers simultaneously place orders for the same stock and get three different prices because of differences in the brokers' capabilities. (Some computers are faster than others.)

The advantage of a market order is that the transaction is processed immediately, and you get your stock without worrying about whether it hits a particular price. For example, if you buy Kowalski, Inc., with a market order, you know that by the end of that phone call (or Web site visit), you're assured of getting the stock. The disadvantage of a market order is that you can't control the price of the stock. Whether you're buying or selling your shares, you may not realize the exact price you expect (especially if you're dealing with a volatile stock).

Market orders get finalized in the chronological order in which they're placed. Your price may change because the orders ahead of you in line cause the stock price to rise or fall based on the latest news.

Stop-loss orders (also known as stop orders)

A *stop-loss order* (also called a *stop order*) is a condition-related order that instructs the broker to sell a particular stock in your portfolio only when the stock reaches a particular price. It acts like a trigger, and the stop order converts to a market order to sell the stock immediately.

The stop-loss order isn't designed to take advantage of small, short-term moves in the stock's price. It's meant to help you protect the bulk of your money when the market turns against your stock investment in a sudden manner.

Say that your Kowalski, Inc., stock rises to $20 per share and you seek to protect your investment against a possible future market decline. A stop-loss order at $18 triggers your broker to sell the stock immediately if it falls to the $18 mark. In this example, if the stock suddenly drops to $17, it still triggers the stop-loss order, but the finalized sale price is $17. In a volatile market, you may not be able to sell at your precise stop-loss price. However, because the order automatically gets converted into a market order, the sale will be done, and you prevent further declines in the stock.

The main benefit of a stop-loss order is that it prevents a major loss in a stock that you own. It's a form of discipline that's important in investing in order to minimize potential losses. Investors can find it agonizing to sell a stock that has fallen. If they don't sell, however, the stock often continues to plummet as investors continue to hold on while hoping for a rebound in the price.

Most investors set a stop-loss amount at about 10 percent below the market value of the stock. This percentage gives the stock some room to fluctuate, which most stocks tend to do on a day-to-day basis.

Trailing stops

Trailing stops are an important technique in wealth preservation for seasoned stock investors and can be one of your key strategies in using stop-loss orders. A *trailing stop* is a stop-loss order that an investor actively manages by moving it up along with the stock's market price. The stop-loss order "trails" the stock price upward. As the stop-loss goes upward, it protects more and more of the stock's value from declining.

A real-life example may be the best way to help you understand trailing stops. Say that you bought Apple (AAPL) in April 2007 for about $90 per share. You would have seen AAPL soar to $200 by the end of 2007 — yup, that iPod would have brought tears to your eyes. If you had a trailing stop on your stock, it would not have been triggered as AAPL trended upward. However, AAPL peaked at that price and then zigzagged downward. Had you continued to do trailing stops along the way, the odds are that you would have been stopped out as AAPL started trending downward.

Practicing discipline with stop-loss orders

I have a stack of several years' worth of investment newsletters in which investment experts made all sorts of calls regarding the prospects of a company, industry, or the economy in general. Some made forecasts that were spectacularly on target, but you should see the ones that were spectacularly wrong — ouch! However, even some of the winners suffered because of a lack of discipline. Those spectacular gains disappeared like balloons at a porcupine convention.

Some of the strongest recommendations made by newsletter experts in 2007 were financial stocks such as Bank of America (BAC). In November 2007, its stock traded at $48. However, BAC had much exposure to subprime debt and derivatives. Even if you didn't know that, you still heard rumblings in the headlines about credit problems in the overall financial sector. Sometimes you don't know a bank has bad debt in its financial picture until it goes bad.

A wary investor would either stay away or at least play it safe if a stock like BAC were in the investor's portfolio.

Fast forward to 2008. The credit and banking crises are in full bloom. BAC's stock price plummets to $19 per share by October 2008. If an investor had placed a stop-loss order at, say, $43 (roughly 10 percent the original price of $48), he would have been saved from a free-fall. BAC hitting $19 means that in less than a year, it fell 60 percent. Right about now you know that some of those newsletter experts are in a new profession asking their clients, "Would you like those loafers in black or brown?"

Investing can be an emotional roller coaster. Keep your sanity and your profits by being disciplined. Use your stop-loss orders and fasten those seat belts.

A trailing stop of, say, 10 percent would have been triggered at $180 in January (10 percent of the AAPL stock price of $200 equals $20, so the stock would have been sold at $180). By March 2008, AAPL stock hit $120 before stabilizing and heading back up. With the trailing stop strategy continuously on, an AAPL investor buying at $90 (April 2007) would have realized a 100 percent gain when the stock was sold in January 2008 at $180. If the investor bought the stock again at the $120 level, she would have witnessed AAPL's rise to $190 in the summer of 2008 before its painful descent back to under $90 in October 2008. Time to trade in that gadget for some antacids.

William O'Neill, founder and publisher of *Investor's Business Daily,* advocates setting a trailing stop of 8 percent below your purchase price. That's his preference. Some investors who invest in very volatile stocks may put in trailing stops of 20 or 25 percent. Is a stop-loss order desirable or advisable in every situation? No. It depends on your level of experience, your investment goals, and the market environment. Still, stop-loss orders are appropriate in most cases, especially if the market seems uncertain (or you do!).

A trailing stop is a stop-loss order that you actively manage. The stop-loss order is good-till-canceled (GTC), and it constantly trails the stock's price as it moves up. To successfully implement trailing stops, you should

- ✔ **Realize that brokers usually don't place trailing stops for you automatically.** In fact, they won't (or shouldn't) place any type of order without your consent. Deciding on the type of order to place is your responsibility. You can raise, lower, or cancel a trailing stop order at will, but you need to monitor your investment when substantial moves do occur to respond to the movement appropriately.

- ✔ **Change the stop-loss order when the stock price moves significantly.** Hopefully, you won't call your broker every time the stock moves 50 cents. Change the stop-loss order when the stock price moves around 10 percent. For example, if you initially purchase a stock at $90 per share, request the broker to place the stop-loss order at $81. When the stock moves to $100, cancel the $81 stop-loss order and replace it at $90. When the stock's price moves to $110, change the stop-loss order to $99, and so on.

- ✔ **Understand your broker's policy on GTC orders.** If your broker usually has a GTC order expire after 30 or 60 days, you should be aware of it. You don't want to risk a sudden drop in your stock's price without the stop-loss order protection. If your broker's time limit is 60 days, note it so that you can renew the order for additional time.

- ✔ **Monitor your stock.** A trailing stop isn't a "set it and forget it" technique. Monitoring your investment is critical. Of course, if the investment falls, the stop-loss order prevents further loss. Should the stock price rise substantially, remember to adjust your trailing stop accordingly. Keep raising the safety net as the stock continues to rise. Part of monitoring the stock is knowing the beta, which you can read more about in the next section.

Using beta measurement

To be a successful investor, you need to understand the volatility of the particular stock you invest in. In stock market parlance, this volatility is also called the beta of a stock. *Beta* is a quantitative measure of the volatility of a given stock (mutual funds and portfolios, too) relative to the overall market, usually the S&P 500 index. (For more information on the S&P 500, see Chapter 5.) Beta specifically measures the performance movement of the stock as the S&P moves 1 percent up or down. A beta measurement above 1 is more volatile than the overall market, while a beta below 1 is less volatile. Some stocks are relatively stable in the price movements; others jump around.

Because beta measures how volatile or unstable the stock's price is, it tends to be uttered in the same breath as "risk" — more volatility indicates more risk. Similarly, less volatility tends to mean less risk.

You can find a company's beta at Web sites that provide a lot of financial information about companies, such as Nasdaq (www.nasdaq.com) or Yahoo! Finance (finance.yahoo.com).

The beta is useful to know when it comes to stop-loss orders because it gives you a general idea of the stock's trading range. If a stock is currently priced at $50 and it typically trades in the $48–$52 range, then a trailing stop at $49 doesn't make sense. Your stock would probably be sold the same day you initiated the stop-loss order. If your stock is a volatile growth stock that may swing up and down by 10 percent, you should more logically set your stop-loss at 15 percent below that day's price.

The stock of a large cap company in a mature industry tends to have a low beta — one close to the overall market. Small and mid cap stocks in new or emerging industries tend to have greater volatility in their day-to-day price fluctuations; hence, they tend to have a high beta. (You can find out more about large, small, and mid cap stocks in Chapter 1.)

Limit orders

A *limit order* is a very precise condition-related order implying that a limit exists either on the buy or the sell side of the transaction. You want to buy (or sell) only at a specified price or better. Period. Limit orders work well if you're buying the stock, and they may not be good for you if you're selling the stock. Here's how they work in both instances:

- ✔ **When you're buying:** Just because you like a particular company and you want its stock doesn't mean that you're willing to pay the current market price. Maybe you want to buy Kowalski, Inc., but the current market price of $20 per share isn't acceptable to you. You prefer to buy it at $16 because you think that price reflects its true market value. What do you do? You tell your broker, "Buy Kowalski with a limit order at $16" (or you can enter a limit order at the broker's Web site). You have to specify whether it's a day order or a GTC order, both of which I discuss earlier in this chapter.

What happens if the stock experiences great volatility? What if it drops to $16.01 and then suddenly drops to $15.95 on the next move? Nothing happens, actually, which you may be dismayed to hear. Because your order was limited to $16, it can be transacted only at $16 — no more or less. The only way for this particular trade to occur is if the stock rises back to $16. However, if the price keeps dropping, then your limit order isn't transacted and may expire or be canceled.

When you're buying a stock, most brokers interpret the limit order as "buy at this specific price or better." Presumably, if your limit order is to buy the stock at $10, you'll be just as happy if your broker buys that stock at $9.95. That way, if you don't get exactly $10 because the stock's price was volatile, you'll still get the stock at a lower price. Talk to your broker to be clear on the meaning of the limit order.

✔ **When you're selling:** Limit orders are activated only when a stock hits a specific price. If you buy Kowalski, Inc., at $20 and you worry about a decline in the share price, you may decide to put in a limit order at $18. If you watch the news and hear that Kowalski's price is dropping, you may sigh and say, "I sure am glad that I put in that limit order at $18!" However, in a volatile market, the share price may leapfrog over your specified price. It could go from $18.01 to $17.99 and then continue its descent. Because the stock price never hit $18 on the mark, it isn't sold. You may be sitting at home satisfied (mistakenly) that you played it smart, while your stock plummets to $15 or $10 or worse! Having a stop-loss order in place is best.

Investors who aren't in a hurry can use a limit order to try to get a better price when they decide to sell. For example, maybe you own a stock whose price is at $50 and you want to sell, but you think that a short-term rally in the stock is imminent. In that case, you can use a limit order such as, "Sell the stock at the sell limit order of $55 and keep the order on for 30 days."

The joys of technology: Advanced orders

Brokers have added sophisticated capabilities to the existing repertoire of orders that are available for stock investors. One example is *advanced orders,* which provide investors with a way to use a combination of orders for more sophisticated trades. An example of an advanced order is something like, "Only sell stock B, and if it sells, use the proceeds to buy stock D." You get the idea. My brokerage firm has the following on its Web site, and I'm sure that more firms will do the same. Inquire with yours and see the benefit of using advanced orders such as the following:

- ✔ **"One Order Cancels Another Order":** This happens when you enter two orders simultaneously with the condition that if one order is executed, the second order is automatically cancelled.

- ✔ **"One Order Triggers Another Order":** Here you submit an order, and if that order is filled, another order is automatically submitted. Many brokers have different names for these types of orders, so ask them if they can provide such an order.

Other types of advanced orders are available, but you get the picture. Talk to your brokerage firm and find out what's available in your particular account. Investors need to know that today's technology allows them to have more power and control over the implementation of buying and selling transactions. I love it!

Buying on Margin

Buying on margin means buying securities, such as stocks, with funds you borrow from your broker. Buying stock on margin is similar to buying a house with a mortgage. If you buy a house at a purchase price of $100,000 and put 10 percent down, your equity (the part you own) is $10,000, and you borrow the remaining $90,000 with a mortgage. If the value of the house rises to $120,000 and you sell (for the sake of simplicity, I don't include closing costs in this example), you make a profit of 200 percent. How is that? The $20,000 gain on the property represents a gain of 20 percent on the purchase price of $100,000, but because your real investment is $10,000 (the down payment), your gain works out to 200 percent (a gain of $20,000 on your initial investment of $10,000).

Buying on margin is an example of using leverage to maximize your gain when prices rise. *Leverage* is simply using borrowed money when you make an asset purchase in order to increase your potential profit. This type of leverage is great in a favorable (bull) market, but it works against you in an unfavorable (bear) market. Say that a $100,000 house you purchase with a $90,000 mortgage falls in value to $80,000 (and property values can decrease during economic hard times). Your outstanding debt of $90,000 exceeds the value of the property. Because you owe more than you own, you're left with a negative net worth.

Leverage is a double-edged sword. Don't forget that you need approval from your brokerage firm before you can go short.

Examining marginal outcomes

Suppose that you think that the stock for the company Mergatroid, Inc., currently at $40 per share, will go up in value. You want to buy 100 shares, but you have only $2,000. What can you do? If you're intent on buying 100 shares (versus simply buying the 50 shares that you have cash for), you can borrow the additional $2,000 from your broker on margin. If you do that, what are the potential outcomes?

If the stock price goes up

This outcome is the best for you. If Mergatroid goes to $50 per share, your investment is worth $5,000, and your outstanding margin loan is $2,000. If you sell, the total proceeds will pay off the loan and leave you with $3,000. Because your initial investment was $2,000, your profit is a solid 50 percent because your $2,000 principal amount generated a $1,000 profit. (For the sake of this example, I leave out any charges, such as commissions and interest paid on the margin loan.) However, if you pay the entire $4,000 upfront without the margin loan, your $4,000 investment generates a profit of $1,000, or 25 percent. Using margin, you double the return on your money.

Leverage, when used properly, is very profitable. However, it's still debt, so understand that you must pay it off eventually, regardless of the stock's performance.

If the stock price fails to rise

If the stock goes nowhere, you still have to pay interest on that margin loan. If the stock pays dividends, this money can defray some of the margin loan's cost. In other words, dividends can help you pay off what you borrow from the broker.

Having the stock neither rise nor fall may seem like a neutral situation, but you pay interest on your margin loan with each passing day. For this reason, margin trading can be a good consideration for conservative investors if the stock pays a high dividend. Many times, a high dividend from $5,000 worth of stock can exceed the margin interest you have to pay from the $2,500 (50 percent) you borrow from the broker to buy that stock.

If the stock price goes down, buying on margin can work against you. What if Mergatroid goes to $38 per share? The market value of 100 shares is then $3,800, but your equity shrinks to only $1,800 because you have to pay your $2,000 margin loan. You're not exactly looking at a disaster at this point, but you'd better be careful, because the margin loan exceeds 50 percent of your stock investment. If it goes any lower, you may get the dreaded *margin call,* when the broker actually contacts you to ask you to restore the ratio between the margin loan and the value of the securities. See the following section for information about appropriate debt to equity ratios.

Maintaining your balance

When you purchase stock on margin, you must maintain a balanced ratio of margin debt to equity of at least 50 percent. If the debt portion exceeds this limit, you're required to restore that ratio by depositing either more stock or more cash into your brokerage account. The additional stock you deposit can be stock that's transferred from another account.

To continue the example from the previous section: If Mergatroid goes to $28 per share, the margin loan portion exceeds 50 percent of the equity value in that stock — in this case, because the market value of your stock is $2,800 but the margin loan is still at $2,000, the margin loan is a worrisome 71 percent of the market value ($2,000 divided by $2,800 = 71 percent). Expect to get a call from your broker to put more securities or cash into the account to restore the 50 percent balance.

If you can't come up with more stock, other securities, or cash, the next step is to sell stock from the account and use the proceeds to pay off the margin loan. For you, that means realizing a capital loss — you lost money on your investment.

The Federal Reserve Board governs margin requirements for brokers with Regulation T. Discuss this rule with your broker to understand fully your (and the broker's) risks and obligations. Regulation T dictates margin requirements set by brokers for their customers. For most listed stocks, it's 50 percent.

Striving for success on margin

Margin, as you can see from the previous sections, can escalate your profits on the up side but magnify your losses on the down side. If your stock plummets drastically, you can end up with a margin loan that exceeds the market value of the stock you used the loan to purchase. In the emerging bear market of 2000–2002, stock losses hurt many people, and a large number of those losses were made worse because people didn't manage the responsibilities involved with margin trading. In 2008, margin debt hit record highs, which means that investors may (again!) be at risk.

If you buy stock on margin, use a disciplined approach. Be extra careful when using leverage, such as a margin loan, because it can backfire. Keep the following points in mind:

✔ **Have ample reserves of cash or marginable securities in your account.** Try to keep the margin ratio at 40 percent or less to minimize the chance of a margin call.

✔ **If you're a beginner, consider using margin to buy stock in large companies that have a relatively stable price and pay a good dividend.** Some people buy income stocks that have dividend yields that exceed the margin interest rate, meaning that the stock ends up paying for its own margin loan. Just remember those stop orders.

✔ **Constantly monitor your stocks.** If the market turns against you, the result will be especially painful if you use margin.

✔ **Have a payback plan for your margin debt.** Taking margin loans against your investments means that you're paying interest. Your ultimate goal is to make money, and paying interest eats into your profits.

Going Short and Coming Out Ahead

The vast majority of stock investors are familiar with buying stock, holding onto it for a while, and hoping its value goes up. This kind of thinking is called *going long,* and investors who go long are considered to be *long on stocks.* Going long essentially means that you're bullish and seeking your profits from rising prices. However, astute investors also profit in the market when stock prices fall. *Going short* (also called *shorting a stock, selling short,* or *doing a short sale*) on a stock is a common technique for profiting from a stock price decline. Investors have made big profits during bear markets by going short. A short sale is a bet that a particular stock is going down.

Most people easily understand making money by going long. It boils down to "buy low and sell high." Piece of cake. Going short means making money by selling high and then buying low. Huh? Thinking in reverse isn't a piece of cake. Although thinking of this stock adage in reverse may be challenging, the mechanics of going short are really simple. Consider an example that uses a fictitious company called DOA, Inc. As a stock, DOA ($50 per share) is looking pretty sickly. It has lots of debt and plummeting sales and earnings, and the news is out that DOA's industry will face hard times for the foreseeable future. This situation describes a stock that's an ideal candidate for shorting. The future may be bleak for DOA, but it's promising for savvy investors.

To go short, you have to be deemed (by your broker) creditworthy — your account needs to be approved for short selling. When you're approved for margin trading, you're probably set to sell short, too. Talk to your broker (or check for this information on the broker's Web site) about limitations in your account regarding going short.

You must understand brokerage rules before you conduct short selling. The broker must approve you for it (see Chapter 7 for information on working with brokers), and you must meet the minimum collateral requirement, which is typically $2,000 or 50 percent of the shorted stock's market value. If the stock generates dividends, those dividends are paid to the stock's owner, not to the person who borrows it to go short. Check with your broker for complete details, and review the resources in Appendix A.

Because going short on stocks has greater risks than going long, I strongly advise beginning investors to avoid shorting stocks until they become more seasoned.

Setting up a short sale

This section explains how to go short. Say that you believe that DOA is the right stock to short — you're pretty sure its price is going to fall. With DOA at $50, you instruct your broker to "go short 100 shares on DOA." (It doesn't have to be 100 shares; I'm just using that as an example.) Here's what happens next:

1. **Your broker borrows 100 shares of DOA stock, either from his own inventory or from another client or broker.**

   That's right. The stock can be borrowed from a client, no permission necessary. The broker guarantees the transaction, and the client/stock owner never has to be informed about it because he never loses legal and beneficial right to the stock. You borrow 100 shares, and you'll return 100 shares when it's time to complete the transaction.

2. **Your broker then sells the stock and puts the money in your account.**

   Your account is credited with $5,000 (100 shares × $50) in cash — the money gained from selling the borrowed stock. This cash acts like a loan on which you're going to have to pay interest.

3. **You buy the stock back and return it to its rightful owner.**

   When it's time to close the transaction (either you want to close it or the owner of the shares wants to sell them, so you have to give them back), you must return the number of shares you borrowed (in this case, it was 100 shares). If you buy back the 100 shares at $40 per share (remember that you shorted this particular stock because you were sure its price was going to fall) and those 100 shares are returned to their owner, you make a $1,000 profit. (To keep the example tidy, I don't include brokerage commissions.)

Oops! Going short when prices grow taller

I bet you guessed that the wonderful profitability of selling short has a flip side. Say that you were wrong about DOA and that the stock price rises from the ashes as it goes from $50 to $87. Now what? You still have to return the 100 shares you borrowed. With the stock's price at $87, that means you have to buy the stock for $8,700 (100 shares at the new, higher price of $87). Ouch! How do you pay for it? Well, you have that original $5,000 in your account from when you initially went short on the stock. But where do you get the other $3,700 ($8,700 less the original $5,000)? You guessed it — your pocket! You have to cough up the difference. If the stock continues to rise, that's a lot of coughing.

How much money do you lose if the stock goes to $100 or more? A heck of a lot. As a matter of fact, there's no limit to how much you can lose. That's why going short can be riskier than going long. When going long, the most you can lose is 100 percent of your money. When you go short, however, you can lose more than 100 percent of the money you invest. Yikes!

Because the potential for loss is unlimited when you short a stock, I suggest that you use a stop order (also called a *buy-stop order*) to minimize the damage. Better yet, make it a good-till-canceled (GTC) order, which I discuss earlier in this chapter. You can set the stop order at a given price, and if the stock hits that price, you buy the stock back so that you can return it to its owner before the price rises even higher. You still lose money, but you limit your losses.

The uptick rule

For many years, the stock market had something called "the uptick rule." This rule stated that you could enter into a short sale only when the stock had just completed an uptick. "Tick" in this case means the actual incremental price movement of the stock you're shorting. For a $10 stock that was just $9.95 a moment ago, the 5-cent difference represents an uptick. If the $10 stock was just $10.10 a moment before, the 10-cent difference is a downtick. The amount of the tick doesn't matter. So, if you short a stock at the price of $40, the immediate prior price must have been $39.99 or lower. The reason for this rule (a Federal Reserve regulation) is

that short selling can aggravate declining stock prices in a rapidly falling market. In practice, going short on a stock whose price is already declining can make the stock price fall even farther. Excessive short selling can make the stock more volatile than it would be otherwise.

In 2007, however, the uptick rule was removed. This has contributed to the increased volatility that investors have seen during 2007–2008. Investors have to adapt accordingly. This means getting used to wider swings in stock price movements on days of heavy activity.

Feeling the squeeze

If you go short on a stock, you have to buy that stock back sooner or later so that you can return it to its owner. What happens when a lot of people are short on a particular stock and its price starts to rise? All those short sellers are scrambling to buy the stock back so that they can close their transactions before they lose too much money. This mass buying quickens the pace of the stock's ascent and puts a squeeze (called a *short squeeze*) on the investors who've been shorting the stock.

Earlier in this chapter, I explain that your broker can borrow stock from another client so that you can go short on it. What happens when that client wants to sell the stock in her account — the stock that you borrowed and which is therefore no longer in her account? When that happens, your broker asks you to return the borrowed stock. That's when you feel the squeeze — you have to buy the stock back at the current price.

Going short can be a great maneuver in a declining (bear) market, but it can be brutal if the stock price goes up. If you're a beginner, stay away from short selling until you have enough experience (and money) to risk it.

Chapter 19

Getting a Handle on DPPs, DRPs, and DCA . . . PDQ

In This Chapter

▶ Buying stock directly from a company

▶ Looking at dividend reinvestment plans

▶ Using dollar cost averaging

*W*ho says you must buy 100 shares of a stock to invest? Do you really have to go through a broker to buy stock, or can you buy direct? What if you only want to put your toe in the water and buy just one share for starters? Can you do that without paying through the nose for transaction costs, such as commissions?

The answer to these questions is that you can buy stocks directly (without a broker) and save money in the process. That's what this chapter is about. In this chapter, I show you how direct purchase programs (DPPs) and dividend reinvestment plans (DRPs) make a lot of sense for long-term stock investors, and I show how you can do them on your own — no broker necessary. I also show you how to use the method of dollar cost averaging (DCA) to acquire stock, a technique that works especially well with DRPs. All these programs are well-suited for people who like to invest small sums of money and plan on doing so consistently in the same stock (or stocks) over a long period of time.

Don't invest in a company just because it has a DPP or DRP. DPPs and DRPs are simply a means for getting into a particular stock with very little money. They shouldn't be a substitute for doing diligent research and analysis on a particular stock.

Being Direct with DPPs

If you're going to buy a stock anyway, why not buy it directly from the company and bypass the broker (and commissions) altogether? Several hundred companies now offer *direct purchase programs* (DPPs), also called DIPs (or direct investment programs), which give investors an opportunity to buy stock directly from these companies. In the following sections, I explain the steps required for investing in a DPP, describe alternatives to DPPs, and warn you of a few minor DPP drawbacks.

DPPs give investors the opportunity to buy stock with little upfront money (usually enough to cover the purchase of one share) and usually no commissions. Why do companies give investors this opportunity? For their sake, they want to encourage more attention and participation from investors. For your purposes, however, a DPP gives you what you may need most: a low-cost entry into that particular company's dividend reinvestment plan, or DRP (which you can read more about in the section "Dipping into DRPs," later in this chapter).

Investing in a DPP

If you have your sights set on a particular company and have only a few bucks to start out, a DPP is probably the best way to make your initial investment. The following steps guide you toward your first stock purchase using a DPP:

1. **Decide what stock you want to invest in (I explain how to do so in Parts II and III) and find the company's contact information.**

   Say that you do your homework and decide to invest in Yumpin Yimminy Corp. (YYC). You can get YYC's contact information through the stock exchange YYC trades on. For example, if YYC trades on the New York Stock Exchange, you can call the NYSE and ask for YYC's contact information, or you can visit the NYSE Web site (www.nyse.com). So, you can contact NYSE to reach YYC for its DPP ASAP. OK?

2. **Find out whether YYC has a DPP (before it's DOA! OK?).**

   Call YYC's shareholder services department and ask whether it has a DPP. If it does, great; if it doesn't, ask whether it plans to start one. At the very least, it may have a DRP. If you prefer, check out the company's Web site, because most corporate Web sites have plenty of information on their stock purchase programs.

3. Look into enrolling.

The company will send you an application along with a prospectus — the program document that serves as a brochure and, hopefully, answers your basic questions. Usually, the enrollment forms are downloadable from the company's Web site.

The processing is typically handled by an organization that the company designates (the plan administrator). From this point forward, you're in the dividend reinvestment plan.

Finding DPP alternatives

Although several hundred companies offer DPPs, the majority of companies don't. What if you want to invest in a company directly and it doesn't have a DPP? The following sections present some alternatives.

Buy your first share through a broker to qualify for DRPs

Yes, buying your first share through a broker costs you a commission; however, after you make the purchase, you can contact that company's shareholder services department and ask about its DRP. After you're an existing stockholder, qualifying for the DRP is a piece of cake.

To qualify for the DRP, you must be on the book of record with the transfer agent. A *book of record* is simply the database the company uses to track every single outstanding share of stock and the stock's owner. The *transfer agent* is the person or organization responsible for maintaining the database. Whenever stock is bought or sold, the transfer agent must implement the change and update the records. In many cases, you must have the broker issue a stock certificate in your name after you own the stock. This is the most common way to get your name on the book of record, hence qualifying you for the DRP.

Sometimes, simply buying the stock isn't enough to get your name on the book of record. Although you technically and legally own the stock, brokers, for ease of transaction, often keep the stock in your account under what's referred to as a *street name*. (For instance, your name may be Jane Smith, but the street name could be the broker's firm name, such as Jones & Co., simply for administrative purposes.) Having the stock in a street name really doesn't mean much to you until you want to qualify for the company's DPP or DRP. Remember to address this point with your broker.

Get started in a DRP directly through a broker

These days, more brokers offer the features of the DRP (like compounding interest) right in the brokerage account itself, which is more convenient than going to the trouble of setting up a DRP with the company directly. This service is most likely a response to the growing number of long-term investors who have fled traditional brokerage accounts for the benefits of direct investing that DPPs and DRPs offer.

The main drawback of a broker-run DRP is that it doesn't usually allow you to make stock purchases through optional cash payments without commission charges (a big negative!). See the section "Building wealth with optional cash payments," later in this chapter, for more on this topic.

Purchase shares via alternate buying services

Organizations have set up services to help small investors buy stock in small quantities. The primary drawback to these middlemen is that you'll probably pay more in transaction costs than you would if you approached the companies directly. Check out the most prominent services, which include the following:

- ✔ First Share at www.firstshare.com
- ✔ Money Paper at www.directinvesting.com
- ✔ National Association of Investors Corporation at www.better investing.org
- ✔ ShareBuilder at www.sharebuilder.com

Recognizing the drawbacks

As beneficial as DPPs are, they do have some minor drawbacks (doesn't everything?). Keep the following points in mind when considering DPPs as part of your stock portfolio:

- ✔ Although more and more companies are starting to offer DPPs, relatively few (approximately 500) companies have them.
- ✔ Some DPPs require a high initial amount to invest (as much as $250 or more) or a commitment of monthly investments. In any case, ask the plan administrator about the investing requirements.
- ✔ A growing number of DPPs have some type of service charge. This charge is usually very modest and lower than typical brokerage commissions. Ask about all the incidents — such as getting into the plan, getting out, and so on — that may trigger a service charge.

Dipping into DRPs

Sometimes, *dividend reinvestment plans* (DRPs) are called "DRIPs," which makes me scratch my head. "Reinvestment" is one word, not two, so where does that "I" come from? But I digress. Whether you call them DRIPs or DRPs, they're great for small investors and people who are truly long-term investors in a particular stock. A company may offer a DRP to allow investors to accumulate more shares of its stock without paying commissions.

A DRP has two primary advantages:

- ✔ **Compounding:** The dividends (cash payments to shareholders) get reinvested and give you the opportunity to buy more stock.

- ✔ **Optional cash payments (OCPs):** Most DRPs give participants the ability to invest through the plan to purchase more stock, usually with no commissions. Some DRPs have the OCP minimum for as little as $25.

Here are the requirements to be in a DRP:

- ✔ You must already be a stockholder of that particular stock

- ✔ The stock must be paying dividends (you had to guess this one!)

In the following sections, I go into more detail on compounding and OCPs, explain the cost advantages of using DRPs, and warn you of a few drawbacks.

Getting a clue about compounding

Dividends are reinvested, offering a form of compounding for the small investor. Dividends buy more shares, in turn generating more dividends. Usually, the dividends don't buy entire shares but fractional ones.

For example, say that you own 20 shares of Fraction Corp. at $10 per share for a total value of $200. Fraction Corp.'s annual dividend is $1, meaning that a quarterly dividend of 25 cents is issued every three months. What happens if this stock is in the DRP? The 20 shares generate a $5 dividend payout in the first quarter (20 shares × 25 cents), and this amount is applied to the stock purchase as soon as it's credited to the DRP account. If you presume for this example that the stock price doesn't change, the DRP has 20.50 total shares valued at $205 (20.50 shares × $10 share price). The dividend payout isn't enough to buy an entire share, so it buys a fractional share and credits that to the account.

Now say that three months pass and that no other shares have been acquired since your prior dividend payout. Fraction Corp. issues another quarterly dividend for 25 cents per share. Now what?

- ✓ The original 20 shares generate a $5 dividend payout.

- ✓ The .50, or half share, in the account generates a 12.5-cent dividend (half the dividend of a full share because it's only half a share).

- ✓ The total dividend payout is $5.125 (rounded to $5.13), and the new total of shares in the account is 21.13 shares (the former 20.50 shares plus .625 shares purchased by the dividend payout and rounded off; the .625 fraction was gained by the cash from the dividends). Full shares generate full dividends, and fractional shares generate fractional dividends.

To illustrate my point easily, the preceding example uses a price that doesn't fluctuate. In reality, stock in a DRP acts like any other stock — the share price changes constantly. Every time the DRP makes a stock purchase, whether it's monthly or quarterly, the purchase price will likely be different.

Building wealth with optional cash payments

Most DRPs (unless they're run by a broker) give the participant the opportunity to make optional cash payments (OCPs), which are payments you send in to purchase more stock in the DRP. DRPs usually establish a minimum and a maximum payment. The minimum is typically very modest, such as $25 or $50. A few plans even have no minimum. This feature makes it very affordable to regularly invest modest amounts and build up a sizable portfolio of stock in a short period of time, unencumbered by commissions.

DRPs also have a maximum investment limitation, such as specifying that DRP participants can't invest more than $10,000 per year. For most investors, the maximum isn't a problem because few would typically invest that much anyway. However, consult with the plan's administrator, because all plans are a little different.

OCPs are probably the most advantageous aspect of a DRP. If you can invest $25 to $50 per month consistently, year after year, at no (or little) cost, you may find that doing so is a superb way to build wealth.

Checking out the cost advantages

In spite of the fact that more and more DRPs are charging service fees, DRPs are still an economical way to invest, especially for small investors. The big savings come from not paying commissions. Although many DPPs and DRPs do have charges, they tend to be relatively small (but keep track of them, because the costs can add up).

Some DRPs actually offer a discount of between 2 percent and 5 percent (a few are higher) when buying stock through the plan. Others offer special programs and discounts on the company's products and services. Some companies offer the service of debiting your checking account or paycheck to invest in the DRP. One company offered its shareholders significant discounts to its restaurant subsidiary. In any case, ask the plan administrator because any plus is . . . well . . . a plus.

Moving money out of DRPs to pay off debt

DRPs are a great way to accumulate a large stock holding over an extended period of time. Moreover, think about what you can do with this stock. Say you accumulate 110 shares of stock, valued at $50 per share, in your DRP. You can, for example, take out $5,000 worth of stock (100 shares at $50 per share) and place those 100 shares in your brokerage account. The remaining 10 shares can stay in your account to keep the DRP and continue with dividend reinvestment to keep your wealth growing. Why remove those shares?

All things being equal, you're better off keeping the stock in the DRP, but what if you have $2,500 in credit card debt and don't have extra cash to pay off that debt? Brokerage accounts still have plenty of advantages, such as, in this example,

the use of margin (a topic I discuss in detail in Chapter 18). If your situation merits it, you can borrow up to 50 percent of the $5,000, or $2,500, as a margin loan and use it to pay off that credit card debt. Because you're replacing unsecured debt (credit card debt that may be charging 15 percent, 18 percent, or more) with secured debt, you can save a lot of money (borrowing against stock in a brokerage account is usually cheaper than credit card debt). Another benefit is that the margin loan with your broker doesn't require monthly payments, as do the credit card balances. Additionally, ask your tax consultant about potential tax benefits — investment interest expense is deductible, but consumer credit card debt is not.

Weighing the pros with the cons

When you're in a DRP, you reap all the benefits of stock investing. You get an annual report, and you qualify for stock splits, dividend increases, and so on. But you must be aware of the risks and responsibilities.

So before you start to salivate over all the goodies that come with DRPs, be clear-eyed about some of the negative aspects to them as well. Those negative aspects include:

✔ You need to get that first share, because that's what's most necessary to get the DRP started (but you knew that).

✔ Even small fees cut into your profits.

✔ Many DRPs may not have certain types of services, such as Individual Retirement Accounts (IRAs). (Chapter 21 offers more information on IRAs.)

✔ DRPs are designed for long-term investing. Although getting in and out of the plan is easy, the transactions may take weeks to process because stock purchases and sales are typically done all at once on a certain day of the month (or quarter).

✔ You need to read the prospectus. You may not consider this a negative point, but for some people, reading a prospectus is not unlike giving blood by using leeches. Even if that's your opinion, you need to read the prospectus to avoid any surprises, such as hidden fees or unreasonable terms.

✔ You must understand the tax issues. There, ya see? I knew I'd ruin it for you. Just know that dividends, whether or not they occur in a DRP, are usually taxable (unless the DRP is in an IRA, which is a different matter). I cover tax issues in detail in Chapter 21.

✔ You need to keep good records. Keep all your statements together and use a good spreadsheet program or accounting program if you plan on doing a lot of DRP investing. These records are especially important at tax time, when you have to report any subsequent gains or losses from stock sales. Because capital gains taxes can be complicated as you sort out short term versus long term, DRP calculations can be a nightmare without good record-keeping.

The One-Two Punch: Dollar Cost Averaging and DRPs

Dollar cost averaging (DCA) is a splendid technique for buying stock and lowering your cost for doing so. The example in Table 19-1 shows that it's not uncommon for investors to see a total cost that reflects a discount to the market value. DCA works especially well with DRPs.

DCA is a simple method for acquiring stock. It rests on the idea that you invest a fixed amount of money at regular intervals (monthly, usually) over a long period of time in a particular stock. Because a fixed amount (say, $50 per month) is going into a fluctuating investment, you end up buying less of that stock when it goes up in price and more of it when it goes down in price. Your average cost per share is usually lower than if you buy all the shares at once.

DCA is best presented with an example. Say you decide to get into the DRP of the company Acme Elevator, Inc. (AE). On your first day in the DRP, AE's stock is at $25, and the plan allows you to invest a minimum of $25 through its optional cash purchase (OCP) program. You decide to invest $25 per month and assess how well (hopefully) you're doing six months from now. Table 19-1 shows how this technique works.

Table 19-1	Dollar Cost Averaging (AE)			
Months	**Investment Amount**	**Purchase Price**	**Shares Bought**	**Accumulated Shares**
1	25	25	1	1
2	25	20	1.25	2.25
3	25	17.5	1.43	3.68
4	25	15	1.67	5.35
5	25	17.5	1.43	6.78
6	25	20	1.25	8.03
Totals	150	N/A	8.03	8.03

To assess the wisdom of your decision to invest in the DRP, ask yourself some questions:

- ✓ **How much did you invest over the entire six months?** Your total investment is $150. So far, so good.

- ✓ **What's the first share price for AE, and what's the last share price?** The first share price is $25, but the last share price is $20.

- ✓ **What's the market value of your investment at the end of six months?** You can easily calculate the value of your investment. Just multiply the number of shares you now own (8.03 shares) by the most recent share price ($20). The total value of your investment is $160.60.

- ✓ **What's the average share price you bought at?** The average share price is also easy to calculate. Take the total amount of your purchases ($150) and divide it by the number of shares you acquired (8.03 shares). Your average cost per share is $18.68.

Be sure to take note of the following:

- Even though the last share price ($20) is lower than the original share price ($25), your total investment's market value is still higher than your purchase amount ($160.60 compared to $150)! How can that be?! Dollar cost averaging is the culprit here. Your disciplined approach (using DCA) overcame the fluctuations in the stock price to help you gain more shares at the lower prices of $17.50 and $15.

- Your average cost per share is only $18.68. The DCA method helped you buy more shares at a lower cost, which ultimately helped you make money when the stock price made a modest rebound.

DCA works in helping you invest with small sums, all the while helping you smooth out the volatility in stock prices. This helps you make more money in your wealth-building program over the long haul. The bottom line for long-term stock investors is that DCA is a solid investing technique and DRPs are a great stock investment vehicle for building wealth. Can you visualize that retirement hammock yet?

Dollar cost averaging is a fantastic technique in a bull market and an okay technique in a flat or sideways market, but it's really not a good consideration during bear markets because the stock you're buying is going down in price and the market value can very easily be lower than your total investment. If you plan on holding onto the stock long term, then simply cease your dollar cost averaging approach until times improve for the stock (and its industry, and the economy). Learn more about industries in Chapter 13 and general economics in Chapter 10.

Chapter 20

Corporate Skullduggery: Looking at Insider Activity

In This Chapter

▶ Using documents to track insider trading

▶ Examining insider buying and selling

▶ Understanding corporate buybacks

▶ Breaking down stock splits

*I*magine that you're boarding a cruise ship, ready to enjoy a hard-earned vacation. As you merrily walk up the plank, you notice that the ship's captain and crew are charging out of the vessel, flailing their arms, and screaming at the top of their lungs. Some are even jumping into the water below. Quiz: Would you get on that ship? You get double credit if you can also explain why (or why not).

What does this scenario have to do with stock investing? Plenty. The behavior of the people running the boat gives you important clues about the near-term prospects for the boat. Similarly, the actions of company insiders can provide important clues into the near-term prospects for their company.

Company *insiders* are key managers or investors in the company. Insiders include the president of the company, the treasurer, or another managing officer. An insider can also be someone who owns a large stake in the company or someone on the board of directors. In any case, insiders usually have a bird's-eye view of what's going on with the company and a good idea of how well (or how poorly) the company is doing.

In this chapter, I describe different kinds of insider activities, such as insider buying, insider selling, corporate stock buybacks, and stock splits. I also show you how to keep track of these activities with the help of a few resources.

Keep tabs on what insiders are doing, because their buy/sell transactions do have a strong correlation to the near-term movement of their company's stock. However, don't buy or sell stock only because you heard that some insider did. Use the information on insider trading to confirm your own good sense in buying or selling stock. Insider trading sometimes can be a great precursor to a significant move that you can profit from if you know what to look for. Many shrewd investors have made their profits (or avoided losses) by tracking the activity of the insiders.

Tracking Insider Trading

Fortunately, we live in an age of disclosure. Insiders who buy or sell stock must file reports that document their trading activity with the Securities and Exchange Commission (SEC), which makes the documents available to the public. You can view these documents at either a regional SEC office (see www.sec.gov/contact/addresses.htm) or on the SEC's Web site, which maintains the EDGAR (Electronic Data Gathering, Analysis, and Retrieval) database (www.sec.gov/edgar.shtml). Just click on the "Search for Company Filings" button. Some of the most useful documents you can view there include the following:

- **Form 3:** This form is the initial statement that insiders provide. They must file Form 3 within ten days of obtaining insider status. An insider files this report even if he hasn't made a purchase yet; the report establishes the insider's status.

- **Form 4:** This document shows the insider's activity, such as a change in the insider's position as stockholder — how many shares the person bought and sold or other relevant changes. Any activity in a particular month must be reported on Form 4 by the 10th of the following month.

- **Form 5:** This annual report covers transactions that are small and not required on Form 4, such as minor, internal transfers of stock.

- **Form 144:** This form serves as the public declaration by an insider of the intention to sell *restricted stock* — stock that the insider was awarded, or received from the company as compensation, or bought as a term of employment. Insiders must hold restricted stock for at least one year before they can sell it. After an insider decides to sell, she files Form 144 and then must sell within 90 days or submit a new Form 144. The insider must file the form on or before the stock's sale date. When the sale is finalized, the insider is then required to file Form 4.

Fighting accounting fraud: The Sarbanes-Oxley Act

Very often, a market that reaches a mania stage sees abuse reach extreme conditions as well. Abuse by insiders is a good example. In the stock market mania of 1997–2000, this abuse wasn't just limited to insider buying and selling of stock; it also covered the related abuse of accounting fraud. (Companies like Enron in 2001 and Fannie Mae in 2008 come to mind.) The top management executives at several prominent companies deceived investors about the companies' financial conditions and subsequently were able to increase the perceived value of the companies' stock. The stock could then be sold at a price that was higher than market value. Congress took notice of these activities and, in 2002, passed the Sarbanes-Oxley Act (SOX). Congress designed this act to protect investors from fraudulent accounting activities by corporations. SOX established a public accounting oversight board and also tightened the rules on corporate financial reporting.

Since passage of SOX, the period of 2003–2007 was relatively quiet on the corporate compliance front, but as I write this, SOX will soon be tested, as Wall Street's financial institutions have been slammed by bankruptcy and alleged management wrongdoing.

Companies are required to make public the documents that track their trading activity. The SEC's Web site offers limited access to these documents, but for greater access, check out one of the many companies that report insider trading data, such as www.marketwatch.com and www.bloomberg.com.

The SEC has enacted the *short-swing profit rule* to protect the investing public. This rule prevents insiders from quickly buying the stock that they just sold at a profit. The insider must wait at least six months before buying it again. The SEC created this rule to prevent insiders from using their privileged knowledge to make an unfair profit quickly, before the investing public can react. The rule also applies if an insider sells stock — he can't sell it at a higher price within a six-month period.

Looking at Insider Transactions

The classic phrase "Actions speak louder than words" was probably coined for insider trading. Insiders are in the know, and keeping a watchful eye on their transactions — both buying and selling their company's stock — can provide you with very useful investing information. But insider buying and insider selling can be as different as day and night; insider buying is simple, while insider selling can be complicated. In the following sections, I present both sides of insider trading.

Breaking down insider buying

Insider buying is usually an unambiguous signal about how an insider feels about his company. After all, the primary reason that all investors buy stock is that they expect it to do well. If one insider is buying stock, that's generally not a monumental event. But if several or more insiders are buying, those purchases should certainly catch your attention.

Insider buying is generally a positive omen and beneficial for the stock's price. Also, when insiders buy stock, less stock is available to the public. If the investing public meets this decreased supply with increased demand, the stock price rises. Keep these factors in mind when analyzing insider buying:

✔ **Identify who's buying the stock.** The CEO is buying 5,000 shares. Is that reason enough for you to jump in? Maybe. After all, the CEO certainly knows how well the company is doing. But what if that CEO is just starting her new position? What if before this purchase she had no stock in the company at all? Maybe the stock is part of her employment package.

The fact that a new company executive is making her first stock purchase isn't as strong a signal urging you to buy as the fact that a long-time CEO is doubling her holdings. Also, if large numbers of insiders are buying, that sends a stronger signal than if a single insider is buying.

✔ **See how much is being bought.** In the preceding example, the CEO bought 5,000 shares, which is a lot of stock no matter how you count it. But is it enough for you to base an investment decision on? Maybe, but a closer look may reveal more. If she already owned 1 million shares at the time of the purchase, then buying 5,000 additional shares wouldn't be such an exciting indicator of a pending stock rise. In this case, 5,000 shares is a small incremental move that doesn't offer much to get excited about.

However, what if this particular insider has owned only 5,000 shares for the past three years and is now buying 1 million shares? Now that should arouse your interest! Usually, a massive purchase tells you that particular insider has strong feelings about the company's prospects and that she's making a huge increase in her share of stock ownership. Still, a purchase of 1 million shares by the CEO isn't as strong a signal as ten insiders buying 100,000 shares each. Again, if only one person is buying, that may or may not be a strong indication of an impending rise. However, if lots of people are buying, consider it a fantastic indication.

An insider purchase of any kind is a positive sign, but it's always more significant when a greater number of insiders are making purchases. "The more the merrier!" is a good rule for judging insider buying. All these individuals have their own, unique perspectives on the company and its prospects. Mass buying indicates mass optimism for the company's future. If the treasurer, the president, the vice president of sales, and several other key players are putting their wealth on the line and investing it in a company they know intimately, that's a good sign for your stock investment as well.

✔ **Notice the timing of the purchase.** The timing of insider stock purchases is important as well. If I tell you that five insiders bought stock at various points last year, you may say, "Hmm." But if I tell you that all five people bought substantial chunks of stock at the same time and right before earnings season, that should make you say, "HMMMMM!"

Picking up tips from insider selling

Insider stock buying is rarely negative — it either bodes well for the stock or is a neutral event at worst. But how about insider selling? When an insider sells his stock, the event can be either neutral or negative. Insider selling is usually a little tougher than insider buying to figure out, because insiders may have many different motivations to sell stock that have nothing to do with the company's future prospects. Just because the president of the company is selling 5,000 shares from his personal portfolio doesn't necessarily mean you should sell, too.

Insiders may sell their stock for a couple reasons: They may think that the company won't be doing well in the near future — a negative sign for you — or they may simply need the money for a variety of personal reasons that have nothing to do with the company's potential. Some typical reasons why insiders may sell stock include the following:

✔ **To diversify their holdings.** If an insider's portfolio is heavily weighted with one company's stock, a financial advisor may suggest that she balance her portfolio by selling some of that company's stock and purchasing other securities.

✔ **To finance personal emergencies.** Sometimes an insider needs money for medical, legal, or family reasons.

✔ **To buy a home or make another major purchase.** An insider may need the money to make a down payment, or perhaps to buy something outright without having to take out a loan.

How do you find out about the details regarding insider stock selling? Although insiders must report their pertinent stock sales and purchases to the SEC, the information isn't always revealing. As a general rule, consider the following questions when analyzing insider selling:

✔ **How many insiders are selling?** If only one insider is selling, that single transaction doesn't give you enough information to act on. However, if many insiders are selling, you should see a red flag. Check out any news or information that's currently available by going to Web sites such as www.marketwatch.com, www.sec.gov, and finance.yahoo.com (along with other sources in Appendix A).

✔ **Are the sales showing a pattern or unusual activity?** If one insider sold some stock last month, that sale alone isn't that significant an event. However, if ten insiders have each made multiple sales in the past few months, those sales are cause for concern. See whether any new developments at the company are potentially negative. If massive insider selling has recently occurred and you don't know why, consider putting a stop-loss order on your stock immediately. I cover stop-loss orders more fully in Chapter 18.

✔ **How much stock is being sold?** If a CEO sells 5,000 shares of stock but still retains 100,000 shares, that's not a big deal. But if the CEO sells all or most of his holdings, that's a possible negative. Check to see whether other company executives have also sold stock.

✔ **Do outside events or analyst reports seem coincidental with the sale of the stock?** Sometimes, an influential analyst may issue a report warning about a company's prospects. If the company's management pooh-poohs the report but most of them are bailing out anyway (selling their stock), you may want to do the same. Frequently, when insiders know that damaging information is forthcoming, they sell the stock before it takes a dip.

Similarly, if the company's management issues positive public statements or reports that contradict their own behavior (they're selling their stock holdings), the SEC may investigate to see whether the company is doing anything that may require a penalty (the SEC regularly tracks insider sales).

Considering Corporate Stock Buybacks

When you read the financial pages or watch the financial shows on TV, you sometimes hear that a company is buying its own stock. The announcement may be something like, "SuperBucks Corp. has announced that it will spend $2 billion dollars to buy back its own stock." Why would a company do that, and what does that mean to you if you own the stock or are considering buying it?

When companies buy back their own stock, they're generally indicating that they believe their stock is undervalued and that it has the potential to rise. If a company shows strong fundamentals (for example, good financial condition and increasing sales and earnings; see Chapter 11 for details) and it's buying more of its own stock, it's worth investigating — it may make a great addition to your portfolio.

Just because a company announces a stock buyback doesn't always mean that one will happen. The announcement itself is meant to stir interest in the stock and cause the price to rise. The stock buyback may be only an opportunity for insiders to sell stock, or it may be needed for executive compensation — recruiting and retaining competent management is a positive use of money.

The following sections present some common reasons a company may buy back its shares from investors, as well as some ideas on the negative effects of stock buybacks.

If you see that a company is buying back its stock while most of the insiders are selling their personal shares, that's not a good sign. It may not necessarily be a bad sign, but it's not a positive sign. Play it safe and invest elsewhere.

Understanding why a company buys back shares

You bought this book because you're looking at buying stocks, but individuals aren't alone in the stock buying universe. No, I don't just mean that mutual funds, pensions, and other entities are buyers; I mean the companies behind the stocks are buyers (and sellers), too. Why would a public company buy stock — especially its own?

Boosting earnings per share

By simply buying back its own shares from stockholders, a company can increase its earnings per share without actually earning extra money (see Chapter 11 and Appendix B for more on earnings per share). Sound like a magician's trick? Well, it is, kind of. A corporate stock buyback is a financial sleight of hand that investors should be aware of. Here's how it works: Noware Earnings, Inc., (NEI) has 10 million shares outstanding, and it's expected to net earnings of $10 million for the fourth quarter. NEI's earnings per share (EPS) would be $1 per share. So far so good. But what happens if NEI buys 2 million of its own shares? Total shares outstanding shrink to 8 million. The new EPS becomes $1.25 — the stock buyback artificially boosts the earnings per share by 25 percent!

The important point to remember about stock buybacks is that actual company earnings don't change — no fundamental changes occur in company management or operations — so the increase in EPS can be misleading. But the marketplace can be obsessive about earnings, and because earnings are the lifeblood of any company, an earnings boost, even if it's cosmetic, can also boost the stock price.

If you watch a company's price-to-earnings ratio (see Chapter 11), you know that increased earnings usually means an eventual increase in the stock price. Additionally, a stock buyback affects supply and demand. With less available stock in the market, demand necessarily sends the stock price upward.

Whenever a company makes a major purchase, such as buying back its own stock, think about how the company is paying for it and whether it seems like a good use of the company's purchasing power. In general, companies buy their stock for the same reasons any investor buys stock — they believe that the stock is a good investment and will appreciate in time. Companies generally pay for a stock buyback in one of two basic ways: funds from operations or borrowed money. Both methods have a downside. For more details, see the section "Exploring the downside of buybacks," later in this chapter.

Beating back a takeover bid

Suppose you read in the financial pages that Company X is doing a hostile takeover of Company Z. A hostile takeover doesn't mean that Company X sends storm troopers armed with mace to Company Z's headquarters to trounce its management. All a *hostile takeover* means is that X wants to buy enough shares of Z's stock to effectively control Z (and Z is unhappy about being owned or controlled by X). Because buying and selling stock happens in a public market or exchange, companies can buy each other's stock. Sometimes, the target company prefers not to be acquired, in which case it may buy back shares of its own stock to give it a measure of protection against unwanted moves by interested companies.

In some cases, the company attempting the takeover already owns some of the target company's stock. In this case, the targeted company may offer to buy those shares back from the aggressor at a premium to thwart the takeover bid. This type of offer is often referred to as *greenmail*.

Takeover concerns generally prompt interest in the investing public, driving the stock price upward and benefiting current stockholders.

Exploring the downside of buybacks

As beneficial as stock buybacks can be, they have to be paid for, and this expense has consequences. When a company uses funds from operations for the stock buyback, less money is available for other activities, such as upgrading technology, making improvements, or doing research and development. A company faces even greater dangers when it uses debt to finance a stock buyback. If the company uses borrowed funds, not only does it have less borrowing power for other uses, but it also has to pay back the borrowed funds with interest, thus lowering earnings figures.

In general, any misuse of money, such as using debt to buy back stock, affects a company's ability to grow its sales and earnings — two measures that need to maintain upward mobility to keep stock prices rising.

Say that Noware Earnings, Inc. (NEI), typically pays an annual dividend of 25 cents per share of stock and wants to buy back shares, which are currently at $10 each, with borrowed money with a 9 percent interest rate. If NEI buys back 2 million shares, it won't have to pay out $500,000 in dividends (2 million × 25 cents). That's money saved. However, NEI has to pay interest on the $20 million it borrowed ($10 per share × 2 million shares) to buy back the shares. The interest totals $1.8 million (9 percent of $20 million), and the net result from this rudimentary example is that NEI sees an outflow of $1.3 million (the difference between the interest paid out and the dividends savings).

Using debt to finance a stock buyback needs to make economic sense — it needs to strengthen the company's financial position. Perhaps NEI could have used the stock buyback money toward a better purpose, such as modernizing equipment or paying for a new marketing campaign. Because debt interest ultimately decreases earnings, companies must be careful when using debt to buy back their stock.

Stock Splits: Nothing to Go Bananas Over

Frequently, management teams decide to do a stock split. A *stock split* is the exchange of existing shares of stock for new shares from the same company. Stock splits don't increase or decrease the company's capitalization; they just change the number of shares available in the market and the per-share price.

Typically, a company may announce that it's doing a 2-for-1 stock split. For example, a company may have 10 million shares outstanding, with a market price of $40 each. In a 2-for-1 split, the company then has 20 million shares (the share total doubles), but the market price is adjusted to $20 (the share price is halved). Companies do other splits, such as a 3-for-2 or 4-for-1, but 2-for-1 is the most common split.

The following sections present the two basic types of splits: ordinary stock splits and reverse stock splits.

Qualifying for a stock split is similar to qualifying to receive a dividend — you must be listed as a stockholder as of the date of record. Keep good records regarding your stock splits in case you need to calculate capital gains for tax purposes. (For information on the date of record, see Chapter 6. See Chapter 21 for tax information.)

Ordinary stock splits

An *ordinary stock split* — when the number of stock shares increases — is the kind investors usually hear about. If you own 100 shares of Dublin, Inc., stock (at $60 per share) and the company announces a stock split, what happens? If you own the stock in certificate form, you receive in the mail a stock certificate for 100 more shares. Now, before you cheer over how your money just doubled, check the stock's new price. Each share is adjusted to a $30 value.

Not all stock is in certificate form. Stocks held in a brokerage account are recorded in book entry form. Most stock, in fact, is in book entry form. A company only issues stock certificates when necessary or when the investor requests it. If you keep the stock in your brokerage account, check with your broker for the new share total to make sure you're credited with the new number of shares after the stock split.

An ordinary stock split is primarily a neutral event, so why does a company bother to do it? The most common reason is that management believes the stock is too expensive, so it wants to lower the stock price to make the stock more affordable and therefore more attractive to new investors. Studies have shown that stock splits frequently precede a rise in the stock price. Although stock splits are considered a non-event in and of themselves, many stock experts see them as bullish signals because of the interest they generate among the investing public.

Reverse stock splits

A *reverse stock split* usually occurs when a company's management wants to raise the price of its stock. Just as ordinary splits can occur when management believes the price is too expensive, a reverse stock split means the company feels that the stock's price is too cheap. If a stock's price looks too low, that may discourage interest by individual or institutional investors (such as mutual funds). Management wants to drum up more interest in the stock for the benefit of shareholders (some of whom are probably insiders).

The company may also do a reverse split to decrease costs. When you have to send an annual report and other correspondence regularly to all the stockholders, the mailings can get a little pricey, especially if you have lots of investors who own only a few shares each. A reverse split helps consolidate shares and lower overall management costs.

A reverse split can best be explained with an example. TuCheep, Inc. (TCI), is selling at $2 per share on the Nasdaq. At that rock-bottom price, the investing public may ignore it. So TCI announces a 10-for-1 reverse stock split. Now what? If a stockholder had 100 shares at $2 (the old shares), the stockholder now owns 10 shares at $20.

Technically, a reverse split is considered a neutral event. However, just as investors may infer positive expectations from an ordinary stock split, they may have negative expectations from a reverse split because a reverse split tends to occur for negative reasons. One definitive negative reason for a reverse split is if the company's stock is threatened to be delisted. If a stock is on a major exchange and the price falls below $1, the stock will face delisting (basically getting removed from the exchange). A reverse split may be used to ward off such an event.

If, in the event of a stock split, you end up with an odd number of shares, the company doesn't produce a fractional share. Instead, you get a check for the cash equivalent. For example, if you have 51 shares and the company announces a 2-for-1 reverse split, odds are that you'll get 25 shares and a cash payout for the odd share (or fractional share).

Chapter 21

Keeping More of Your Money from the Taxman

In This Chapter

▶ Checking out the tax implications of your investments

▶ Paying taxes on your investments

▶ Taking your tax deductions

▶ Investing for your retirement

*A*fter conquering the world of making money with stocks, now you have another hurdle — keeping your money. Some people may tell you that taxes are brutal, complicated, and counterproductive. Others may tell you that they're a form of legalized thievery, and still others may say that they're a necessary evil. And then there are the pessimists. In any case, this chapter shows you how to keep more of the fruits from your hard-earned labor.

Keep in mind that this chapter isn't meant to be comprehensive. For a fuller treatment of personal taxes, refer to the latest edition of *Taxes For Dummies* (published by Wiley). You should also check with your personal tax advisor and get the publications referenced in this chapter by either visiting the IRS Web site at www.irs.gov or calling the IRS publications department at 800-829-3676.

However, in this chapter, I cover the most relevant points for stock investors, such as the tax treatment for dividends and capital gains and losses, common tax deductions for investors, some simple tax-reduction strategies, and pointers for retirement investing.

Tax laws can be very hairy and perplexing, and at press time, the rumblings in Washington, DC, are for the potential expiration of tax cuts. Higher (and more complicated) taxes generally aren't good for stock investors or the economy at large, so give the legislative folks a piece of your mind. A good way to do this is through taxpayer advocacy groups like the National Taxpayers Union (www.ntu.org). 'Nuff said.

Paying through the Nose: The Tax Treatment of Different Investments

This section tells you what you need to know about the tax implications you face when you start investing in stocks. It's good to know in advance the basics on ordinary income, capital gains, and capital losses because it may affect your investing strategy.

Understanding ordinary income and capital gains

Profit you make from your stock investments can be taxed in one of two ways, depending on the type of profit:

- **Ordinary income:** Your profit could be taxed at the same rate as wages — at your full, regular tax rate. If your tax bracket is 28 percent, that's the rate at which your ordinary income investment profit is taxed. Two types of investment profits get taxed as ordinary income (Check out IRS Publication 550, "Investment Income and Expenses," for more information):

  - **Dividends:** When you receive dividends (either in cash or stock), they're taxed as ordinary income. This is true even if those dividends are in a dividend reinvestment plan (see Chapter 19 to find out more about dividend reinvestment plans, or DRPs.) If, however, the dividends occur in a tax-sheltered plan, such as an IRA or 401(k) plan, then they're exempt from taxes for as long as they're in the plan. (Retirement plans are covered in the section "Taking Advantage of Tax-Advantaged Retirement Investing," later in this chapter.) Keep in mind that qualified dividends are taxed at a lower rate than non-qualified dividends.

  - **Short-term capital gains:** If you sell stock for a gain and you've owned the stock for one year or less, the gain is considered ordinary income. To calculate the time, you use the *trade date* (or *date of execution*). This is the date that you executed the order, not the settlement date. (For more on important dates, see Chapter 6.) However, if these gains occur in a tax-sheltered plan, such as a 401(k) or an IRA, no tax is triggered.

- **Long-term capital gains:** These are usually much better for you than ordinary income as far as taxes are concerned. The tax laws reward patient investors. After you've held the stock for at least a year and a day (what a difference a day makes!), your tax rate is reduced. Get more information on capital gains in IRS Publication 550, "Investment Income and Expenses."

You can control how you manage the tax burden from your investment profits. Gains are taxable only if a sale actually takes place (in other words, only if the gain is "realized"). If your stock in GazillionBucks, Inc., goes from $5 per share to $87, that $82 appreciation isn't subject to taxation unless you actually sell the stock. Until you sell, that gain is "unrealized." Time your stock sales carefully and hold onto stocks for at least a year to minimize the amount of taxes you have to pay on them.

When you buy stock, record the date of purchase and the *cost basis* (the purchase price of the stock plus any ancillary charges, such as commissions). This information is very important come tax time should you decide to sell your stock. The date of purchase (the date of execution) helps establish the *holding period* (how long you own the stocks) that determines whether your gains are considered short term or long term.

Say you buy 100 shares of GazillionBucks, Inc., at $5 and pay a commission of $18. Your cost basis is $518 (100 shares times $5 plus $18 commission). If you sell the stock at $87 per share and pay a $24 commission, the total sale amount is $8,676 (100 shares times $87 less $24 commission). If this sale occurs less than a year after the purchase, it's a short-term gain. In the 28 percent tax bracket, the short-term gain of $8,158 ($8,676 – $518) is also taxed at 28 percent. Read the following section to see the tax implications if your gain is a long-term gain.

Any gain (or loss) from a short sale is considered short term regardless of how long the position is held open. For more information on selling short, check out Chapter 18.

Minimizing the tax on your capital gains

Long-term capital gains are taxed at a more favorable rate than ordinary income. To qualify for long-term capital gains treatment, you must hold the investment for over one year (in other words, for at least one year and one day).

Recall the example in the previous section with GazillionBucks, Inc. As a short-term transaction at the 28 percent tax rate, the tax is $2,284 ($8,158 × 28 percent). After you revive, you say, "Gasp! What a chunk of dough. I better hold off a while longer." You hold onto the stock for at least a year to achieve the status of long-term capital gains. How does that change the tax? For anyone in the 28 percent tax bracket or higher, the long-term capital gains rate of 15 percent applies. In this case, the tax is $1,224 ($8,158 × 15 percent), resulting in a tax savings to you of $1,060 ($2,284 less $1,224). Okay, it's not a fortune, but it's a substantial difference from the original tax.

Capital gains taxes *can* be lower than the tax on ordinary income, but they're not higher. If, for example, you're in the 15 percent tax bracket for ordinary income and you have a long-term capital gain that would normally bump you up to the 28 percent tax bracket, the gain is taxed at your lower rate of 15 percent instead of a higher capital gains rate. Check with your tax advisor on a regular basis because this can change due to new tax laws.

Don't sell a stock just because it qualifies for long-term capital gains treatment, even if the sale eases your tax burden. If the stock is doing well and meets your investing criteria, hold onto it.

Coping with capital losses

Ever think that having the value of your stocks fall could be a good thing? Perhaps the only real positive regarding losses in your portfolio is that they can reduce your taxes. A *capital loss* means that you lose money on your investments. This amount is generally deductible on your tax return, and you can claim a loss on either long-term or short-term stock holdings. This loss can go against your other income and lower your overall tax.

Say you bought Worth Zilch Co. stock for a total purchase price of $3,500 and sold it later at a sale price of $800. Your tax-deductible capital loss is $2,700.

The one string attached to deducting investment losses on your tax return is that the most you can report in a single year is $3,000. On the bright side, though, any excess loss isn't really lost — you can carry it forward to the next year. If you have net investment losses of $4,500 in 2008, you can deduct $3,000 in 2008 and carry the remaining $1,500 loss over to 2009 and deduct it on your 2009 tax return.

Debt and taxes: Another angle

If you truly need cash but you don't want to sell your stock because it's doing well and you want to avoid paying capital gains tax, consider borrowing against it. If the stock is listed (on the New York Stock Exchange, for example) and is in a brokerage account, you can borrow up to 50 percent of the value of marginable securities at favorable rates (listed stocks are marginable securities). The money you borrow is considered a margin loan (see Chapter 18 for details), and

the interest you pay is low (compared to credit cards or personal loans) because it's considered a secured loan (your stock acts as collateral). On those rare occasions when I use margin, I usually make sure I use stocks that generate a high dividend. That way, the stocks themselves help to pay off the margin loan. In addition, if the proceeds are used for an investment purpose, the margin interest may be tax-deductible. See IRS Publication 550 for more details.

Before you can deduct losses, they must first be used to offset any capital gains. If you realize long-term capital gains of $7,000 in stock A and long-term capital losses of $6,000 in stock B, then you have a net long-term capital gain of $1,000 ($7,000 gain less the offset of $6,000 loss). Whenever possible, see whether losses in your portfolio can be realized to offset any capital gains to reduce potential tax. IRS Publication 550 includes information for investors on capital gains and losses.

Here's your optimum strategy: Where possible, keep losses on a short-term basis and push your gains into long-term capital gains status. If a transaction can't be tax free, at the very least try to defer the tax to keep your money working for you.

Evaluating gains and losses scenarios

Of course, any investor can come up with hundreds of possible gains and losses scenarios. For example, you may wonder what happens if you sell part of your holdings now as a short-term capital loss and the remainder later as a long-term capital gain. You must look at each sale of stock (or potential sale) methodically to calculate the gain or loss you would realize from it. Figuring out your gain or loss isn't that complicated. Here are some general rules to help you wade through the morass:

- ✔ If you add up all your gains and losses and *the net result is a short-term gain,* it's taxed at your highest tax bracket (as ordinary income).

- ✔ If you add up all your gains and losses and *the net result is a long-term gain,* it's taxed at 15 percent if you're in the 28 percent tax bracket or higher. If you're in the 15 percent tax bracket or lower, the tax rate on long-term capital gains is 0 percent in 2008.

- ✔ If you add up all your gains and losses and *the net result is a loss,* it's deductible as follows: If your loss is $3,000 or less, it's fully deductible against other income. If you're married filing separately, your deduction limit is $1,500.

- ✔ If you add up all your gains and losses and *the net result is a loss that exceeds $3,000,* you can only deduct up to $3,000 in that year; the remainder goes forward to future years.

Sharing Your Gains with the IRS

Of course, you don't want to pay more taxes than you have to, but as the old cliché goes, "Don't let the tax tail wag the investment dog." You should buy or sell a stock because it makes economic sense first and consider the tax implications as secondary issues. After all, taxes consume a relatively small portion of your gain. As long as you experience a *net gain* (gain after all transaction costs, including taxes, brokerage fees, and other related fees), consider yourself a successful investor — even if you have to give away some of your gain to taxes.

Try to make tax planning second nature in your day-to-day activities. No, you don't have to consume yourself with a blizzard of paperwork and tax projections. I simply mean that when you make a stock transaction, keep the receipt and maintain good records. When you make a large purchase or sale, pause for a moment and ask yourself whether you'll have to face any tax consequences. (Refer to the section "Paying through the Nose: The Tax Treatment of Different Investments," earlier in this chapter, to review various tax scenarios.) Speak to a tax consultant beforehand to discuss the ramifications.

In the following sections, I describe the tax forms you need to fill out, as well as some important rules to follow.

Filling out forms

Most investors report their investment-related activities on their individual tax returns (Form 1040). The reports that you'll likely receive from brokers and other investment sources include the following:

- **Brokerage and bank statements:** Monthly statements that you receive
- **Trade confirmations:** Documents to confirm that you bought or sold stock
- **1099-DIV:** Reporting dividends paid to you
- **1099-INT:** Reporting interest paid to you
- **1099-B:** Reporting gross proceeds submitted to you from the sale of investments, such as stocks and mutual funds

You may receive other, more obscure forms that aren't listed here. You should retain all documents related to your stock investments.

The IRS schedules and forms that most stock investors need to be aware of and/or attach to their Form 1040 include the following:

- **Schedule B:** To report interest and dividends
- **Schedule D:** To report capital gains and losses
- **Form 4952:** Investment Interest Expense Deduction
- **Publication 17:** Guide to Form 1040

You can get these publications directly from the IRS at 800-829-3676, or you can download them from the Web site (www.irs.gov). For more information on what records and documentation investors should hang onto, check out IRS Publication 552, "Recordkeeping for Individuals."

If you plan to do your own taxes, consider using the latest tax software products, which are inexpensive and easy to use. These programs usually have a question-and-answer feature to help you do your taxes step by step, and they include all the necessary forms. Consider getting either TurboTax (www.turbotax.com) or TaxCut (www.taxcut.com) at your local software vendor or the companies' Web sites.

Playing by the rules

Some people get the smart idea of, "Hey! Why not sell my losing stock by December 31 to grab the short-term loss and just buy back the stock on January 2 so that I can have my cake and eat it, too?" Not so fast. The IRS puts the kibosh on maneuvers like that with something called the *wash-sale rule*. This rule states that if you sell a stock for a loss and buy it back within 30 days, the loss isn't valid because you didn't make any substantial investment change. The wash-sale rule applies only to losses. The way around the rule is simple: Wait at least 31 days before you buy that identical stock back again.

Some people try to get around the wash-sale rule by doubling up on their stock position with the intention of selling half. Therefore, the IRS makes the 30-day rule cover both sides of the sale date. That way, an investor can't buy the identical stock within 30 days just before the sale and then realize a short-term loss for tax purposes.

Discovering the Softer Side of the IRS: Tax Deductions for Investors

In the course of managing your portfolio of stocks and other investments, you'll probably incur expenses that are tax-deductible. The tax laws allow you to write off certain investment-related expenses as itemized expenses on Schedule A — an attachment to IRS Form 1040. Keep records of your deductions and retain a checklist to remind you which deductions you normally take. IRS Publication 550 ("Investment Income and Expenses") gives you more details.

The following sections explain common tax deductions for investors: investment interest, miscellaneous expenses, and donations to charity. I also list a few items you *can't* deduct.

Investment interest

If you pay any interest to a stockbroker, such as margin interest or any interest to acquire a taxable financial investment, that's considered investment interest and is usually fully deductible as an itemized expense.

Keep in mind that not all interest is deductible. Consumer interest or interest paid for any consumer or personal purpose isn't deductible. For more general information, see the section covering interest in IRS Publication 17.

Miscellaneous expenses

Most investment-related deductions are reported as miscellaneous expenses. Here are some common deductions:

- Accounting or bookkeeping fees for keeping records of investment income

- Any expense related to tax service or education

- Computer expense — you can take a depreciation deduction for your computer if you use it 50 percent of the time or more for managing your investments

- Investment management or investment advisor's fees (fees paid for advice on tax-exempt investments aren't deductible)

- Legal fees involving stockholder issues

- Safe-deposit box rental fee or home safe to hold your securities, unless used to hold personal effects or tax-exempt securities

- Service charges for collecting interest and dividends

- Subscription fees for investment advisory services

- Travel costs to check investments or to confer with advisors regarding income-related investments

You can deduct only that portion of your miscellaneous expenses that exceeds 2 percent of your adjusted gross income. For more information on deducting miscellaneous expenses, check out IRS Publication 529.

Donations of stock to charity

What happens if you donate stock to your favorite (IRS-approved) charity? Because it's a noncash charitable contribution, you can deduct the market value of the stock.

Say that last year you bought stock for $2,000 and it's worth $4,000 this year. If you donate it this year, you can write off the market value at the time of the contribution. In this case, you have a $4,000 deduction. Use IRS Form 8283, which is an attachment to Schedule A, to report noncash contributions exceeding $500.

To get more guidance from the IRS on this matter, get Publication 526, "Charitable Contributions," by calling 800-829-3676.

Knowing what you can't deduct

Just to be complete, here are some items you may think you can deduct, but, alas, you can't:

- ✔ Financial planning or investment seminars
- ✔ Any costs connected with attending stockholder meetings
- ✔ Home office expenses for managing your investments

Taking Advantage of Tax-Advantaged Retirement Investing

If you're going to invest for the long term (such as your retirement), you may as well maximize your use of tax-sheltered retirement plans. Many different types of plans are available; I touch on only the most popular ones in the following sections. Although retirement plans may not seem relevant for investors who buy and sell stocks directly (as opposed to a mutual fund), some plans, called self-directed retirement accounts, allow you to invest directly.

IRAs

Individual Retirement Accounts (IRAs) are accounts you can open with a financial institution, such as a bank or a mutual fund company. An IRA is available to almost anyone who has earned income, and it allows you to set aside and invest money to help fund your retirement. Opening an IRA is easy, and virtually any bank or mutual fund can guide you through the process. Two basic types of IRAs are traditional and Roth.

Traditional IRA

The traditional Individual Retirement Account (also called the deductible IRA) was first popularized in the early 1980s. In a traditional IRA, you can make a tax-deductible contribution of up to $5,000 in 2008. In addition, individuals age 50 and older can make additional "catch-up" investments of $1,000. For 2009 and beyond, the limits will be indexed to inflation.

The money can then grow in the IRA account unfettered by current taxes, because the money isn't taxed until you take it out. Because IRAs are designed for retirement purposes, you can start taking money out of your IRA in the year you turn $59^1/_2$. (Hmm. That must really disappoint those who want their money in the year they turn $58^3/_4$.) The withdrawals at that point are taxed as ordinary income. Fortunately, you'll probably be in a lower tax bracket then, so the tax shouldn't be as burdensome.

Keep in mind that you're required to start taking distributions from your account when you reach age $70^1/_2$, and after that point you may no longer contribute to a traditional IRA. Again, check with your tax advisor to see how this affects you personally.

If you take out money from an IRA too early, the amount is included in your taxable income, and you may be zapped with a 10 percent penalty. You can avoid the penalty if you have a good reason. (The IRS provides a list of reasons in Publication 590, "Individual Retirement Arrangements.")

To put money into an IRA, you must earn income equal to or greater than the amount you're contributing. *Earned income* is money made either as an employee or a self-employed person. Although traditional IRAs can be great for investors, the toughest part about them is qualifying — they have income limitations and other qualifiers that make them less deductible based on how high your income is. See IRS Publication 590 for more details.

Wait a minute! If IRAs usually involve mutual funds or bank investments, how does the stock investor take advantage of them? Here's how: Stock investors can open a self-directed IRA with a brokerage firm. This means that you can buy and sell stocks in the account with no taxes on dividends or capital gains. The account is tax-deferred, so you don't have to worry about taxes until you start making withdrawals. Also, many dividend reinvestment plans (DRPs) can be set up as IRAs as well. See Chapter 19 for more about DRPs.

Roth IRA

The Roth IRA is a great retirement plan that I wish had existed a long time ago. Here are some ways to distinguish the Roth IRA from the traditional IRA:

- The Roth IRA provides no tax deduction for contributions.

- Money in the Roth IRA grows tax free and can be withdrawn tax free when you turn $59^1/_2$.

- The Roth IRA is subject to early distribution penalties (although there are exceptions). Distributions have to be qualified to be penalty and tax-free.

The maximum contribution per year for Roth IRAs is the same as for traditional IRAs. You can open a self-directed account with a broker as well. See IRS Publication 590 for details on qualifying.

401(k) plans

Company-sponsored 401(k) plans (named after the section in the tax code that allows them) are widely used and very popular. In a 401(k) plan, companies set aside money from their paychecks that employees can use to invest for retirement. Generally, in 2008 you can invest as much as $15,500 of your pretax earned income and have it grow tax-deferred. Those over age 50 can contribute an additional $5,000 as a "catch-up" contribution. For 2009 and beyond, check with the IRS and/or your tax advisor.

Usually, the money is put in mutual funds administered through a mutual fund company or an insurance firm. Although most 401(k) plans aren't self-directed, I mention them in this book for good reason.

Because your money is in a mutual fund that may invest in stocks, take an active role in finding out the mutual funds in which you're allowed to invest. Most plans offer several types of stock mutual funds. Use your growing knowledge about stocks to make more informed choices about your 401(k) plan options. For more information on 401(k) and other retirement plans, check out IRS Publication 560.

Keep in mind that a mutual fund is only as good as what it invests in. Ask the plan administrator some questions about the funds and the types of stocks the plan invests in. Are the stocks defensive or cyclical? (For more information on defensive and cyclical stocks, see Chapter 13.) Are they large-cap or small-cap? If you don't make an informed choice about the investments in your plan, someone else will (such as the plan administrator), and that someone probably doesn't have the same ideas about your money that you do.

Part V
The Part of Tens

The 5th Wave   By Rich Tennant

Looks like the market's about to take a downturn.

In this part . . .

This wouldn't be a *For Dummies* book if I didn't include a Part of Tens. Here you find quick reference lists of many of the most basic stock investing concepts and practices. I explain how to profit before others do, describe methods for protecting those profits, tell you about investing red flags, and show you how to handle both investing challenges and opportunities. Check the information in this part when you don't have time to read the denser parts of the book or when you just need a quick refresher on what to do before, after, and even during your stock investing pursuits.

Chapter 22

Ten Ways to Profit before the Crowd Does

- -

In This Chapter

▶ Noting good reports from the media and stock analysts

▶ Looking at higher earnings

▶ Observing industries, megatrends, and politics

▶ Checking in on insider buying and institutional investing

- -

*I*f you find a stock that has all ten points listed in this chapter going for it, back up the truck and load up! Don't forget to tell me about it! Well . . . you don't need all ten of these points to give you the flashing buy signal, but the more, the better.

Use Your Instincts

Look at the world around you. Remember that you're a daily participant in the economy. Your savvy consumer instincts tell you much about what goods and services are great . . . or not so great. What do you like? What products do you see flying off the shelves? Do you see anything that throngs of fellow consumers are lining around the block to buy? One of the greatest investors of our time, Peter Lynch, used to go with his wife to various stores and consumer outlets. He watched how consumers responded to what was offered. Whatever he found that was popular became a subject of research, which lead to great stock picks for the Fidelity Magellan Fund, a stock mutual fund that he managed very successfully for years.

Take Notice of Praise from Consumer Groups

A company is only as good as the profit it generates, and the profit it generates is only as good as the revenues it generates. The revenues are based on whether customers are accepting (and shelling out money for) the company's products or services. Therefore, if what the company offers is popular with consumers, that bodes well for profits and, ultimately, higher stock prices.

When you're ready to invest in stocks, look for high consumer satisfaction. Review consumer publications and Web sites such as Consumer Reports (www.consumerreports.org) and read the surveys and consumer feedback information. Good publicity and word-of-mouth consumer satisfaction are things that investors should be aware of. Stock-picking expert Lynch sees this popularity with consumers as very valuable stock-picking information. He likes to see what consumers buy because that's where the company's success starts.

Check Out Powerful Demographics

If you know that a company generates lots of profit from the teenage market and you find out that the teenage market is going to expand by 10 percent per year for the foreseeable future, what would you do? Exactly — you'd buy that company's stock. If a company has strong fundamentals and appealing products or services and its market is expanding, that company has a winning combination.

Stay alert to growing trends in society. How are demographics changing? Which sectors of the population are growing or shrinking? What shifts are expected in society in terms of age or ethnicity? Check out the data freely available at the Department of Commerce's Web site for the U.S. Census Bureau (www.census.gov).

A market that's growing in size isn't an indicator all by itself (in fact, no indicator gives you the green light all by itself), but it should alert you to do some research. The fact that a strong company sees improving demographic shifts (translation: more potential customers) in its marketplace is a big plus.

Look for a Rise in Earnings

If a company earned $1 per share for the past three years and its earnings are now $1.20 per share (a 20 percent increase), consider this increase a positive harbinger. As the saying goes, "Earnings drive the market," so you need to pay attention to a company's profitability. The more a company makes, the greater the chance that its stock price will increase.

Some people wonder whether to invest in a company that was losing money and then finally turns a profit. Perhaps you're considering the stock of a company involved in new, untested technology. My advice is that you need to be careful in this situation. In such a case, predicting whether a second year of profits will show up is hard, but of course, that's what investors are hoping.

For the serious investor, a track record of positive earnings is important. Several years of earnings (especially growing earnings) are crucial in the decision-making process. As earnings rise, make sure that the growth is at a rate of 10 percent or higher.

Say that you're looking at the stock Buckets-o-Cash, Inc. (BOC). BOC had earnings of $1 per share in 2006, $1.10 in 2007, and $1.21 in 2008. First, you can see that the company is a profitable enterprise. Second (and more important), you can see that the earnings grew 10 percent each year. The fact that earnings grew consistently year after year is important because it indicates that the company is being managed well. Effective company management has a very positive effect on the stock price as the market notices the company's progress.

Growing earnings are important for another reason — inflation. If a company earns $1 per share in each year, that's better than earning less or losing money. But inflation erodes money's purchasing power. If earnings stay constant, the company's ability to grow decreases because the value of its money declines as a result of inflation.

Check out Chapter 11 for an introduction to the importance of earnings.

Analyze Industries

Become a regular and informed watcher of a specific industry that shows great promise. Being aware of an industry's progress and its promising potential is a great starting point to find a great stock before the rest of the crowd does. Start reading the trade magazines (ask your librarian for help), regularly peruse the industry's Web sites, and (if possible) attend trade shows and conferences. It's easier to find a good stock this way than trying to scan the thousands of companies that span the entire economy. For more on analyzing industries, check out Chapter 13.

Stay Aware of Positive Publicity for Industries

When the media report that a company is doing well financially or that its products and services are being well-received by both the media and the market, that news lets you know that the company's stock may be going places. This positive publicity ties in nicely with the point made earlier in this chapter about consumer acceptance for the company's products and services.

Positive press and consumer acceptance are important because they mean that the company is doing what's necessary to please its customers. The positive media coverage also may attract new customers to the company. Gaining customers means more sales and more earnings, which translates into a higher stock price. You can find corporate publicity articles at Web sites such as www.prnewswire.com, and you can track the industries at www.hoovers.com.

Watch Megatrends

Watching the news and reading the headlines for megatrends (a trend that affects an entire country or major subsections of it) isn't just an activity to pass the time. It's a profitable pursuit because noticing what society at large is doing is a great early warning system. This is one of my favorite ways to pick winning stocks. I've even done some of the work for you (you can thank me later). Take a look at emerging opportunities in Chapter 14.

Keep Track of Politics

The storm clouds or pending sunshine in today's political sphere can mean lots of rain or lots of light in the markets the following day. Stock markets tend to be reactive to positive or negative scuttlebutt in the world of politics. Politicians get a lot of coverage, especially during election season, which gives the stock investor an idea of what's coming down the pike. When politicians of all stripes start talking about, say, the need to be environmentally sensitive and how industry should go green, that tells you something (like that you should invest in eco-friendly companies). When politicians get elected and their agenda becomes obvious (raise taxes, increase regulations, provide incentives for activity X, and so on), those actions deserve further investigation for investment potential.

Keep a regular eye on popular publications and Web sites that delve into the world of politics. Web sites such as www.cnn.com, www.drudgereport. com, and www.realclearpolitics.com should be visited regularly. Some financial publications, such as the Kiplinger Letter (www.kiplinger.com), also make a point of watching political trends. Flip to Chapter 15 for more on the effect of politics on stock investing.

Recognize Heavy Insider or Corporate Buying

Company insiders (such as the CEO and the treasurer) know more about the company's health than anyone else. If insiders are buying stock by the boatload, these purchases are certainly a positive sign for investors. Chapter 20 thoroughly covers insider trading, but I highlight the main points here. Insiders can do one of two things:

- **Buy stock for themselves:** If individuals such as the CEO or the treasurer are buying stocks for their personal portfolios, you can assume that they think the stock is a good investment.

- **Buy stock as a corporate decision:** A corporation buying its own stock is usually considered a positive move. The corporation may see its own stock as a good investment. Additionally, corporate stock buying reduces the number of shares available in the market, potentially pushing the stock price higher.

All things being equal, either of these situations will have a positive impact on the stock price. Odds are that you won't see a stampede of insiders buying the stock in a day or week, but you may see it over a period of months. This is generally true simply because each insider has different circumstances, and insider buying is usually done on an individual basis. An accumulation of purchases tells you that members of the management team believe so strongly that the company will do well that they're willing to put their own money at risk.

Follow Institutional Investors

You can generally break down the market into two basic groups: retail and institutional. Retail is you, me, and millions of other individuals. The institutional group includes mutual funds, hedge funds, pensions, and other large entities. These large entities aren't just private, corporate organizations — they now include governmental entities such as the newly-formed sovereign wealth funds created by national governments that are becoming direct participants in the markets. Institutional investors can have a big impact on markets because they can move millions (sometimes even billions) of dollars in and out of markets.

To find out more about the actions of institutional investors, you can use resources such as Institutional Investor News (www.iinews.com), search engines on the Internet, and resources in Appendix A to get you started.

Chapter 23

Ten (Or So) Ways to Protect Your Stock Market Profits

In This Chapter

▶ Using long-term investing strategies

▶ Considering orders, triggers, and options

▶ Selling your stocks if you absolutely must

*W*hew! When you see the headlines out there, you tend to think that your money is like a balloon in a room full of porcupines — headed for trouble. Fortunately, successful stock investing (or just plain avoiding losses) isn't that difficult to accomplish, even in a crazy market. This chapter lists some things to keep in mind when you want to be defensive about your hard-earned stock market profits.

Accrue Cash

Always try to have some extra cash on the sideline no matter how tempted you are to be 100 percent fully invested. You never know when buying opportunities may show up, especially in stocks you already own. Being in cash is its own form of diversification away from market risk.

Spread Your Money across Several Stocks

You should never have too much tied to a single stock because it's too risky. Spread your money elsewhere. As a general rule of thumb, you shouldn't have more than 10 percent of your financial assets tied to a single company.

Buy More of a Down (Yet Solid) Stock

Gadzooks! Your stock just went down like a lemming off a cliff! What a rotten day in the market. Now what do you do? Well, if you've chosen well (profitable company, good industry, and so on), then why not buy more? If you bought a solid, profitable stock at $44, then why not buy some more at $33? That way you can dollar-cost average a bit and end up with a better cost basis. When the inevitable rebound in the stock price occurs, you're looking pretty smart.

Apply Long-Term Logic

Even if you've done your homework and chosen well, you may still find yourself scratching your head and saying, "Holy Moly! My stock just went down. What the heck happened?!" It's happened to me many times. You may make what you think is the greatest choice in stock market history and still see the price decline. What's a prudent investor to do? Believe it or not, wait. Wait? Yes . . . wait. Markets move in irrational ways in the short term, but rationality finally kicks in after a longer time horizon (such as 12, 18, or 24 months or longer).

Common sense takes over regarding a stock price over a protracted period. Long term, good choices go up and bad choices go down. Sooner or later, market participants (millions of both big and small investors) finally notice good companies and invest accordingly. The best way to remember this point is to keep in mind that pithy phrase, "Choose right and sit tight." This is why successful stock investing and long-term stock investing tend to be a good marriage.

Use the Almighty Stop-Loss Order

Getting jittery about the market? What's happening with your stock? Keep in mind that success with your stocks isn't just based on what you invest in — it's also based on how you invest. The stop-loss order is a perennial standby, and you should reach for it as often as the police commissioner reaches for the superhero hotline.

A *stop-loss order* is simply a conditional order that you put in with your brokerage firm on a stock you hold in your account. If the stock is at, say, $50 per share, you can put a stop-loss order in at $45 so that if your stock falls and hits $45, it's automatically sold. Keep in mind that a stop-loss order is also a time-related order; you can stipulate that it can be a *day order* or a *good-till-cancelled* (GTC) order. The day order expires at the end of trading that day, while the GTC order expires at a much later time (determined by the broker). Find out more about stop-loss orders in Chapter 18.

Use the Almighty Trailing Stop Order

The *trailing stop order* is a nice variation on the stop-loss order that I discuss in the preceding section. This order takes the stop-loss order a step further by making it move upward with the stock but not budging on the down side. In other words, the stop loss trails the stock's price upward but won't adjust downward. You set the trailing stop at a percentage (or dollar amount) below the stock price.

For example, say your stock is at $50; you can set the trailing stop at 10 percent below and make it a GTC order. If the stock falls to $45 (which is 10 percent below $50), it's then automatically sold to prevent further losses. But if the stock rises to, say, $60, the trailing stop adjusts upward and would then be at $54 (10 percent below the stock's new price). Should the stock reverse and then fall, the trailing stop stays put at $54 and a sell order is then triggered. At that point you've protected 100 percent of your original investment ($50 per share) and the $4 profit, too. Find out more about trailing stops in Chapter 18.

Place a Limit Order

The *limit order* is another order available to anyone who has a stock brokerage account. It has some similarity to the stop-loss order in that you set a sales price (or a purchase price) for the stock in question. If the stock is rising and hits $48, for example, you can have your brokerage firm set limit prices for that stock. If you want to sell it, you can put a limit order at, say, $46 ($2 below) or at $50 ($2 above) and, again, make it a GTC order. That way, you won't settle for a price; you get what you want.

Limit orders give you the ability to get your price (up or down), but they require discipline and patience, because sometimes the market doesn't move the way you think it will. I provide details on limit orders in Chapter 18.

Set Up Broker Triggers

Don't be gun-shy about *broker triggers* (like that pun?). These are just orders and/or e-mail alerts that brokers use to help their customers navigate the market environment. Is some news hitting your stock or its particular industry? Triggers act like an early warning system when certain events and conditions occur so that you can act on them (by buying or selling your stock). Many brokerage firms have Web sites that allow you to customize your orders. In addition, Web sites such as www.marketwatch.com and www.bloomberg.com can e-mail you news alerts on stocks and market news. You can find out more about broker orders (such as trade triggers) in Chapter 18.

Consider the Put Option

A *put option* is a speculative vehicle that helps you make money when you bet on an investment (such as a stock) going down. Put options are beyond the scope of this book, but that doesn't mean that I can't whet your appetite about something that I feel is a good alternative to simply watching your investment decrease. The type of put option I want to mention is referred to as a *protective put*.

Many people buy puts when they're betting (and hoping) that a particular stock will go down. Of course, if you own that particular stock, you certainly aren't hoping that it goes down, but you can get a protective put as a form of insurance in case the stock does decline. In this case you buy a put on your own stock. If the stock goes down (temporarily), your protective put goes up. You can then hold onto the stock and sell the put option at a profit. The profit you make on the put can offset (wholly or partially) the temporary decline in the stock.

Check Out the Covered Call Option

Writing covered call options is a good way to generate income from an existing stock in your portfolio. Simply stated, a *covered call option* is a vehicle that gives you a chance to make money from stocks in your brokerage account. It's an ultra safe way to generate more income — as much as 10 percent, 15 percent, or more — from your stock position.

Covered call options are beyond the scope of this book, but I strongly recommend that you look into them, as they can be a safe wealth-building feature, even in portfolios that are temporarily down. You can find excellent tutorials and beginners' information on both covered call options and protective puts (the topic of the preceding section) at places such as the Chicago Board Options Exchange (www.cboe.com) and the Options Industry Council (www.888options.com). For more on options in general, see *Stock Options For Dummies* by Alan R. Simon and *Futures & Options For Dummies* by Joe Duarte (both published by Wiley).

When All Else Fails, Sell

The most successful investors in history have taken their lumps. As the old adage goes, "Keep your winners and sell your losers." You sell losers to minimize the downside. It's easier to recoup a 10 percent or 20 percent loss in your portfolio on the whole than it is to recoup a huge loss in a particular stock. In addition, for what it's worth, the losses are usually tax-deductible, which can at least help minimize the pain at tax time. (See Chapter 21 for details on handling taxes.)

Chapter 24

Ten Red Flags for Stock Investors

In This Chapter

▷ Seeing a slowdown in earnings and sales

▷ Keeping an eye out for high debt or low bond ratings

▷ Staying aware of industry or political troubles

▷ Investigating insider selling and questionable accounting practices

*H*ave you ever watched a movie and noticed that one of the characters coughs excessively throughout the entire film? To me, that's a dead giveaway that the character is a goner. Or maybe you've seen a movie in which a bit character annoys a crime boss, so right away you know that it's time for him to "sleep with the fishes." Stocks aren't that different. If you're alert, you can recognize some definite signs that your investment may be ready to kick the bucket.

Let the tips in this chapter serve as a symptoms checklist on your stock investment. This chapter helps you catch your stock as it starts to cough so that you can get out before it sleeps with the fishes. (I just can't help you with mixed metaphors.)

Earnings Slow Down or Head South

Profit is the lifeblood of a company. Of course, the opposite is true as well — lack of profit is a sign of a company's poor financial health. Watch the earnings. Are they increasing or not? If they aren't, find out why. Keep in mind that if the general economy is experiencing a recession, stagnant earnings are still better than robust losses — everything is relative. Earnings slowdowns for a company may very well be a temporary phenomenon. If a firm's earnings are holding up better than its competitors and/or the market in general, you don't need to be alarmed.

Nonetheless, a company's earnings are its most important measure of success. Keep an eye on the company's P/E ratio (see Chapter 11 for details on this ratio). It could change negatively (go up) as a result of one of two basic scenarios:

- ✔ The stock price goes up as earnings barely budge.
- ✔ The stock price doesn't move, yet earnings drop.

Both of these scenarios result in a rising P/E ratio that ultimately has a negative effect on the stock price.

A P/E ratio that's lower than industry competitors' P/E ratios makes a company's stock a favorable investment.

Don't buy the argument that "Although the company has losses, its sales are exploding." This argument is a variation of "The company may be losing money, but it'll make it up on volume." For example, say that Sweet Patootee, Inc. (SPI), had sales of $1 billion in 2008 and that the firm expects sales to be $1.5 billion in 2009, projecting an increase of 50 percent. But what if SPI's earnings were $200 million in 2008 and the company actually expects a loss for 2009? The business wouldn't succeed, because sales without earnings aren't enough — the company needs to make a profit. Remember that if you put your money in the stock of a company that's losing money today with hopes that it will become profitable tomorrow, you're not investing, you're speculating.

Sales Slow Down

Before you invest in a company, make sure that sales are strong and rising. If sales start to decline, that downward motion ultimately affects earnings (see the previous section). Although a firm's earnings may go safely up and down, sales should consistently rise. If they cease to rise, a variety of reasons may be to blame. First, the situation may be temporary because the economy in general is having tough times. However, it may be more serious. Perhaps the company is having marketing problems, or a competitor is eating away at its market share. Or maybe a new technology is replacing its products and services. In any case, falling sales raise a red flag you shouldn't ignore.

By the way, when I talk sales, I'm talking about the sales of what the company usually offers (its products or services). Sometimes a company may sell something other than what it normally offers (such as equipment, real estate, or a subdivision of its business), and this sale may make the total sales number temporarily blip upward. Watch for this because it can fool your perception of the company's financial strength. Maybe the unusual sale is due to financial or cash flow problems that the company's experiencing. The bottom line is to simply check it out.

Debt Is Too High or Unsustainable

Excessive debt is the kiss of death for a struggling company. During 2000–2002, many companies that experts thought were invincible went bankrupt. During 2007 and 2008, many prominent businesses struggled with high debt, including brokerage firms (longtime Wall Street power-houses Bear Stearns and Lehman Brothers collapsed into bankruptcy in early 2008), large regional banks (Indymac Bank in California), and that old standby, General Motors (GM was fighting off bankruptcy in mid-2008). It's getting so that stock investing is riskier than hang gliding in a hurricane!

Be aware of a company's debt and solvency. Chapter 12 and Appendix B can help you read and understand a company's financial data clearly so that you can make an informed decision about buying or selling its stock.

Analysts Are Exuberant Despite Logic

Too often, analysts give glowing praise to stocks that any logical person with some modest financial acumen would avoid like the plague. Why is this? In many instances, the analysts have, alas, a dark motive (or something not so dark such as . . . ugh . . . stupidity). In any case, remember that analysts are employed by firms that earn hefty investment banking fees from the very companies that these analysts tout. In that situation, issuing a less-than-complete or less-than-accurate report can be easy.

In fact, you should be wary of analysts' views, especially the analysts who make positive recommendations even when the company in question has wor-risome features, such as no income and tremendous debt. It seems like a para-dox: Sell a stock when all the pros say to buy it? How can that be? The merits of any stock should speak for themselves. When a company is losing money, all the great recommendations in the world can't reverse its fortunes.

Also, keep in mind that if everybody is buying a particular stock — the current analysts' favorite — who's left to buy it? When the stock turns out to be a dud, you aren't able to sell it because all the other suckers already own it (thanks to analysts' recommendations). And if they already own it, they're probably already aware of the company's flaws. What happens then? You got it: More and more people end up selling it. When more people are selling than buying a stock, its price declines.

Insider Selling

Heavy insider selling is to a stock what garlic, sunrises, and crosses are to vampires: an almost certain sign of doom! If you notice that increasing numbers of insiders (such as a company's president, treasurer, or vice president of finance, for instance) are selling their stock holdings, you can consider it a red flag. In recent years, massive insider selling has become a telltale sign of a company's imminent fall from grace. After all, who better to know the company's prospects for success (or lack thereof) than its high-level management? What management does (selling stock, for example) speaks louder than what management says. (Do you hear that loud and persistent coughing again?) For more information on insider trading, see Chapter 20.

A Bond Rating Cut

It may seem odd, but the prospects for a company's bonds are an indicator of the prospects for the company's stock. Many firms issue bonds so they can borrow money to fund operations or new ventures. These corporate bonds are usually rated by major bond-rating agencies such as Standard and Poor's. These agencies issue a rating on the bond with this question in mind: "Does the issuer of the bond (the company) have the financial wherewithal to pay back the bond principal and interest in full according to the terms of the bond indenture (the bond agreement)?"

If a company is rated as financially strong, the bond-rating agency will issue a high bond rating (such as AAA or AA). If the agency's view of the company is generally negative, the bond rating for the company will be lower (such as BBB or lower). If you see a company's bonds being downgraded, that's definitely a red flag for investors. Check out Chapter 9 for more information on bond ratings.

Increased Negative Coverage

You may easily recognize unfavorable reports of a company's stock as a sign to unload that stock. Or you may be a contrarian and see bad press as an opportunity to scoop up some shares of a company victimized by negative reporting. In any case, take the negative reports as a signal to further investigate the merits of holding onto the stock or as a sign for selling it so that you can make room in your portfolio for a more promising stock choice.

Industry Problems

Sometimes, being a strong company doesn't matter if that company's industry is having problems. If the industry is in trouble, the company's decline probably isn't that far behind. Tighten up those trailing stops (see Chapter 18 to find out how).

Also, try to be aware of industries that are intimately related to the industry of a company's stock you own or are considering buying. Very often, problems in one industry can affect or spread to a related industry. For example, plummeting auto sales may have a negative effect on prospects for auto parts or auto services companies. To find out more about industries, check out Chapter 13.

Political Problems

Political considerations are always a factor in investing. Be it taxes, regulations, or other government actions, politics can easily break a company and sink its stock. If your company's stock is sensitive to political developments, be aware of potential political pitfalls. Reading *The Wall Street Journal* and regularly viewing major financial Web sites can help you stay informed. (I give you lists of sources in Appendix A.)

In recent years, drug and tobacco stocks in general suffered because of prevailing political attitudes. Also, the prices of certain stocks in particular (Microsoft in the late 1990s comes to mind) have dropped drastically because the companies were targets of government actions for such reasons as antitrust concerns and public safety issues. To find out more about political considerations affecting stocks, go to Chapter 15.

Funny Accounting: No Laughing Here!

Throughout this book, I discuss the topic of accounting as an important way to see how well (or how poorly) a company is doing. Understanding a company's balance sheet and income statement and making a simple comparison of these documents over a period of several years can give you great insights into the company's prospects. You don't have to be an accountant to grasp key concepts. Enron is a perfect example of how you can avoid a stock investing disaster with some rudimentary knowledge of accounting.

Despite the fact that Enron hid many of its financial problems from public view, the information that was available made the message clear: "Danger Will Robinson! Houston, we have a problem!" If investors had done some simple homework, they would have plainly seen the following revealing points in 2000, over a year and a half before the collapse:

- **Enron's price-to-earnings (P/E) ratio hit 90 in 2000.** This stratospheric P/E kept most value investors (including myself) away.

- **Its price to book (P/B) ratio hit 12.** For investors, this ratio means that the market value of the company, compared to the company's book value (also called *accounting value*), was 12 to 1 — for every $12 of market value, investors were getting only $1 in book value. When you consider that a P/B ratio of 3 or 4 is considered nosebleed territory for value investors, you can see that Enron's P/B ratio was screaming, "Watch out below!"

- **The price to sales (P/S) ratio hit an incredible 22.** This ratio means that investors paid $22 in market value for every $1 of sales the company generated. When a P/S of 5 or 10 is considered too high, 22 is nosebleed territory!

I found this information in public filings that anyone could have seen. To understand these points more fully (along with other equally incisive and lucid accounting and financial points) and to discover how to use the information to avoid similar mistakes in the future, see Chapters 11 and 12 and Appendix B.

Chapter 25

Ten Challenges and Opportunities for Stock Investors

In This Chapter

▶ Understanding the most pressing concerns for stock investors

▶ Recognizing other markets that can affect stocks

▶ Spotting hidden opportunities with new economic megatrends

*O*ver the years, I've found that the easiest way to make money with stocks (or to avoid losing money with stocks) is to simply be aware of the economic environment in which they operate. Stocks can be the best (or worst) investment depending on the economic/political environment. Many economic challenges face the stock market, including what's happening with government policy, societal trends, and national/international geopolitical conditions. In this chapter, I discuss the most important issues or megatrends that can affect you and your loved ones, as well as your stock investments.

You need to be aware of the big picture by regularly checking in with great Web sites such as Financial Sense (www.financialsense.com), Free-Market News Network (www.freemarketnews.com), and the Mises Institute (www.mises.org). See Appendix A for more resources.

Debt, Debt, and More Debt

In the summer of 2008, the U.S. Gross Domestic Product (GDP) surpassed the $14 trillion mark. Great! However, the total level of debt in the country surpassed $40 trillion. Ugh . . . NOT great. What has kept the economy afloat and "growing" during the past eight to ten years is massive and pervasive debt that must be dealt with. Debt in just about every category is at record levels, including mortgage, consumer, margin, corporate, and government debt. The problem is that this debt must be either paid off or wiped out through bankruptcy. In 2008, you've seen financial catastrophes with debt gone bad in the banking and brokerage industries. The chickens have come home to roost!

Make sure that you're dealing with your debt level now. Reduce it as much as possible, and make sure that you're analyzing your stocks in the same light. Companies that carry too much debt are at great risk. If a company sinks, your stock will follow. If the company goes into bankruptcy, your stock's value will be vaporized.

If you want to see something fascinating (and scary at the same time), check out the total debt figures by viewing the Grandfather Economic Report by Michael Hodges at `http://mwhodges.home.att.net` (if the Web site is no longer active, feel free to e-mail me at `paul@mladjenovic.com` and I'll get the info for you). It's sobering stuff!

Derivatives

Deriv . . . what? You may say, "What the hell are they?" unless, of course, you're my church's pastor. *Derivatives* are the largest financial market in the world. As of September 2008, the total dollar value exceeds $500 trillion. It easily dwarfs the world economy. Easily! Now, you don't have to understand them, but you should be aware of what could go wrong if a derivatives problem occurs. Companies such as Enron, Bear Stearns, and AIG imploded very quickly, primarily because of tragic errors in their derivatives portfolio. I would love to explain derivatives more fully, but it would take a whole chapter by itself. If you want a detailed explanation, sources such as `www.wikipedia.com` and `www.investopedia.com` do a fairly good job. Derivatives "accidents" have dotted the financial landscape over the past 10 to 15 years, and they had (and will have) the potential to do major damage to the stock market.

There's no use fretting about derivatives. While you're at it, you may as well worry about meteors and presidential campaigns. Just take common sense approaches to protect your portfolio as you grow your wealth. Stay away from firms that have large derivatives positions (typically banks and brokerage firms). Look into diversifying, trailing stops, and the other strategies discussed in this book and in the resources cited.

Real Estate

Real estate is one challenge the experts warned you about during 2004–2005. By the time you read this, everyone will realize that the real estate industry is down dramatically from its former bubble highs, and it's languishing with record levels of foreclosures and unsold inventories of property (as of mid-2008). If you're tempted to jump in, tread carefully, because a full, healthy recovery in a slow-moving market like real estate tends to take a long time. You're better off waiting until the data from the industry becomes more positive.

The message to you at this point is clear: Make sure you have your mortgage under control and your debt at manageable levels. Make sure that the real estate industry is showing signs of solid recovery before you buy any stock of any related companies.

Some early signs of a recovery are at least three consecutive quarters of rising building permits and a steady shrinkage of the national inventory of unsold real estate, among others. Some good Web sites on real estate include www.realtor.com and realestate.yahoo.com.

Inflation

Inflation is indeed a major megatrend as I write this. The real-world rate 1of inflation (as of September 2008) is in the 9 to 11 percent range. High (and rising) inflation is now a worldwide phenomenon because most major countries are increasing their money supply at double-digit levels. What do stock investors do?

Reassess your portfolios and avoid companies that may get hurt from rising inflation (such as mortgage companies and other fixed-debt securities). Consider shifting more of your portfolio to companies that benefit from inflation (or at least don't get hurt by it), such as those in the food, water, energy, and precious metals sectors.

Pensions and Unfunded Liabilities

The year 2008 is more than just an election year; it's also the year that the first wave of 78 million baby boomers retire. The problem is that pensions for these folks will likely fall short. The latest data shows that many pensions are underfunded, and many future retirees are in for a rude awakening.

In addition, Social Security and Medicare are certain to be gigantic challenges during the next few decades. As of July 2008, the total liabilities for these mammoth programs exceed $50 trillion. That's not a typo; it's a combined liability that's nearly four times the nation's gross domestic product (GDP). Current beneficiaries will likely not be affected, but anyone under 65 will certainly be. Let's face it: We're living longer than ever before, and we need to be more proactive about our personal responsibility in our senior years.

To find out more, review your rights and responsibilities with the Social Security Administration (www.ssa.gov) and Medicare (www.medicare.gov). Also check out some excellent private sites such as www.social security.org, www.medicare.org, and www.medicarenewswatch.com.

The message is clear: People need to save and invest more to fill in the financial gaps that seem to be inevitable. Stocks are a wealth-building tool that's well-suited for long-term needs such as your retirement concerns. Start now, because the future has a way of sneaking up on you faster than you think.

The Growth of Government

Every economy has two components: private (consumers and producers) and public (government). No matter how you slice it, government is supported (think taxes) by the private sector. The total combined budget for federal, state, and local governments in the U.S. exceeds $5 trillion as of September 2008. The trend is for larger and more activist government, which entails higher overall taxes, increased regulations, and other government growth (inflation, spending, and so on). History tells us that this isn't a positive trend and that it can weigh very heavily on the finances of the private sector (translation: the stock market goes down). What's an investor to do?

I repeat the message from throughout this book: Stick to stocks from companies whose products or services address basic human needs, and understand the good, the bad, and the ugly of government and its effect on the economy and financial markets (Chapters 10 and 15 are good places to start).

Recession/Depression

Recessions and depressions are actually a tie-in to the point in the previous section — they're symptoms of excessive government growth and intervention. In any event, Americans have been trying to fend off a recession throughout much of 2008. I think that struggling economic times will still be evident when you read these words.

In rough economic times, the best stocks are defensive (food, beverage, utilities, and so on) because people buy these things no matter how good or bad the economy is. Cyclical stocks will get beaten down, so it may be a good idea to shop around for real values after the economy turns around. Meanwhile, deploy protective strategies with your money, and play it safe with solid, financially sound companies.

Commodities

A shrewd man once said, "History may not repeat itself, but it can often rhyme" (okay, it was me!). In many respects, this decade resembles the 1970s. Stocks were having a dreadful time as inflation, the energy crisis, and international tensions escalated. However, it was a great time to invest in energy, precious metals, and commodities. Gold and silver hit all-time highs by the end of the 1970s. Stock investors who scooped up shares of companies in these specific industries racked up tremendous gains.

The lesson for investors to understand is that conditions in this decade offer opportunities in natural resources that mirror the late 1970s. In addition, China and India are growing, and they'll need more commodities (grains, base metals, energy, water, and so on) for their expanding economies and populations. As demand continues to outpace supply, the stocks of companies that provide products and services in natural resources will shine.

Energy

Oil hit a recent high of $147 per barrel in early summer 2008. Although the price corrected (it's at approximately $65 as of mid-October 2008), the world's appetite for energy (oil, gas, and so on) has caused prices to hit record highs, and the coming years promise more demand. The energy markets are experiencing a sea change that makes current conditions far more different and more serious than in recent decades. Our society has entered the age of Peak Oil (see more about this at www.peakoil.net), which means that cheap and readily available energy is a thing of the past.

For stock investors, this at least means the chance to grow your money both directly (energy companies, obviously) and indirectly (alternate energy companies). If you want your wealth to grow, you need to understand the impact that energy has on your portfolio. (See Chapter 14 for more on emerging sector opportunities.)

Dangers from Left Field

Gee, after being beaten up by the previous nine points, what else is needed? This reminds me of the episode of "Get Smart" where the arch villain says, "You've been whipped, beaten, and tortured, but the picnic is over!" (I still use that great line at parties.) In any case, I hope that I've impressed upon you that it's a brave new world fraught with dangers for the clueless but filled with wealth-building opportunities for the clued in. The fact is that no one knows what will hit our economy and society from out of the blue. Events such as 9/11, the tsunami in Asia, and Hurricane Katrina certainly tell us that the world has unseen perils for us and our prosperity. Terrorism and other factors will have an impact. Fortunately, you can make changes — even slight changes — that can protect or grow your wealth.

Whether you're talking about healthcare stocks that boom in response to new health threats or concerns (such as mad cow disease) or stocks of companies that prosper because of homeland security issues, your stock investing program can survive and thrive. Stay informed and understand that successful stock investing doesn't happen in a vacuum.

Part VI
Appendixes

The 5th Wave   By Rich Tennant

That's the Harrisons. Never have I seen an investment portfolio start so strong and go south so quickly.

In this part . . .

Check out the appendixes for resources that aid you in making informed investment decisions. Whether the topic is stock investing terminology, economics, or avoiding capital gains taxes, I include a treasure trove of resources to assist you in your research. Whether you go to a bookstore, the library, or the Internet, Appendix A gives you some great places to turn to for help. In Appendix B, I explain financial ratios. These important numbers help you better determine whether to invest in a particular company's stock.

Appendix A

Resources for Stock Investors

· ·

*G*etting and staying informed is an ongoing priority for stock investors. The lists in this appendix represent some of the best information resources available.

Financial Planning Sources

To find a financial planner to help you with your general financial needs, contact the following organizations:

Certified Financial Planner Board of Standards
1425 K St. NW, Suite 500
Washington, DC 20005
800-487-1497
www.cfp.net
Get a free copy of the CFP Board's pamphlet *10 Questions to Ask When Choosing a Financial Planner*. Be sure to ask for a financial planner who specializes in investing.

Financial Planning Association (FPA)
1600 K St. NW, Suite 201
Washington, DC 20006
800-322-4237
www.fpanet.org

National Association of Personal Financial Advisors
3250 N. Arlington Heights Rd., Suite 109
Arlington Heights, IL 60004
847-483-5400
www.napfa.org

The Language of Investing

Standard & Poor's Dictionary of Financial Terms
By Virginia Morris and Kenneth Morris
Published by Lightbulb Press, Inc.
A nicely laid out A-to-Z publication for investors mystified by financial terms.
It explains the important investing terms you come across every day.

Investing for Beginners
beginnersinvest.about.com
This site offers good basic information for novice investors.

Investopedia
www.investopedia.com
An excellent site with plenty of information on investing for beginning and
intermediate investors.

Investor Words
www.investorwords.com
One of the most comprehensive sites on the Internet for beginning and
intermediate investors for learning words and phrases unique to the
financial world.

Textual Investment Resources

Stock investing success isn't an event; it's a process. The periodicals and
magazines listed here (along with their Web sites) have offered many years of
guidance and information for investors, and they're still top-notch. The books
and pamphlets provide much wisdom that's either timeless or timely (covering problems and concerns every investor should be aware of now).

Periodicals and magazines

Barron's
www.barrons.com

Forbes magazine
www.forbes.com

Investor's Business Daily
www.investors.com

Kiplinger's Personal Finance **magazine**
www.kiplinger.com

Money **magazine**
www.money.com

SmartMoney
www.smartmoney.com

The Wall Street Journal
www.wsj.com

Books and pamphlets

Common Stocks and Uncommon Profits
By Philip A. Fisher
Published by John Wiley & Sons, Inc.

Elliott Wave Principle: Key to Market Behavior
By Robert Prechter and A. J. Frost
Published by New Classics Library

Forbes Guide to the Markets
By Marc M. Groz
Published by John Wiley & Sons, Inc.

How to Pick Stocks Like Warren Buffett: Profiting from the Bargain Hunting Strategies of the World's Greatest Value Investor
By Timothy Vick
Published by McGraw-Hill Professional Publishing

The Intelligent Investor: The Classic Text on Value Investing
By Benjamin Graham
Published by HarperCollins

Invest Wisely: Advice From Your Securities Regulators (pamphlet)
www.sec.gov/investor/pubs/inws.htm
This publication provides basic information to help investors select a brokerage firm and sales representative, make an initial investment decision, monitor an investment, and address an investment problem.

Secrets of the Great Investors (audiotape series)
Published by Knowledge Products
800-876-4332
www.knowledgeproducts.net/html/inv_files/invest.cfm

Security Analysis: The Classic 1951 Edition
by Benjamin Graham and David Dodd
Published by the McGraw-Hill Companies
This book is a classic, and most investors in this uncertain age should
acquaint themselves with the basics.

Standard & Poor's Stock Reports (available in the library reference section)
Ask your reference librarian about this excellent reference source, which
gives one-page summaries on the major companies and has detailed financial reports on all major companies listed on the New York Stock Exchange,
American Stock Exchange, and Nasdaq.

The Wall Street Journal Guide to Understanding Money & Investing
By Kenneth Morris and Virginia Morris
Published by Lightbulb Press, Inc.

Special books of interest to stock investors

These titles provide more in-depth information for Chapters 10, 13, 14, 15,
and 25.

*The Coming Collapse of the Dollar and How to Profit from It: Make a
Fortune by Investing in Gold and Other Hard Assets*
By James Turk and John Rubino
Published by Doubleday

Crash Proof: How to Profit from the Coming Economic Collapse
By Peter Schiff
Published by John Wiley & Sons, Inc.

The ETF Book: All You Need to Know About Exchange-Traded Funds
By Richard Ferri
Published by John Wiley & Sons, Inc.
Considering the marketplace, ETFs are better choices than stocks for some
investors, and this book does a good job of explaining them.

Hot Commodities: How Anyone Can Invest
Profitably in the World's Best Market
By Jim Rogers
Published by Random House

Precious Metals Investing For Dummies
By Paul Mladjenovic
Published by John Wiley & Sons, Inc.
My shameless plug for another great book. Seriously, the book covers an area that will become an important part of the financial landscape in the coming months and years (can you say "inflation"?). Yes, common stocks and exchange-traded funds (ETFs) involved in precious metals are covered.

Profit from the Peak: The End of Oil and the Greatest Investment Event of the Century
By Brian Hicks and Chris Nelder
Published by John Wiley & Sons, Inc.

Twilight in the Desert: The Coming Saudi Oil Shock and the World Economy
By Matthew R. Simmons
Published by John Wiley & Sons, Inc.

Investing Web Sites

How can any serious investor ignore the Internet? You can't and you shouldn't. The following are among the best information sources available.

General investing Web sites

Bloomberg
www.bloomberg.com

CNN Money
www.money.cnn.com

Financial Sense
www.financialsense.com

Forbes
www.forbes.com

Free-Market News Network
www.freemarketnews.com

MarketWatch
www.marketwatch.com

Money Central
www.moneycentral.com

SmartMoney
www.smartmoney.com

Stock investing Web sites

Allstocks.com
www.allstocks.com

CNBC
www.cnbc.com

Contrarian Investing.com
www.contrarianinvesting.com

DailyStocks
www.dailystocks.com

Investools
www.investools.com

Morningstar GrowthInvestor (known for mutual funds but also has great
research available on stocks as well)
www.morningstar.com

Quote.com
www.quote.com

Raging Bull
www.ragingbull.com

Standard and Poor's
www.standardandpoors.com

The Street
www.thestreet.com

Super Money Links
www.supermoneylinks.com

Yahoo! Finance
www.finance.yahoo.com

Investor Associations and Organizations

American Association of Individual Investors (AAII)
625 N. Michigan Ave.
Chicago, IL 60611-3110
800-428-2244, 312-280-0170
www.aaii.com

National Association of Investors Corp. (NAIC)
711 W. 13 Mile Rd.
Madison Heights, MI 48071
877-275-6242, 248-583-6242
www.betterinvesting.org

Stock Exchanges

American Stock Exchange
www.amex.com

Nasdaq
www.nasdaq.com

New York Stock Exchange
www.nyse.com

OTC Bulletin Board
www.otcbb.com

Finding Brokers

The following sections offer sources to help you evaluate brokers and an extensive list of brokers (with telephone numbers and Web sites) so that you can do your own shopping.

Choosing brokers

SmartMoney magazine
www.smartmoney.com
SmartMoney does a comprehensive annual review and comparison of stockbrokers.

Stock Brokers
www.stockbrokers.com

Brokers

Charles Schwab & Co.
800-435-4000
www.schwab.com

Citi Smith Barney
800-221-3636
www.smithbarney.com

E*TRADE
800-387-2331
www.etrade.com

Fidelity Brokerage
800-343-3548
www.fidelity.com

Merrill Lynch
800-637-7455
www.ml.com

Muriel Siebert & Co.
800-872-0444
www.siebertnet.com

Options Xpress
888-280-8020
www.optionsxpress.com

R.F. Lafferty & Co., Inc.
800-221-8601
www.laffertyny.com

Scottrade
800-619-7283
www.scottrade.com

TD Ameritrade
800-669-3900
www.tdameritrade.com

thinkorswim
866-839-1100
www.thinkorswim.com

TradeKing
877-495-5464
www.tradeking.com

Vanguard Brokerage Services
877-662-7447
www.vanguard.com

Wachovia Securities
866-927-0812
www.wachoviasecurities.com

Wall Street Access
800-709-5929
www.wsaccess.com

Fee-Based Investment Sources

The following are fee-based subscription services. Many of them also offer excellent (and free) e-mail newsletters tracking the stock market and related news.

The Bull & Bear
www.thebullandbear.com

The Daily Reckoning (Agora Publishing)
www.dailyreckoning.com

The Elliott Wave Theorist
770-536-0309
www.elliottwave.com

Hulbert Financial Digest
www.hulbertdigest.com
Part of MarketWatch.com

InvestorPlace
www.investorplace.com

Louis Rukeyser's Wall Street
www.rukeyser.com

Mark Skousen
www.mskousen.com

Money and Markets
www.moneyandmarkets.com

The Motley Fool
www.fool.com

Richard Russell's Dow Theory Letters
www.dowtheoryletters.com

The Value Line Investment Survey
800-654-0508
www.valueline.com

Dividend Reinvestment Plans

BUYandHOLD, Inc.
www.buyandhold.com

DRIP Central
www.dripcentral.com

First Share
www.firstshare.com

ShareBuilder (ING Direct)
www.sharebuilder.com

Sources for Analysis

The following sources give you the chance to look a little deeper at some critical aspects regarding stock analysis. Whether it's earnings estimates and insider selling or a more insightful look at a particular industry, these sources are among my favorites.

Earnings and earnings estimates

Earnings Whispers
www.earningswhispers.com

Thomson Reuters
www.thomsonreuters.com

Zacks Summary of Brokerage Research
www.zacks.com

Industry analysis

Hoover's
www.hoovers.com

MarketWatch
www.marketwatch.com

Standard & Poor's
www.standardandpoors.com

Factors that affect market value

Understanding basic economics is so vital to making your investment decisions that I had to include this section. These great sources have helped me understand the big picture and what ultimately affects the stock market (see Chapters 10 and 15 for more details).

Economics and politics

American Institute for Economic Research (AIER)
P.O. Box 100
Great Barrington, MA 01230
www.aier.org
Note: AIER also has great little booklets for consumers on budgeting, social security, avoiding financial problems, and other topics.

Center for Freedom and Prosperity
www.freedomandprosperity.org

Federal Reserve Board
www.federalreserve.gov

Financial Sense
P.O. Box 1269
Poway, CA 92074
858-486-3939
www.financialsense.com

Foundation for Economic Education
30 S. Broadway
Irvington, NY 10533
800-960-4333
www.fee.org

Le Metropole Café
www.lemetropolecafe.com

Ludwig von Mises Institute
518 W. Magnolia Ave.
Auburn, AL 36832
334-321-2100
www.mises.org

Moody's Economy.com
121 N. Walnut St., Suite 500
West Chester, PA 19380-3166
866-275-3266
www.economy.com

Securities and Exchange Commission (SEC)
www.sec.gov
The SEC has tremendous resources for investors. In addition to providing information on investing, the SEC also monitors the financial markets for

fraud and other abusive activities. For stock investors, it also has EDGAR (Electronic Data Gathering, Analysis, and Retrieval system), which is a comprehensive, searchable database of public documents that are filed by public companies.

Federal laws

Go to any of these sites to find out about new and proposed laws. The on-site search engines will help you find laws either by their assigned number or a keyword search.

Library of Congress
Thomas legislative search engine
http://thomas.loc.gov

U.S. House of Representatives
www.house.gov

U.S. Senate
www.senate.gov

Technical analysis

Big Charts (Provided by www.marketwatch.com)
www.bigcharts.com

The Elliott Wave Theorist
www.elliottwave.com

LiveCharts
www.livecharts.com

StockCharts.com, Inc.
www.stockcharts.com

Insider trading

Free EDGAR
www.freeedgar.com

Securities and Exchange Commission (SEC)
www.sec.gov

StreetInsider
www.streetinsider.com

10-K Wizard
www.10kwizard.com

Tax Benefits and Obligations

Americans for Tax Reform
www.atr.org

Fairmark
www.fairmark.com

Fidelity Investments
www.401k.com

J.K. Lasser's series of books on taxes
By J.K. Lasser
Published by John Wiley & Sons, Inc.
www.wiley.com

National Taxpayers Union
www.ntu.org

Roth IRA
www.rothira.com

Taxes 2008 For Dummies
By Eric Tyson, Margaret A. Munro, and David J. Silverman
Published by John Wiley & Sons, Inc.
www.dummies.com, www.wiley.com

Fraud

Federal Citizen Information Center
www.pueblo.gsa.gov
Investing publications for consumers from the Federal Citizen Information
Center catalog are available for free downloading at this Web site.

Financial Industry Regulatory Authority (FINRA)
1735 K St. NW
Washington, DC 20006
800-289-9999
202-728-8000
www.finra.org
This Web site gives you information and assistance on reporting fraud or other abuse by brokers.

National Consumers League's Fraud Center
www.fraud.org

North American Securities Administrators Association
888-846-2722
www.nasaa.org

Securities and Exchange Commission (SEC)
www.sec.gov
The government agency that regulates the securities industry.

Securities Industry and Financial Markets Association
1101 New York Ave. NW, 8th Floor
Washington, DC 20005
202-962-7300
www.sifma.org

Securities Investor Protection Corporation (SIPC)
www.sipc.org
SIPC has the role of restoring funds to investors with assets in the hands of bankrupt and otherwise financially troubled brokerage firms (make sure that your brokerage firm is a member of SIPC).

Appendix B

Financial Ratios

$\mathbf{C}$onsidering how many financial catastrophes have occurred in recent years (and continue to occur in the current headlines), doing your homework regarding the financial health of your stock choices is more important than ever. This appendix should be your go-to section when you find stocks that you're considering for your portfolio. It lists the most common ratios that investors should be aware of and use. A solid company doesn't have to pass all these ratio tests with flying colors, but at a minimum, it should comfortably pass the ones regarding profitability and solvency:

- **Profitability:** Is the company making money? Is it making more or less than it did in the prior period? Are sales growing? Are profits growing?

  You can answer these questions by looking at the following ratios:

  - Return on equity

  - Return on assets

  - Common size ratio (income statement)

- **Solvency:** Is the company keeping debts and other liabilities under control? Are the company's assets growing? Is the company's net equity (or net worth or stockholders' equity) growing?

  You can answer these questions by looking at the following ratios:

  - Quick ratio

  - Debt to net equity

  - Working capital

While you examine ratios, keep these points in mind:

- Not every company and/or industry is the same. A ratio that seems dubious in one industry may be just fine in another. Investigate and check out the norms in that particular industry. (See Chapter 13 for details on analyzing industries.)

✔ A single ratio isn't enough on which to base your investment decision. Look at several ratios covering the major aspects of the company's finances.

✔ Look at two or more years of the company's numbers to judge whether the most recent ratio is better, worse, or unchanged from the previous year's ratio. Ratios can give you early warning signs regarding the company's prospects. (See Chapter 11 for details on two important documents that list a company's numbers — the balance sheet and the income statement.)

Liquidity Ratios

Liquidity is the ability to quickly turn assets into cash. Liquid assets are simply assets that are easy to convert to cash. Real estate, for example, is certainly an asset, but it's not liquid because converting it to cash could take weeks, months, or even years. Current assets such as checking accounts, savings accounts, marketable securities, accounts receivable, and inventory are much easier to sell or convert to cash in a short period of time.

Paying bills or immediate debt takes liquidity. Liquidity ratios help you understand a company's ability to pay its current liabilities. The most common liquidity ratios are the current ratio and the quick ratio; the numbers to calculate them are located on the balance sheet.

Current ratio

The current ratio is the most commonly used liquidity ratio. It answers the question, "Does the company have enough financial cushion to meet its current bills?" It's calculated as follows:

Current ratio = Total current assets ÷ Total current liabilities

If Schmocky Corp. (SHM) has $60,000 in current assets and $20,000 in current liabilities, the current ratio is 3, meaning the company has $3 of current assets for each dollar of current liabilities. As a general rule, a current ratio of 2 or more is desirable.

A current ratio of less than 1 is a red flag that the company may have a cash crunch that could cause financial problems. Although many companies strive to get the current ratio to equal 1, I like to see a higher ratio (in the range of 1–3) to keep a cash cushion should the economy slow down.

Quick ratio

The quick ratio is frequently referred to as the "acid test" ratio. It's a little more stringent than the current ratio in that you calculate it without inventory. I'll use the current ratio example discussed in the preceding section. What if half of the assets are inventory ($30,000 in this case)? Now what? First, here's the formula for the quick ratio:

Quick ratio = (Current assets less inventory) ÷ Current liabilities

In the example, the quick ratio for SHM is 1.5 ($30,000 divided by $20,000). In other words, the company has $1.50 of "quick" liquid assets for each dollar of current liabilities. This amount is okay. *Quick liquid assets* include any money in the bank, marketable securities, and accounts receivable. If quick liquid assets at the very least equal or exceed total current liabilities, that amount is considered adequate.

The acid test that this ratio reflects is embodied in the question, "Can the company pay its bills when times are tough?" In other words, if the company can't sell its goods (inventory), can it still meet its short-term liabilities? Of course, you must watch the accounts receivable as well. If the economy is entering rough times, you want to make sure that the company's customers are paying invoices on a timely basis.

Operating Ratios

Operating ratios essentially measure a company's efficiency. "How is the company managing its resources?" is a question commonly answered with operating ratios. If, for example, a company sells products, does it have too much inventory? If it does, that could impair the company's operations. The following sections present common operating ratios.

Return on equity (ROE)

Equity is the amount left from total assets after you account for total liabilities. (This can also be considered a profitability ratio.) The *net equity* (also known as shareholders' equity, stockholders' equity, or net worth) is the bottom line on the company's balance sheet, both geographically and figuratively. It's calculated as

Return on equity (ROE) = Net income ÷ Net equity

The net income (from the company's income statement) is simply the total income less total expenses. Net income that isn't spent or used up increases the company's net equity. Looking at net income is a great way to see whether the company's management is doing a good job growing the business. You can check this out by looking at the net equity from both the most recent balance sheet and the one from a year earlier. Ask yourself whether the current net equity is higher or lower than the year before. If it's higher, by what percentage is it higher?

For example, if SHM's net equity is $40,000 and its net income is $10,000, its ROE is a robust 25 percent (net income of $10,000 divided by net equity of $40,000). The higher the ROE, the better. An ROE that exceeds 10 percent (for simplicity's sake) is good (especially in a slow and struggling economy). Use the ROE in conjunction with the ROA ratio in the following section to get a fuller picture of a company's activity.

Return on assets (ROA)

The ROA may seem similar to the ROE, but it actually gives a perspective that completes the picture when coupled with the ROE. The formula for figuring out ROA is

Return on assets = Net income ÷ Total assets

The ROA reflects the relationship between a company's profit and the assets used to generate that profit. If SHM makes a profit of $10,000 and has total assets of $100,000, the ROA is 10 percent. This percentage should be as high as possible, but it will generally be less than the ROE.

Say that the company has an ROE of 25 percent but an ROA of only 5 percent. Is that good? It sounds okay, but a problem exists. An ROA that's much lower than the ROE indicates that the higher ROE may have been generated by something other than total assets — debt! The use of debt can be a leverage to maximize the ROE, but if the ROA doesn't show a similar percentage of efficiency, then the company may have incurred too much debt. In that case, investors should be aware that this situation could cause problems (see the section "Solvency Ratios," later in this appendix). Better ROA than DOA!

Sales to receivables ratio (SR)

The sales to receivables ratio (SR) gives investors an indication of a company's ability to manage what customers owe it. This ratio uses data from both the income statement (sales) and the balance sheet (accounts receivable, or AR). The formula is expressed as

Sales to receivables ratio = Sales ÷ Receivables

Say that you have the following data for SHM:

Sales in 2007 are $75,000. On 12/31/07, receivables stood at $25,000.

Sales in 2008 are $80,000. On 12/31/08, receivables stood at $50,000.

Based on this data, you can figure out that sales went up 6.6 percent, but receivables went up 100 percent! In 2007, the SR was 3 ($75,000 divided by $25,000). However, the SR in 2008 sank to 1.6 ($80,000 divided by $50,000), or was nearly cut in half. Yes, sales did increase, but the company's ability to collect money due from customers fell dramatically. This information is important to notice for one main reason: What good is selling more when you can't get the money? From a cash flow point of view, the company's financial situation deteriorated.

Solvency Ratios

Solvency just means that a company isn't overwhelmed by its liabilities. Insolvency means "Oops! Too late." You get the point. Solvency ratios have never been more important than they are now because the American economy is currently carrying so much debt. Solvency ratios look at the relationship between what a company owns and what it owes. Here are two of the primary solvency ratios.

Debt to net equity ratio

The debt to net equity ratio answers the question, "How dependent is the company on debt?" In other words, it tells you how much the company owes and how much it owns. You calculate it as follows:

Debt to net equity ratio = Total liabilities ÷ Net equity

If SHM has $100,000 in debt and $50,000 in net worth, the debt to net equity ratio is 2. The company has $2 of debt to every dollar of net worth. In this case, what the company owes is twice the amount of what it owns.

Whenever a company's debt to net equity ratio exceeds 1 (as in the example), that isn't good. In fact, the higher the number, the more negative the situation. If the number is too high and the company isn't generating enough income to cover the debt, the business runs the risk of bankruptcy.

Working capital

Technically, working capital isn't a ratio, but it does belong to the list of things that serious investors look at. *Working capital* measures a company's current assets in relation to its current liabilities. It's a simple equation:

Working capital = Total current assets − Total current liabilities

The point is obvious: Does the company have enough to cover the current bills? Actually, you can formulate a useful ratio. If current assets are $25,000 and current liabilities are $25,000, that's a 1-to-1 ratio, which is cutting it close. Current assets should be at least 50 percent higher than current liabilities (say, $1.50 to $1.00) to have enough cushion to pay bills and have some money for other purposes. Preferably, the ratio should be 2 to 1 or higher.

Common Size Ratios

Common size ratios offer simple comparisons. You have common size ratios for both the balance sheet (where you compare total assets) and the income statement (where you compare total sales):

- ✔ **To get a common size ratio from a balance sheet,** the total assets figure is assigned the percentage of 100 percent. Every other item on the balance sheet is represented as a percentage of total assets. For example, if SHM has total assets of $10,000 and debt of $3,000, then debut equals 30 percent (debt divided by total assets, or $3,000 ÷ $10,000, which equals 30 percent).

- ✔ **To get a common size ratio from an income statement (or profit and loss statement),** you compare total sales. For example, if SHM has $50,000 in total sales and a net profit of $8,000, then you know that the profit equals 16 percent of total sales.

Keep in mind the following points with common size ratios:

- ✔ **Net profit:** What percentage of sales is it? What was it last year? How about the year before? What percentage of increases (or decreases) is the company experiencing?

> ✔ **Expenses:** Are total expenses in line with the previous year? Are any expenses going out of line?
>
> ✔ **Net equity:** Is this item higher or lower than the year before?
>
> ✔ **Debt:** Is this item higher or lower than the year before?

Common size ratios are used to compare the company's financial data not only with prior balance sheets and income statements but also with other companies in the same industry. You want to make sure that the company is not only doing better historically but also as a competitor in the industry.

Valuation Ratios

Understanding the value of a stock is very important for stock investors. The quickest and most efficient way to judge the value of a company is to look at valuation ratios. The type of value that you deal with throughout this book is the *market value* (essentially the price of the company's stock). You hope to buy it at one price and sell it later at a higher price — that's the name of the game. But what's the best way to determine whether what you're paying for now is a bargain or is fair market value? How do you know whether your stock investment is undervalued or overvalued? The valuation ratios in the following sections can help you answer these questions. In fact, they're the same ratios that value investors have used with great success for many years.

Price-to-earnings ratio (P/E)

The price-to-earnings ratio can also double as a profitability ratio because it's a common barometer of value that many investors and analysts look at. I cover this topic in Chapter 11, but because it's such a critical ratio, I also include it here. The formula is

P/E ratio = Price (per share) ÷ Earnings (per share)

For example, if SHM's stock price per share is $10 and the earnings per share are $1, the P/E ratio is 10 (10 divided by 1).

The P/E ratio answers the question, "Am I paying too much for the company's earnings?" Value investors find this number to be very important. Here are some points to remember:

- ✔ Generally, the lower the P/E ratio, the better (from a financial strength point of view). Frequently, a low P/E ratio indicates that the stock is under-valued, especially if the company's sales are growing and the industry is also growing. But you may occasionally encounter a situation where the stock price is falling faster than the company's earnings, which would also generate a low P/E. And if the company has too much debt and the industry is struggling, then a low P/E may indicate that the company is in trouble. Use the P/E as part of your analysis along with other factors (such as debt, for instance) to get a more complete picture.

- ✔ A company with a P/E ratio significantly higher than its industry average is a red flag that its stock price is too high (or that it's growing faster than its competitors).

- ✔ Don't invest in a company with no P/E ratio (it has a stock price, but the company experienced losses). Such a stock may be good for a specula-tor's portfolio but not for your retirement account.

- ✔ Any stock with a P/E ratio higher than 40 should be considered a specu-lation and not an investment. Frequently, a high P/E ratio indicates that the stock is overvalued.

When you buy a company, you're really buying its power to make money. In essence, you're buying its earnings. Paying for a stock that's priced at 10 to 20 times earnings is a conservative strategy that has served investors well for nearly a century. Make sure that the company is priced fairly, and use the P/E ratio in conjunction with other measures of value (such as the ratios in this appendix).

Price to sales ratio (PSR)

The price to sales ratio (PSR) helps to answer the question, "Am I paying too much for the company's stock based on the company's sales?" This is a useful valuation ratio that I recommend using as a companion tool with the company's P/E ratio. You calculate it as follows:

PSR = Stock price (per share) ÷ Total sales (per share)

This ratio can be quoted on a per-share basis or on an aggregate basis. For example, if a company's market value (or market capitalization) is $1 billion and annual sales are also $1 billion, the PSR is 1. If the market value in this example is $2 billion, then the PSR is 2. Or, if the share price is $76 and the total sales per share are $38, the PSR is 2 — you arrive at the same ratio whether you calculate on a per-share or aggregate basis. For investors trying to make sure that they're not paying too much for the stock, the general rule is that the lower the PSR, the better. Stocks with a PSR of 2 or lower are considered undervalued.

Be very hesitant about buying a stock with a PSR greater than 5. If you buy a stock with a PSR of 5, you're paying $5 for each dollar of sales — not exactly a bargain.

Price to book ratio (PBR)

No, this doesn't have anything to do with beer, although I am enjoying a cold Pabst Blue Ribbon as I write this! The price to book ratio (PBR) compares a company's market value to its accounting (or book) value. The book value refers to the company's net equity (assets minus liabilities). The company's market value is usually dictated by external factors such as supply and demand in the stock market. The book value is indicative of the company's internal operations. Value investors see the PBR as another way of valuing the company to determine whether they're paying too much for the stock. The formula is

Price to book ratio (PBR) = Market value ÷ Book value

An alternate method is to calculate the ratio on a per-share basis, which yields the same ratio. If the company's stock price is $20 and the book value (per share) is $15, then the PBR is 1.33. In other words, the company's market value is 33 percent higher than its book value. Investors seeking an undervalued stock like to see the market value as close as possible to (or even better, below) the book value.

Keep in mind that the PBR may vary depending on the industry and other factors. Also, judging a company solely on book value may be misleading because many companies have assets that aren't adequately reflected in the book value. Software companies are a good example. Intellectual properties, such as copyrights and trademarks, are very valuable yet aren't fully covered in book value. Just bear in mind that, generally, the lower the market value is in relation to the book value, the better for you (especially if the company has strong earnings and the outlook for the industry is positive).

Index

• *Numerics* •

$10,000 to $50,000, asset allocation, 230
$50,000 or more, asset allocation, 230–231
52-week high column, stock tables, 87–88
52-week low column, stock tables, 87–88
401(k) plans, 32, 293–284
529 & Other College Savings Plans For Dummies (Margaret A. Munro), 227
1099-B, tax reporting document, 278
1099-DIV, tax reporting document, 278
1099-INT, tax reporting document, 278

• *A* •

account executives, 99–101
accounting value. *See* book value
accounts receivable, 161
accumulate, broker recommendation, 106
adjustable-rate mortgages (ARMs), 26, 197
advanced orders, stock trading, 243–244
advisory services
  broker's role, 98, 100, 102
  stock trading, 221
age 40 plus, strategies, 227–228
aggressive and bearish approach, 201
aggressive and bullish approach, 200
AgnicoEagle (AEM), gold stock, 194
alternative energy, 193, 206–207
American International Group, Inc. (AIG), government intervention, 208
American Stock Exchange (AMEX), 72–73, 78–79
analysts, 117, 301
annual growth rate, asset liquidity, 22–24
annual reports
  company identity data, 171
  company's offerings, 169–170
  CPA opinion letter, 171
  financial statements, 170–171
  Form 5, 262
  letter from the chairman of the board, 168–169
  management issues, 171
  obtaining, 167–168
  stock data, 171
  summary of past financial figures, 171
appreciating assets, balance sheet, 27
appreciation, capital gains, 42–43
asset allocations
  $10,000 to $50,000, 230
  $50,000 or more, 230–231
  less than $10,000, 229
  risk versus return, 62
assets
  annual growth rate, 22–24
  appreciating, 27
  balance sheet item, 20, 157–158
  depreciating, 27
  emergency fund, 21
  garage sales, 28
  liquidity order, 22–24
  long-term, 23
  market value, 22–23
  reallocating, 29
auctions, unproductive asset reduction strategy, 28
Austrian school, economic philosophy, 145
automobiles
  bearish opportunities, 199
  cyclical industry, 180–181
  economic barometer, 187

• *B* •

balance sheets
  accounts receivable, 161
  analysis points, 27–28
  assets, 21–24
  debt, 157–158
  derivatives, 157
  emergency fund, 21
  equity, 157–158
  financial assets, 157–158
  financial strength over time assessment, 158–159
  inventory, 157

balance sheets *(continued)*
  liabilities, 24–26, 158
  net worth calculations, 26
  net worth determinations, 154, 156–159
  total assets, 157–158
bank statements, 278
banking services, 98, 188
banks, 43, 198–199
Barron's
  broker comparisons, 103
  information research, 177
bear markets
  consumer discretionary sectors, 196–197
  credit services, 198–199
  cyclical stocks, 199
  defined, 11
  dollar cost averaging (DCA), 258–260
  real estate, 197–198
beta, stock's, 223, 242
Bloomberg, financial news resource, 84
Bombay Stock Exchange, 70
bond ratings, income stocks, 131–132
bonds, 50, 302
book of record, direct purchase programs
    (DPPs), 253
book value, stockholder's equity, 153
bottom line. *See* earnings; net profit
brand recognition, growth stocks, 113
broad-based index, 64
broker triggers, 296
brokerage accounts, 25, 103–105
brokerage firms, 198–199
brokerage orders
  advanced orders, 243–244
  buy/sell triggers, 58
  buying on margin, 244–247
  condition-related, 238–243
  day orders, 236
  dividend reinvestment plans (DRPs),
    253–258
  DPP alternative, 253–254
  going short, 247–250
  good-till-canceled (GTC), 237–238, 241
  limit orders, 238, 242–243
  market orders, 238–239
  stock trading tool, 221
  stop-loss orders, 239–242
  time-related, 236–238
  trailing stops, 240–241

brokerage reports, 175–177
brokerage statements, 278
brokers
  advisory services, 98
  banking services, 98
  churning, 101
  commissions, 98, 101–102
  discount, 101–102
  Financial Industry Regulatory Authority
    (FINRA), 98
  full service, 99–101
  institutional versus personal, 97–98
  margin interest charges, 98
  recommendation analysis, 106–108
  recommendation ratings, 106
  Securities and Exchange Commission
    (SEC), 98
  Securities Investor Protection
    Corporation (SIPC), 98
  selection guidelines, 102–103
  service charges, 98
BSE SENSEX (India), 70
bull markets
  alternative energy, 193
  commodities, 191–192
  defense industry, 195–196
  dollar cost averaging (DCA), 258–260
  gold, 194
  healthcare, 195
  oil and gas, 192–193
  precious metals, 194
Bunge Limited (BG), commodities, 191
Bureau of Labor Statistics
  Consumer Price Index (CPI), 211–212
  National Unemployment Report, 211
business debt, 198–199
buy, broker recommendation, 106
buy activities, insider trading, 264–265
buying on margin. *See* margins
buying services, 254
buy-stop order, going short, 249

• C •

CAC-40 (France), 71
call options, stock trading, 218–219
capital appreciation, stock investment, 109

capital gains
  aggressive investment approach, 46
  growth investing, 42–43
  long-term, 274–276
  short-term, 274
  tax strategies, 275–277
capital losses, tax issues, 276–277
capitalization-weighted index, 64
Case, Doug, gold analyst, 194
cash accounts, brokerage firms, 103–104
cash accrual, investment strategies, 293
cash assets, emergency fund, 21
cash flow statements
  401(k) plan payments, 32
  analysis questions, 33
  income sources, 29–31
  negative versus positive cash flow, 29–30
  outgo categories, 29, 31–32
  versus profit and loss statement, 30
cause and effect, economic concepts,
    81–82, 142
certificate of deposit (CD)
  income stock alternative, 126
  low-yield investment, 28
  short-term goals, 40
chairman of the board letter, 168–169
charitable donations, tax deductions, 281
Charles Schwab, discount broker, 101–102
China
  commodities, 191–192
  Halter USX China Index, 71
churning, commission concerns, 101
closing date, dividend reports, 93
Coca-Cola, niche market, 113
commissions, brokerage fees, 98, 101–102
commodities
  bullish opportunities, 191–192
  investment concerns, 309
common size ratios, 334–335
common stock, voting rights, 12
companies
  accounting practices, 303–304
  bond rating cut, 302
  corporate stock buybacks, 266–269
  direct purchase programs (DPPs),
    252–254

dividend reinvestment plans (DRPs),
    255–258
  earnings/sales red flags, 299–300
  excessive debt, 301
  increased negative coverage, 302
  industry problems, 303
  insider sales, 302
  political problems, 303
  stock splits, 269–271
company identity data, 171
company's offerings, 169–170
comparative financial analysis, accounting
    principle, 80
composite index, 64
compounding, dividend reinvestment
    plans (DRPs), 255–256
computers, technology stocks, 187–188
condition-related orders, 238–243
Conference Board, Leading Economic
    Indicators (LEI), 139
conservative and bearish approach, 201
conservative and bullish approach, 200
conservative investors
  identifying, 45
  income stocks, 124
consumer debt, 198–199
consumer discretionary sectors, 196–197
Consumer Price Index (CPI)
  I bonds, 226
  monitoring, 211–212
consumer publications, 117
Consumer Reports, product/service ratings,
    117, 288
core sales, income statement, 160
corporate stock buybacks, 266–269
cost basis, stock purchases, 275
covered call options, strategies, 296–297
CPA opinion letter, annual reports, 171
credit cards, 25–26
cultural trends, information, 86–87
current ratio, liquidity ratio, 330
customer health, interest rate risk, 51
cyclical industries, rising/falling with the
    economy, 180–181
cyclical stocks, 199

• D •

date of declaration, 93–94
date of execution, 93, 274
date of record, dividend reports, 93–94
DAX (Germany), 64, 71
Day Last column, stock tables, 92
day orders, 236, 295
debt load, interest rate risk, 51
debt reduction, 59–60
debt to net equity, solvency ratio, 333–334
debts
    balance sheet item, 157–158
    bearish opportunities, 198–199
    fixed versus variable interest, 26
    growth stock fundamentals, 114
    interest rate risks, 52
    investment concerns, 305–306
    liability determinations, 24–26
    market loans, 28
    red flags, 301
    secured versus unsecured, 25
    U.S. debt statistics, 27
deductions, taxes, 280–281
defense industry, 195–196
defensive industries, 181
defensive stocks. *See* income stocks
demand, economic concepts, 140
demographics, investment strategies, 288
depreciating assets, reasons for selling, 27
depression, investment concerns, 309
deregulation, industry benefits, 185
derivatives
    balance sheet item, 157
    financial statements, 170
    investment concerns, 306
direct funding, industry benefits, 185
direct investment programs (DIPs),
        252–254
direct purchase programs (DPPs), 252–254
discount brokers, 101–102
Div (Dividend) column, stock tables, 87, 89
diversification
    investment strategy, 228–229
    risk reduction strategy, 60–61
dividend rates, income stocks, 124

dividend reinvestment plans (DRPs)
    dollar cost averaging (DCA), 258–260
    income stocks, 124
    pros/cons, 255–258
    stock purchase program, 17
dividend reports, date information, 93–94
dividends
    income investing approach, 43–44
    income stocks, 124
    ordinary income, 274
    preferred stocks, 12
    stock payments, 39
    versus interest, 39, 43, 128
documents
    annual report, 167–172
    brokerage reports, 175–177
    Form 10K, 173
    Form 10Q, 174
    Form 144, 262
    Form 3, 262
    Form 4, 262
    Form 5, 262
    government reports, 210–212
    insider reports, 174
    Moody's Handbook of Common Stocks, 175
    proxy materials, 172
    resource library, 177–178
    S&P Bond Reports, 175
    S&P Industry Survey, 175
    S&P Stock Reports, 175
    SEC filings, 172–174, 262–263
    Standard & Poor's (S&P), 174–175
    tax forms, 278
    tax schedules, 278
    Value Line Investment Survey, 174
dollar cost averaging (DCA), 258–260
dot(.)com companies, 30
doubt, failing stock sales factor, 232
Dow Jones Industrial Average (DJIA), 65–68
Dow Jones Transportation Average
        (DJTA), 68
Dow Jones Utilities Average (DJUA), 68
down stocks, investment strategies, 294
Duarte, Joe (*Futures & Options For
        Dummies*), 297
dynamic analysis, 141

• E •

earnings. *See also* profits
  corporate stock buyback per share, 267–268
  growth stock fundamentals, 114, 116
  income statement item, 159, 161–162
  price-to-earnings ratio (P/E), 153–154, 163–165
  red flags, 299–300
earnings rise, 289
economics
  Austrian school, 145
  cause and effect, 81–82, 142
  dynamic analysis, 141
  government actions, 82, 146
  gross domestic product (GDP), 85
  inflation, 146–147
  investment success factor, 15
  Keynes school, 143–144
  Leading Economic Indicators (LEI), 86, 139
  learning from past mistakes, 82–84
  macroeconomics, 138–139
  Marx school, 142–143
  microeconomics, 138
  research resources, 137–138
  static analysis, 141
  supply and demand, 81, 140
  wants and needs, 140–141
effects, economic concepts, 142
electric utilities, 51
Electronic Data Gathering, Analysis, and Retrieval system (EDGAR), 122
electronics, technology stocks, 187–188
emergency fund
  Federal Deposit Insurance Corporation (FDIC) backing, 27
  guidelines, 21
  risk reduction strategy, 59
emotional baggage, 231–232
emotional risk, identifying, 56–58
energy sector
  alternative energy, 193
  high-dividend stocks, 125
  oil and gas, 192–193
  royalty trusts, 135
energy stocks, 309–310

entertainment trends, 86–87
entry barriers, growth stocks, 114
environment, investment success factor, 15
equity, balance sheet item, 157–158
equity growth, 116
events, stock price cause and effect, 81–82
exchange-traded funds (ETFs)
  conservative and bullish approach, 200
  index investment method, 72–73
  industrial investments, 181
  stock investment alternative, 60
  XLE, 193
ex-dividend date, 93–94
expenses
  cash flow statements, 29, 31–32
  income statement item, 159, 161
  reduction strategies, 33
  tax deductions, 280–281
Exxon Mobil (XOM), 156

• F •

face rate, interest rate risks, 50
Fannie Mae, 198–199
fear, emotional risk, 56–57
Federal Deposit Insurance Corporation (FDIC), 27
Federal Express, high entry barrier, 114
Federal Mortgage Assurance Corporation (FRE), bear market, 198–199
Federal National Mortgage Association (FNM), bear market, 198–199
fees, brokers, 98, 101–102
Fidelity Magellan Fund, Peter Lynch, 287
financial assets, balance sheet item, 157
financial consultants, 99–101
financial goals
  intermediate-term, 40–41
  long-term, 41–42
  short-term, 39–40
  stock type/investment matching, 38–39
Financial Industry Regulatory Authority (FINRA), brokers, 98
financial institutions
  bearish opportunities, 198–199
  financial disasters, 206
financial news, 84–87

financial risk, identifying, 48–49
financial services, investment cautions and
   concerns, 188
financial statements, 170–171
fixed-interest debt, 26
Fontanills, George A. (*Trading Options For
   Dummies*), 220
foods, defensive industry, 181
Forbes, information research, 177
Ford Motor Company (F), 199
Form 3, SEC filings, 262
Form 4, SEC filings, 262
Form 5, SEC filings, 262
Form 10K, SEC filings, 173
Form 10Q, SEC filings, 174
Form 144, SEC filings, 262
Form 4952 (Investment Interest Expense
   Deduction), 278
forward P/E, value analysis, 165
France, CAC-40 Index, 71
Freddie Mac, 198–199
FTSE-100 (Great Britain), 71
fuel cells, bullish opportunities, 193
full service brokers, 99–101
fundamental analysis, value investors, 152
fundamentals
   growth stocks, 114
   stock trading versus investing, 215, 217
Futures & Options For Dummies (Joe
   Duarte), 297

• G •

garage sales, 28
gas stocks, 192–193
General Motors Corporation (GM)
   bearish opportunities, 199
   financial health, 156
geothermal, alternative energy, 193
Germany, DAX Index, 71
glossaries, stock exchange service, 78
goal achievement, full service broker, 100
goal setting, investing element, 34–35
goals, rate of return factors, 61–62
going long, stock purchases, 247
going short, investment strategies, 247–250
Gold Corp (GG), gold stock, 194

gold, 194
good-till-canceled (GTC) order
   going short, 249
   investment strategies, 295
   stock trading, 237–238, 241
   trailing stops, 118
government
   economic effects, 82
   information gathering resource, 86
   intervention impact, 146
   investment concerns, 308
   nonsystemic effects, 207–208
   systemic effects, 208–209
   risk identification, 54–55
government debt, 198–199
government reports, monitoring, 210–212
government-sponsored enterprises (GSEs),
   financial disasters, 206
Great Britain, FTSE-100 Index, 71
greed, emotional risk, 56
greenmail offers, 268
gross domestic product (GDP)
   economic health indicator, 85
   monitoring, 210–211
growth investing, capital gains, 42–43
growth rate, 22–23
growth stocks
   analysts' attention, 117
   capital appreciation, 109
   company versus industry growth, 113
   consumer publications, 117
   continued growth, 118–119
   earnings growth, 116
   equity growth, 116
   fundamentals, 114
   insider buying, 116
   institutional buying, 117
   learning from history, 119
   management evaluation, 115–116
   market risk, 53
   megatrend leaders, 112–113
   newsletter recommendations, 117
   niche markets, 113–114
   return on equity (ROE), 115–116
   trailing stops, 118
   value-oriented approach, 110–111
   versus value stocks, 110–111

• H •

Halter USX China Index (China), 71
Hang Seng Index (Hong Kong), 71
Hazlitt, Henry, Austrian economist, 145
healthcare, 181, 195
hedging, stock trading, 222
high-interest debt, 25–26, 28
high-yield investments, U.S. savings
    bonds, 28
hold, broker recommendation, 106
holding period, stocks, 275
home equity loans, 25, 28
Hong Kong, Hang Seng Index, 71
hostile takeovers, 268
Hot Commodities (Jim Rogers), 192
*How to Read a Financial Report: Wringing
    Vital Signs Out of the Numbers* (John A.
    Tracy), 178
Hubbert, Marion King, Peak Oil, 193

• I •

I bonds, variable interest rate, 226
illiquid investments, real estate, 22
income, 29–33
income and expense statements, versus
    cash flow statement, 30
income investing, dividends versus
    interest, 43
income mutual funds, income stock
    alternative, 126
income statements
  core sales, 160
  earnings, 159, 161–162
  expenses, 159, 161
  forward P/E, 165
  nonrecurring items, 162
  operational earnings, 162
  profitability determinations, 154, 159–162
  research and development (R&D), 159
  sales, 159–161
  total earnings, 162
  trailing P/E, 165
income stocks
  bond ratings, 131–132
  defensive stocks, 125

diversification, 132
  dividend-paying stocks, 123–124
  inflation effects, 126
  interest-rate sensitivity, 125–126
  investor profiles, 124
  needs determinations, 127–128
  non-stock alternatives, 126
  payout ratio, 130–131
  pros/cons, 125–127
  real estate investment trusts (REITs),
    133–135
  royalty trusts, 135
  taxes, 127
  utilities, 133
  yield determinations, 128–130
index mutual funds, index investment
    method, 72
indexes. *See* market indexes
India
  BSE SENSEX Index, 70
  commodities, 191–192
Individual Retirement Account (IRA)
  retirees, 282–283
  tax reduction benefits, 33
industries
  automotive, 187
  codependency factors, 184
  computers, 187–188
  cyclical, 180–181
  defensive, 181
  deregulation benefits, 185
  direct funding benefits, 185
  electronics, 187–188
  established leaders versus
    innovators, 184
  financials, 188
  growth factors, 183–184
  growth research resources, 181–182
  megatrend research, 183
  real estate, 186–187
  sunrise versus sunset, 183
  tax decrease benefits, 185
  tech, 187–188
industry analysis
  investment strategies, 289–290
  stock exchange service, 78

inflation
  economic impact, 146–147
  income stock effects, 126
  investment concerns, 307
  risk, identification, 54
information gathering
  cultural trends, 86–87
  dividend reports, 92–95
  economic concepts, 81–84
  entertainment trends, 86–87
  financial news, 84–87
  governmental actions, 86
  gross domestic product (GDP), 85
  leading economic indicators (LEI), 86
  societal trends, 86–87
  stock exchanges, 78–79
  stock investing, 12–13
  stock tables, 87–92
  tip/advice evaluation, 95–96
initial public offerings (IPOs), avoiding, 120–121
innovation, aggressive investment approach, 46
insider buying, growth stocks, 116
insider reports, SEC filings, 174
insider sales, red flags, 302
insider trading
  buy activities, 264–265
  corporate stock buybacks, 266–269
  investment strategies, 291
  investment success factor, 16–17
  Sarbanes-Oxley Act (SOX), 263
  SEC filings, 262–263
  short-swing profit rule, 263
  stock sales, 265–266
  stock splits, 269–271
instinct, investment strategies, 287
institutional brokers, versus personal brokers, 97–98
institutional buying, growth stock value indicator, 117
institutional investors, investment strategies, 292
insurance, risk reduction strategy, 60
intangibles, investment concerns, 310
interest
  tax deductions, 280
  versus dividends, 39, 43, 128

interest owed
  fixed versus variable debts, 26
  secured versus unsecured debts, 25
interest rate risk, identifying, 49–52
interest rates, U.S. Treasury bonds, 226
interest-rate sensitivity, income stocks, 125–126
interest-sensitive stocks, 51
intermediate-term goals, 34, 40–41
intermediate term, trading time frame, 216
Internal Revenue Service (IRS)
  investment-related forms and schedules, 278
  Publication 17 (Form 1040 Guide), 278
  Publication 526 (Charitable Contributions), 281
  Publication 550 (Investment Income and Expenses), 274
  Publication 560 (Retirement Plans), 283
intrinsic value, market value comparison, 153
inventory, balance sheet item, 157
investing, versus speculating, 53
investment decisions, 100–101
investment grade, bond ratings, 132
investment interest, tax deductions, 280
investment newsletters, cautions/concerns, 240
investment strategies. *See also* stock investing
  asset allocation, 228–231
  broker triggers, 296
  brokerage orders, 235–244
  buying on margin, 244–247
  cash accrual, 293
  consumer group praise, 288
  corporate stock buybacks, 266–269
  covered call option, 296–297
  demographics, 288
  direct purchase programs (DPPs), 252–254
  diversification, 228–229, 293
  dividend reinvestment plans (DRPs), 253–258
  dollar cost averaging (DCA), 258–260
  down stocks, 294
  earnings rise, 289
  going short, 247–250

industry analyzation, 289–290
insider trading, 291
institutional investors, 292
investor profiles, 225–228
keep winners/sell losers, 297
limit orders, 295
long-term logic, 294
low versus high yield, 28
megatrends, 290
politics, 290–291
positive publicity, 290
protective put option, 296
put options, 296
stock sales, 231–233
stock splits, 269–271
stop-loss order, 294–295
trailing stop order, 295
trusting your instincts, 287
Investopedia, investment practice, 59
investor profiles
 $10,000 to $50,000, 230
 $50,000 or more, 230–231
 less than $10,000, 229
 life situation factors, 62
 married w/dependents, 227
 over age 40, 227–228
 retirees, 228
 single w/no dependents, 226–227
Investor's Business Daily (William O'Neill),
 84, 177, 241

• J •

Japan, Nikkei Index, 71
job security, risk reduction strategy, 60
junk bonds, bond ratings, 132

• K •

Keynes school, philosophy, 143–144
knowledge
 investment success factor, 15
 market correction versus fear of loss, 57
 market tracking, 59
 risk reduction factor, 58–59

• L •

large caps
 conservative and bullish approach, 201
 stock value, 14
leadership, conservative investing
 approach, 45
Leading Economic Indicators (LEI)
 economic health indicator, 86
 macroeconomics, 139
Lefevre, Edwin (*Reminiscences of a Stock
 Operator*), 223
legislation, information gathering, 86
less than $10,000, asset allocation, 229
leverage, buying on margin, 244–245
liabilities
 balance sheet element, 20, 24–26, 158
 fixed-interest debt, 26
 secured debts, 25
 unsecured debts, 25
 variable-interest debt, 26
life situations, investor profile element, 62
limit orders
 investment strategies, 295
 stock trading, 222, 238, 242–243
liquidity
 assets, 22–24
 ratios, 330–331
loans, buying on margin, 244–247
long-term
 assets, liquidity order, 23
 capital gains, taxes, 274–276
 goals, identifying, 34, 41–42
 logic, investment strategies, 294
 trading time frame, 216
love (of stock) affairs, emotional risks, 58
low-yield investments, CDs, 28
Lynch, Peter, Fidelity Magellan Fund, 287

• M •

macroeconomics, big picture, 138–139
management evaluation, growth stocks,
 115–116
management trends, annual reports, 171
margin accounts, brokerage firms, 104–105

margin calls, buying on margin, 245–246

margin debt
  bearish opportunities, 198–199
  interest rate risk, 52

margin interest charges, brokers, 98, 102

margin loans, cash flow increase, 276

margins
  disciplined approach, 246–247
  outcomes, 245
  ratio balancing, 246
  stock purchases, 244–247

market capitalization. *See also* market
    value
  stock categories, 14
  stock type/investment matching, 38–39

market corrections, 57

market indexes
  broad-based, 64
  BSE SENSEX (India), 70
  CAC-40 (France), 71
  composite, 64
  DAX (Germany), 71
  Dow Jones Industrial Average (DJIA),
      64–68
  Dow Jones Transportation Average
      (DJTA), 68
  Dow Jones Utilities Average (DJUA), 68
  exchange-traded funds (ETFs), 72–73
  FTSE-100 (Great Britain), 71
  Halter USX China Index (China), 71
  Hang Seng Index (Hong Kong), 71
  index mutual funds, 72
  market-value weighted, 64
  Nasdaq, 64, 69–70
  Nasdaq 1000 Index, 70
  Nikkei (Japan), 71
  performance-based, 64
  price-weighted, 64
  Russell 1000, 70
  Russell 2000, 70
  Russell 3000, 70
  SSE Composite Index (Shanghai), 71
  Standard & Poor's 500, 64, 68–69
  tracking methods, 72
  weighting methods, 64
  Wilshire 5000 Equity Index, 64, 69

market leadership, conservative investing
    approach, 45

market loans, debt reduction strategy, 28

market orders, stock trading, 238–239

market perform, 106

market risk, identifying, 52–53

market size, conservative investing
    approach, 46

market tracking
  indexes, 72
  knowledge attainment method, 59

market value. *See also* market
    capitalization
  asset liquidity determinations, 22–23
  stock quote, 152

Marketocracy, investment practice, 59

market-value weighted index, 64

MarketWatch, financial news resource, 84

married w/dependents, investment
    strategies, 227

Marx school, economic philosophy,
    142–143

megatrends
  growth stocks, 112–113
  investment strategies, 290
  investment success factor, 15

Merck, research and development
    (R&D), 114

Merrill Lynch, full service broker, 99–101

micro cap, stock value, 14

microeconomics, small details, 138

Microsoft, niche market, 113

mid cap
  aggressive and bullish approach, 200
  stock value, 14

miscellaneous expenses, tax deductions,
    280–281

Mladjenovic, Paul (*Precious Metals
    Investing For Dummies*), 194

money managers, $50,000 or investment
    level, 231

money market accounts, emergency
    funds, 27

Moody's Handbook of Common Stocks,
    stock/bond research, 175

Morgan Stanley, full service broker, 99–101

Morningstar, index mutual funds, 72

mortgage debt
  bearish opportunities, 198–199
  variable versus fixed interest, 26

mortgage resets, real estate concerns, 197

moving averages, stock trading indicators, 220

Munro, Margaret A. (*529 & Other College Savings Plans For Dummies*), 227

Murphy, Bill, Gold Anti-Trust Action Committee, 194

mutual funds
  index investment method, 72
  market risk, 53
  real estate investment trusts (REITs) similarities, 133–134

• *N* •

Name (Symbol) column, stock tables, 87, 89

Nasdaq 1000 Index, market-value weighted, 70

Nasdaq Composite Index
  information resource, 78–79
  market-value weighted, 64, 69–70

National Unemployment Report, monitoring, 211

needs, economic concepts, 140–141

Net Chg (Net change) column, stock tables, 92

net income, income statement item, 80, 160

net profit, income statement item, 160

net worth
  assets minus liabilities, 79–80
  balance sheet results, 20, 26

neutral, broker recommendation, 106

New York Stock Exchange (NYSE)
  composite index, 64
  information resource, 78–79

Newmont Mining (NEM), gold stock, 194

newsletters, growth stock value indicator, 117

niche markets, growth stocks, 113–114

Nikkei (Japan), international market index, 71

nominal rate, interest rate risks, 50

nonrecurring items, income statements, 162

novice investors, income stocks, 124

nuclear energy, bullish opportunities, 193

• *O* •

ocean currents, alternative energy, 193

odd lots, share purchases, 229

oil stocks, bullish opportunities, 192–193

O'Neill, William (*Investor's Business Daily*), 241

operating ratios, 331–333

operational earnings, income statements, 162

option accounts, brokerage firms, 105

optional cash payments (OCPs), dividend reinvestment plans (DRPs), 256

options
  aggressive and bearish approach, 201
  stock trading, 218–219

ordinary income, tax issues, 274

ordinary stock splits, 270

outgo (expenses), cash flow statements, 29, 31–32

over age 40, strategies, 227–228

• *P* •

P/E ratio column, stock tables, 87, 91–92

payment date, dividend reports, 93–94

payout ratio, income stocks, 130–131

payroll taxes, cash flow statements, 31–32

Peak Oil, oil/gas research, 192–193

pensions, unfunded liabilities, 308

performance, conservative investing approach, 46

performance-based index, 64

personal brokers, versus institutional brokers, 97–98

personal loans, unsecured debt, 25

personal risk, identifying, 55–56

Pfizer, research and development (R&D), 114

politics
  alternative energy, 207
  climate indicators, 206–207
  economic effects, 82
  government reports, 210–212
  information gathering resource, 86
  investment strategies, 290–291
  nonsystemic effects, 207–208
  price controls, 209
  red flags, 303
  risk, identification, 54–55
  stock investing effects, 204–209
  systemic effects, 208–209
positive publicity, strategies, 290
potential, aggressive investment
    approach, 46
Precious Metals Investing For Dummies
    (Paul Mladjenovic), 194
precious metals, bullish opportunities, 194
preferred stock, dividend priority, 12
press releases, stock exchange service, 78
price controls, cautions/concerns, 209
price to book (PBR), valuation ratio, 337
price-to-earnings (P/E), valuation ratio,
    153–155, 163–165, 335–336
price to sales (PSR), valuation ratio, 153–
    154, 165–166, 336–337
price-weighted index, 64
pride, failing stock sales factor, 232
profit and loss statements, versus cash
    flow statement, 30
profits, income statement item, 161–162
protective put options, investment
    strategies, 296
proxy materials, absentee voting, 172
psychology, stock trading versus
    investing, 217
purchasing power risk. *See* inflation risk
put options
  aggressive and bearish approach, 201
  investment strategies, 296
  stock trading, 218–219

• Q •

quick ratio, liquidity ratio, 331

• R •

rate of return, goal planning, 61–62
ratings
  bonds, 131–132, 302
  broker recommendations, 105–108
ratios
  analytical tool, 154, 162–166
  common size, 334–335
  current, 330
  debt to net equity, 333–334
  liquidity, 330–331
  margin calls, 245–246
  operating, 331–333
  price to book (PBR), 337
  price-to-earnings (P/E), 153–155, 163–165,
    335–336
  price to sales (PSR), 153–154, 165–166,
    336–337
  quick, 331
  return on assets (ROA), 332
  return on equity (ROE), 331–332
  sales to receivables (SR), 332–333
  solvency, 333–334
  valuation, 335–337
  working capital, 334
real estate
  bellwether industry, 186–187
  cautions/concerns, 197–198
  cyclical industry, 180–181
  illiquid investment, 22
  interest-sensitive stock, 51
  investment concerns, 307
  mortgage resets, 197
Real Estate Investment Trust Act
    of 1960, 134
real estate investment trusts (REITs)
  advantages/disadvantages, 134–135
  high-dividend stocks, 125
  income stocks, 133–135
  mutual fund similarities, 133–134
  stock similarities, 133
  trust designation, 134
recession, investment concerns, 309

registered reps, full service brokers, 99–101

Relative Strength Indicators (RSI), stock trading, 220

Reliance Steel & Aluminum Co. (RS), commodities, 191

Reminiscences of a Stock Operator (Edwin Lefevre), 223

research access, full service broker, 100

research and development (R&D)
  growth stocks, 114
  income statement item, 159

research, investment success factor, 15

resources
  associations, 319
  books, 315–317
  brokers, 319–321
  dividend reinvestment plans, 322
  earnings/earnings estimates, 323
  fee-based investments, 321–322
  financial planning, 313
  fraud, 326–327
  government reports, 210–212
  industry analysis, 323
  insider trading, 325–326
  investment language, 314
  investment Web sites, 317–319
  magazines, 314–315
  market value factors, 323–325
  organizations, 319
  pamphlets, 315–316
  periodicals, 314–315
  stock exchanges, 319
  tax benefits/obligations, 326
  technical analysis, 325

restricted stock, Form 144, 262

retirees
  401(k) plans, 283–284
  income stocks, 124
  Individual Retirement Accounts (IRAs), 282–283
  investment strategies, 228
  Roth IRAs, 283

retirement, conservative and bullish approach, 201

return on assets (ROA), operating ratio, 332

return on equity (ROE)
  growth stocks, 115–116
  operating ratio, 331–332

returns, versus risks, 61–62

reverse stock splits, reasons for, 271

risk
  debt reduction, 59–60
  diversification strategies, 60–61
  emergency funds, 59
  emotional, 56–58
  financial, 48–49
  governmental, 54–55
  growth stocks versus value stocks, 110–111
  inflation, 54
  initial public offerings (IPOs), 120–121
  insurance coverage, 60
  interest rate, 49–52
  job security, 60
  knowledge, 58–59
  market, 52–53
  personal, 55–56
  political, 54–55
  small cap stocks, 120
  tax, 54
  versus returns, 61–62

Rockefeller, Barbara (_Technical Analysis For Dummies_), 220

Rogers, Jim (_Hot Commodities_), 192

Roth IRA
  retirees, 283
  tax reduction benefits, 33

Rothbard, Murray, Austrian economist, 145

round lots, share purchases, 229

royalty trusts, pros/cons, 135

Russell 1000 Index, 70

Russell 2000 Index, 70

Russell 3000 Index, 70

Russell Investments Group, 70

• _S_ •

S&P Bond Reports, bond ratings, 175

S&P Industry Survey, 175

S&P Stock Reports, 175
sales
  growth stock fundamentals, 114
  income statement item, 159–161
  red flags, 300
  top line analysis, 160
sales to receivables (SR), operating ratio, 332–333
sales value, price to sales ratio (PSR), 153–154, 165–166
Sarbanes-Oxley Act (SOX), insider trading, 263
savings bonds, safe investment, 226
savings, versus investing/speculating, 35
Schedule B, tax reporting document, 278
Schedule D, tax reporting document, 278
schedules, investment-related, 278
Schlumberger Limited (SLB), oil drilling/ services, 192
sector mutual funds, conservative and bullish approach, 200
secured debt, interest strategies, 25
securities
  common stock, 12
  preferred stock, 12
Securities and Exchange Commission (SEC)
  brokers, 98
  documents, 172–174, 262–263
  short-swing profit rule, 263
Securities Investor Protection Corporation (SIPC), brokers, 98
sell, broker recommendation, 106
separation anxiety, failing stock sales factor, 232
September 11, 2001, investment lessons, 57
service charges, brokers, 98, 101–102
settlement date, dividend reports, 93
Shanghai, SSE Composite Index, 71
shareholders, interest versus dividends, 43
shares
  odd lots, 229
  round lots, 229
short sales, uptick rule, 249
short squeeze, going short, 250
short term, trading time frame, 216
short-swing profit rule, insider trading, 263

short-term
  bond funds, high-yield investment, 28
  capital gains, ordinary income, 274
  goals, identifying, 34, 39–40
silver, bullish opportunities, 194
Simon, Alan R. (*Stock Options For Dummies*), 105
Sinclair, James, gold analyst, 194
single w/no dependents strategies, 226–227
small caps
  aggressive and bullish approach, 200
  aggressive investment approach, 46
  analyzing before investing, 122
  initial public offerings (IPOs), 120–121
  performance tracking, 121
  research resources, 122
  risks/rewards, 120
  stock value, 14, 19
SmartMoney, 103, 177
societal trends, 86–87
solvency ratios, 333–334
speculating, 35, 41, 53, 200–201
SSE Composite Index (Shanghai), 71
stagflation, defined, 185
Standard & Poor's 500
  broad-based index, 64, 68–69
  independent rating agency, 131–132
start-up IPO, avoiding, 120–121
static analysis, economic concepts, 141
staying power, 45
stock data, annual reports, 171
stock exchanges, 78–79
stockholder's equity, book value, 153
stock investing. *See also* investment strategies
  aggressive and bearish approach, 201
  aggressive and bullish approach, 200
  aggressive approach, 46
  asset reallocation, 29
  bear market, 11
  buying into a company, 109–110
  capital appreciation, 109
  cash flow statement, 29–33
  commodities, 309
  conservative and bearish approach, 201
  conservative and bullish approach, 200

conservative approach, 45
debt concerns, 305–306
derivatives, 306
diversification, 60–61
dividend reinvestment plans, 17
energy stocks, 309–310
fundamental analysis, 152
goal setting, 34–35
government growth concerns, 308
inflation concerns, 307
information gathering, 12–13
intangible concerns, 310
market capitalization, 14–15
political effects, 204–209
real estate concerns, 307
recession/depression concerns, 309
risk identification, 48–58
September 11, 2001 lessons, 57
short-term rise/fall, 16
success factors, 15–16
technical analysis, 152
value investors, 152
value recognition, 13
versus saving/speculating, 35
versus stock trading, 215–220
yield calculations, 44
Stock Options For Dummies (Alan R.
    Simon), 105
stock price, cause and effect events, 81–82
stock quotes, stock exchange service, 78
stock sales
    going short, 247–250
    insider trading, 265–266
    investment strategies, 231–233
    limit orders, 243
    wash-sale rule, 279
stock splits, investment strategies, 269–271
stock tables
    52-week high column, 87–88
    52-week low column, 87–88
    Day Last column, 92
    Div (Dividend) column, 87, 89
    Name (Symbol) column, 87, 89
    Net Chg (Net change) column, 92
    P/E ratio column, 87, 91–92
    Volume column, 87, 89–91
    Yield column, 87, 91

stock tips, cautions/concerns, 95–96
stock tracking, stock exchange service, 78
stock value, market capitalization, 14–15
Stock, Futures and Options magazine, 221
stocks
    book value, 153
    borrowing against, 276
    charitable donations, 281
    cost basis, 275
    direct purchase programs (DPPs),
        252–254
    dividend reinvestment plans (DRPs),
        255–258
    dividends, 39
    DJIA (Dow Jones Industrial Average),
        65–66
    dollar cost averaging (DCA), 258–260
    earnings value, 153–154
    financial goal matching, 38–39
    going long, 247
    going short, 247–250
    growth investing approach, 42–43
    holding period, 275
    income investing approach, 43–44
    interest-sensitive, 51
    intermediate-term investments, 40–41
    long-term goals, 34
    long-term investments, 41–42
    macro effects, 203
    market value, 152–153
    micro effects, 203
    ordinary stock splits, 270
    ownership certificate, 12
    real estate investment trusts (REITs), 133
    reverse stock splits, 271
    sales value, 153–154
    shareholders, 43
    short squeeze, 250
    uptick rule, 249
    wash-sale rule, 279
    yield calculations, 44
stock's beta, volatility measurement,
    223, 242
stop-loss order
    going short, 249
    investment strategies, 294–295
    stock trading, 222, 239–242

street name, direct purchase programs (DPPs), 253
strong buy, broker recommendation, 106
summaries, annual reports, 171
sunrise industry, 183
sunset industry, declining growth, 183
supply and demand
  economic concepts, 81, 140
  market risk, 52–53

• T •

takeover bids, 268
tax decreases, 185
tax risk, identifying, 54
TaxCut, tax preparation, 279
taxes
  capital losses, 276–277
  charitable donations, 281
  deductions, 279–281
  income stocks, 127
  investment success factor, 16
  IRS forms, 278
  IRS schedules, 278–279
  long-term capital gains, 274–276
  ordinary income, 274
  payroll, 31–32
  reduction strategies, 33
  retirement investing, 281–284
  short-term capital gains, 274
  stock sales factor, 231–232
  tax preparation software, 279
  wash-sale rule, 279
Taylor, Jay, gold analyst, 194
TD Ameritrade, discount broker, 101–102
tech stocks
  bearish opportunities, 199
  computers/related electronics, 187–188
Technical Analysis For Dummies (Barbara Rockefeller), 220
technical analysis, 152, 220–221
technical indicators, stock trading, 218
terrorism, September 11, 2001 lessons, 57
time factors, stock trading versus investing, 216
time-related orders, stock trading, 236–238

top line analysis, sales evaluation, 160
Tracy, John A. (*How to Read a Financial Report: Wringing Vital Signs Out of the Numbers*, 6th Edition), 178
trade date, short-term capital gains, 274
trading
  advanced orders, 243–244
  advisory services, 221
  brokerage orders, 221
  brokerage orders, 235–244
  cash commitment, 222
  condition-related orders, 238–243
  discipline/patience, 222
  hedging, 222
  limit orders, 222
  market moving events, 222
  moving averages, 220
  options, 218–219
  planning, 222
  profit taking, 222
  psychology factors, 217
  Relative Strength Indicators (RSI), 220
  rules, 222–223
  stock trading history, 222
  stock's beta, 223, 242
  stop-loss orders, 222
  technical analysis, 220–221
  technical indicators, 218
  time factors, 216
  time-related orders, 236–238
  transaction costs, 222
  versus stock investing, 215–220
Trading Options For Dummies (George A. Fontanills), 220
traditional IRA, retirees, 282–283
trailing P/E, value analysis, 165
trailing stops
  good-till-canceled (GTC) order, 118
  growth stocks, 118
  investment strategies, 295
  stock sales, 233
  stock trading, 240–241
transfer agents, direct purchase programs (DPPs), 253
TurboTax, tax preparation software, 279
tutorials, stock exchange service, 78

Type 2 account. *See* margin accounts
Type 3 account. *See* option accounts

• *U* •

U.S. Department of Commerce, GDP (gross domestic product) report, 210
U.S. Treasury securities
emergency funds, 27
high-yield investment, 28
income stock alternative, 126
safe investment advantages, 226
ultra cap, stock value, 14
underperformance, stock sale reason, 232
unexpected expenditures, stock sale, 232
United Parcel Service, 114
unsecured debt, 25
uptick rule, stock purchases, 249
uranium, bullish opportunities, 194
utilities
defensive industry, 181
dividend payout ratio, 133
geographic location, 133
high-dividend stocks, 125
income stocks, 133

• *V* •

valuation ratios, 335–337
value investors
balance sheets, 154, 156–159
debt load, 155
fundamental analysis, 152
income statements, 154, 159–162
ratio analysis, 154, 162–166
stock picking technique, 151–152
value measurements, 152–154
Value Line Investment Survey, 174
value stocks, versus growth stocks, 110–111
values
book, 153
earnings, 153–154
forward P/E, 165
intrinsic, 153

market, 152–153
price-to-earnings ratio (P/E), 153–155, 163–165
price to sales ration (PSR), 153–154, 165–166
sales, 153–154
trailing P/E, 165
variable-interest debt, 26
volatility, market risk, 52–53
Volume column, stock tables, 87, 89–91
von Mises, Ludwig, economic philosophy, 145
voting rights, common stock, 12

• *W* •

Wall Street Journal, The, 84, 177
wants and needs, economic concepts, 140–141
wash-sale rule, stock purchases, 279
Web sites
American Institute for Economic Research, 210
American Stock Exchange (AMEX), 73, 79, 181
Association for the Study of Peak Oil & Gas, 193
beta measurement, 242
Bloomberg, 71, 84, 192
Bombay Stock Exchange, 70
Bureau of Labor Statistics, 211
Business Week, 163
Charles Schwab, 163
Chicago Board Options Exchange, 123, 196, 201, 297
cnn.com, 291
commodities, 192
Conference Board, 139, 212
Consumer Reports, 288
corporate publicity articles, 290
Dismal Scientist, 137
djindexes.com, 65
Doug Noland (prudentbear.com), 188
drudgereport.com, 291
E*TRADE, 101, 163
economic data, 212

Web sites *(continued)*
economics research, 137–138
EDGAR (Electronic Data Gathering, Analysis, and Retrieval system), 262
Edgar Online, Inc., 173
Elliott Wave International, 221
Federal Reserve, 212
Financial Industry Regulatory Authority (FINRA), 98
Financial Sense, 138, 305
First Share, 254
Foundation for Economic Education, 138
Free Lunch, 212
FreeEDGAR, 173
Free-Market News Network, 305
futuresource.com, 192
Gold Anti-Trust Action Committee, 194
gold-eagle.com, 194
Grandfather Economic Report, 306
Hoover's, 182, 290
Institutional Investor News, 292
Internal Revenue Service (IRS), 273
international indexes, 71
Investopedia, 59, 306
Kiplinger Letter, 291
kitco.com, 194
lemetropolecafe.com, 194
Library of Congress, 86
Library of Congress/THOMAS search engine, 212
Marketocracy, 59
MarketWatch, 84, 163, 182
marketwatch.com, 71
Medicare, 308
The Mises Institute, 138, 145
Money Paper, 254
Moody's, 210
Morningstar, 72
Nasdaq, 69, 79, 156, 163
National Association of Investors, 254
National Taxpayers Union, 86, 273
New York Stock Exchange (NYSE), 79
Options Industry Council, 201, 297
Peak Oil, 193, 310

politics, 291
prnewswire.com, 290
realclearpolitics.com, 291
realestate.yahoo.com, 307
realestatetopsites.com, 198
realtor.com, 198, 307
Russell Investments Group, 70
Scottrade.com, 101
Securities and Exchange Commission (SEC), 98
Securities Investor Protection Corporation (SIPC), 98
Shadow Government Statistics, 138, 210
ShareBuilder, 254
Social Security Administration, 308
Standard & Poor's, 69, 182
stock screening tools, 163
stock trading advisory services, 221
Stock, Futures and Options magazine, 221
superpages.com, 103
TaxCut, 279
10K Wizard, 173
thinkorswim.com, 101
THOMAS search engine, 212
TradeKing.com, 101
TurboTax, 279
U.S. House of Representatives, 212
U.S. & World Early Warning Report, 196
U.S. Census Bureau, 133, 288
U.S. Department of Commerce, 210, 212
U.S. Senate, 212
U.S. Treasury Bonds, 226
Value Line, 174
The Wall Street Journal, 182
White House, 212
wikipedia.com, 306
Wilshire 5000 Equity Index, 69
Yahoo!, 163
Yahoo! Finance, 182
weighting, market indexes, 64
Wilshire 5000 Equity Index, 64, 69
wind energy, bullish opportunities, 193
without dividend, 93
working capital, solvency ratio, 334

• X •

XLE, exchange-traded funds, 193

• Y •

yield, 44, 128–130
Yield column, stock tables, 87, 91

• Z •

Zimbabwe, inflation rate, 147

Notes

BUSINESS, CAREERS & PERSONAL FINANCE

Accounting For Dummies, 4th Edition*
978-0-470-24600-9

Bookkeeping Workbook For Dummies†
978-0-470-16983-4

Commodities For Dummies
978-0-470-04928-0

Doing Business in China For Dummies
978-0-470-04929-7

E-Mail Marketing For Dummies
978-0-470-19087-6

Job Interviews For Dummies, 3rd Edition*†
978-0-470-17748-8

Personal Finance Workbook For Dummies*†
978-0-470-09933-9

Real Estate License Exams For Dummies
978-0-7645-7623-2

Six Sigma For Dummies
978-0-7645-6798-8

Small Business Kit For Dummies,
2nd Edition*†
978-0-7645-5984-6

Telephone Sales For Dummies
978-0-470-16836-3

BUSINESS PRODUCTIVITY & MICROSOFT OFFICE

Access 2007 For Dummies
978-0-470-03649-5

Excel 2007 For Dummies
978-0-470-03737-9

Office 2007 For Dummies
978-0-470-00923-9

Outlook 2007 For Dummies
978-0-470-03830-7

PowerPoint 2007 For Dummies
978-0-470-04059-1

Project 2007 For Dummies
978-0-470-03651-8

QuickBooks 2008 For Dummies
978-0-470-18470-7

Quicken 2008 For Dummies
978-0-470-17473-9

Salesforce.com For Dummies,
2nd Edition
978-0-470-04893-1

Word 2007 For Dummies
978-0-470-03658-7

EDUCATION, HISTORY, REFERENCE & TEST PREPARATION

African American History For Dummies
978-0-7645-5469-8

Algebra For Dummies
978-0-7645-5325-7

Algebra Workbook For Dummies
978-0-7645-8467-1

Art History For Dummies
978-0-470-09910-0

ASVAB For Dummies, 2nd Edition
978-0-470-10671-6

British Military History For Dummies
978-0-470-03213-8

Calculus For Dummies
978-0-7645-2498-1

Canadian History For Dummies, 2nd Edition
978-0-470-83656-9

Geometry Workbook For Dummies
978-0-471-79940-5

The SAT I For Dummies, 6th Edition
978-0-7645-7193-0

Series 7 Exam For Dummies
978-0-470-09932-2

World History For Dummies
978-0-7645-5242-7

FOOD, GARDEN, HOBBIES & HOME

Bridge For Dummies, 2nd Edition
978-0-471-92426-5

Coin Collecting For Dummies, 2nd Edition
978-0-470-22275-1

Cooking Basics For Dummies, 3rd Edition
978-0-7645-7206-7

Drawing For Dummies
978-0-7645-5476-6

Etiquette For Dummies, 2nd Edition
978-0-470-10672-3

Gardening Basics For Dummies*†
978-0-470-03749-2

Knitting Patterns For Dummies
978-0-470-04556-5

Living Gluten-Free For Dummies†
978-0-471-77383-2

Painting Do-It-Yourself For Dummies
978-0-470-17533-0

HEALTH, SELF HELP, PARENTING & PETS

Anger Management For Dummies
978-0-470-03715-7

Anxiety & Depression Workbook
For Dummies
978-0-7645-9793-0

Dieting For Dummies, 2nd Edition
978-0-7645-4149-0

Dog Training For Dummies, 2nd Edition
978-0-7645-8418-3

Horseback Riding For Dummies
978-0-470-09719-9

Infertility For Dummies†
978-0-470-11518-3

Meditation For Dummies with CD-ROM,
2nd Edition
978-0-471-77774-8

Post-Traumatic Stress Disorder For Dummies
978-0-470-04922-8

Puppies For Dummies, 2nd Edition
978-0-470-03717-1

Thyroid For Dummies, 2nd Edition†
978-0-471-78755-6

Type 1 Diabetes For Dummies*†
978-0-470-17811-9

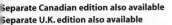

WILEY

INTERNET & DIGITAL MEDIA

AdWords For Dummies
978-0-470-15252-2

Blogging For Dummies, 2nd Edition
978-0-470-23017-6

**Digital Photography All-in-One
Desk Reference For Dummies, 3rd Edition**
978-0-470-03743-0

Digital Photography For Dummies, 5th Edition
978-0-7645-9802-9

**Digital SLR Cameras & Photography
For Dummies, 2nd Edition**
978-0-470-14927-0

**eBay Business All-in-One Desk Reference
For Dummies**
978-0-7645-8438-1

eBay For Dummies, 5th Edition*
978-0-470-04529-9

eBay Listings That Sell For Dummies
978-0-471-78912-3

Facebook For Dummies
978-0-470-26273-3

The Internet For Dummies, 11th Edition
978-0-470-12174-0

Investing Online For Dummies, 5th Edition
978-0-7645-8456-5

iPod & iTunes For Dummies, 5th Editi
978-0-470-17474-6

MySpace For Dummies
978-0-470-09529-4

Podcasting For Dummies
978-0-471-74898-4

**Search Engine Optimization
For Dummies, 2nd Edition**
978-0-471-97998-2

Second Life For Dummies
978-0-470-18025-9

Starting an eBay Business For Dumm
3rd Edition†
978-0-470-14924-9

GRAPHICS, DESIGN & WEB DEVELOPMENT

**Adobe Creative Suite 3 Design Premium
All-in-One Desk Reference For Dummies**
978-0-470-11724-8

**Adobe Web Suite CS3 All-in-One Desk
Reference For Dummies**
978-0-470-12099-6

AutoCAD 2008 For Dummies
978-0-470-11650-0

**Building a Web Site For Dummies,
3rd Edition**
978-0-470-14928-7

**Creating Web Pages All-in-One Desk
Reference For Dummies, 3rd Edition**
978-0-470-09629-1

**Creating Web Pages For Dummies,
8th Edition**
978-0-470-08030-6

Dreamweaver CS3 For Dummies
978-0-470-11490-2

Flash CS3 For Dummies
978-0-470-12100-9

Google SketchUp For Dummies
978-0-470-13744-4

InDesign CS3 For Dummies
978-0-470-11865-8

**Photoshop CS3 All-in-One
Desk Reference For Dummies**
978-0-470-11195-6

Photoshop CS3 For Dummies
978-0-470-11193-2

Photoshop Elements 5 For Dummie
978-0-470-09810-3

SolidWorks For Dummies
978-0-7645-9555-4

Visio 2007 For Dummies
978-0-470-08983-5

Web Design For Dummies, 2nd Edit
978-0-471-78117-2

Web Sites Do-It-Yourself For Dumm
978-0-470-16903-2

Web Stores Do-It-Yourself For Dumm
978-0-470-17443-2

LANGUAGES, RELIGION & SPIRITUALITY

Arabic For Dummies
978-0-471-77270-5

Chinese For Dummies, Audio Set
978-0-470-12766-7

French For Dummies
978-0-7645-5193-2

German For Dummies
978-0-7645-5195-6

Hebrew For Dummies
978-0-7645-5489-6

Ingles Para Dummies
978-0-7645-5427-8

Italian For Dummies, Audio Set
978-0-470-09586-7

Italian Verbs For Dummies
978-0-471-77389-4

Japanese For Dummies
978-0-7645-5429-2

Latin For Dummies
978-0-7645-5431-5

Portuguese For Dummies
978-0-471-78738-9

Russian For Dummies
978-0-471-78001-4

Spanish Phrases For Dummies
978-0-7645-7204-3

Spanish For Dummies
978-0-7645-5194-9

Spanish For Dummies, Audio Set
978-0-470-09585-0

The Bible For Dummies
978-0-7645-5296-0

Catholicism For Dummies
978-0-7645-5391-2

The Historical Jesus For Dummies
978-0-470-16785-4

Islam For Dummies
978-0-7645-5503-9

**Spirituality For Dummies,
2nd Edition**
978-0-470-19142-2

NETWORKING AND PROGRAMMING

ASP.NET 3.5 For Dummies
978-0-470-19592-5

C# 2008 For Dummies
978-0-470-19109-5

Hacking For Dummies, 2nd Edition
978-0-470-05235-8

Home Networking For Dummies, 4th Edition
978-0-470-11806-1

Java For Dummies, 4th Edition
978-0-470-08716-9

**Microsoft® SQL Server™ 2008 All-in-One
Desk Reference For Dummies**
978-0-470-17954-3

**Networking All-in-One Desk Reference
For Dummies, 2nd Edition**
978-0-7645-9939-2

**Networking For Dummies,
8th Edition**
978-0-470-05620-2

SharePoint 2007 For Dummies
978-0-470-09941-4

**Wireless Home Networking
For Dummies, 2nd Edition**
978-0-471-74940-0

OPERATING SYSTEMS & COMPUTER BASICS

Mac For Dummies, 5th Edition
978-0-7645-8458-9

Laptops For Dummies, 2nd Edition
978-0-470-05432-1

Linux For Dummies, 8th Edition
978-0-470-11649-4

MacBook For Dummies
978-0-470-04859-7

**Mac OS X Leopard All-in-One
Desk Reference For Dummies**
978-0-470-05434-5

Mac OS X Leopard For Dummies
978-0-470-05433-8

Macs For Dummies, 9th Edition
978-0-470-04849-8

PCs For Dummies, 11th Edition
978-0-470-13728-4

Windows® Home Server For Dummies
978-0-470-18592-6

Windows Server 2008 For Dummies
978-0-470-18043-3

**Windows Vista All-in-One
Desk Reference For Dummies**
978-0-471-74941-7

Windows Vista For Dummies
978-0-471-75421-3

Windows Vista Security For Dummies
978-0-470-11805-4

SPORTS, FITNESS & MUSIC

Coaching Hockey For Dummies
978-0-470-83685-9

Coaching Soccer For Dummies
978-0-471-77381-8

Fitness For Dummies, 3rd Edition
978-0-7645-7851-9

Football For Dummies, 3rd Edition
978-0-470-12536-6

GarageBand For Dummies
978-0-7645-7323-1

Golf For Dummies, 3rd Edition
978-0-471-76871-5

Guitar For Dummies, 2nd Edition
978-0-7645-9904-0

**Home Recording For Musicians
For Dummies, 2nd Edition**
978-0-7645-8884-6

**iPod & iTunes For Dummies,
5th Edition**
978-0-470-17474-6

Music Theory For Dummies
978-0-7645-7838-0

Stretching For Dummies
978-0-470-06741-3

Get smart @ dummies.com®

- Find a full list of Dummies titles
- Look into loads of FREE on-site articles
- Sign up for FREE eTips e-mailed to you weekly
- See what other products carry the Dummies name
- Shop directly from the Dummies bookstore
- Enter to win new prizes every month!

Separate Canadian edition also available
Separate U.K. edition also available

Available wherever books are sold. For more information or to order direct: U.S. customers visit www.dummies.com or call 1-877-762-2974.
U.K. customers visit www.wileyeurope.com or call (0) 1243 843291. Canadian customers visit www.wiley.ca or call 1-800-567-4797.